Contesting Nietzsche

Contesting Nietzsche

Christa Davis Acampora

The University of Chicago Press CHICAGO & LONDON

CHRISTA DAVIS ACAMPORA is associate professor of philosophy at
Hunter College and the Graduate Center of the City University of New York.

The University of Chicago Press, Chicago 60637
The University of Chicago Press, Ltd., London
© 2013 by The University of Chicago
All rights reserved. Published 2013.
Printed in the United States of America

22 21 20 19 18 17 16 15 14 13   1 2 3 4 5

ISBN-13: 978-0-226-92390-1 (cloth)
ISBN-13: 978-0-226-92391-8 (e-book)

Library of Congress Cataloging-in-Publication Data
Acampora, Christa Davis, 1967–
    Contesting Nietzsche / Christa Davis Acampora.
        pages ; cm
    Includes bibliographical references and index.
    ISBN 978-0-226-92390-1 (hardcover : alkaline paper) —
  ISBN 978-0-226-92391-8 (e-book)   1. Nietzsche, Friedrich Wilhelm,
    1844–1900.   2. Struggle.   I. Title.
B3317.A24 2013
193—dc23   2012015846

♾ This paper meets the requirements of ANSI/NISO Z39.48-1992
(Permanence of Paper).

To Max, who regularly schools me in joyful struggle

To be incapable of taking one's enemies, one's accidents, even one's misdeeds seriously for very long—that is the sign of strong, full natures in whom there is an excess of the power to form, to mold, to recuperate and to forget . . . here alone genuine "love of one's enemies" is possible—supposing it to be possible at all on earth. How much reverence has a noble man for his enemies!—and such reverence is a bridge to love.

FRIEDRICH NIETZSCHE, *On the Genealogy of Morality*

CONTENTS

ACKNOWLEDGMENTS

At the end of his forty-fourth year, Nietzsche surveyed the presents it brought: three works of which he was especially proud and for which he was profoundly grateful. For the interleaf of *Ecce Homo* he writes: "On this perfect day, when everything is ripening and not only the grape turns brown, the eye of the sun just fell upon my life: I looked forward, I looked backward, and never saw so many good things at once." The passage calls to mind another one in which he was beginning a new year rather than burying one. It appears at the beginning of the fourth book of *Die fröhliche Wissenschaft*, the last book in the first edition of the volume, which would conclude heralding the arrival of Zarathustra. His thoughts on a new year include the words: "what it is that I want from myself today, and what was the first thought to run across my heart this year—what thought shall be for me the reason, warranty, and sweetness of my life henceforth. I want to learn more and more to see as beautiful what is necessary in things; then I shall be one of those who make things beautiful. *Amor fati*: let that be my love henceforth!" In many ways, *Ecce Homo* is about realizing that vision, that gaze that beautifies by loving and results in immense gratitude.

In the midst of my own forty-fourth year, I look back on a life very different from Nietzsche's but with no less need to be thankful. This project has haunted, irritated, seduced, and excited me for virtually all my professional life to date. Reworking it for the last time before burying it (or setting it free?), I am reminded of how much living occurred during its writing; just how much traveling we—the manuscript and I—have done together; how many deaths and births we have seen; how many restless nights, sleepy mornings, and afternoons filled with peals of laughter have transpired. For the development and writing of this book is woven into, bound up with all those experiences, nearly omnipresent, even when collecting dust in moving boxes, covered with papers to grade, or forsaken for other manuscripts to read or write. So it is that as I bid farewell to this project and all the living over which it presided I come to share Nietzsche's question at the end of his interleaf in *Ecce Homo*—"*How could I fail to be grateful to my whole life?*"

Looking backward and looking forward, I see many whose presence is bound up with the necessity of the course the living, thinking, and writing took. Having good philosophical friends capable of encouraging me but more important challenging me, and even more crucially pushing me to the point of saying no, is truly a good fortune I enjoyed. For this, I am especially grateful to Keith Ansell-Pearson, Daniel Conway, Lawrence Hatab, Paul S. Loeb, Alan Schrift, Herman Siemens, and Paul van Tongeren. Others showed generosity and tremendous patience with me in reading earlier (some, *much earlier*) drafts of this work, including Alexander Nehamas, David Owen, John Richardson, Gary Shapiro, and Robert Solomon.

Nickolas Pappas introduced me to Nietzsche, offered feedback on portions of this project, and continues to inspire me as a colleague.

Thomas Flynn, Richard Patterson, Donald Rutherford, and Steven Strange helped germinate many of these ideas when I began to develop what I call the *agonistic framework* while a graduate student. Richard Schacht supported translation work I did at the time, which forced me to consider Nietzsche's ideas in a broader context and enabled me to find them elsewhere in his writings.

Hunter College and the City University of New York have proved to be places where research can flourish. I am grateful to provost Vita Rabinowitz and president Jennifer Raab, who provided funding to support the manuscript preparation and travel for research. My department chairpersons over the years, especially Frank Kirkland and, more recently, Laura Keating, never once complained about and even sought to increase my reassigned time just when I needed it. Students and research assistants from Hunter and the Graduate Center helped with organizing materials and discussed drafts of sections. Among the hundred or so students with whom I discussed these ideas, I am particularly grateful to Ben Abelson, Jonathan Berk, David Cerequas, Brian Crowley, Adam Israel, Adele Sarli, and Greg Zucker.

Significant work on the final manuscript occurred during several leaves and fellowships, including a PSC-CUNY grant from the CUNY Research

Foundation and fellowships in residence at the Institute for Advanced Studies at Durham University and at Warwick University.

Several audiences provided thoughtful critical feedback. I am particularly grateful to those at Greifswald University, New School University, Nijmegen University, Oxford University, Southampton University, and Warwick University. Fellow panelists and participants at a variety of professional meetings contributed greatly to the development of my ideas. I owe many debts to members and friends of the Friedrich Nietzsche Society and the Nietzsche Research Group in Nijmegen for criticism and direction.

Ideas for most chapters began as articles or contributions to other volumes. Germs, sketches, and early drafts of some of what appears here can be found in the list of my publications appearing in the bibliography, and I am grateful to those publishers and editors for providing me with venues (and deadlines) for developing this work.

For guidance and encouragement (and even more deadlines), I am grateful to Elizabeth Branch Dyson, my editor at the University of Chicago Press, and to the anonymous reviewers who generously provided critical direction that spurred me to make the book better than it would have been otherwise.

Finally, in completing this project, it was crucial for me to have the very good fortune of a supportive family. Ralph Acampora, our parents, and our extended kinfolk provided cheer, encouragement, child care, and all kinds of reinforcements that made thinking and writing compatible with the demands of daily life. To them—*thank you* very much.

ABBREVIATIONS AND CITATIONS OF NIETZSCHE'S WORKS

References to Nietzsche's texts are given in the text, not the notes. References to his unpublished writings are standardized, whenever possible, to refer to the most accessible print editions of his notebooks and publications:

KSA Giorgio Colli and Mazzino Montinari, gen. eds., *Kritische Studienausgabe*, 15 vols. (Berlin: Walter de Gruyter, 1980);

KGW Giorgio Colli and Mazzino Montinari, gen. eds., *Werke: Kritische Gesamtausgabe*, 9 pts. to date (Berlin: Walter de Gruyter, 1967–).

In reviewing the text, particularly unpublished writings, I have also consulted and compared

Friedrich Nietzsche, *Digital Critical Edition of the Complete Works and Letters*, ed. Paolo D'Iorio, http://nietzschesource.org, which is based on *KGW*.

When citing that text, I include the abbreviation *eKGWB* and provide the stable text identification.

Full titles of Nietzsche's works are given in their original German; short titles and abbreviations follow familiar and widely used English translations, as indicated below.

In references to Nietzsche's works, roman numerals denote the volume number of a set of collected works or standard subdivision within a single work, and arabic numerals denote the relevant section number. In cases in which Nietzsche's prefaces are cited, the letter *P* is used followed by the relevant section number, where applicable. When a section is too long for the section number alone to be useful, the page number of the relevant translation is also provided. In the cases in which the *KSA* is cited, references provide the volume number followed by the relevant fragment number and any relevant aphorism.

ABBREVIATIONS FOR TITLES OF PUBLISHED WORKS

A O M *Vermischte Meinungen und Sprüche*, in *Menschliches, Allzumenschliches* II (*Assorted Opinions and Maxims*)

B G E *Jenseits von Gut und Böse* (*Beyond Good and Evil*)

B T *Die Geburt der Tragödie* (*The Birth of Tragedy*)

C W *Der Fall Wagner* (*The Case of Wagner*)

D *Morgenröthe* (*Daybreak* or *Dawn*)

D S *David Strauss*, in *Unzeitgemäße Betrachtungen* I

G M *Zur Genealogie der Moral* (*On the Genealogy of Morals* or *On the Genealogy of Morality*)

G S *Die fröhliche Wissenschaft* (*The Gay Science* or *The Joyful Wisdom*)

H H *Menschliches, Allzumenschliches* (*Human All-Too-Human*)

H L *Vom Nutzen und Nachtheil der Historie für das Leben*, in *Unzeitgemäße Betrachtungen* II

R W B *Richard Wagner in Bayreuth*, *Unzeitgemäße Betrachtungen* IV

T I *Götzen-Dämmerung* (*Twilight of the Idols*); references to this work also include an abbreviated section name

W S *Der Wanderer und sein Schatten*, in *Menschliches, Allzumenschliches* II (*The Wanderer and His Shadow*)

Z *Also sprach Zarathustra* (*Thus Spoke Zarathustra*); references to this work also include an abbreviated section name

ABBREVIATIONS FOR OTHER FREQUENTLY CITED PRIVATE PUBLICATIONS, AUTHORIZED MANUSCRIPTS, AND COLLECTIONS OF NIETZSCHE'S UNPUBLISHED WRITINGS AND NOTES

A *Der Antichrist* (*The Antichrist* or *The Antichristian*)

E H *Ecce Homo*; references to this work also include a section name

H C "Homer's Wettkampf" ("Homer's Contest")

N C W *Nietzsche contra Wagner*

P P P *Die vorplatonischen Philosophen* (*The Pre-Platonic Philosophers*)

W P H "Wir Philologen" ("We Philologists" or "We Classicists")

INTRODUCTION

This book has modest aims. I do not claim to have discovered some previously unknown dimension of Nietzsche's thought; I offer no key to unlock his texts. My goal is not to show that all or most past scholarship has been wrong or wrongheaded. Indeed, I expect to stand on the shoulders of giants, of what are now at least four generations of scholarship in English on Nietzsche. Some battles simply are not fought any longer—such as whether Nietzsche can seriously hold perspectivism and still make assertions he thinks are true. Some are not openly engaged much any longer—such as whether *how* Nietzsche writes is relevant to *what* he argues philosophically. (Of course, the fact that few argue about these matters does not mean that they are not worthy objects of investigation or that all the important questions about them are resolved.) And there are some debates that show no signs of dwindling anytime soon, particularly, as discussed at length in this book, those concerning Nietzsche's conception of agency and the nature and extent of his naturalism. This book builds on many of the fine studies that precede it and jumps into debates that are among the most lively.

"Giants" to whom I am particularly indebted include Alexander Nehamas, John Richardson, and Robert Pippin, whose books on Nietzsche are immediately relevant to my focus, especially *Nietzsche's System*, in which Richardson elaborates Nietzsche's "power ontology," and *Nietzsche, Psychology, and First Philosophy*, in which Pippin applies and extends his well-known work on expressivism.[1] Richardson's book elaborates the notion of will to power as applied to "drives and power points," which form dynamic and relational organizations and patterns of activity. My own book focuses on one pattern of activity that was a frequent and intensive object of Nietzsche's interest—the agon, or contest—by comparison to which he assessed structures of opposition and affiliation more generally. But, whereas Richardson *begins* with will to power, I work to show how Nietzsche's earlier ideas led him to that descriptive observation. The effect, I think, is that important facets and dimensions of Nietzsche's "proposition" of "will to power" (*BGE* 36) and what it means to hold it come to the fore.

Pippin's work examines Nietzsche's alternative conception of agency, what follows from it, and what problems it generates. He shows how reading Nietzsche as a particular kind of expressivist both draws out important points in his moral psychology and facilitates recognizing distinctive features of his critique of modern conceptions of morality and agency. I argue that Nietzsche develops an agonistic conception of self that is compatible with an expressivist view and that Nietzsche conceives of agonistic relations as *one way* in which the multiplicity of drives that we are might be joined to become one.

There is, perhaps, no one who has given a more elaborate account of how an entity composed of the "most multifarious" drives[2] potentially becomes something unique, incomparable, and rare—*something*, some *one* at all—than Alexander Nehamas.[3] His *Nietzsche: Life as Literature* provides extended reflection on *how one becomes what one is* by virtue of becoming something of a work of art, demonstrating the depths and vast reaches of Nietzsche's views about creativity and how they animate the questions he raises and solutions he scouts.[4] I see my work as related in at least three ways. The account I offer seeks to show how *resistance*—in the form of reflection on its significance and as a source of motivation that organizes his work—plays a major role in the development and pursuit of Nietzsche's philosophical projects. Because such resistance might include some measure of destruction, my study might be thought to pursue an opposing perspective on his writings, but, since I think his agonism ultimately aspires to be affirmative and creative, I do not think that there is any serious conflict here. In that case, then, Nietzsche's agonism might be regarded as a species of creativity that combines aspects of affirmation and negation. I explore that possibility explicitly in chapters 2 and 5. Nehamas's efforts to provide a detailed account of what it means for Nietzsche to create and pursue a life worth living and the body of literature that has focused on undermining "self-creationist" views have motivated my efforts to consider how the agon provides Nietzsche with a way of accounting for one particular way in which difference can be cultivated at the same time that it potentially taps a *binding* force.

I begin by observing that at least three basic assumptions underlie Nietzsche's philosophical projects: human existence is characterized by ineradicable struggle; human beings seek meaning in the struggle of existence; and such struggle is tolerable, even potentially estimable and affirmable, insofar as it is meaningful. I examine how Nietzsche's philosophy grows out of these assumptions, specifically as they are combined in his reflections on contest, his agonism. The main argument of the book, then, is fairly simple: Nietzsche's views of the agon shape what he argues and how. I gather support for my claim by examining his explicit remarks about types of contests, qualities of contestants, and the conditions in which both thrive or deteriorate, and I demonstrate how he draws on those very same ideas in organizing his philosophical projects and his critical assessments of others. I work from case studies, the results of which are cumulative: after laying out the basic structure of Nietzsche's explicit discussion of agonism, I build on it and enhance it. My sensitivity to the development of his ideas intends to show that what he learns from one application of his views of contest, for example, in the case of art and his analysis of the agonal basis of the creative forces of tragedy, leads him to adopt a different approach and scope in the next, as, for example, when he considers viewing all of existence as potentially engaged in organizing struggles and begins to explicitly develop his ideas of will to power. I aim to show how he shifts both the targets and the means of reaching them as he engages various monumental contests throughout his career. The studies that form the basis of the core chapters demonstrate how he applies his agonistic framework and enhances it throughout his writings. The particular points of focus I have chosen—his contests with Homer, Socrates, Paul, and Wagner—also allow me to cover a wide range of his interests through applications to his aesthetic and cultural views, his reflections on metaphysical concerns, his critique of morality and anticipation of its replacement, and the legacy and implications of his moral psychology. I emphasize the constitutive role of struggle and conflict, and I think this helps explain or dissolve what is an apparently paradoxical tension in Nietzsche's work, namely, that the agent as will to power both affirms overcoming resistance and remains mindful of the context in which any and all such successes are decisive and meaningful; that is, agents want both to win and to be perpetually overcoming, not simply to *have overcome*. This book aims to elaborate how this is supposed to occur and how affirmation is possible in such a process.

It was precisely this curious tension that gripped Nietzsche in his early reflections on the nature and significance of the contest, which he located at the center of the Homeric vision of human achievement. In considering how contest provided a means for the creation of value in an ancient Greek context, he found a model for the production and proliferation of values more generally, and he began to examine various structures that support such development as well as what undermines and diminishes it. He both examined and contended monumental exemplars of such activities and the historical and cultural situations that made them possible, leading him to his ultimate view that very many, if not all, values are produced and maintained agonistically, that is, through contests of various kinds. How such contests are achieved, which are most effective, and whether and how they can be sustained preoccupied him throughout his writings.

From early in his career Nietzsche was interested in how human capacities for and tendencies toward aggression, struggle, and resistance could be channeled, sublimated, or redirected. Both the invention of the agon as a worthy enterprise and its effectiveness as a mechanism for generating and distributing significance (or meaning) to other dimensions of human experience impressed Nietzsche to such a degree that it served as his standard by which other forms of opposition and conflict were measured and future forms anticipated. As he examines the variety of contexts in which monumental struggles occur, he develops a rich and detailed conception of the limits and possibilities of agonistic engagement, its necessary conditions, its vulnerabilities, and its fragility. This obviously bears on his conception of power. I am quite mindful of the problematic temptation to try to tame or soften Nietzsche's ideas about power, which include raw descriptions and seek ultimately reassessments of what might be regarded by us as brutal expressions of power (*BGE* 230). Like Richardson, I see Nietzsche's "agon argument" as potentially tempering or qualifying these ideas, and I similarly try to tread with care.[5] The agonistic framework I find Nietzsche advocating might be indexed to one rare but especially effective set of "activity patterns" or organizations. Productive agonism is one among many types of power relations rather than a usual and regular occurrence, and even it may include a measure of what we might regard as violence. Ultimately, I show how Nietzsche's agonism is at the heart of his concerns about the circuits of value production and change—how human activity becomes significant or meaningful, how values and meanings become shared, and how they animate forms of life—and how these insights bear on persistent questions in ethics, politics, and our conception of human nature.

Nietzsche's most direct and focused discussion of the agon occurs in his unpublished preface titled "Homer's Wettkampf," which I discuss at length in chapter 1 and repeatedly throughout the case studies. Since my book utilizes ideas drawn from an unpublished writing as the starting point for its analysis, some further justification of my approach is necessary for those readers who are duly suspicious of interpretations based on Nietzsche's unpublished notebooks. It should be clear that I take "Homer's Wettkampf" *as a starting point* and that my claims are supported in the published writings (as I show). Moreover, I think there are more subtle distinctions to be drawn among the sorts of materials found in the body of writing that constitutes Nietzsche's *Nachlass*. Despite garnering increased attention during the decade or so that I have spent writing about it, "Homer's Wettkampf" is still underappreciated for what it contributes to our understanding of Nietzsche's corpus. Its use in opening interpretations of his work should not be subject to the same criticisms as the compilation of notes translated into English as *The Will to Power*, which acquired its structure and organization on the basis of decisions made by editors drawing on plans Nietzsche explicitly abandoned and rejected.[6] Unlike many sketches and plans for projects that appear in his notebooks, "Homer's Wettkampf" is a work that he considered finished.[7] It is one of five prefaces collectively titled "Five Prefaces to Five Unwritten Books" ("Fünf Vorreden zu fünf ungeschriebenen Büchern").[8] Nietzsche polished and considerably reworked the material before presenting it to Cosima Wagner as a Christmas gift in 1872. He described it in letters and promised to send it to others. He knew well—and, we might speculate, *anticipated with delight*—that, like others the Wagners received, his present would be displayed and read for the enjoyment of other guests at the Wagners' home. For this reason, "Homer's Wettkampf" should be viewed as *publicly shared writing*, not on a par with his published books, yet neither an excerpt from his notebooks nor a finished work he decided to keep only for himself, and certainly not something tossed in the trash, as is the case with some material published in compilations of his notebooks. Nietzsche thought "Homer's Wettkampf" was complete, and he shared it with a limited audience.

After 1872, Nietzsche continued to work on the ideas explored in "Homer's Wettkampf." Drafts and plans for *Unzeitgemäße Betrachtungen* include one to be titled "Der Wettkampf." He anticipated incorporating some of these same ideas in the book he never completed on the pre-Platonic philosophers since he regarded the development of pre-Platonic philosophy (including the thought of Socrates) as unfolding through philosophical contest, depicting the cosmos as a site of struggle between forces or elements.[9] Later, portions of "Homer's Wettkampf" were incorporated in other published works.[10] Virtually every significant idea I draw from "Homer's Wettkampf" is amplified and elaborated in other published writings.

Nietzsche was fascinated by the formal function of the ancient Greek agon and how it seemed to underwrite so many cultural institutions—education, politics, art, and even philosophy. It provided him with a graphic image of how meaning could be publicly produced and reproduced and how such a mechanism could supply the basis of culture. He also recognized its potential for creation of a community; that is, he had an interest in how eris, a powerful drive in competition, could also be related to eros in the form of drawing together those who might otherwise have very diverse interests, values, and aspirations. As I discuss at greater length in the chapters that follow, this interest in the agon certainly informed his conception of power, but his initial and early reflections on the contest did not simply focus on the justification or glorification of expressions of power, as some might imagine. Instead, Nietzsche examined the relation between conflict and culture as he thought it worked in ancient Greece because that dynamic appeared to supply a basis of meaningful relations among people and enabled more than just the participants in the conflict to recognize human possibilities and affirm and pursue them as their own. What motivated and nourished his interest in this facet of Greek culture was the social and public good of competition, not the ways in which competitive institutions celebrated individuality and personal accomplishment.

Increasingly, Nietzsche's readers have come to appreciate how his interest in agon reverberates throughout his writings, from his early appeals for cultural rejuvenation through his later polemics on self-overcoming, and how it illuminates his own theoretical tactics.[11] Those making casual references to "Homer's Wettkampf" nearly always emphasize the *disruptive* features of the agon—namely, how it affords opportunities for what some call *contestability*. According to such a view, if one succeeds in drawing something into a contest, then one has opportunities to confront and possibly overthrow it. This possibility is particularly enticing to political theorists, literary critics, and those pursuing a variety of liberatory projects. But my analysis emphasizes the creative alongside the disruptive potential of the agon. What initially intrigued Nietzsche about the competitive nature of Greek culture was how the agon created opportunities to ground judgments of excellence that were not contingent on some external authority and to share them with others. This possibility is less explored in the literature on agonism generally and Nietzsche's agonism particularly, yet I think it is among the more promising for further applications to contemporary philosophical concerns. Although the value of having a means for challenging hegemonic power is of great interest to many readers of "Homer's Wettkampf," what seems most interesting *to Nietzsche* is the link between agonism and meaning-making, which is a dominant theme of this book. The perpetual creation and re-creation of value and significance, to which many are bound by gratitude and indebtedness to others, tantalized the young author and continued to tempt him as he matured.

I think this sheds considerable light on how Nietzsche regards the cultural work (or function) of art, the nature of philosophy and its connection to meaningful and purposeful living, the structure of valuation (meaning-giving practices generally, particularly in light of his vague proposal for philosophical value creation), and the moral psychology that supports these activities. The articulation of an analytic framework of agonism also sheds light on *how* Nietzsche pursues his major philosophical concerns. Specifically, I argue that a partial explanation of the differences in argumentative approach and style that are evident in Nietzsche's writings can be found in his effort to effect himself as a certain kind of agonist and generate and control his own opposition. Thus, the agon motif gives us insight into Nietzsche's overarching philosophical project, how he pursues it, how we might evaluate it in light of those aims and aspirations, and how we might engage it ourselves if our assessment supports it. Moreover, I find these particular insights applicable and relevant to several concerns in contemporary philosophy, particularly in the areas of aesthetics, ethics, epistemology, and political theory. So, while this book is chiefly an interpretation of the philosophical projects of Nietzsche, it has aspirations to facilitate work beyond Nietzsche studies.

I begin by outlining the organizational model of the agon Nietzsche identifies in "Homer's Wettkampf" and then elaborate the basic terms of the analytic framework that grows out of it in his subsequent published writings. He distinguishes productive and effective struggle from that which is not. This provides a preliminary framework for applications to his contests with Homer, Socrates, Paul, and Wagner, which are evident in his analyses of various phenomena, including struggles at the heart of tragic art; the contest for truth in Socratic and Platonic philosophy and how it bears on conceptions of life, growth, and development; the adaptation of spiritualized struggle in Christian morality; and his reflections on his own development and postmoral psychology. Nietzsche considers striving and struggle to be basic conditions of existence, not merely for human beings, but for everything there is. Given this ineluctable feature of existence, he considers what forms of struggle might advance human possibilities generally. Throughout, I show how he develops and applies evaluative criteria that he uses to compare a variety of forms of opposition and overcoming resistance, thereby deepening and enhancing the initial sketch in "Homer's Wettkampf" as he expands his scope.

How Nietzsche thinks about contest substantially informs how he raises and pursues axiological, epistemological, and metaphysical questions. Throughout the book, I show how his agonism influences his conception of what it means to engage in philosophical thinking and draw others into it. Specifically, he creates historical agones to advance his philosophical development and provoke similar contestation for his readers. I describe this as Nietzsche's own *agonistic practice*.

An important goal of this study is to foster deeper understanding of the subtlety of Nietzsche's conception of power and, more precisely, how he constantly grapples with articulating the spectrum in which creativity and destruction are situated as ends. This examination yields conceptual resources applicable to relational social and ethical theory, strands of radical democratic political theory (which does not necessarily commit Nietzsche to having a preference for democracy), coherentist epistemologies, and studies of education and conflict that could be useful for confronting contemporary issues of violence and aggression. While such applications are beyond the scope of this book, the work here supports future extensions. A well-developed conception of agonism can lead to more refined conceptions of power and conflict that facilitate the advancement of other important social and political conceptual work, including developing alternative forms of political organization and meaningful political discourse, conceiving alternative models of subjectivity in ways that are morally and socially relevant, and constructing institutions that enable and foster creative activity while minimizing aggressive and destructive tendencies. A larger goal of this book is to supply a framework for more fully appreciating the significance of the idea of contest that underwrites Nietzsche's critical activities and constructive projects and to provide criteria for challenging and moving past him.

How Nietzsche develops criteria for what constitutes a productive competitive engagement is at the core of chapter 1, in which I identify the basic features of the agon as described in "Homer's Wettkampf" and highlight what I call a *typology of contests*. Not all struggles are agones: Nietzsche distinguishes contests on the basis of the organization of their supporting institutions (i.e., how the contests are structured) as well as how participants act within them. In "Homer's Wettkampf," he takes up at least three main concerns. The first is the curious entwinement of what we conceive as natural and what is distinctive of human culture. Nietzsche challenges the separation we often suppose, and he emphasizes the mutual dependence and interplay of these two aspects of human existence. The second is the striking way in which agonistic interactions, which obviously entail separation and opposition, can also generate values that can be shared and thereby bring about and strengthen a sense of common purpose and community. And, finally, Nietzsche notices

how this general orientation of evaluation and its transmission and reproduction of values differed from his contemporary culture, specifically, in how the
earlier evaluative scheme centered on contingent human activity rather than
external divine sanction. With "Homer's Wettkampf," he commences a lifelong project to understand structures of valuation and how they can change.
This early text articulates the basis of his subsequent reflections on both the
general terms of organization that define and regulate agonistic exchange and
the modes of activity available for participants.

Throughout his writings, Nietzsche is particularly interested in how values
generated by and in the course of various specific kinds of struggles are dis-
seminated and influence other values. Since his initial exemplar of productive
agonism is located in ancient Greek culture, I provide examples drawn from
studies of antiquity to elaborate how agonistic values have been investigated
as radiating from their sources in institutionalized contexts, proliferating the
field of values more generally. I do not argue that Nietzsche uncovered some
novel invention by the Greeks or that his depiction of ancient Greek culture is
necessarily historically accurate. Rather, I use contemporary studies to vivify
the model of an economy of values he describes and further elaborate how
agonism potentially plays an integral role in supplying a context that lends
actions and relations to others their meanings.

Chapter 2 focuses on Nietzsche's engagement with Homer as turning
on the question of whether there can be an aesthetic justification of life.
Nietzsche considers how Homer revalues the significance of human existence
by replacing the conception of human life as essentially a form of punishment
from which only death can provide relief. He takes Homer as an exemplary
affirmative revaluator who achieved this distinction by introducing a means
of social and cultural organization that facilitated pursuit of positive higher
values—namely, *excellence through contest.* On Nietzsche's account, the identification of such human values and the creation of means to attain them made
the "affirmation of life" possible. In his assessment of modern culture following the death of God and the deflation of all values that such a death entails
(the problem of nihilism), Nietzsche regards the possibility of life affirmation
as one of the most difficult for moderns to achieve.[12] His agon with Homer
focuses on the relation between art and the value of human existence, and it
is organized in terms of his effort to surpass Homer so as to make the kind of
affirmation he inspired possible once again.

In *Die Geburt der Tragödie*, Nietzsche characterizes tragic insight as ultimately derived from a monumental agon with the Homeric affirmation of existence. The outcome is a refinement and further intensification of Homeric

culture rather than a defeat of it, insofar as it does not turn a blind eye to suffering and cruelty or the apparently inherent senselessness of human existence. Nevertheless, the dramatic display of this tension and struggle between the Apollinian and the Dionysian can be beautiful, and the drama of humanity can thereby be affirmed even as it faces up to its more gruesome aspects. Nietzsche also specifically discusses the significance of the agonistic form of this engagement between these two basic facets of existence. It is not simply that the infusion of the Dionysian gives us a sobering dose of reality. Just as in "Homer's Wettkampf" Nietzsche admires the Greek agon for its positive effects in coordinating, organizing, and channeling otherwise destructive tendencies, he sees the *Kampf* between the Apollinian and the Dionysian as productively directing (*without denying, avoiding, or ignoring*) that which might otherwise undermine our senses of ourselves as distinct and worthwhile individuals and communities. Once these processes of collection and division are appreciated as a form of *refinement* of these characteristics, it becomes possible to see how it is precisely this capability that Nietzsche associates with creative power and that he sets as his task to recuperate.

Nietzsche's account of Homeric achievement goes beyond its depiction and display of the shining glory of a few exceptional warriors and the glowing optimism captured in the recurrent Homeric epithet *rosy-fingered dawn*. In his analysis, the resultant aesthetic justification of existence is not simply naively cheerful, and the affirmation of human conditions and possibilities does not simply take the form of maintaining optimism. Nietzsche is fascinated by what he regards as an ultimately *positive form of pessimism*, what he later calls a "pessimism of strength" (*BT* "Attempt at a Self-Criticism," 1; cf. *GS* 370) as exhibited in the tragic contest of the Homeric Apollinian and Dionysian. While the Homeric perspective might be thought of as founded on a celebration and cult of the individual in the form of the idealized hero, the Dionysian marks the dissolution of such distinction. From out of this struggle between creation and destruction, affirmation and negation, clarity and opacity, a new form of affirmation develops and with it a new logic for insight into the meaning of all sorts of things.[13] I explore this idea at some length in the context of tragedy, in which it is most frequently discussed, and apply it in later chapters.

There are at least two dimensions of Nietzsche's investigation of tragedy's constitutive agon that are relevant to his contest with Socrates, the subject of chapter 3. Nietzsche wanted to understand how the Socratic perspective disrupted the agon at the core of tragedy and what replaced it. He wanted to explain how such a change in valuation could be possible and consider how the reversal revalued not just human existence (as had been the case with Homer) but the *whole* of existence itself. Once again he is concerned to examine and assess the form of the contest Socrates initiates *and* how it affects possibilities for agonistic participation and organization more generally. The outcome of this assessment is that Nietzsche concludes that the Platonic Socrates diminishes contestability, constricts the possibilities for agonistic engagement, and fixes in advance the potential outcomes; thus, the regenerative potency of agonism (the organizing powers he so admired in the Homeric and tragic contexts) was lost. Moreover, he was concerned about the precise content of ideas that marked the end of robust agonism, the Socratic worldview, and its implications for the affirmation of existence.

Nietzsche considered the artistic forces of the Apollinian and the Dionysian as expressive of general tendencies rather than solely artistic forces or plastic powers. Thus, he thought the world as such could be viewed as caught up in the struggle of these forces (the ability to extrapolate such vast generalizations was part of what he admired about "philosophy in the tragic age of the Greeks"). As his interest in science intensified along with his critique of unjustified and unquestioned metaphysical assumptions he associated with a Platonic legacy, he began to experiment with ways of conceptualizing and depicting evolutionary forces and developmental processes in terms similar to his analysis of the development of art. The result is his attempt to describe *agonistically* both human existence and existence more generally and to explore how this affects the potential meaning and value of existence. His conception of gay science and his hypotheses concerning will to power are the results of this larger project.

Nietzsche experiments with practicing *Wissenschaft* in a way that captures a discernible character of the world (such as that of contesting forces) and attends to the relation between such conceptualizations and their possibilities for meaning (i.e., the potential of such ideas to be affirmative). I identify this practice as the primary way Nietzsche engages Socrates as an agonist. Given that he regards the Socratic worldview as having overcome and brought about the demise of the tragic, he considers his task as contending with and defeating what he sees as the dominant way of interpreting and evaluating the world. The outcome of this engagement is a new conception of philosophy that includes an explicit commitment to philosophical agonism as well as a reconsideration of the relation between philosophy, art, and science. In this new scheme, philosophy is regarded as a potential contributor to rather than a replica of science because it generates basic concepts that are both adequate and enabling in their descriptive and explanatory powers (again, Nietzsche speculates that the concept of will to power might exemplify the practice of this activity). Such conceptual work is both critical and creative and, thus, constitutes a philosophical form of artistry. I designate this *artful naturalism*, and I offer an illustration of how Nietzsche attempts to practice it. "Future philosophy" is anticipated as taking this form, specifically in contrast with Platonic metaphysics and Socratic dialectic.

One of the ways Nietzsche characterizes Socrates as having overcome the tragic worldview is as seizing control and direction of the very mechanism that channeled and appropriated aggression—the agon. Providing further evidence that the agon is a concern for him from early to late, Nietzsche specifically pinpoints this maneuver in his late work *Götzen-Dämmerung*, in which Socrates is characterized as having preyed on the Greeks' familiarity with and eagerness to participate in agonistic interactions in establishing the dialectical contest as the only one with stakes that mattered (*TI* "Socrates" 8). But several features of this contest are particularly worrisome to him. Formally, it is destructive—the Platonic character Socrates is supposed to be exemplary as a replacement for the Homeric hero,[14] but, like the *Republic*'s Thrasymachus, Nietzsche thinks that Socrates "wins" only by diminishing his opposition, by tearing down others' views, not by positively offering an alternative he successfully defends as superior. So the structure of the agon that Socratic dialectic and philosophic practice supposedly inaugurates is problematic, and these concerns are intensified when one considers that Socrates shifts the field of agonism from the social to the psychic. This relocation of the agon from the public sphere to the psychic realm diminishes the communal benefits of agonism, and what replaces it is ultimately self-destructive and liable to a particularly intense form of self-directed violence.

Such violence is precisely what Nietzsche charts in his agon with Paul. Nietzsche's contest with Homer is organized around the possibilities for the significance of human existence. That concern is extended to existence more generally in his engagement with Socrates. In the agon with Paul, however, he intensively focuses on the development of moral values specifically, their relation to epistemic values, and the processes and organization involved in producing or generating these values. Having already identified an agonistic structure in valuation more generally and a variety of specific forms this can take (as evident particularly in the cases of Homer and Socrates, among others), Nietzsche assesses the Pauline engine of values in terms of the productive possibilities he discovers in his earlier agones. In his assessment of Paul, he charts the escalation of violent action that is legitimized and encouraged in the *agonies* of Christ and the immense cache of debt thus generated.

The economy of debt Paul expands and regulates in the development of Christianity stands in sharp contrast with the economy of value Nietzsche finds in ancient Greek agonism, and it utilizes a currency of pain that converts an extant set of corporal equivalences to psychic ones. Put coarsely, there is hell to pay for redemption even though it is a debt that can never be repaid. Nietzsche thinks our current conceptions of responsibility and guilt are coeval with this development (*GM* II). Moreover, they bolster and exploit other seemingly nonmoral concepts that are also important in inquiry, including causality and agency. What results is a rise toward the pinnacle of the process of our moralization: the emergence of the agent who is capable of (and punitively responsible for) forming, communicating, and executing intent. A perverse outcome, but one that is intelligible in light of Nietzsche's hypotheses about will to power, is that pain and suffering become desirable insofar as their value is acquired and increases by virtue of their standing as currency in this economy.[15] In short, pain and suffering can be affirmed while the value of human existence in itself cannot. The basis of Nietzsche's agon with Paul is his contention with this ultimate assessment of life—Paul sanctifies human suffering rather than transfiguring it, as Nietzsche saw in the case of Homer. Nietzsche presents our familiar models of intentional agency as part and parcel of the Pauline economy of guilt and debt; redemption from this suffering might well require a reconceptualization of moral agency. While Nietzsche scholars have been very reluctant to relinquish the conception of intentional agency Nietzsche criticizes (indeed, some have been loathe to even acknowledge his criticisms), I argue this is vital to his contention with Pauline morality.

Nietzsche began to contest the Pauline assessment scheme by utilizing the philosophical practice he anticipated in the course of his agon with Socrates. (He did not complete the project, though he planned to do so.) Specifically, he experiments with alternative conceptions of the subject that facilitate different conceptions of agency and responsibility. These are crystallized in his lifelong agon with Wagner. But the passing of moralized versions of these ideas, which Nietzsche believes are so central to our thinking that they are evident in the very structure of language (e.g., our presumption of a "doer behind the deed" in nearly everything we observe and not just human action), does not necessarily entail their disappearance. What is needed is the creative development of new varieties of these concepts without the taint of the devaluation of life inherent in the current scheme. This is precisely what Nietzsche endeavors to achieve in his account of his becoming what he is. His agon with Wagner sharpened both his skills and his sense of what it means to fight.

Nietzsche's account of his own development provides significant insight into his anticipation of a postmoral subject and the revised conceptions of freedom and responsibility such would entail. In Nietzsche's unfinished autobiography, *Ecce Homo*, Wagner plays a significant role in his account of his own becoming—both loving him and resisting him, opposing dispositions that Nietzsche thinks are entirely compatible, helped make Nietzsche who he is. He explicitly describes his practice of philosophical agonism—what he calls his "Kriegs-Praxis" (or "practice of war"). In this work, Nietzsche portrays his own development in the context of considering "how one becomes what one is" in terms that are both fatalistic and suggestive of a form of freedom realized in agonistic activity. I explore this apparent tension and explain how Nietzsche's contest with Wagner exemplifies this and defines his conception of himself as agonist. This also provides an opportunity to assess *Nietzsche's* efforts to revitalize or realize for the first time the agonistic practices he claims to admire and to apply his evaluative criteria to his own activities. The results are mixed. While it is clear that Nietzsche *strives* to create contests with productive aims, it is less clear that he *realized* such goals or that his own actions in fact model those he admires and claims he seeks to advance. These concerns are discussed in detail throughout chapter 5.

Nietzsche's story of his own becoming compares in very interesting ways with his early account of *Wagner's* becoming in the fourth *Unzeitgemäße Betrachtungen*, *Richard Wagner in Bayreuth*. Even though Nietzsche claims (in *Ecce Homo*) that this earlier account is the story of his own development, it differs in important respects since the two presentations deploy different conceptions of life struggles and their role in shaping and defining him. These differences reflect the further development of his agonism, in which his later view challenges some of his earlier aspirations for a revitalized Homeric culture that might produce great individuals and bears on important concerns about his views of agency and freedom. I examine these ideas at length in the context of discussions in the current scholarship, and I use this examination as a basis for suggesting promising paths for contemporary reflection on these important concerns. By tracing the import of his agonism, we are in a better position to understand how Nietzsche identified and tackled his major concerns, and this sheds new light on the challenges he sought to create as part of his legacy.

CHAPTER ONE

Agon as Analytic, Diagnostic, and Antidote

1.1 VALUING ANIMALS

Nietzsche's interests in history and development led him to focus on the entwinement of nature and culture. He underscores precisely this relation at the head of his unpublished preface "Homer's Wettkampf," where he begins: "When one speaks of *humanity*, underlying this idea is the belief that it is humanity that *separates* and distinguishes human beings from nature. But, there is, in reality, no such distinction: the 'natural' qualities and those properly called 'human' grow inseparably. The human, in his highest and noblest capacities, is wholly nature and bears within himself its uncanny dual character" (HC, p. 783).[1] Such uncanniness is surely equally vexing today, although it takes different forms in contemporary discussions of philosophical naturalism. Nietzsche was greatly influenced by then emerging discussions of evolutionary biology and rapid developments in modern physiology, zoology, and neurology as well as applications of these ideas in theories of human cultural and social development.[2] He was particularly keen to explore an agonistic relation between the cultural and the biological in the realm of values.

It is clear from his work that Nietzsche did not think the specific values we hold issue from some inherent value of the world as such: values are products of human creativity and ingenuity that develop historically and are preserved and transmitted culturally. This does not make them any less real. What we value, why we value in that way, and how we hold such values have immense consequences on a grand scale. Some values are enduring (e.g., the value of truth); others are relatively fleeting and rare. One possible way of organizing a historical account of human existence is to focus on shifts in evaluative *axes*, the major terms or poles of human cultural value. And Nietzsche thinks this perspective on history can hang together and is illuminating because it is characteristic of human beings that they seek value; they are *valuing animals.*[3]

As Nietzsche gains familiarity with theories of evolutionary origins and development, both cultural and biological, he becomes increasingly intrigued by and concerned about what such accounts assume and imply about the ultimate value of existence. By this, I mean the presumed or suggested general end or ends of existence, what is supposed as that toward which human development is oriented, if not progressing, rather than some inherent value that life itself actually has. Even nonteleological accounts that do not regard such development as actual improvement still rely on philosophical assumptions that influence how such views characterize the causal mechanism of change—the concept of selection, for example, can smuggle in suspicious notions of agency (e.g., that some thing, some agent *selects* with some *intent*) and teleology even while endeavoring to avoid such implications.[4] Moreover, there would seem to be an implicit value or set of values linked with what is identified as the basis of selection (e.g., the highest good) and the level(s) on which it occurs (species, organisms, parts of organisms). How we think about these matters is relevant to how we might regard the nature of this process and future human cultural as well as biological prospects. These are all critical concerns Nietzsche raises even as he maintains positive interest in evolutionary and developmental sciences and integrates dimensions of them in his conception of human nature.

In the sphere of cultural development, Nietzsche is particularly concerned about *how* culture and nature are entwined in characterizations of the natural history of morality, particularly in the tendency to focus on altruism as the allegedly advantageous trait that became part of our basic constitution when it was selected for its contribution to preserving the species more generally. This presumed biological advantage became the explanatory focus for the development of human morals, law, and society. Accounting for the development of altruism within an evolutionary framework that is supposed to favor *self*-preservation and its relation to the development of morality provides much grist for those "English psychologists" Nietzsche challenges at the beginning of *Zur Genealogie der Moral,*[5] as discussed in chapters 4 and 5 below. This general concern endures in contemporary evolutionary ethics and cross-species studies of behavior.[6] That evolutionary psycho- and neurobiology will mark the end of philosophical ethics is increasingly advanced in both popular and academic literature. Nietzsche's reflections are germane to such discussions and considerations of whether and to what extent such scientific views are free of ethical content or import. Nietzsche criticizes the association of value and *advantage* with *conservation*, that is, the *preservation* of existence. Thus, he considers the two dominant developments in (what he regards as *Darwinian*) evolutionary theory as valuing the *extension* of life above all else, positing as the highest goal life at all costs, and he challenges these suppositions. Moreover, he appears to think that human beings suffer acutely when cultural and biological axes of valuation are at odds or in conflict.

As a form of organized or stylized struggle, the ancient Greek model of contest—the agon—provides Nietzsche with some analytic measures to examine and evaluate forms of human cultural interaction for social adaptability. The most vivid historical example of agonism shows that certain contingent cultural conditions are essential to the efficacy of the agon for specific forms of productivity. For the agon to be an effective means of producing shared cultural values, the community itself must have significant involvement in virtually all its dimensions since it is the community that creates and sanctions the institutions or forums in which agonistic encounters can occur. Thus, it is the *community* and not any great individual competitor that founds this form of interaction. The community has this priority by virtue of the fact that it provides the conditions for the possibility of meaningful agonistic exchange—it provides the judges, the grounds for deciding outcomes, and the conditions for participation. And so the community defines and delimits the agonistic arena. As it facilitates and supports (or not) prospective competitors, relevant measures, and mechanisms to determine outcomes, it founds and grounds the ethos that supports the economy of agonistic exchange, which I shall elaborate below.

When Nietzsche examines monumental agonists and *ant*agonists, he is analyzing organizations of values that make it possible for individuals to become who they are rather than simply lionizing or vilifying them. While it is true that individuals compete in the great agones he investigates, it is also the case that they all rise and fall on cultural conditions that make them possible and determine, in some large measure, their possible outcomes. This becomes clear in his nearly dialectical account of the trajectory of the development of agonism from Homer to Socrates to Paul and his self-assessment and conception of his own development in relation to his agon with Wagner. In each case, the connections between cultural conditions and the possibilities for action they provide are also essential to understanding his own projects.

1.2 "HOMER'S WETTKAMPF" AND THE GOOD OF THE SECOND ERIS

The locus classicus for Nietzsche's conception of the agon is the discussion in "Homer's Wettkampf." Prefiguring the notion that would years later make his Basel colleague Jacob Burckhardt famous, Nietzsche examines the significance of the agon for ancient Greek culture, considers how it animated Greek ethics, education, art, and philosophy, and briefly contrasts that orientation with the cultural aims of his contemporaries.[7] Of particular interest to him is how a dynamic of localization and circulation of power, specifically put to creative and constructive purposes, is cultivated in ancient culture through contest. And he is especially interested in how that mechanism degenerates and becomes deformed as the contest is utilized for other purposes in Platonic philosophy and Christian morality.

Scholars have trodden some well-worn paths through "Homer's Wettkampf." Those discussing Nietzsche's agonism frequently make reference to his account of the text of Hesiod's *Works and Days* that Pausanias is supposed to have seen during his travels in Greece. That text, unlike the one many of Nietzsche's fellow philologists considered authentic, describes two Eris goddesses.[8] Eris is ordinarily associated with strife, conflict, and war. She is depicted in Hesiod's (presumably earlier) *Theogony* as the source of envy and jealous rage. What is curious about Pausanias's reference to an alternative account of the genealogy of strife is that the hitherto unknown Eris sister is considered to be good: she spurs human beings to action, to competition that enhances rather than destroys. Thus conceived, dissension bears a very strong family resemblance to a fruitful desire, namely, the urge to excel.[9] Nietzsche maps the original Eris to what he describes as a desire to bring about complete destruction of what one opposes—*Vernichtungslust*, "a thirst for destruction"—while he identifies the second as summoning a drive for excellence by motivating a superlative performance in response to opposition. He links the second Eris to *Wettkampf*. Examples of the latter, he thinks, are evident in the relations among similarly skilled opponents, for example, struggles between rivals worthy of each other.

Struggles can have either creative or destructive ends and corresponding means to reach them. In *Der Wanderer und sein Schatten*, Nietzsche further distinguishes different kinds of contests when he highlights modes of action as *elevating above* (*erheben*) and *forcing back* (*herabdrücken*) what one opposes: "Someone who is envious senses another's every protrusion beyond the common measure and wants to force him back to it [bis dahin herabdrücken]—or to elevate himself to it [sich bis dorthin erheben]: out of which there arise two different modes of action [Handlungsweisen], which Hesiod designated as the evil and the good Eris" (*WS* 29).[10] One can defeat an opponent in at least two ways: either by summoning a superlative performance from oneself, thereby winning by surpassing one's opposition, or by diminishing the capacities of one's opponent, thereby undercutting his excellence and overcoming by diminishing one's opposition. An effect of the latter is to lower the bar for what stands as the best. Just as individuals can manifest these modes of action, cultures and institutions can regulate, facilitate, and encourage different forms of contest that promote and reward different forms of activity.

If we look back once more on Hesiod's Eris goddesses, we notice that the earlier sense of Eris as bad is retained in *Works and Days* and that her presence accounts for why humans are subject to the miseries of war, senseless suffering, cruelty, and seemingly endless toil. But Pausanias's copy of Hesiod's text casts the other Eris as worthy of praise for the fruit she brings to bear in the form of prosperous labor. The second Eris gives meaning to human struggles; her gifts take the form of inspiration, aspiration, and motivation toward the pursuit of overcoming what impedes excellence. Whereas the bad Eris provokes human beings to be destructive, the good one incites them to be creative and productive. In "Homer's Wettkampf," Nietzsche suggests the introduction of this second Eris conceptually enabled the ancient Greeks to eventually direct what had been recognized as a source of misery—the effort required to engage the daily struggle to sustain life—into a channel that led to pursuit of the highest forms of human possibilities. He speculates, in line with Burckhardt's thesis, that the proliferation of outlets organized on an agonistic model (which he identified as the form of contest best suited to fostering and rewarding the activity of *elevating above*) accounts for the monumental accomplishments in ancient Greek culture.

Nietzsche goes beyond simply admiring a little healthy competition. Although it is common for those citing "Homer's Wettkampf" to point to the distinction he highlights between the good and the bad Eris goddesses, less critical attention is paid to the more general context and purpose of his discussion. He is not merely suggesting that there are good contests and bad ones and that the good ones are those in which the truly superlative competitor emerges as the victor. He goes beyond the banal assertion that competition is a good source of motivation. Nietzsche cites Hesiod's account of the two Erises—depicting one as a gift and the other as a curse—specifically to draw attention to what he regards as a monumental distinction between his own culture and what Hesiod indicated in the relevant passage from *Works and*

Days: with the introduction of the second Eris, the highest values are tied to human activity and not divine sanction.

It is especially noteworthy that the Eris twins share the same name. The ancient Greeks demonstrated time and again that they lacked no imagination when it came to creating new gods or adopting from other cultures gods with whom they became acquainted. Finding themselves in need of a goddess who would spur productivity, they might have created a new one or invited a relevant neighboring deity to receive their gifts and offerings in exchange for patronage. Interestingly, the good Eris emerges out of the same spirit as her sister, but she takes on a different personality and cultivates different proclivities. Nietzsche reads the birth or conception of creative contention as indicative of the recognition that what inspires us to fight can also be the very thing that inspires us to pursue excellence: destruction and creation are the poles of a continuum of the expression of the same drive. Arguably, it is this "uncanny dual character" (HC, p. 783) of human existence that preoccupies Nietzsche throughout his creative life; zeal for understanding that dynamic, its possible configurations, animates nearly every one of his inquiries.

The view that envy could have a productive and positive function in the economy of human desires also reflects what Nietzsche identifies as a different ethical orientation, a different ethical "coloring": what distinguishes the Eris goddesses from each other are their contributions specifically to the good of humankind in its own right. The one sort of envy is good because it creatively draws excellence out of human beings, at its best inspiring them not simply to *outdo* each other in any way possible but to do so in such a way that advances human possibilities generally. This can be accomplished without requiring competitors to give up their own aspirations for success. In other words, playing to win and playing well *might* be, but are not *necessarily*, mutually exclusive goals. A competitive institution comprises more than just the competitors and their intentions. Through reward and punishment, recognition and dishonor by the judges and the community, competitive institutions direct and influence modes of action that are realized in particular agonistic exchanges. As we shall see in coming chapters, this subtle point lies at the heart of Nietzsche's evaluations of the contests established in Socratic philosophy and Christian morality.

The bad Eris arouses concern about the disparity between oneself and another just as the good Eris does, but she inspires a destructive response: her answer to what offers itself as a manifestation of excellence is annihilation. Thus, the bad Eris effectively obliterates the necessity of surpassing opposition in order to win. "Homer's Wettkampf" highlights the fact that it is in the interest of humankind, of raising humanity collectively to its peak, that the differences between the two Erises are highlighted. This particular distinction in Greek culture is crucial: human excellence is at the center of the Greek view, whereas it is subordinate to the will of a supernatural other in Judeo-Christian morality.

Some of Nietzsche's critics make him out as a modern Thrasymachus or Callicles, holding the view that *might makes right*.[11] What Nietzsche has to say about why the second Eris is especially good should lead us to reconsider such characterizations. He sees the good of the second Eris both in terms of the motivation she provides in order to make humans more productive and in terms of the localization of moral concern that her birth or appearance seems to indicate. Plato's *Republic* thematically presents an opposition between an ethic organized around drives of outdoing (*pleonexia*) and that of doing well (*eupraxia*). Nietzsche's response to the account offered by the *Republic*'s Socrates might be that what is problematic is not outdoing as such but rather how it is cultivated and directed. The Socrates of the *Republic* and Nietzsche are not in significant disagreement on this point.

One of the tasks of the *Republic* is to consider both how justice might be defined and *what kind of thing* it is. The three main definitions advanced in book 1 are considered both in terms of the content given the conception of justice (i.e., justice is telling the truth and repaying debts [Cephalus], doing good to friends and harming enemies [Polemarchus], the advantage of the stronger [Thrasymachus]) and in terms of how justice is implicitly conceived more generally (i.e., justice is a specific set of actions [Cephalus], a general rule [Polemarchus], a kind of power [Thrasymachus]). Socrates engages both considerations in his refutations; for example, we realize in the refutation of Cephalus that it is not only that he is mistaken about which set of actions is really just but also that a project of defining justice in terms of *any* set of actions simply will not suffice.

When Thrasymachus identifies justice as a certain kind of power, he conceives power as that which allows one to outdo others in order to get what one wants. Socrates ultimately offers a refutation of Thrasymachus's position, although it takes him the entire stretch of the *Republic* to do so, and it is debatable whether he succeeds. However, he ultimately rejects only the nature of what is sought in such striving (i.e., power over others), not the striving itself. In other words, the *Republic*'s Socrates arguably agrees with Thrasymachus that justice is properly conceived as a certain kind of power, which manifests itself in a certain sort of agon, the contours of which are sketched to some extent in the core books of the *Republic* (see esp. bks. 4–5, 9). Only at the end of the dialogue, once he ultimately concludes the "contest between the 'just' and the 'unjust' man," do we see that the basis of the disagreement between him and Thrasymachus is that they have different ideas about what constitutes power and what makes power good.[12]

Nietzsche is sometimes thought to simply equate power with goodness, but his reflections on agon indicate something different, and in the next chapters I elaborate how this matter bears on his conception of a third sense in which the second Eris brings about something good: insofar as she draws us toward the creation of competitive institutions, she grants the occasion for the exercise of judgment, for negotiating the standards of what becomes designated as good. Thus, agon is one way in which values are created, justified, and shared.

1.3 WHAT IS AN AGON? A TYPOLOGY OF NIETZSCHE'S CONTESTS

Nietzsche articulates several features of productive contest, although he never offers a full exposition of what makes some contests better than others. In the following chapters, I show how he persistently develops and repeatedly utilizes these features to analyze forms of contest he finds in most spheres of human existence. What we can gather from "Homer's Wettkampf" and some other early writings as they relate to identification of types of competition are the following:

1. There are at least two different ways of competing: one aims to win by destroying what opposes (i.e., it engages the activity of forcing back [*herabdrücken*] what poses a challenge); the other aims to win by excelling what opposes (i.e., it engages the activity of elevating above [*erheben*] opposition).

2. *Forcing back* is an expression of an annihilative desire (*Vernichtungslust*), and *excelling* is the expression of a competitive, agonistic drive reminiscent of Nietzsche's view of early Greek modes of contest (*Wettkämpfe*).

3. The agonistic mode of competing can be embraced as good, not only for the competitor, but also for its promotion of the general welfare because competition of that sort *potentially* advances human possibilities generally; that is, it *can*—provided a relevant goal is sought—promote meaningful excellence.

In order to fully appreciate how Nietzsche makes use of these critical distinctions, in order to link agon with superior accomplishment and recognize institutionalized agon as culturally productive, we need to specify what constitutes agonistic interaction and distinguish it from other potentially non-destructive contests. Contests of chance, games of mimicry, and self-induced vertigo are modes of playful activity that do not typically involve competition in which opponents face off and try to beat each other.[13] For example, a lottery contestant engages in play and might reap great rewards, but success in the lottery indicates little about the character or value of the person who, by chance, happens to win. A lottery winner might be wealthier, but there is little reason to believe that that kind of success makes the person better; at least, there is not any obvious intrinsic connection between winning the lottery and being a productive contributor to the cultural development of a society. Furthermore, it is not clear that there is any way in which *playing* the lottery makes one a better person or contributes to the development of productive skills. Finally, while the winner of a lottery might think her new wealth makes life worth living, such a disposition would seem to be significantly different from the positive valuation of life Nietzsche identifies with the ancient Greeks. Thus, there is some work to do in identifying precisely what constitutes an agon and how one engages it.

Agonistic engagement is organized around the test of specific qualities competitors possess. When two runners compete, the quality tested is typically speed or endurance; when artists compete, it might be creativity or mastery of a particular style; craftsmen test their skills; etc. The contest has a specific set of rules and criteria for determining (i.e., measuring) which person has excelled above the others in the relevant way. This is not to say that the criteria could not be a source of disagreement among competitors, judges, or spectators (if there are any). The point is that it is essential to there being a competition that success criteria exist so that their satisfaction or excellence can be ascertained, so that a *decision* can be reached. This would be true even in cases in which the criteria are vague or poorly defined. What is tested is a quality the competitive parties (either individually or as a team) themselves express; external assistance is not permitted.

Ideally, agonistic endeavors draw from competitors their best performances, their greatest capabilities. Although agonistic competition could occur in the form of a zero-sum game in which the winner takes all, Nietzsche, at least in his early and most concentrated study, focuses on how it occurs that all who participate are enhanced by competition.[14] Winning must be a significant goal of participation in agonistic contests, but it would seem that winning might be only one, and not necessarily or always the most important one, among many reasons to participate in such competitions—one can play for the sake of playing, one can play to win, and one can desire to *play well*. In his later writings, Nietzsche is particularly interested in thinking about how the structures of contests or struggles can facilitate different possibilities for competing well within them. In other words, he considers whether the structure of the game might both limit and motivate the way in which one is able to compete. As we shall see in discussion of the agonies of Christianity and Nietzsche's contest with Paul, Nietzsche's study of slavish morality illuminates especially well the dynamic relation between forms of contest and kinds of actions they make possible and cultivate.

Those who look to "Homer's Wettkampf" for guidance about how Nietzsche thinks about power also sometimes refer to what he says there about ostracism. What he cites as the original meaning of *ostracism* is supposed to be evidence of the fact that the Greeks were conscious, at least to some extent, of the importance of their new discovery in their invention of the second Eris. While he grants that ostracism later became a way for tyrants to minimize their opposition, he follows Heraclitus's account of its origin. Diogenes Laertius reports that Heraclitus complained that his friend Hermadorus was forced into exile by his native Ephesians when his accomplishments became so great that no one could even hope to better him.[15] Allegedly, the Ephesians did this because they were concerned about cultivating the pursuit of excellence on a broad scale, not because they despised greatness itself. The value and merits of others in the community were to be affected by ever extending the prospect of being able to earn a title to greatness, not through reduction to the lowest common denominator. In making such a prospect real—that is, making it sufficiently motivating—it had to be reasonably possible for at least some people to consider themselves prospective victors. And, to be so accommodating, there must necessarily be a certain amount of flexibility or fluidity in that standard of excellence.

This notion of how the best is determined further extends prospective participation in creating the standard for what would count as best. Moreover, such standards themselves can be renegotiated in the course of rendering decisions because every decisive agonistic exchange summons the judgment of the community that sanctions and legitimizes the contest. Nietzsche cites the most exemplary contestants as those who both offered exceptional performances in the contest and set new standards by which others were later judged. His admiration of these features of contest makes it clear that he is not simply nostalgic for a heroic ethic of nobility lost and not just pining for a return to the good old days of Homer (even though he might harbor such views).

He relishes the agon because of its potential for what he later describes as the "revaluation of values." This key feature of "Homer's Wettkampf," which the ostracism example illustrates, is crucial for understanding Nietzsche's development and appreciating what he conceives as the prospects for revaluation, as we shall see in each of his engagements with his own agonists.

Thus, Nietzsche considers ostracism to be a social mechanism for regulating political power and contentious relations more generally; the origin of the practice was allegedly designed to protect the dynamism of the contest itself even if its later use was clearly to *avoid* serious competition, precisely the opposite of what he seems to admire. In the event that anyone became so dominant that he could not be seriously challenged, he had to be excluded from the community of prospective contestants—exiled. The sanction functioned foremost as protection for the *institution* that allowed striving contestants their exercise, not to secure the position or authority of any particular one of its *participants*. Nietzsche infers that the creation of the institution of ostracism is an expression of the recognition of the essential role contest played in the health and vitality of Greek cultural life.

Agonistic contest, Nietzsche speculates, is a productive force that regulates without subjugating the interests of individuals, coordinating them without reducing them to the interests of the community, and providing radical openness for the circulation of power that avoids ossification into tyranny. It also provides a means for producing individuals by allowing participants to distinguish themselves through their pursuits within competitive interactions. In this way, agonistic relations create a context in which distinctive performances emerge; understood in this light, they quite literally *activate* the process of individualization, the basis of distinguishing one from another. Moreover, the agon also produces communities insofar as it generates social significance through relations between individuals and the community of judges who bear witness to and sanction the action produced in agonistic exchange. Nietzsche envisions the best possible situation as one in which these interests are reciprocal and in tension: the community desires the production of greatness cast in terms it establishes; the most potent competitors achieve the affirmation of the community that provides the conditions for the possibility of their victories, but they also aspire to become standard bearers and thereby bring about a reformation of judgment generally. Although its advantages are great, Nietzsche thinks, agonism is an extremely fragile condition to maintain. The agon's sustenance requires, first, preservation of the viability of challenge and, second, flexibility sufficient to generate decisions about excellence that are both relative to past performances and in accordance with new standards that are derived through subjecting the prevailing standards of measure to contest.

While this second feature of the agon is especially attractive to contemporary theorists looking to Nietzsche for instruction about the role of dissent and progressive contention in a democracy, I am ambivalent about this particular application of insights drawn from his work. On the one hand, I am wary of the use of Nietzsche or "Nietzscheanism" for projects that strive to articulate *democratic* practices because he is quite clearly and relentlessly a critic of democracy,[16] although I appreciate the compatibility of democracy with a number of Nietzsche's other claims about freedom. On the other hand, I think the very articulations of radical democratic political theory that look to the agon specifically as Nietzsche discussed it or at least in that same spirit are, ironically, not Nietzschean enough and, if they had some interest in being true to the ultimate possibilities they find in radical contestability, they would do well to follow Nietzsche *all the way down* to the heart of the matter. In other words, despite protests otherwise, democratic political theorists who view the agon as a means of legitimizing contingent values seem unwilling to admit as contestable the larger democratic values of freedom and equality. If agonism is a means of legitimizing, promulgating, and sharing values and one turns to it as the alternative to a foundational scheme or specific procedure, then no value can be sacrosanct, no value spared from *possible* agonistic contention. This is not to say that such theorists could not argue for yet another basis for founding democracy's core values (for agon need not be the only way in which one comes to hold or share a value) or that the values supporting the institution of an agonistic framework are not enduring. Indeed, such values must have longevity; otherwise, there would be no reason to prefer the agon (or anything for that matter) to its alternatives. But, if the values in question emerge, are created, and acquire their legitimacy through contestation, then they all must potentially be subject to it at some point.[17] Nevertheless, prior to mounting such arguments, one must be clear about precisely what Nietzsche thinks an agon is, how it potentially organizes human life, what it contributes to culture, how it is deployed in morality, and wherein lies its interpretive power, which are precisely the aims of this book. Fortified by an appreciation of the breadth, depth, and expanse of Nietzsche's agonistic meditations, we might be better prepared to grasp new insights in fields in which Nietzsche's work has long been fashionable, such as political theory and moral psychology, and at the same time find some ways to put his work in dialogue with a less familiar scope of concerns.

1.4 LESSONS FROM PINDAR: THE ECONOMY OF AGONISTIC VALUES AND THE CIRCULATION OF POWER

The Greek word ἀγών appears in the Homeric corpus twenty-nine times, generally designating an assembly or gathering place. The noun stems from the verb meaning "to lead or to bring with one." Later, ἀγών came to indicate a particular kind of assembly, the public gatherings for the games. Eventually, the word was used to refer to all manner of contests or struggles, including spiritual and religious struggles with decadent and malevolent forces that lie externally in the world and within oneself.[18]

Epinician praise poetry, which memorializes victories in sacred games, supplies further insight into the significance of contest and the ways in which competition gathers other values. We catch a glimpse of how competitive interactions provide contexts in which meanings are generated, relations formed and regulated, and truths manifested.[19] Of special interest is Pindar's "Olympian 10," which celebrates the victory of Hagesidamos, the boys' boxing victor in 476 BCE. Pindar sets the stage for appreciating Hagesidamos's achievement by describing the legendary origin of organized games in Greek culture, the founding of the sacred games at Olympia.[20] A vast community and complex set of relations are gathered in the text, including legendary figures, gods, spiritual intermediaries, and the boy's immediate relations. The meaning and significance of Hagesidamos's accomplishment is inextricably bound to those who supported and trained him, those who gave him the opportunity to compete for his polis, those who founded the games, and the poet himself, who preserves the victory for others to remember.

Throughout the ode, Pindar elaborates and relies on a sophisticated economy of value, weaving together themes of honor, gratitude, memory, truth, and time. The poem begins playfully as Pindar calls to mind the debt he owes (the promise he has made) to produce a "honeyed song" for Hagesidamos. He has forgotten the boy's name, he explains, perhaps as an excuse for a delay, and, lest he be thought a liar or a cheat, he appeals to Alētheia for redemption—that is, he asks to be reminded, relieved of his forgetting, so that he can pay his debt and be true to his word. On this basis, he admonishes the victorious youth *to not forget* the debt of gratitude he owes his trainer and all others who made his achievement possible.

The appeal to the goddess Alētheia is more than a matter of piety. The Greek word *alētheia* is derived from *lēthē*—forgetting—so *alētheia* literally means "not forgetting."[21] In English, this word is often translated as *truth*.

Pindar wants to do more than simply call to mind the fact that he has already received payment from the boy's father and therefore is obliged to produce the poem. He aspires to do something more, to give added value, provide some surplus. What he *does* in the poem, Pindar will ultimately claim by its conclusion, constitutes an achievement in its own right, one that entitles *him* praise as well. This is suggested already in the first stanza where the poet announces his intent to pay his debt *with interest*. Understanding what it is that Pindar thinks he does and how it is possible that he is able to do it yields further insight into the broader set of relations in which he places the young boy's victory. This account also provides some clues about the ethos supporting agonistic institutions and how competition produces and reproduces values.

Instead of flattering Hagesidamos or championing his specific virtues, Pindar educates him about the importance of paying his debts; more specifically, he teaches him about the nature of the web of relations in which he now finds himself. He makes the boy's victory sweeter in at least two respects: he enlightens him in the ways in which glory commands obligation along with authority, and the boy's achievement is made even greater by joining it with the successes of the quintessential, legendary agonist, Herakles. This is especially apropos since the games at which Hagesidamos competed and won, those at Olympia, were themselves a tribute by Herakles to honor his father, Zeus, who made it possible for him to prevail in struggles with others. Pindar reminds Hagesidamos that he is indebted to his trainer, Ilas, just as Patroklos was to Achilles for providing the motivation to strive as he did. Others help us by sharpening our skills as well as stirring us to use them. Debts of gratitude run deep for those who "whet another's ambition" and "inspire [. . .] to prodigious feats."[22] Being grateful to them and remembering one's debts will play an important role in Pindar's claim to his own achievement.

Following his introduction, Pindar makes reference to the city that shares Hagesidamos's glory and title to recognition for its role in cultivating his talent. The Lokrians are identified as "honest" (having "strict integrity")[23] and as simultaneously fostering culture (Calliope) and war (Ares). Appealing to these qualities and values is part of Pindar's task. Culture and war are not depicted as opposed, although uniting and maintaining them present challenges. With that said, Pindar goes on to illustrate the games as an example of such a union and to prepare Hagesidamos for further participation in this kind of society. After raising the topic of the founding of the Olympic games, Pindar recounts a protracted series of events leading up to it, showing how the culture of games and athletic contests is related to war and not simply as preparation for its physical and mental challenges but as a kind of redemption of it.

The founding of the Olympic games occurs as recompense and tribute to Zeus for standing by (in the sense of supporting and aiding at critical moments) Herakles in his struggles with King Augeas. Fixing on these details, combined with commentary from the poet, suggests a kind of agonistic *Bildung* that guides Hagesidamos in the ways of being a great victor and instructs him in how to avoid certain dangers that come with such success.

Modern audiences are generally more familiar with Herakles' twelve labors than they are with what happens thereafter, but the legends ascribe to him a long life full of struggle, conflict, and battle, punctuated by contests and play. Augeas figures in what is known as Herakles' "fifth labor," but that particular episode is mentioned only indirectly in "Olympian 10"; it is what comes later that is most important for Pindar's account. Herakles' troubles with Augeas began when Eurystheus ordered him to clean out in a single day the stables housing Augeas's vast herd of oxen. Herakles accomplished what was regarded as a supremely degrading and impossible task by diverting two rivers to wash the stable clean. In exchange for this work, he was supposed to receive a tenth of Augeas's oxen. But Augeas refused to pay what was owed. Ancient sources offer conflicting accounts of what happened next, but it would appear that Herakles swore revenge and, at some point after his other labors, gathered an army to attack Augeas's kingdom in Elis. This campaign was unsuccessful, and Herakles and his men were violently repelled, but eventually Herakles managed to kill Augeas's nephews in ambush.[24] Herakles then led a successful campaign against Augeas that completely destroyed the city: Augeas, "deceiver of strangers, saw his wealth-laden country bow beneath the sword-stroke and remorseless fire, his own city sinking into the torrent of ruin."[25] He was ultimately captured and died.

Herakles oversaw the gathering of the spoils of his victory. Pindar then describes in rather specific detail how Herakles "marked out a precinct sacred to his father, fenced the Altis apart in the clear and made the plain around a place for feasting, honoring the ford of Alpheos and the twelve lordly gods." And he pays further tribute by giving this place a name, "Kronos' Hill," in recognition of the fact that "in former times, when Oinomaos ruled, it had lain beneath deep drifts of snow, without a name."[26] Herakles not only pays his debt to his father; he uses the occasion to set other accounts in order. And then, of the booty, its "first fruits," "the choicest portion," he set aside as sacrifice for Zeus, thereby passing on the greatest measure of his own title to the one who made it possible.

The Herakles example is clearly intended to illustrate what it means to pay a debt and why it is important to do so, how it is that victors are not only entitled but also indebted, and the disastrous consequences that can befall both individuals and cities when debts go unpaid, not remembered. Throughout this account, Pindar also makes observations that resemble maxims to guide future action as well as epithets that draw attention to certain salient features of the events he describes. In addition to the earlier comment about how victors can be grateful to others who ignite their ambition and spur them to great achievements, Pindar also notes that, although the gods sanction and sometimes even provide direct support for such activity, effort and exertion are required for such success.[27] Competitors in the Olympic games might be "praying for victory in [their] thoughts," but success depends on "seizing it by [their] deed." Preceding the account of the epic struggle with Augeas, Pindar briefly mentions Herakles' engagement with Kyknos, in which, he says, "even champion Herakles recoiled once."[28] A plausible inference is that Pindar is underscoring the importance of fighting at the right time since his opponent is described elsewhere in ancient literature as "insatiable in war," refusing Herakles' appeal to take a break. And Pindar gives Augeas the epithet "deceiver of strangers," "betrayer of guests," indicating that he has not only failed to pay a specific debt owed (for cleaning the stable) but also violated the custom of guest-friendship, hospitality. This suggests that, in breaking his word to Herakles, Augeas diminished an important social practice of honoring reciprocal relations more generally. A very important part of telling these events involves reiterating and restoring that order.

Cementing Herakles' founding act of the games, as Pindar tells the story, is the presence of the Moirai, the Fates: "the Moirai stood by, and next to them the one who alone proves Truth true, Time."[29] The Moirai—Lachesis, Clotho, and Atropos—dispense lots, create the fabric of the present, and orient the course of the future. In effect, they govern and shape the dimensions of significant temporality in establishing the horizon of past, present, and future that gives events their temporal context.[30] Immediately following the lines concerning the Moirai, the feats of the first victors are recounted. They are also indebted to Herakles not only because he created the physical place in which the games occurred but also because this provided the semantic space that lent their actions meaning. In other words, recalling the origins of the word ἀγών, we might say that establishing games created a gathering place for meaning-making insofar as it instituted a framework through which otherwise mundane activities could acquire new significance. The early victors Pindar recalls in his ode for Hagesidamos are indebted to Herakles for creating conditions that made it possible for them to engage in meaningful struggle, for their struggles to be *strivings*. In creating an institution that for-

malized competitive interactions, Herakles established a whole context of significance that radiated beyond the sacred space he marked out. Following the
list of achievements of the first victors, Pindar writes: "And then the radiance
of the moon's beautiful eye made evening shine. All the precinct rang with
music, sung at the feast in the mode of praise" much as Pindar's song "rains
sweet words" and "lent [. . .] a hand in [. . .] zeal" to "the Lokrian people and
bathed their heroic town in music."[31] Pindar's honey song both praises and
pays debts—his own and that of the poem's subject. He not only marks the
boy's glory; he ensures that it *grows*.[32]

   This particular contribution highlights an important feature of this mode
of evaluation. Put in economic terms, it is oriented toward *abundance*, maxi-
mizing value, rather than the *conservation* of finite resources. As Dana Burgess
argues, Pindar is able to praise himself not simply by diminishing the subject
of the poem.[33] Rather, in the course of praising Hagesidamos, and in drawing
out the broader community that made his victory possible, Pindar stakes a
claim to his own glory; he does not vie for or claim the glory that Hagesidamos has earned. I think it is possible for us to take this a step further to imagine on what basis it is that Pindar might seek title to this glory that constitutes
the "interest" on his debt. Paying debts is important, as Pindar reminds us in
highlighting the honesty of those who live in the Lokroi region from which
Hagesidamos hails. Pindar will be true to his word, teach Hagesidamos about
how to be true to the spirit of competition, and summon for all to witness the
debts they share to the most honorable competitors of the past. And, for doing all of this, Pindar stakes his own claim to fame.

   Others have noted the pedagogical function of the ode as well as Pindar's
self-praise that is evident in it.[34] My reading endeavors to highlight what else
is implied about how such positive values are generated and sustained in the
social relations sketched out and implied in the text. It is interesting to note
that there is no zero-sum game in the circulation of honor. Pindar can discharge his debts while simultaneously elevating himself, Hagesidamos, and
poetry itself. Pindar's own value increases by the end but not at the expense of
Hagesidamos. Burgess demonstrates how part of what is taught here is "that
honoring obligations need not be inconsistent with personal advantage."[35] I
would go even further. I think Pindar's account of Herakles shows that honoring obligations is, in fact, essential in this economy: without honoring there
are fewer advantages to be sought and won.

   Pindar is surely prideful, but he is not merely self-congratulatory. He carves
out his place within this system of values by virtue of having done something
himself that is worthwhile and estimable. *What* he has done, I suggest, and

what serves as the basis for his title, is that he has *told the truth* in remembering by making manifest Herakles' achievement. His payment is also a contribution to the agonistic economy. This is a distinctive sense of truth-telling, more nuanced than simply relating a historical record that corresponds to actual events. It includes holding in memory, as represented explicitly in Pindar's ode, as well as being attentive to salient detail. In Pindar's account, Herakles is held up as great not because he is a fierce fighter or because he is clever or strong or has distinctive personal qualities other than reverence for this form of honoring relations. Bernard Williams underscores the nexus of concern for "vigilance and memory" in which "accuracy" involves attention to what is most relevant as bound up in the sense of truth found in archaic Greek uses of *alētheia*.[36] I think we find something similar here in Pindar, and this is related to the kind of responsibility and authority that he claims toward the poem's conclusion.

A basic orientation toward gratitude, rather than guilt, is found in the agonistic model, and it entails a different sense of responsibility. One can claim responsibility on the basis of achievement, but this includes mindfulness that such achievements are possible, become manifest, meet the conditions for being worthy of truth, only because of others, only by virtue of dependence and *shared* responsibility. Each victor's achievement also rests on his ability to shelter the economy that makes his victory possible. Such sheltering does not require the victor to explicitly seek to preserve the agon by cultivating competition that will prove superior and represent his ultimate defeat (though that *will* often be the eventual result)—rather, it involves an obligation to express gratitude. And it ends in love, as Pindar compares his subject to one of the most beautiful and most beloved of all mortals, Ganymede. This is an important observation because both scholarly literature on ancient Greece and contemporary work in moral philosophy often assume that evaluative systems that prize competition tend to be hostile to virtues and actions requiring cooperation. Showing how these are not only compatible but also perhaps mutually reinforcing is part of the effort of this book.

Distinguishing *kudos* from *kleos*, Leslie Kurke has described this means of cultural organization in terms of "a circulation of powers and honors whose goal is to achieve a harmonious sharing of this special commodity within the city." *Kudos* hereby signifies "special power bestowed by a god that makes a hero invincible," whereas *kleos* is fame bestowed by human beings.[37] *Kudos*, Kurke argues, is a special kind of potency, available only to the living, a kind of power acquired in victorious struggle, especially for crown winners in sacred games. But such power does not belong to the individual alone: the victor returns to his polis to extend and redistribute this power to the city through the rituals of the crowning ceremony, the ceremonial reentry of the victor in the city, and the statuary and poetic memorials. Such an economy reflects the political negotiations of the aristocracy within communities that were increasingly placing greater value on the rule of the *demos*, the common free citizenry. At the heart of ancient Greek identity, Kurke claims, is a desire to have a stake in this economy and view all social interactions as negotiations for this power.

Relations between and among individuals and communities were significantly bound in agonistic institutions—winning was important both because it led to individual distinction and because it brought a certain kind of power to the victor's city. Individuals distinguished themselves by virtue of *bearing* and *sharing* the fruits of this potency, not simply by besting their competition. Thus, individual victories and distinction strengthened the bonds between a person and his community rather than further separating him from it. The nature of this circulation of power and significance, rather than simply the emergence of distinguishing characteristics or individual glory, was of great interest to Nietzsche, and, in the chapters that follow, I elaborate how the agon provides him with a model for producing meaning and mediating relations more generally.

1.5 THE END OF THE GAME: *HYBRIS* AND VIOLENCE

While Nietzsche found immense benefits in creating and sustaining agonistic relations, he recognized that even the effects of good Eris, who spurs the desire to compete, have their limits. His typology of contests allows him to distinguish creative from destructive modes of action and differentiate productive and harmful cultural relations—the interactions between agonistic institutions and the societies that support them and make them possible. He further entertains another feature that shows just how fragile the relations are between a culture and the exemplary agonists who are upheld as the standard bearers of ultimate value. His concerns about the dangers of *hybris* further indicate the fragility of contest and the dangerous limits of agonism, which are important features of his critical framework.

Succumbing to what we might call the *Miltiades complex*,[38] the Greeks were, on Nietzsche's account, already losing their capacity to sustain agonistic relations even prior to the meddling of which Socrates is repeatedly accused in Nietzsche's works (especially in *Die Geburt der Tragödie* and *Götzen-Dämmerung*). In "Homer's Wettkampf," Nietzsche offers the *hybris* of

Miltiades as evidence that the Greeks were waning in their capacity to properly cultivate the agonistic spirit: although they could produce a great victor such as Miltiades (the Athenian general credited with the victory over the Persians at the decisive battle of Marathon), they could not sustain the institutional framework necessary to support and ultimately contain him. Legend has it that Miltiades was struck down when he challenged the gods by stealing into a temple at night to consort with the priestess Timo. He is supposed to have suffered a mortal wound when, panic struck while leaping over the temple walls, he fell. For Nietzsche, Miltiades' fate exemplifies a victor escaping the boundaries and limits of the agonistic arena that made his achievements possible. His *arete* became limitless. Reflecting back on the language of Pindar's "Olympian 10," Miltiades became a liar; he somehow forgot the debt he owed to the community and failed to hold true the idea that his excellence was contingent on the participation and judgment of the community. Without this limit, and lacking proper understanding of the limits and conditions of his excellence, Miltiades became reckless and destructive. Both he and his city, Athens, suffered gravely as a result.

By achieving such enormous success, Miltiades effectively propelled himself to an insurmountable status—no one could challenge him. Finding no other outlet for his ambition, he challenged the gods, a competition against which the Greeks were warned in countless myths. Through his audacious actions, he aroused the dreaded *envy of the gods*, a kind of envy believed to crush humankind. Nietzsche describes it thus: "godly envy is inflamed when it spots a human being without a rival, unopposed, on a solitary peak of fame" (HC, p. 792).[39] And, like the example of ostracism, the sanctions attending *hybris* suggest to Nietzsche that agonistic institutions were valued so highly that they had to be protected from destruction when indomitable victors threaten—if the state did not take care of the situation, the gods would. Miltiades succumbed to *hybris*, and he was crushed by its weight. But his ruin is also suggestive to Nietzsche of a larger failure. It shows that the ancient Greeks ultimately lacked the cultural resources to support the agonistic needs of a person such as Miltiades; it is symptomatic of the weakening of the agonistic element in Greek culture; thus, Nietzsche has no bald nostalgia for "returning to the Greeks."[40]

The disappearance of agon is bad not only for the individuals who lack an outlet to distinguish themselves but also for the community as a whole. Nietzsche thinks the agon effectively channeled aggression, coordinated it with productive goals, and, once it disappeared, violence ensued. In "Homer's Wettkampf," he points toward the brutal and violent end of agonistic culture as crystallized in the example of Athens at Aegospotamoi. In the Persian War, the Athenian leader Xanthippos ordered the torture and murder of his opponent Artauktes and his son.[41] Later, in 405 BCE, near the end of the Peloponnesian War, the Athenians were devastated by the Spartans at the same site. Herodotus reports that this was widely interpreted throughout the Greek world as divine retaliation for the brutality of Athens in the preceding war as well as the *hybris* it exhibited after its earlier immense victory. Following the Persian War, the Greek city-states formed the Delian League, led by Athens, which eventually subjected the other member states to immense taxes that it used for its own benefit. The devastation of Athens by the Spartans weakened the political power of the entire region: ultimately, the Delian League, which had been indomitable, was unable to resist the Macedonian conquest and, eventually, Roman rule.[42]

What Nietzsche highlights here is the dwindling and decay of what has been described by others as *agonistic respect*.[43] The events at Aegospotamoi were brutal and devastating. Athens never recovered from its defeat, and it could no longer sustain the major role it had played in promoting and facilitating interstate agonism because it could no longer be a viable competitor among its fellow city-states. Thus, Nietzsche writes: "just as Miltiades perishes, so the noblest city-states perish, when, through merit and fortune, they arrive at the temple of Nike from the race track" (HC, p. 792).[44] While the Greek states were able to compete with each other, they experienced comparable peace and unsurpassed cultural achievement. When one of those states seized an abundance of power, it effectively brought that competition to a close. The result was an overall decline in political power even though individual states continued to achieve cultural successes in the years following. Nietzsche interprets those events as examples of Athens's resignation of a genuine contesting spirit and found in them an explanation of its ultimate decline.

Exceptional victory has a tendency to induce *hybris*, a belief in invincibility that can lead to violence and diminished respect for one's opponents and the institutions that provide the means for legitimizing claims to victory.[45] Too much or too little competition leads to destruction, Nietzsche thinks. In his notes, he writes: "the agonistic element is also the danger in every development; it overstimulates the creative drive.—The luckiest thing in development; when several men of genius mutually impose limits on each other" (*KSA* 8:5[146]).[46] Thus, in some respects, the culture that would give prominent place to agonism as a mechanism for determining its values and distributing its goods risks itself: it invites its destruction at the hands of the tyrannical victor that such intensive competition might produce. The significance of the mutual imposition of limits mentioned here, how the meanings of such limits (and the significance of whatever else lies in relation to them) are acquired, is relevant to how we think about the value of competition generally, especially in light of various strands of contemporary ethical and political theory that are keen on eradicating (or at least minimizing) competitive contention and emphasizing cooperation. Nietzsche thinks competitive striving plays an important role in the creation of relational contexts that spur creative action. The Greek agon, for him, gathered more than just a few good men; it served as a site for the production of meaning, for making and remaking the social order and cultural fabric, and for articulating the range of individual possibilities. In his later writings, as discussed in the following chapters, Nietzsche uses this model of relation as a measure of the vitality and creative potential of cultures and societies, and eventually he applies it to the social structures of what he calls "the soul."

1.6 AGON MODEL AS DIAGNOSTIC

In his contemporaries, Nietzsche recognizes a different but related example of the cultural decline he observed in the ancient Greeks. In the first of his *Unzeitgemäße Betrachtungen*, he offers a diagnosis of contemporary German culture: German victory in the Franco-Prussian War led to complacency, self-satisfaction, and destructive self-deception. "The German," in particular, has become a cultural philistine who "perceives around him nothing but needs identical with and views similar to his own; wherever he goes he is at once embraced by a bond of tacit conventions in regard to many things especially in the realms of religion and art." The philistine not only lacks creative energy; he acts as a cultural impediment: "a swamp to the feet of the weary, a fetter to all who would pursue lofty goals" (*DS* 1, pp. 8–9). He celebrates the common as the height of accomplishment.

Nietzsche links what he identifies as narrow-minded self-contentment in his contemporaries with Germany's inability to endure its victory in the Franco-Prussian War. "Human nature," he claims, "finds it harder to endure a victory than a defeat" (*DS* 1, p. 8). On his account, the Germans erroneously convinced themselves that their victory over France was not simply a military success but also evidence of their cultural superiority. This was harmful, not simply because it was deceptive, but because this particular deception was also *destructive*. German success led to stupefaction and stagnation: "everyone is convinced that struggle and bravery are no longer required, but that, on the contrary, most things are regulated in the finest possible way and that in any case everything that needed doing has long since been done." With victory, German culture "feels itself not merely confirmed and sanctioned, but almost sacrosanct" (*DS* 1, p. 4). Germany is no longer able to question and challenge itself, Nietzsche argues, and the courage required to overcome any opposing threat was deemed unnecessary. (He offers similar analyses in *BGE* in "On Peoples and Fatherlands," in *TI* in the sections entitled "What the Germans Lack," and in *EH* in "The Untimely Ones.") Germany suffers, according to him, because it fails to recognize varieties of struggles and their value in cultural life and, moreover, because it believes that all forms of future struggle are needless—it believes its victory is decisive and final.

Relevant here are Nietzsche's evaluative criteria for assessing contests and forms of struggle in terms of their prospects for serving as effective means of institutionalized value production and in terms of the ethos such institutions facilitate. Recall that Nietzsche thinks that human beings, generally speaking, strive at some basic level to improve their lot, but he disagrees with his contemporary Darwinians that self-preservation is always the ultimate aim. And he observes that social institutions always have to manage, channel, or direct this energy according to the intents and purposes of the cultural or political arrangement. For example, negotiating potential conflicts between the perceived good of individuals and the good of the whole is something that all political organizations must face. Something Nietzsche finds particularly interesting about institutionalized agonism is that it appears to be a way to direct human aggression into potentially productive channels, using it as a means to creative rather than mutually destructive ends. He regards the ancient Greek example as successfully achieving this, albeit quite briefly.

Such arrangements are precarious, Nietzsche thinks, for two basic reasons. They potentially overstimulate what drives human beings to excel, and institutions can have difficulty containing such individuals, as the example of Miltiades suggests. And stagnation can occur if it becomes impossible for participants to rise to challenge indomitable victors because productive agonism is dependent on the actual capabilities of participants who must manifest them in order for them to be meaningful indicators of value. Nietzsche's remarks on the function and practice of ostracism illustrate this other tendency. Thus, the cases of *hybris* and ostracism underscore the fragility of these arrangements: they mark out boundaries of productive agonism and its capacity to stimulate and regulate such striving. These conditions provide some explanatory evidence for Nietzsche as to how and why agonistic arrangements decay and decline and the possible results of such in cultures in which this occurs.

Nietzsche's analyses of various domains of human culture (including art, philosophy, science, and morality) focus on how they manage this character-istic of human existence, that is, how they characterize, organize, and direct human striving. He finds various ways of doing this, obviously, but there are some general tendencies in how management of struggle occurs: institutions can organize human striving around certain terms of excellence (e.g., human well-being and thriving) or in terms of struggles *against* basic features of hu-man existence and mortality (e.g., human desires, limitations, and possibilities issuing from our embodiment etc.). So the institutional structures themselves can be variously oriented around creative or destructive projects, depending on how they cast the aims, limits on and qualifications for participation, and terms of exercising judgment and reaching decisions.

Moreover, Nietzsche makes use of this analytic framework for distinguish-ing and assessing the activity of individuals, comparing those who diminish their opposition (forcing back [*herabdrücken*] what poses a challenge) with those who surpass their opponents by excelling (i.e., the activity of elevating above [*erheben*] opposition). The *bad Eris*, discussed above, fuels *Vernich-tungslust*, the desire not merely to conquer but to annihilate. But her twin enhances human existence in the form of propelling one toward excellence however it comes to be defined. Competition of that sort, Nietzsche appears to believe particularly early on, *potentially* advances human possibilities generally.

1.7 WRESTLING WITH THE PAST: NIETZSCHE'S AGONISTIC CRITIQUE AND USE OF HISTORY

Nietzsche's interest in the agon is clearly evident in his conception of history, its utility and its misuse. These ideas inform a methodological pursuit of phil-osophical questioning through agonistic engagement with various historical figures and the cultural movements for which they are catalysts. Nietzsche an-ticipates a history that is *effective*, informing how we think about ourselves in the present and our possible goals for the future. Although the precise route to pursue it changes throughout his works, his sights remain fixed on the re-lation between historical inquiry (from philology to genealogy) and the pro-duction and perpetuation of values. An abiding goal of his historical practice is to produce contention. One way he does this is by distancing his readers (e.g., the ancient Greeks are not just our better noble selves) and connecting them to other potent legacies that allow them to combat current enemies (e.g., battling the tendency toward modern decadence by recognizing the creative potential that is part of an ancestry previously shrugged).[47]

Historical study and presentation not only discover values of the past and disclose something of their transmission but also constitute acts of valuation themselves. That is to say, when we engage in historical inquiry, we remake values, form new ones, at the same time as we learn about those held by others. Historical inquiry itself changes history at the same time as it potentially changes us. This connection between valuation and history is at the center of Nietzsche's best-known and most extended and direct discussion of history, his 1874 essay *Vom Nutzen und Nachteil der Historie für das Leben* (*History in the Service and Disservice of Life*). This essay, particularly understood in the context of the other three independently published *Unzeitgemässe Betrachtungen* (*Untimely Meditations*), helps illuminate his method of cultural critique and therapy, which draws on and extends the agonistic model he earlier describes.

Human history can be charted in terms of overcomings—temporary victories, decisions—in the continuous struggle that is living. When Nietzsche explores the ways in which humans organize culture in terms of stylized struggles of various kinds, including war, games, and other forms of play, he is interested in what such choices reveal about those who so choose and their possible relations to others. As he describes it in his second *Meditation*, history takes three forms: (1) exemplary or monumental ("relevant to the man of action and ambition"), (2) antiquarian (relevant "to the man who preserves and venerates"), and (3) critical (relevant "to the man who suffers and needs liberation") (*HL* 2, p. 95). Each type of history serves different needs. When Nietzsche discovers (and creates) exemplary artistic models in his *Die Geburt der Tragödie* and thereby redefines what should be preserved and venerated from the past, he draws on antiquarian history to serve the end of a monumental history. And he develops these ideas about history when he utilizes historical examples as foils to critique and contest the present.

This description of the workings of history is strikingly similar to the dynamic of opposing tendencies Nietzsche identifies in tragedy: "*The unhistorical and the historical are equally necessary to the good health of a man, a people, and a culture*" (*HL* 1, p. 90). History can be especially useful for someone, perhaps such as Nietzsche himself, who "needs exemplars, teachers, and comforters, and is unable to find them among his companions and contemporaries" (*HL* 2, p. 95). By a mixture of the historical and the unhistorical, he seems to have in mind a combination of *Wissenschaftlich* fact, with which he associates the antiquarian history practiced by his contemporaries, and a creative history that is inspirational. He writes: "a man becomes human only by using the past for the purpose of life and by making history anew from events.

[. . .] No artist would ever paint a picture, no general would win a victory, no people would gain its freedom without first having longed for and struggled toward that end in such an unhistorical condition" (*HL* 1, p. 91). The unhistorical condition is not only a forward-looking projection but also a creative interpretation or extrapolation of events and personages of the past.

Nietzsche argues that a combination of various kinds of history is needed; none is sufficient alone. Monumental history is insufficient because, when it is the only kind of history we employ, it becomes indistinguishable from myth and disarms the power that history exercises on us as the ultimate truth about our past. Antiquarian history, as Nietzsche characterizes it, functions chiefly as a preservative of the past; it cannot be creative. For him: "it always undervalues becoming because it lacks the divining instinct for it—the instinct which exemplary history, for instance possesses" (*HL* 3, p. 102). Critical history entails a form of forgetting. It destroys elements of the past that impede creative action, for example, those that might suggest that a certain kind of progressive action is impossible or unattainable. Just as Nietzsche thinks the Dionysian and the Apollinian must be combined such that their mutual resistance achieves creative results, he argues that the various practices of history must be combined in the interest of creating and serving an affirmative form of life.

Different modes of historical investigation adopt different perspectives on the past as well as relations between the past and the present, and Nietzsche is keen to emphasize how such differences bear on what one can *do* with history. That is, he sees differing perspectives as enabling and facilitating different kinds of actions. This prefigures his later appeal to the advantages that come to one who is able to see something from multiple perspectives and thereby able to take different actions.[48] The various kinds of history bring with them distinctive insights and are susceptible to differing limitations. Antiquarian history focuses a narrow perspective. In striving to preserve the past simply because it has passed, antiquarian history lacks a "criterion of value" and a "sense of proportions applied to things." It preserves and holds dear all it can discern in the past without any reason for preferring or admiring one aspect of that past over any other: "it simply does not notice most things, and the little it does see, it sees in isolation and much too closely. It cannot measure anything, and hence regards everything as equally important, and hence each single detail as excessively important" (*HL* 3, p. 101). It is clear from what Nietzsche writes later in his career about scholars that he views professional philology as primarily limited to this practice.

Critical history is a perspective that grows from a need to "disintegrate a past." When we assume this interpretive stance, we call together aspects of the past in order to challenge and ultimately condemn them. We rightly reject "human violence and weakness," Nietzsche claims, but we cannot sustain this perspective if we strive to overcome that past and provide a different legacy for those who follow us. Critical history is practiced in order to purge the needs demanded by the present. Often, these are needs to eradicate past injustices when "it becomes extremely clear precisely how unjust it is that certain things—a privilege, a caste, or a dynasty, for instance—exist at all, and how thoroughly they deserve destruction." When we practice critical history, we confront that injustice, and "we attack its roots with a knife; then [...] we cruelly trample on all the pieties of the past. The process is always dangerous, dangerous even to life itself" (*HL* 3, pp. 102–3). One danger we face when practicing critical history is that we might become overwhelmed by the process, intoxicated by destructive acts, and abandon the task of asserting what is valuable in human life. Engaging in nothing but critical history diminishes our own power; it is a "lack of self-mastery, [...] what the Romans call *impotentia*" (*HL* 5, p. 112). Once the needs that generate critical history have been dissolved, we must employ a creative form of history if we are to redeem the past with a history of which we deem ourselves worthy, of which we *want* to be worthy.

We take a monumental perspective on the human past when we "attempt to give ourselves a past *a posteriori*, as it were, a past from which we prefer to be descended, as opposed to the past from which we did descend" (*HL* 3, p. 103). This practice of history requires us to forget, even if only temporarily, what is acknowledged in antiquarian and critical modes. Monumental history lies closest to the unhistorical sense Nietzsche associates with Greek accomplishments: "That famous small people of the not-so-remote past—I mean the Greeks—had, during the period of their greatest vigor, stubbornly preserved an unhistorical sense" (*HL* 4, p. 105). The fact that Nietzsche calls the Greeks a "small people" who experienced extraordinary "vigor" is significant. His *Die Geburt der Tragödie* is an attempt to extend that same prospect for his contemporaries, to simultaneously put the Greeks' accomplishment within reach (in the "not-so-remote past") while describing the enormous effort required to get there. In this respect, he charts what he regards as the agonistic potential of historical inquiry. He repeatedly engages this practice, for example, when he looks back to ancient Greek tragedy and the historical conditions from which it emerged to critically inquire about the "music of the future" and when he invents a prehistoric past depicting the birth of morality and the human soul in order to engage inquiry into what might lie "beyond good and evil."

Monumental history is essentially an artistic enterprise that gives meaning to the past. It is a "spirited retelling, enhancing, and heightening of a familiar or even ordinary theme, an everyday tune, into a comprehensive symbol, and thereby intimating in the original theme the presence of a whole world of profound meaning, power, and beauty" (*HL* 6, p. 117). In *Die Geburt der Tragödie*, Nietzsche illustrates two artistic types—the Dionysian and the Apollinian—and the reigning form of their manifestation in the theoretical type Socrates represents (i.e., the Socratic theoretical man currently holds the title of victory in contest between the Dionysian and the Apollinian). The robust practice of history, understood as a commingling of the historical and the unhistorical, creates a tension of constructive and destructive aims. When either task is abandoned, the service of history for life is jeopardized: "If no constructive urge is at work behind the historical urge; unless demolition and clearing away are carried out in the hope that a future, already alive in hope, may build its home on the cleared ground; if justice alone rules, then the creative instinct is weakened and discouraged." Nietzsche continues, "historical research inevitably reveals so much falsehood, coarseness, inhumanity, absurdity, and violence," all traits associated in *BT* with the Dionysian, "that the compassionate atmosphere of illusion," what he describes as characteristic of the Apollinian, "indispensable to everything that wants to live, necessarily vanishes" (*HL* 7, p. 119). *Die Geburt der Tragödie* reflects his attempt to transform ancient Greek history into a work of art in order to awaken a creative instinct that might allow his contemporaries to project the possibilities this history holds for them.

The ancient Greek agon serves Nietzsche as a great example of stylized struggle for a variety of reasons. Foremost is the pervasiveness of the contest in Greek antiquity: the Greeks are almost always at war, the major literary sources that anchor Greek cultural identities are linked to struggles that inaugurated and sustained their existence, the Greeks' gods served as monumental exemplars of grand struggles and conflicts, and their forms of worship included athletic and artistic contests that served as tribute to their exemplary agonists. Major forms of play and recreation were based on reenactments of these struggles, and eventually social and civic life was organized around performance in contests whose structure and values were transferred from these earlier forms of struggle. We can examine how various spheres of contest are related and interdependent. Observation of changes and devolutions of agonistic relations allows us to appreciate their fragility and develop a finer set of distinctions for use in analyses. The deformations are particularly instructive since they are not the result of the acts of specific individuals despite Nietzsche's tendency to characterize them this way. In all such cases, the necessary institutional conditions eroded. New developments emerge in the context of reactions to and against these structural changes, as evident in the development Nietzsche identifies from Homer to Socrates to Paul, and the disappointing results we find in his attempts to reengage, revive, and catalyze new contests with these agonists and the self-assessment he undertakes in his agon with Wagner, as discussed in chapter 5 below.

1.8 INTRODUCING NIETZSCHE'S AGONISTS

Homer is Nietzsche's exemplar for two key crucial concerns throughout his works: creativity and power. The potency of Homer's poetic transformation of human toil and struggle both fascinated and spurred Nietzsche to try to capture and command the same kind of force. Nietzsche's Homer is not simply the founder of a certain form of culture; he is a revolutionary, a reformer, someone who effects a tremendous revaluation. Thus, it is important in Nietzsche's account that Homer is *late*.[49] Here, *late* means that Nietzsche regards the emergence of what is classically considered Homeric as standing at the end of a significant period of cultural development rather than at the beginning. As I elaborate in the next chapter, Nietzsche regards Homer as having *overcome* dominant cultural traditions that developed prior to his arrival on the scene. Thus, he considers Homeric literature to be a late development in Greek culture rather than its founding moment. The life of struggle, previously portrayed by Hesiod as a kind of punishment for all of human existence, comes to have glorious new possibilities when (certain kinds of) struggles are arranged that allow humans to be so great as to be enviable by the gods.[50] In other words, Homer makes a virtue of what Hesiod sees as a curse. Although Hesiod and Homer both regard struggle as inescapable, Homer is distinctive in making it a route to glory. He is exemplary in Nietzsche's historical account because he is a successful competitor in a larger contest over the value of human existence, overcoming the worldview typified by Hesiod.

Moreover, *what* he offers as replacement values are particularly creative and affirmative. Nietzsche regards the significance or value of Homeric existence as potentially surpassing that of the gods—the gods cannot achieve the status of the heroes because they cannot risk their lives. And the replacement values for the glory of contest created an engine for value production that was particularly fruitful. So there are three major facets to the case of Homer that Nietzsche presents:

1. *Homer is an exemplary revaluator.* In overcoming the prior worldview that regards human existence as a kind of punishment, Homer provides a model, a touchstone, for the creation of new values. Nietzsche defines his own tasks in light of what he thinks Homer accomplishes and in light of how he sees those who wrestle with the Homeric legacy, particularly Plato.

2. *Homer affirms life; he gives a positive value to human existence.* The worldview evident in Homeric poetry epitomizes affirmation, what Nietzsche later calls *yes-saying*: it offers a redemption of human existence that is tangible and meaningful in the real world, the here and now; it does not need an otherworldly or afterworldly anchor. The obvious contrast to this will be Nietzsche's characterization of Christianity and its model of redemption that casts human beings as lacking the resources to save themselves. In this respect, human beings are no longer damned, but they are eternally *guilty*. Insofar as Homer depicts human possibilities as even greater than those of the gods (because gods cannot take the relevant great risks), he offers a maximally rich conception of the meaning and purposes of human existence. Thus, Homer is Nietzsche's model of the ultimate life affirmer.

3. *Homeric values are renewable, and the agonistic arena supplies a forum for further revaluation.* The standards of excellence for engaging in contest are derived from past performances (prior contests) and the extraordinary performances that call for a revision of those measures in any given contest. Thus, values derived in agonistic contexts are contingent and eminent; they are perpetually renewable. Although Nietzsche does not directly state it, this feature of Homer's contest is the most enticing for him. Such values are tangible, derived from specific cases, and motivating, insofar as one seeks to manifest or realize them for oneself or to become the new standard bearer. Old values can be renewed in agonistic interaction, and new values can be created when specific engagements call for a reformulation of the exercise of judgment.

The Homeric achievement is contested, as Nietzsche tells the story, by Socrates (the Platonic Socrates, or more likely the Socrates evident in *Socratism*—that is, what Socrates has come to mean or stand for). The engagement of Homer and Socrates turns on what is valued (e.g., the heroic life) as well as how it is valued (e.g., through public contests). That Socrates succeeds in his resistance demonstrates that he is also exemplary in his ability to transform values, to revalue them. But how he goes about it (through promulgation of dialectic) and why (because it better prepares one for death rather than life) are highly problematic for Nietzsche. The case of Socrates can be measured against that of Homer, and it too has at least three facets:

1. *Socrates is an exemplary revaluator.* Nietzsche is awed by the success of Socratic revaluation, but he finds it particularly puzzling and in need of an explanation. He considers Socratic values so alien and at odds with earlier standards of excellence. This problem is captured in a set of questions that organize Nietzsche's contest with Socrates: If the Greeks were really so superior because of their orientation toward the *arete* Homeric agonism made possible, how was it that Socrates was able to be successful in replacing heroic values with philosophical virtues? How did Socrates convince the Greeks that their enemies and most important battles resided *within* themselves rather than among or outside those in their community? How was it that he was so seductive? In his investigation of these problems, Nietzsche explores the significant change in taste that Socrates inaugurated. What it means to live the good life changes quite dramatically as Nietzsche sees it, and Socrates earns the credit (or defamation) for instigating this monumental shift. With Socrates, the Greeks acquire a "taste for dialectic" (*TI* "Socrates" 5) that exceeds their taste for heroism. Nietzsche investigates the background conditions that would make this possible and what such ultimately indicate about what the Greeks valued and why.

2. *Socrates is a life-denier—he regards the struggle of life as reaching satisfactory resolution only in death.* For Nietzsche, Socrates ultimately views life as a disease (*GS* 340). This is a view Nietzsche advances throughout his writings, beginning with his first book, and becoming even more nuanced in his later writings. The evidence for this is supposed to be that Socrates seeks to "correct existence" in large measure because of his equation of the good, the true, and the beautiful. While there is certainly much that Nietzsche admires about Socrates—particularly his "silence"—what he sees as this underlying motivation ultimately causes him to reject Socrates.

3. *Socrates is an antagonist, and, thus, he effectively shuts down the mechanism for the rejuvenation of values Nietzsche thinks Homer inaugurated.* Nietzsche sees Socrates as blocking the channels of productive agonism,

not only because he diminishes the value of the ends of contests that emerged from Homeric culture but also because he alters the means of striving. He regards the emergence of Plato's Socrates as an ideal type that affects both the efficacy of the institutionalized structure of cultural agonism and the modes of action that are definitive of social participation. Thus, for example, Socrates diminishes the value of competing in and striving to win the contests that were such an imiportant facet of ancient Greek life, including the artistic festival contests of the tragedies and the athletic contests of the religious games. Nietzsche regards dialectic as essentially destructive, debilitating, and ultimately incapacitating in an agonistic context.[51]

Nietzsche's case against Socrates begins with reflection on his position in light of the cultural conditions he inherits from Homer.

Similarly, Nietzsche critically engages Pauline theosophy specifically in its relation to the development of Socratic values. But, whereas he regards Socratic philosophy as standing *opposed* and providing an alternative to the Homeric worldview, he sees the Pauline interpretation of existence as an advancement and intensification of certain destructive features of Socratism, thereby bringing about a complete annihilation of the Homeric. There are at least three parallel features of Nietzsche's account of Paul as agonist:

1. *Paul completes the Socratic devaluation of Homeric glory.* Whereas mortality was an essential ingredient of Homeric glory (the value of life could be weighed and measured according to risks assumed), the site of mortality—the human body, *flesh*—was transfigured as a site of decadence, sin. No glory in *this* life could be attained; such was reserved only for another, other world.
2. *Paul invents the "evil enemy" and limits the agon to internal struggle.* The Socratic agon is viewed as taking on not only external enemies but also internal ones. With Paul, Nietzsche thinks, this process of turning inward is completed when the soul becomes the *only* battleground. The characterization of the enemy also shifts in the Pauline worldview. Rather than struggling against imperfection, as is the case with Socrates, Paul fights an enemy who is evil. Thus, the only recourse is destruction; *Vernichtungslust* is the primary motivation for action in this contest.
3. *Paul is the life-denier par excellence.* Nietzsche figures Socratic dialectic as essentially destructive—it attains its victory by destroying opposition rather than by surpassing it. Pauline values put a premium on violence

and destruction and ultimately diminish to the point of vanishing the significance of human existence.

His account of Pauline theosophy is both a critical engagement with the past and an assessment of our current situation, since Nietzsche thinks that Pauline Christianity has come to be the dominant worldview and paradigm for values, at least in the West, and particularly in Europe. The agonistic development I trace through most of the book comes to a certain end, or at least rest, in the engagement with Paul. Nietzsche opposes virtually every facet of this development: he regards Paul's *ant*agonism as the near perfect antithesis of the agonism he admired in Homer—Paul obliterates the form of contest as well as the ethos that would facilitate and sustain a robust agonism.

Nietzsche's agon with Wagner, then, does not simply trace the further decline of the agon since Homer but rather (finally, eventually) anticipates its possible place and future from out of the ruins of its maximal decay. This agon is particularly reflective of Nietzsche's own struggles against himself, but not exclusively so (furthermore, the other agones might also offer evidence of Nietzsche struggling against his own tendencies). What begins in opposition to Pauline moralism ends in the anticipation of a postmoral psychology in which Nietzsche reconsiders certain key facets of his earlier views of agonism, including the heroic form of struggle as well as the centrality and ends of agonism. I show how Nietzsche offers accounts of *how one becomes what one is* by pitting his own biography against that of Wagner, an account of his own development compared and contrasted with earlier and later depictions of Wagner that he creates. The heart of this contest is a fight over the entitlement to Wagner, his significance, what Wagner might mean to us, what use we can make of him, what his appearance indicates about us, and what future we might claim on that basis. It is ultimately a fight for the future that indicates something about *how a future becomes ours*.

We might expect at the end of it all to see Nietzsche vying for the title of the replacement to Pauline valuation. But Paul's project is complete. It simply is not possible to play the same game any longer. There is no outdoing him; he corrupted the whole enterprise. Paul is not to be defeated or surpassed; he has to be *passed by*. Nietzsche's struggle with Wagner reflects his efforts to make that transition and scout possibilities to be found in the aftermath of Christian morality and its influence in virtually every aspect of human culture and inquiry.

Nietzsche evaluates each of his agonists in terms of their own projects of revaluation and mindful of how his engagement with them *produces or gener-*

ates certain kinds of contests of its own. New contests can generate new terms of evaluation as well as create opportunities for an agonistic culture insofar as our current culture depends on the preeminence, the continued reign, of these values. Learning how they acquired their supremacy might also provide insight into how they can be overcome. The way in which Nietzsche portrays his agonists is related to the kind of contest he strives to effect and the purposes to which he puts those contentions. A dialectical development is discernible. In the chapters that follow, I show how his reflections on these different models and modes of contest organize and animate the major philosophical projects in which he engaged, including exploring the relation between art and culture to understand practices of making meaning or creating values (the engagement of and with Homer); investigating the relation between philosophy and other modes of inquiry, particularly science, and how this bears on the value of truth itself (Socrates); examining the relations among values, particularly moral values and how they organize entire forms of life (Paul); and considering alternative conceptions of subjectivity and agency that might be available beyond the morality of good and evil (Wagner).

Nietzsche's account of the development of Greek culture, art, and science, broadly conceived, figures Homer as offering the first monumental revaluation of human existence through his depiction of human struggle as *potentially* modeled on contests, the stakes of which were the highly prized commodities of honor and glory. What is particularly important to Nietzsche is not only that Homer revalued human existence, even though such is quite a feat in itself, but also the legacy of that valuation, particularly insofar as it provided a medium through which other revaluations might occur. In other words, the contest Homer valorizes not only provides the conditions for esteeming human life in light of its exemplary and exceptional struggles but also fuels prospects for revising, reenvisioning, and reevaluating such ideals as it draws others to contest the aims and ends of struggles that characterize human life. Nietzsche's Homer is an exemplary contestant because he accomplishes a great feat—he sets new standards for what constitutes cultural production (in terms of commanding the tastes and aspirations that define a culture and organizing life around their pursuit), and he supplies a means for the perpetual renewal and revaluation of values.

The case of Socrates illustrates certain facets of Homer's success insofar as Nietzsche regards Platonic Socratic philosophy as fundamentally organized in terms of contesting Homer. Ultimately at stake is philosophy's entitlement (as opposed to poetry's) to determine the whither and for what of humanity. Pauline morality represents a certain intensification and exaggeration of this struggle, endeavoring to wrest this power from the philosophers to give it to the priests.[52] We see this general historical view of the broad sweep and development of Western values reflected time and again in Nietzsche's works. Understanding that account in terms of the development, deployment, and deformation of agon can help us appreciate the terms of his critical analyses as well as what he envisions for a possible future he eventually anticipates in his struggle with, against, and for the meaning of Wagner and in his reflections on a moral psychology beyond good and evil. From Homer to Socrates to Paul to Wagner, Nietzsche sees the emergence of a creative mechanism for producing values and positively valuing human existence that is ultimately transformed into something nearly its opposite. Once we stake out this vantage point, we are able to witness his struggles to imagine and articulate some possibilities that lie beyond it.

CHAPTER TWO

Contesting Homer:
The Poiesis of Value

2.1 HOMER'S CONTEST AS EXEMPLARY REVALUATION

Homer stands as Nietzsche's exemplar of Apollinian artists, as described in his first book *Die Geburt der Tragödie*. Nietzsche admires him not only or even primarily for depicting and celebrating what was already noble but also for staking a claim to the creation of nobility itself. Homer's idealization of the life of glory and his articulation of vehicles for achieving it, namely, through contest, effected a transformation of the mundane trials and tribulations of life that might otherwise seem meaningless. Nietzsche argues that Homer's valorization of the agon produced new forms of possible relations that allowed people to forge significant attachments among individuals and groups and between people, the city, and the powerful forces of the gods. And in this way even ordinary existence acquired an altogether different connotation. In short, Nietzsche credits Homer with making it possible to affirm life, specifically *human* life: the new world of values he shaped afforded possibilities that one might be able to create a life one desires as one's own.

Of special concern to Nietzsche is understanding how Homer stands as a *victor* over something prior and, thus, epitomizes *victorious overcoming* as such: Homer redeems, he revalues, he sets the standard for redemption. Moreover, the rise and fall of Homeric agonism, evident in the great sweep of history Nietzsche depicts, is itself illustrative of how a value scheme can develop to such a point that it begins to undermine itself, insofar as the Homeric view is ultimately contested, reasserted, united with its opposition at its height, and then ruined. This resembles a process Nietzsche later describes as "self-overcoming," which he thinks is characteristic of all existence.[1]

In *Die Geburt der Tragödie*, much of which was written after Nietzsche's plans for "Homer's Wettkampf" were already organized, Homer is credited with overcoming an earlier expression of a modified version of the Hobbesian view of the state of nature—namely, that for humans life is nasty, brutish, and (not) short (enough). Nietzsche finds this view crystallized in the so-called wisdom of Silenus, who tells Midas that "what is best for humans is to never have been born and second best is to die soon."[2] Silenus and Hesiod testify that human life is marked by relentless toil and struggle, meaningless labor and strife, and the best one can hope for is to get out of it as quickly as possible. But guided by Homer, Nietzsche claims, we witness the significance of the labors of human existence deliberately transformed and placed into the hands of humans themselves. The Homeric perspective extends the possibility of evaluating human life differently. From this new point of view, it might very well be that human beings are fated to struggle, but they nevertheless have the power to craft labors of their own that enhance the character and meaning of their existence. Evidence of this, and an index of the intensity of this value, is the abundance of literary testimony that through such labors human beings potentially attracted the jealousy of the gods. Thus conceived, life becomes full of possibilities to seek and win, and the wisdom of Silenus is overcome, replaced with the worldview expressed in Homeric literature. Homer's revaluation of human existence has it that what is best is to never die—to achieve some unforgettable victory. Second best is to not die too soon—that is, to live long enough to secure the meaning of one's life through significant action.

For Nietzsche, Homer vivifies an exemplary model of productive valuation—he creates values that affirm life and also provide a means for further value generation.[3] In "Homer's Wettkampf," *Die Geburt der Tragödie*, and other early writings, Homer rises as the first deliberate transformer of values, a figure who fundamentally redirects the conception of the significance of human life. But Nietzsche credits Homer with even more than that—the *kind* of values he offered were different insofar as they opened possibilities for others to engage in revaluation by tapping the transformative potential of the agon. That is, the agon was both the result of a new evaluation of the more significant possibilities of human existence and a mechanism or means for creating other values—in short, it provided an engine for further revaluation. On these grounds, Nietzsche extols Homer as an exemplary poet who inspires others to practice the art of transfiguration themselves. He is lured to contest Homer by seeking to surpass his accomplishment, not by diminishing it. Homer is an exemplary agonist Nietzsche strives to exceed.

No figures in antiquity knew more about the agonistic way of life than Homer's struggling heroes. It was thanks to Homer that the Greeks thought they knew so much about the mythical age of the great heroes, the people who allegedly lived in the age before his own.[4] As M. I. Finley describes it in his influential book vivifying the Homeric worldview: "everything pivoted on a single element of honour and virtue: strength, bravery, physical courage, prowess. Conversely, there was no weakness, no unheroic trait, but one, and that was cowardice and the consequent failure to pursue heroic goals."[5] Reputation was a paramount concern; achieving heroic recognition was a public affair. James Redfield goes so far as to claim that one can recognize in Homeric literature the view that only through public competition could individuals fully realize the height of human existence.[6] In these respects, we can think of the agon as providing a site where *human being* gathers its meaning, its value as worthwhile, respectable, desirable. To be a hero one had to be willing to stake everything—including one's life—in a struggle to acquire greater prestige. Consequently, the immortal gods could not be heroes or even be genuinely brave. The heroic life was exclusively the provenance of the human.

This culture of contest and revaluation provides the model for one source of a regenerative power Nietzsche aims to yoke in art and philosophy, a theme that persistently occupies his writings. Homer's victory over Silenus and the projection of the heroic ideal become the quintessence of the creative force that he famously associates with the Apollinian. In *Die Geburt der Tragödie*, the agon of the Apollinian and the Dionysian is initially characterized in terms of a contest of creative forces of nature. Nietzsche then moves on to discuss how the phenomenon is manifest in art, Greek art in particular. He uses the example of Doric art as particularly evincing rigid opposition to the Dionysian festivals in Greece and beyond, noting that, while the agon of the Apollinian and the Dionysian might result in temporary reconciliations, these in no way bring the two forces any closer together and in fact sharpen and clarify their distinguishing characteristics. In other words, the apparent cessation of conflict serves only to intensify the opposition. Given what I discussed earlier about the significance for Nietzsche of *sustaining* agonism, intensification of opposition might seem as though it should be desirable to him. Exploring this with the benefit of the agon analytic allows us to more fully appreciate the achievement that Nietzsche endeavors to highlight in his admiration of the tragic and to see how these earlier contests (and their reconciliations) differ from what occurs in the case of tragedy.

Applying the distinctions between forms of contest and ways of competing, we might see how what occurs in the particular kind of deepening and sharpening of differences that Nietzsche flags as the result of these truces could result in a propensity toward *Vernichtungslust*: As the contestants are increasingly defined in terms of diametric opposition and absolute difference, they are increasingly less tolerant and receptive to actual engagement. The temporary reconciliations Nietzsche acknowledges in the history of the contest of the Apollinian and the Dionysian in ancient Greek art serve to push the two forces further apart and fuel their claims to exclusive authority. A possible result of such development could be that the participants become agon-aversive rather than spurred to *Wettkampf*. In such a case, the conflict would fail to be sufficiently robust to fully tap the potentially productive power Nietzsche associates with agonistic relations.

But perhaps the sharpening of differences Nietzsche highlights in the early sections of *Die Geburt der Tragödie* reflects not a series of failures or missed opportunities but rather preparation for the later full-blown contest he highlights in ancient Greek tragedy. He describes the emergence of the Dionysian dithyramb and how it is consonant with a view of life evident in ancient literature and the Titanic world order. He highlights the development of a contrasting view in depictions of the Olympian gods, which he characterizes as expressing a "fantastic excess of life" in which "all things are deified," triumphantly, with exuberance (*BT* 3). He specifically emphasizes the visual and imagistic elements of what he regards as the ultimate expression of the Apollinian at this point.

The Olympian world serves as a "transfiguring mirror" that reflects back a glorified, deified projection of human life. It can be seen as an idealization of human existence itself rather than an image in comparison to which human life is shown to be fundamentally base and defective: the gods glorify humans by *living out* human-like lives in which both good and evil are beautiful. What motivates such production, the needs that drive its expression, is of special interest to Nietzsche. He is particularly keen to point out that this "oneness of man with nature" evident in the Olympian vision "is by no means a simple condition that comes into being naturally and as if inevitably." It is important for his account that the Olympian vision is *produced* (not the result of some necessary development)—a creative product that harnesses and deploys significant resources. Such resources are inherent in the culture; thus, they are not the work of a lone creative genius of the sort that might have preoccupied Nietzsche's contemporaries. But neither is their expression simply the natural progression of a culture: "It is not a condition that, like a terrestrial paradise, *must* necessarily be found at the gate of every culture." The Olympian world produced in Homeric literature represents "the complete victory of Apollinian illusion" (*BT* 3), not naïveté.

When the Homeric/Apollinian cultural forces collided with their opposite, the Archilochean/Dionysian, so the story goes in *Die Geburt der Tragödie*, each fought for domination. Nietzsche maps this struggle to the development of art and its various expressions as manifestations of temporary victories of one or the other of these forces. Periodically, one outdoes the other, and the loser is submerged, just waiting for the right moment to try again to get the upper hand. On Nietzsche's now familiar account, tragedy somehow managed to bring forth and harness both opponents. It was not primarily the expression of just one of the creative forces—both were expressed simultaneously. Remaining opposed, in tragic art, hostility was converted to creativity as each agonist worked to pursue its own aims by repurposing the resources of the other. The tragic contest thus described crystallizes the productive cultural model Nietzsche identifies in "Homer's Wettkampf": tragic art manages to gather creative energies from both opposing forces without eradicating conflict. It achieves such a union without contriving a compromise that diminishes opposition. And it expresses these energies in a way that was extraordinarily transformative, all because it effects a contest that brought out the simultaneous maximal expression of these opposing tendencies.

Several features of Nietzsche's account of this struggle, elaborated below, were especially controversial among his fellow philologists since the details were at odds with received ways of formulating some of the core concerns of the discipline. This includes how his account bears on the classic Homeric Question and its implications for the problem of beauty in tragic art. His portrayal of Homer as a victor over earlier pessimistic views, specifically those expressed by Hesiod, affects the dating of the Homeric tradition and requires Homer to be considered *late*, as Nietzsche puts it. Thus, recall that, on Nietzsche's account, Homer does not stand at the beginning of ancient Greek civilization; he is not its genius founder. It is important for Nietzsche's story that Homer overcomes and conquers something that *is already* distinctively Greek.

Moreover, how Nietzsche characterizes the fundamental dynamic of the struggle between the Apollinian and the Dionysian and its attraction in ancient Greek tragedy has significant implications for the received view of Aristotle about the source of the pleasure derived from consuming this art. The problem of beauty in tragedy is to explain why the depiction of such horrific images of human destruction should be beautiful to us, pleasurable. Nietzsche's view is that the tragedies are pleasing not by virtue of the fact that they provide moral purification of pity and fear—catharsis, as Aristotle describes—or because such scenes satisfy a craving for violence but rather because they have transformative effects and positively induce a feeling of creative power. As we shall see, this was not simply association with the power stemming from a superior destructive force—this is another reason why it is important to bear in mind that *both* the Apollinian and the Dionysian play a significant role. On Nietzsche's account, ancient Greek tragic art created an arena in which the best was drawn out of each opponent in a dynamic through which neither was allowed to dominate. Nietzsche thought the pleasure derived from tragedy was the result of the experience of poiesis—of poetic power exercised so as to supply human existence with meaningful content that was inaccessible solely through the idealized imagery of the Apollinian or the rapturous ecstasy of the Dionysian (*BT* 22; cf. *BT* 7).

The more familiar arguments of *Die Geburt der Tragödie* can be coordinated with the previously elaborated criteria for evaluating contests in terms of their organization and the kinds of actions they facilitate. While the basic argument of *Die Geburt der Tragödie* has been extensively treated in the secondary literature,[7] its connection to a detailed and broader conception of agonism has not been discussed in any extended and substantial way. If we apply the insights achieved through focused attention on Nietzsche's conception of agonism, certain assumptions and persistent characterizations of the work, including perhaps his own later assessment of it as too much influenced by Schopenhauer's pessimism and as substantially distant from his later philosophy, become suspect. A more thorough examination of the agon at the heart of *Die Geburt der Tragödie* shows how that book initiates a more expansive investigation of competitive institutions and their relations to culture that stretches across Nietzsche's entire oeuvre. With this text, Nietzsche commences an abiding two-pronged investigation in which he explores the possibility that all of existence can be described in terms of forces that are in opposition and cooperation (in which culture and practices of self-constitution reflect appropriations of these forces) and how philosophy might involve creatively developing the concepts through which the diverse researches of scientific inquiry might be coordinated and combined. The second prong of this project becomes an increasingly urgent concern for Nietzsche immediately following his work on *Die Geburt der Tragödie*, and it is discussed at greater length in following chapters. Reading *Die Geburt der Tragödie* illuminated by Nietzsche's agonism allows us to confront some persistently thorny issues in ongoing discussions of his views. Informed by a richer conception of his agonism, we are better poised to address the issue of pessimism in his philosophy and his alleged conservatism and assess the degree to which his affirmation of agonism is *merely* romantic machismo or reckless nostalgia for a Greece that remains idealized and racist, even if it is reformed.

2.2 THE APOLLINIAN (AND THE DIONYSIAN): THE AGON BEGINS

Clearly, the most significant aspects of tragedy for Nietzsche are its massive artistic resources, which it utilizes to facilitate *transformations*. These involve generating new and different meanings and affording different felt qualities for the experience of being human. Briefly put, tragedy provides a means for what Nietzsche later calls *revaluation*: It provides a positive form of redemption of human existence that he later contrasts with the Christian model. It involves a direction of desire and revision of the purposes around which we organize our lives and in accordance with which we might affirm something as valuable and worthwhile. What gives tragedy this affective, organizational force is, we shall see, its agonistic structure. Although tragedy is composed of two essential ingredients (the Apollinian and the Dionysian) and the exclusion of the Dionysian plays a monumental role in his well-known story about the demise of tragedy, Nietzsche thinks that tragic art never would have emerged, its most potent possibilities never realized, were it not for the way in which the *Apollinian* manifests itself specifically in Homeric literature. Thus, although the Dionysian is emphasized in his later philosophy and its absence is painfully felt in his account of what followed Attic tragedy, the Apollinian has a more prominent place than what is often considered, as suggested in the heading for this section. This is an important part of the story to tell, but obviously not the only part, for, while Nietzsche works hard to distinguish his opponents, he also provides ample clues that their distinction is only one way of regarding a process in which both elements are thoroughly entwined. Apollo and Dionysus symbolize differing aspects, competing tendencies, but they are not two essentially separate and distinct entities.

Recall some of the distinguishing features in Nietzsche's characterization of Homer. As Nietzsche approaches the classic "problem of Homer" or Homeric Question, he speculates about ways of thinking and forms of evaluation that the appearance of the Homeric stories made possible. The emergence of the Homeric worldview makes it possible to at least *imagine* that one might be able to create a life one desires as one's own. When Nietzsche examines life as depicted by Hesiod, he concludes that a Homeric form of affirmation was previously simply inconceivable. Thus, he depicts Homer as a *victor*—but of a different kind from the type he brought to life. By identifying at least some struggles as evidence of excellence, worthy of both public and divine recognition, Homer fought and won against an earlier pessimistic assessment of the aims and purposes of human existence. Because such distinction was attached to *action*, because it was contingent on being manifest and evident rather than exclusively an entitlement of birth, it had a particularly tangible character. (Of course, slaves, women, children, and countless others were not permitted to vie for this recognition, so it is not as though circumstances of birth played no role.) Moreover, the benefits of this enterprise extended beyond the honor accrued by individuals or the communities who claimed them as their own. The explicitly public nature of the activity also engaged the community in a common exercise of judgment that was regenerative: values could be reinforced and reaffirmed, or they could be reformulated. The Homeric model of competitive engagement was enacted in a different way in tragedy, as Nietzsche tells the story, because then the Apollinian activity of idealization and distinction that Homer exemplified was itself contested by the Dionysian tendency to dissolve distinctions.

The characteristics of the primary agonists of tragedy, the Apollinian and the Dionysian, are well-known. Less prominent are discussions of the precise form of their engagement in tragic art and the end toward which this contest unfolds. If we ask about the aims of the Apollinian and the Dionysian, we find the traditional view that the Apollinian seeks to build up a beautiful image and the Dionysian seeks its destruction or annihilation. But, if we keep in mind that these forces are distinguished in and through contest, a fact that is obscured as each force has its turn in dominating the other but that is fully apparent in the case of tragedy, then we need to understand how their simultaneous engagement organizes the work. This provides new insight into the terms of the agon at the core of tragedy. In particular, this perspective leads us to consider what might be at stake for each agonist, what might be thought as the prize each seeks. In focusing on Apollo and Dionysus as *contestants*, we might ask, *What is it that the Apollinian and the Dionysian want?*

The claim that the Apollinian and the Dionysian each pursue in Nietzsche's story is *entitlement to symbolization*. Each strives to become the arbiter of meaning, to express the character of the world cast in its own terms. This is evident in the overarching dynamic Nietzsche sketches in the very first paragraph of *Die Geburt der Tragödie*, where he writes: "the continuous development of art is bound up with the *Apollinian* and *Dionysian* duality—just as procreation depends on the duality of the sexes, involving perpetual strife with only periodically intervening reconciliations" (*BT* 1). What is at stake in the contest for symbolization and just how transformative it can be become clear early in *Die Geburt der Tragödie* when, in the second section, Nietzsche imagines the initial Greek reception of the alien Dionysian perspective on existence conveyed in the gestures and movements it was thought to inspire. The Dionysian tendency casts the world in terms of a unity that obliterates individual distinctions and disintegrates singular identities. Through dance and rhythmic movement, the Dionysian introduces a new symbolism of the body and puts into play what hitherto prevailed (*BT* 2). Although this new means of symbolization seemed strange to the Greeks, as Nietzsche tells the story, to their own amazement—and, considering the reputation of the Dionysian as it was expressed abroad, undoubtedly to their horror—they were able to understand this uncanny force. In short, they were able to meet the Dionysian because they recognized themselves in it and the predominant features of their culture as draped over it. To account for this possibility of how they could recognize themselves in the Dionysian, Nietzsche provides a sketch of what precedes the formal introduction of the Dionysian in Greek culture by "dismantl[ing] that artistic structure of *Apollinian culture*, stone by stone" (*BT* 3). Thus, he begins by asking what produced Apollinian culture in the first place. What need did it seek to satisfy?

The answer is quite familiar to Nietzsche scholars: the need was one of overcoming fear, surmounting terror. The Greeks did this not by denying that world from which they sought relief—a perspective on nature and its grasp on human beings that Nietzsche finds exemplified in portrayal of the Titans—but rather by *inserting* a world, a middle world, between the Titanic and their own, namely, the world of the Olympians (*BT* 3).[8] The human world was thereby justified on the basis of being lived by the gods themselves. Nietzsche claims that Homer's depiction of the Olympian world should not be considered the product of naïveté, as Schiller characterizes it; rather, the Homeric worldview represents an *accomplishment* Nietzsche identifies as "the complete victory [Sieg] of Apollinian illusion" (*BT* 3).

Schiller draws the relevant distinction in his "On Naive and Sentimental Poetry" (1795). Nietzsche's insistence that Homer is *not* naive is related to his effort to dismiss the idea that the vision of the beautiful found in Homeric literature somehow stems from its author's (or, more precisely, authors') greater proximity to nature or that Homer had special access to nature because he did not have certain cultural impediments that needed to be overcome (as in the case of the poets Schiller described as *sentimental*). Schiller argues that sentimental poetry is more admirable, "higher," because it represents a more significant accomplishment (overcoming the obstacles to nature) and that ancient poetry can be best understood as naive. I will return to a comparison of Nietzsche and Schiller shortly in the context of understanding the different ways they conceive the workings of aesthetic experience. What is significant to note at this point is that, for Nietzsche, what is distinctively Homeric is more than just the peak of a "natural" evolution of views that emerged out of the historical, social, and material circumstances of the ancient Greeks. Homer brings about something new. Nietzsche takes great pains to characterize the Homeric perspective as reflecting a monumental victory in a battle fought (*kämpfte*) against its "artistically correlative talent for suffering and the wisdom of suffering"—"that entire philosophy of the forest" over which Silenus presides (*BT* 3).

Drawing on what he has learned from Schopenhauer, Nietzsche explains that the Greeks can recognize the *unheimlich* Dionysian revelers as their fellows because they, too, have felt what the revelers' wild and rhythmic movements express. Ultimately, the two opposed artistic forces are the mutually necessary expressions of the "mysterious ground of our being": *Will*. And what we recognize as art or culture reflects the vicissitudes of the ongoing struggle between the perspective of the world as primal unity and the world considered from the perspective of individuation. One seeks the obliteration of difference; the other draws measure and "delineation of boundaries." Both are locked in eternal contradiction, "the father of things," as both Heraclitus and Schopenhauer would have it. In *Die Geburt der Tragödie*, the whole struggle seems to aim at a "summit and purpose" in Attic tragedy, imbued with dramatic dithyramb. Nietzsche describes it as a "mysterious matrimonial union [geheimnissvolles Ehebündniss]" (*BT* 4). But the marriage is not blissful; rather, it appears as a kind of tense binding together of opposites, a desire to permanently bond what would otherwise seek the destruction of its mate. The love-hate situation Nietzsche envisions in the contest of the Apollinian and the Dionysian results in both forces needing each other, both seeking to dominate the other, and this engagement is mutually enhancing insofar as it provides the condition for the possibility of regeneration and growth.[9]

There is no question that Nietzsche's tale is heavily influenced by Schopenhauer's metaphysics, but there is more to Nietzsche's account than just a simplistic application of Schopenhauer's ideas. Nietzsche translates Schopenhauer's metaphysics in his own aesthetic theory in order to account for the development of art: from folk wisdom (the traditional stories of the Titans) to the emergence and success of Homerica (i.e., from myth to poetry), from the influx of Dionysian elements from other cultures to the rise of Doric architecture (i.e., from chaos to order) and, finally, to the culminating period of Attic tragedy (i.e., a philosophical poetry that synthesizes and overcomes the prior stages of development). Each break in this history is supposed to be effected by the resurgence or counterattack of one artistic principle over the other. Human agency is minimized in Nietzsche's description. What we appear to have instead is nonpersonified creative force turning or doubling back on itself.[10] Individuation is the appearance of Willing; the "sphere of beauty" created by beings that perceive themselves to be individuated is merely the *appearance of appearance*, an image of an image. Since this illusion rests on a primordial unity that can be perceived only as suffering (because it represents the end or obliteration of what we cling to as our own, as what is our ownmost), what we have is a tremendous vacillation between illusion and perception of its basis. Thus, the perspective Schiller associates with naïveté is, on Nietzsche's account, not based on ignorance, and it is not lacking in complexity of insight; rather, it is a form of overcoming, and at this point Nietzsche parts company with Schopenhauer.

The fact that Nietzsche's Apollo and Dionysus might very well resemble at times thinly disguised personifications of Schopenhauer's "Representation" and "Will," respectively, does not mean that Nietzsche's philosophy follows Schopenhauer's all the way to its particular pessimistic end, as some would have it.[11] I follow those who claim that Nietzsche *transforms* at the same time as he deploys Schopenhauerian language and concepts.[12] Insofar as Nietzsche's Apollinian (akin to Schopenhauer's Representation [Vorstellung]) emerges from and can be seen as a response to a need, it is at odds with how Schopenhauer thinks about Representation. And, because he associates the erotic desire of the Dionysian with an aspect of insight or intelligence and with what is artistic and creative, Nietzsche breaks from Schopenhauer's conception of Will, which is essentially purposeless and blind, a relentless and meaningless tempest of craving and longing. Moreover, he further distances himself in his insistence on the practical function of art, in which the transfiguring and redemptive features reverberate or resound back into and throughout our ordinary existence. Art, for Nietzsche, is more than a means to escape; it differs from Schopenhauer's conception of the arts as momentarily stilling or distracting Will.[13] This redemptive aspect of Nietzsche's account of tragedy best exemplifies his surpassing of Schopenhauer's pessimism, as I elaborate later in this chapter.

The aesthetic pleasure of the contest of tragedy lies, for Nietzsche, in activating and creatively appropriating the desirous strivings characteristic of what are personified as Apollo and Dionysus. What one prospectively undergoes in the aesthetic experience afforded by tragedy is essentially *the play of meaning and measure.* The quintessential features of the Apollinian are alternately suspended and reasserted in the tragic, namely, through measure and identification. Recall Nietzsche's account of the birth of the Apollinian. (Notice, however, that there can be no presumption of providing an actual history of events since there is no birth of either the Apollinian or the Dionysian. As differing perspectives or aspects of the same primal unity that serves as the basis of all existence, they necessarily exist together simultaneously; i.e., the Apollinian and the Dionysian are dimensions of existence.) As the "apotheosis of individuation," the Apollinian "knows but one law"; its distinguishing characteristic is its response to "the delineation of the boundaries of the individual, *measure* in the Hellenic sense [die Einhaltung der Grenzen des Individuums, das Maass im hellenischen Sinne]" (*BT* 4).

Attention to the significance of this play with measure and excess can yield a creative appreciation for Nietzsche's account of the *pleasure* of tragedy and the subtleties of the dialectic that is being described. The aesthetic pleasure of the tragic does not lie in the insight it provides concerning some moral lesson, or in the release of pity and fear it might afford us, or in some consolation for our own struggles. Instead, the tragic work of art offers appreciation of the claims of measure, intelligibility, the comfort that comes from having a compass for our actions and our pursuits of knowledge, *while at the same time* affording the sense that the claims of measure are malleable, capable of relocation, and admit of being reissued in light of a reorganization of desirable ends. This point bears repeating since it is frequently misunderstood: Nietzsche locates the pleasure of tragedy in the *entire agon* of the Apollinian and the Dionysian, not, as others have asserted (or accused), in the destruction wrought by the Dionysian.[14] Association of the pleasure of tragedy strictly or solely with Dionysian destruction is somewhat like mistaking the end of a climatic phrase for the crescendo in a musical work. What such listeners fail to grasp is that a crescendo is constituted by the sweep of the entire passage that leads to such climax. It is the *whole struggle* of the Apollinian and the Dionysian that produces the pleasure of tragedy for Nietzsche, not simply the Dionysian puncturing, deflating, or destroying, which is but part of that contest.

The tragic contest between the Apollinian and the Dionysian makes possible the redirection of desire that animates and enables the value-giving and meaning-making activities that allow us to find our lives to be significant, worthwhile, and meaningful. This is further indicated in how Nietzsche describes the so-called birth of Homeric naïveté and how it is accomplished: "Homeric 'naïveté' can be understood only as the complete victory [Sieg] of Apollinian illusion [Illusion]: this is one of those illusions which nature so frequently employs to achieve her own ends. The true goal is veiled by a phantasm [Wahnbild]: and while we *stretch out our hands* for the latter, nature attains the former by means of our illusion" (*BT* 3; emphasis added). In "stretch[ing] out our hands," we come to *want* something else; we come to have other desires, different needs. This is significant because what Nietzsche imagines is not simply an emotional outburst or a whimsical psychological shift. The nature of our desires influences the kinds of pursuits we uphold as worthwhile and thereby indicates courses of action in light of such fulfillment. It is, thus, that *direction of desire* potentially informs different courses, different ways of life. Such reorientations of the means and ends of human existence constitute the ways in which we distinguish our lives as *our own*.

In this respect, the new symbolism of the body (*BT* 2), mentioned above, is even more significant than it might otherwise seem. When we gain access to a new symbolism of the body, we acquire different metaphoric possibilities for conceiving ourselves and our possible relations to others. Nietzsche identifies at least two examples: in terms of our sense of ourselves as the kind of *animals* we are and our possible relations to the human community that we ordinarily take as our own. Concerning our animality, he writes: "In song and dance man expresses himself as a member of a higher community; he has forgotten [verlernt] how to walk and speak and is on the way toward flying into the air, dancing" (*BT* 1). Regarding our civic identity, he claims: "the dithyrambic chorus is a chorus of the transformed [Verwandelten] whose civic past and social status have been totally forgotten" (*BT* 8; translation emended). When we have recourse to new symbolic forms, we potentially gain different resources to remake the world and our place within it. Nietzsche's remarks about the new symbolism of the body that tragedy affords are germane to two features of tragedy already described: (1) the *play of meaning and measure* associated with Nietzsche's characterization of the pleasure of tragedy and (2) the *entitlement to symbolization* that is part of the goal that motivates (or, if a less volitional term is wanted, *activates*) the Apollinian and the Dionysian in the peak artistic contest, or agon, of tragedy.

Pleasure in the agon of the Apollinian and the Dionysian in *Die Geburt der Tragödie* potentially stems from being permitted, momentarily, to be released from the claims and limitations of measure that define one's life. Since the suspension is temporary, one does not suffer the complete and utter annihilation of the boundaries that make meaningful action possible. That would be perfect nihilism, in which nothing could be meaningful because all the boundaries and relational contexts in which anything could stand out or potentially be significant in relation to things have been obliterated. Thus, because it is a momentary experience, the tragic dissolution of boundaries transforms a potentially terrifying experience into one that is potentially liberating and enabling.[15]

What makes the "new symbolization of the body" distinctively pleasurable is the incomparable exercise of imagination it affords. If Nietzsche is drawing on, while at the same time transforming, Schopenhauerian concepts and language in his work, then we should briefly consider what the significance of the body is for Schopenhauer—that which is closest to us, that which, in its relation to Will, gives us a window on the thing-in-itself (our body is a representation of Will, of the thing-in-itself that we are). Thus, what is so momentous about being able to act as if one had actually entered into another body, to see oneself transformed before one's own eyes, is that it is the most relevant and *personally interested* possibility of our creative powers. We have the power not only to create stories about other fictional beings but also to become works of art ourselves, and not only in the stories we tell ourselves about ourselves but also in the immediate and visceral experience of who and what we are and how we could be in the future.[16]

The illusion of the Apollinian is punctured, ruptured, and fragmented within the frame or context of the tragic production. The world measured and meted according to the customary limits of justice abides—thus, we can return to it at the end—but the limits defining it are temporarily suspended. In the case of tragedy, it is not as though we fulfill a fantasy of vicariously living the life of Oedipus or that we achieve the satisfaction of having our customary views justified or vindicated in the words of the chorus that admonishes and reproaches the figures suffering tragic fate. Rather, *the entire play* of these forces and perspectives constitutes a process of transfiguration that fuels the pleasurable experience of tragedy. This includes the interplay of the transgression of boundaries that the hero commits and the reassertion of those limits by the chorus and the gods.

In the course of this play, new economies of wants and needs and possibilities for satisfaction emerge and become shared with others, those with whom we share in the production of our cultural fabric and social relations. Creating marvelously tied knots in these interrelations, encircled by magical effects that make possible the seemingly impossible, tragic action affords its audience opportunities to achieve satisfaction by participating in unraveling "dialectical" riddles (*BT* 9). Such is the agon that forms the heart of tragedy for Nietzsche. The dialectical riddles are not epistemic—they are not puzzles that knowledge resolves. Rather, they are ethical dilemmas in the broadest and most fundamental sense, riddles about how to live our lives, how to *define* our ends and the means to their satisfaction.

2.3 DEADLY MODIFICATIONS AND THE END OF AGON

Tragic art delivers to those who witness it opportunities to participate in the transformative magic of creative production, to engage the poetic creativity at the heart of the work of art. Nietzsche's fable of the contest of the Apollinian and the Dionysian includes an account of its end or demise when the element most vital to its production was eliminated. The question is whether this critical loss is solely one of the individual competitors—the Dionysian—or whether it is the disruption of the artistic agon that is most relevant. Nearly inexplicably, Nietzsche blames this on Euripides (*BT* 10). I use the qualification *nearly* here because it *seems* as though Euripides more than any other ancient tragedian takes Dionysus quite seriously. He is, after all, the only one to bring him visibly to the stage. And the powerful capabilities of Dionysus are clearly evident in Euripides' work. This makes Nietzsche's claim that Euripides kills tragedy by eradicating the Dionysian highly implausible, to some nonsensical.[17] But one could argue that Euripides' preoccupation with the Dionysian is more demonizing than celebratory. Although it is true that Dionysus gets the upper hand in the *Bacchae*, Pentheus's dismemberment by his Dionysian-crazed mother does not so much convey the message "don't mess with Dionysus" as it serves to admonish us that, if we are not more vigilant about *restraining* Dionysus, he might very well destroy us all. Although much has been written that is critical of Nietzsche's account of the rise and fall of tragedy, it is still instructive to consider how Nietzsche considers the tragic contest to have been transformed because it will contribute detail to the agon analytic I am describing. In recounting this, we make progress in further understanding how Nietzsche's fable of the birth of tragedy symbolizes the possibilities the agon has in relation to art and its appropriation for cultural development.

One of the most common interpretations of Nietzsche's *Die Geburt der Tragödie* is that it advances the claim that tragic art collapsed with the diminution of the Dionysian. But this, at best, tells only half the story. We can better appreciate the argument of the book and the overall place of the book in Nietzsche's oeuvre if we focus on the effect of the abandonment of Dionysus on the most crucial element of the tragic—namely, *the contest* between the Dionysian and the Apollinian. Tragic art is supposed to be so powerful because it creates a contest of equally fundamental forces in which, to cite "Homer's Wettkampf," the opposing parties "incite each other to reciprocal action as they keep each other within the limits of measure" (HC, p. 789).[18] We can compare this with *HH* 158, where Nietzsche writes: "The most fortunate thing that can happen in the evolution of an art is that several geniuses appear together and keep one another in bounds; in the course of this struggle the weaker and tenderer natures too will usually be granted light and air."[19] Nietzsche's interests in drawing boundaries, mutual containment, and managing transgressive excess are relevant to discussion of the logic of the contest, described below. They also play a prominent role in the account of desire and the erotic nature of the agon as discussed throughout the book. Nietzsche accuses Euripides of disrupting tragedy's agon, allegedly under the influence of Socratic optimism, which Nietzsche associates with having a kind of faith that ambiguity and unintelligibility can be surmounted and eradicated. How it is that Euripides brings about "the suicide of tragedy" by undermining its agon repays investigation if for no other reason than it helps readers understand his agonism.[20]

Tragedy is vulnerable to assault on two fronts. Recall that it is supposed to be organized around a contest between two competitors who ordinarily seek to annihilate each other but have somehow been magnificently "enflamed," "bridled," and "restrained" (HC, p. 790). Following the account of the relevant components of agonistic exchange in the preceding chapter, we can see that the agon of the Apollinian and the Dionysian is characterized by (1) the qualities of its competitors and (2) its formal structure. Nietzsche's evaluation of the contest in the hands of Euripides unfolds along the lines of the two general features of agonistic action and the form of contestatory relations already noted. Nietzsche accuses Euripides of corrupting both essential features of the contest, of having mounted a twofold attack on tragedy: (1) he seriously compromises the capacities of one of its competitors, Dionysus, and (2) he dictates new rules of engagement for the contest itself. Nietzsche's readers have easily and often noticed his claims about the first of these points, but the second aspect is less recognized and, I argue, more important for appreciating what Nietzsche himself finds to be so important about his own critique and how he applies it in his later writings.

Because Euripides allegedly sought to diminish the "unintelligible" and "unmeasured," which are precisely what the Dionysian brings to the work, he minimized expression of Dionysian elements whenever he could. Again, some close readers of the *Bacchae* find this claim utterly ridiculous, but Nietzsche thinks the *Bacchae* is exceptional. That work indicates Euripides' *surrender* on Nietzsche's account; it reveals Euripides' aversion to Dionysus. The Dionysian is allowed to run amok, wreaking havoc anywhere and everywhere it is allowed expression. This, for Nietzsche, is just further evidence that Euripides really *fears* the Dionysian and thinks it must be incapacitated and thoroughly restrained lest it destroy everyone it finds on its path. But, once Euripides "abandoned Dionysus, Apollo abandoned him" (*BT* 11), Nietzsche claims. In other words, once the Apollinian could no longer achieve its effects through the music of the Dionysian, its possible contributions to tragic production were also compromised. Euripides sought the reign of the intelligible, illuminated, and insightful. In pursuit of that aim, he pitted his pale Dionysus against the Socratic rather than the Apollinian (which would not have been able to rise to the challenge in any event).

With the introduction of this new competitor, the rules of engagement were also revised so as to diminish encounters in which the antipodes could exploit the resources of the other for the completion of its own ends. (In *BT* 6, Nietzsche provides a powerful description of how, in tragic art, Dionysian music finds its reflection in the Apollinian, in which the appearance of will is the form of its longing, and desire is brought forth. The Apollinian depends on the music, and the music endures the conceptualization manifest in the Apollinian.) With the new contest that Euripides is supposed to have initiated, one element of the Apollinian is engaged, intensified, localized, and atrophied, and the other legitimate contestant in the tragic agon is replaced with an imposter. This imposter's actions within the contest demonstrate that he does not seek to prove himself to be superior to the Dionysian but rather *pursues his opponent's annihilation*. An emaciated Dionysus is pitted against a Cycloptic Socrates (transmogrified by his atrophied rationality) in a struggle in which neither can emerge as truly better for having engaged in the fight. Thus, as Nietzsche tells the story, the new Euripidean contest brings forth dystrophic, unworthy contestants who are merely shadowboxing under corrupted rules of engagement. All features of vibrant agonistic exchange wane—both the tension of the competing parties and the possibilities for action circumscribed by the nature of the contest evaporate. What Nietzsche then seeks, of course, is a route to revivifying the tragic agon, which he imagines as potentially realizable through innovations Wagner brings to the opera when he makes music itself a character.

2.4 THE AGON: PESSIMISM, CONSERVATISM, AND RACISM

Emphasis in the scholarly literature on Nietzsche's early Dionysianism and widespread, albeit not universal, acceptance of the idea that his book was written largely under the spell of Schopenhauer's metaphysics lead many to conclude that the so-called early Nietzsche shares Schopenhauer's pessimistic view about the value and character of human existence. Since most commentators also highlight his emphasis on value creation and a corresponding critique of what he calls "life denying" after the publication of *Die Geburt der Tragödie*, they often find themselves needing to explain how and when Nietzsche rejects the Schopenhauerian pessimism he allegedly expressed in his first book. An interpretation that is both attentive to the particularities of his appropriation of Schopenhauer and sensitive to the centrality of the agon and the way it provides aesthetic pleasure can show that, even in *Die Geburt der Tragödie*, his views stand far away from the conclusions of his intellectual mentor while recognizing the development of his ideas over time.[21] Some obvious clues lie in his references to a pessimism of strength as described most memorably, if still cryptically, in his writings from 1886 on and in the assessment of Schopenhauer in *Jenseits von Gut und Böse*, in which he claims that Schopenhauer simply did not take his pessimism *far enough* (*BGE* 56). That extra distance he imagines as traversed in his own idea of eternal recurrence, which could strike some as a pessimistic, possibly nihilistic, commitment to fatalism, but which he imagines in the character of Zarathustra as joyfully embraced and a basis of meaning creation. I explore this in greater detail in the next chapter. The focus here is on how the agonistic model bears on issues pertaining to Nietzsche's early work and the additional insight it allows us to gather, and we can further notice that, when Nietzsche returned to *Die Geburt der Tragödie* to write a new preface for the 1886 edition, he recast the subtitle, replacing "Out of the Spirit of Music" with "or, Hellenism and Pessimism." Hellenism, rather than a simplistic and serene expression of cheerful optimism, issues forth, he claims, from a deeply pessimistic need, which produces what might be described as a pessimism of strength realized in the union of the Apollinian and the Dionysian in tragedy.

One of the most important gains to be realized at this point is a perspective on how and why Nietzsche considered agonistic relations to be *generative*. For all his references to value creation and revaluation and the oceans of ink commentators have spilled in reiterating these ideas, there is little discussion either in Nietzsche's works or in the scholarly literature regarding more specifically how such activity takes place. With Nietzsche, readers often remain focused on the critical discussions of the monstrous or decadent ways in which valuation happens or the pitfalls of *failing* to engage in revaluation, at the expense of considering the affirmative aspects of Nietzsche's thinking and the positive models that serve as the basis for his comparisons. Beyond simply admiring the ancient Greeks, what does Nietzsche think antiquity supplies in the way of direction for the future? The agon structure, including the relations it makes possible and the mechanism it supplies for the development and exercise of judgment, is prominent. Appreciating this is helpful for addressing some thorny issues in the scholarship, including Nietzsche's pessimism, conservatism, and possible racism.

If one associates the Dionysian exclusively with pessimism and the tragic with the Dionysian, then it would appear that *Die Geburt der Tragödie* is, indeed, ultimately pessimistic. But, as I have argued, neither of these associations capture Nietzsche's views. The Dionysian retains a sense of creativity for Nietzsche, and the tragic is essentially a *union* of the Apollinian and the Dionysian, not simply a resurgence of the latter. As I have already discussed, what so distinguishes tragic art for Nietzsche is that it successfully draws on and *sustains* both artistic drives. Indeed, as described above, it is their struggle for dominance—which is thoroughly unresolved in favor of either force—that gives tragic art its special force.

We might inquire further about what Nietzsche thinks is significant about tragic insight, why it might be necessary, what need it might fulfill. Consider the wisdom of Silenus, the view that human existence is valueless, not worth the pain it requires one to endure—the best life ends as quickly as possible; even better is to avoid life entirely. Nietzsche's Homer makes it possible to see human existence as glorious—maximally so, even better than the life of a god. However, such lives are rare, and it is a terrible fate to suffer dying before one can realize such glory. Tragic insight allows one to hold both perspectives: to acknowledge the wisdom of Silenus and recognize that human life has no inherent value while recognizing that human beings can create meaning even if it appears to be fleeting. Tragic drama not only depicts such creative action; it also instantiates it not merely through the production of heroic deeds but rather through the creation of works of art.

Tragic insight makes it possible to hold the view that knowledge of the world as it is shows that it lacks (inherent) value, but it does not necessarily follow from this that life is not worth living. The latter view is characteristic of precisely the kind of nihilism that concerns Nietzsche; it is exactly where he sees his contemporary culture heading as the redemptive proclamations and prescriptions of religious institutions lose their sway and the significance of artistic institutions becomes eclipsed by militarism and vapid nationalism. Just because something has no inherent value stemming from an eternal essence or guaranteed by some divine arbiter does not mean that values themselves do not exist, cannot be given or transformed. In fact, we cannot make much sense of the significance of tragedy for Nietzsche, of why he so admired the Greek solution to the problem of existence, without presupposing the latter. Tragic art *produces* rather than *discovers* in the world an affirmative response to the value of human existence. Far from being merely subjective fancies, such values have real and lasting effects that bind together a community and supply the basis for the development of individual identities and productive forms of life. How is such valuation possible? What makes it work? How could it be possible in the future? What would we need to do in order to realize this ourselves? These questions—rather than illusions of grandeur, machismo, narcissism, or megalomania—are what drive Nietzsche's investigations. It is not that Nietzsche himself wishes to seize or celebrate the power to remake the world in his image; rather, he wishes to understand how one might distinguish between individual fantasy or subjective preference and the creation of shared desires and interests that bind people together and move them to pursue common ends. The agonistic model provides him with one example of how such production, transmission, and reappropriation is possible.

Nietzsche does not have to reject the Apollinian because its presentation of the value of existence is superficial, a sham, a lie. Of course, he admires the ancient Greeks for their superficiality—a reference to their ability "to stop courageously at the surface, the fold, the skin, to adore appearance" (*GS* P:4) and their ability to transform values. He is not hostile to redemption per se. His *Zur Genealogie der Moral* urgently raises the question of how redemption might be accomplished beyond the practices and values of the ascetic priests. But he thinks it matters very much what the mechanism of redemption is and what serves as the basis of its legitimation. Otherworldly solutions to the problem of existence are, indeed, problematic because they tend to debase what is here and now and, consequently, ultimately fail to satisfactorily *redeem*, in the sense of *enhancing* the affirmative value of, the world in which we must live. Nietzsche clearly admires Homeric redemption as it is extended in the production of honor and glory in contest precisely because it locates salvation, justification of human life, in the very world it seeks to redeem. The challenge with which he wrestles virtually throughout his entire career is identifying how such redemptive practices truly enhance human existence. Although he entertains a variety of prospective approaches—for example, artistic metaphysics (as in the case of *Die Geburt der Tragödie*), poeticized science (as in the case of *Die fröhliche Wissenschaft*), and axiology beyond good and evil (as envisioned in *Zur Genealogie der Moral*)—the general concern persists, and each deploys and utilizes the agonal model.

Recognizing how the agon supplies Nietzsche with a structural model for

deriving meanings and significance sheds light on his Hellenism (and pessimism) and his understanding of the relation between studies of antiquity and
his own culture. His view is sometimes associated with romantic tendencies
to idealize the Greeks, even when he also emphasizes their tendencies toward
cruelty and acts associated with barbarism (as opposed to their so-called noble simplicity, yet another variety of romantic Hellenism).[22] My account of
his interest in the Greeks in *Die Geburt der Tragödie* and other early writings
has emphasized the degree to which much of what he writes appears to be a
fable or set of fables he constructs—fictional stories that are much less about
the historical peoples who lived in antiquity than about forms of human life
and relations that might be pursued in the future. Even his Homer is a figure
largely of his invention. Yet the portrayal is not wholly fictive or substantially
contradicted by archaeological and anthropological evidence and philologi-
cal research advanced even after Nietzsche lived. If we consider his aim as
illuminating possibilities for development in contemporary times, rather than
providing an *explanation* for the appearance of a historical phenomenon, his
idealizations take on a particularly pragmatic character. He admires the agon
less for what it might have been than for what it might become. Its function
in the narrative of *Die Geburt der Tragödie* is to characterize a possible set
of relations (which may not necessarily be constituted precisely in the way
he describes). It allows us to understand something about the possibilities
for valuation, how we might participate in such a process, and the difference
such might make in our lives. In the next chapter, I shall more directly address
Nietzsche's use of fiction and artifice for the purpose of disclosing something
he believes to be true.

Thus, Nietzsche's interest in the agon is fundamentally progressive rather
than conservative. It does not baldly hail the values of the past or simply herald the return of some long-lost nobility. Instead, his interest in the agon aims
to supply a mechanism for reinvesting with significance what we claim to uphold as meaningful.[23] Nietzsche searches, perhaps unsuccessfully, to find a
way to escape the tyrannical and stultifying effects that such values can have
when we take them to be inherently true and without need for justification.
And he reconsiders the limits of how we think about the world and relate to
each other, how we orient our actions and determine what is worthy of pursuit. The abundant secondary literature on his interest in revaluating values
would be helpfully supplemented by an account of the role the agon plays in
his vision of such a process. The agon signals more than his fondness for the
ancient Greeks because it focuses on disclosing future possibilities and realizing them instead of simply admiring or glorifying the past. This much should

be clear in the account of the agon at the heart of *Die Geburt der Tragödie* discussed here, and I shall elaborate the application and function of this mechanism of valuation throughout the remainder of this book.

In this light, we can also explore whether Nietzsche's admiration of the agon is essentially and primarily in the service of an elitist or racist agenda favoring a kind of social Darwinism that excludes those who are deemed not to be among the fittest. In such a case, the agon might, in fact, be thought to supply a means for further justifying and authorizing the abuse and mistreatment of those over whom such elites already enjoy greater social power and physical strength. While it is true that the battles Nietzsche considers are generally among those who wield an extraordinary amount of power, it is not the case that he envisions the agon as reinforcing the *standing distribution of power*. Indeed, as I have already discussed in light of his reference to ostracism and its function in relation to the agon as effectively undermining hegemonic power, it is clear he identifies one of the strengths of agonistic institutions to lie in how they facilitate resistance to domination. He does not praise ostracism on account of its function in purging a city or an institution of its weak or decadent elements. In fact, ostracism serves the interest of promoting the growth and enhancement of those who might be, relative to the standing organization of power, too weak or poorly constituted to challenge the reigning power. We can contrast the function of ostracism as regulating by *increasing* productive conflict with forms of political and social organization modeled on immunity, in which case the community seeks *protection* from (through dissolution of) threats and conflicts. The notion of immunity in the context of analysis of forms of political power and organization can be found in a variety of thinkers who are especially interested in what is distinctive about modern political organizations, something that was certainly a concern that Nietzsche shared and that motivated his examinations of ancient Greek history and philosophy.[24] Of course, he does not think the agon *protects* the weakest and least abled, but that does not mean that he is specifically and inherently ill disposed toward such individuals either (cf. *HH* 158). He emphasizes the circulation and redistribution of power rather than its concentration, and this is graphically illustrated in his account of the agon and the ways in which it organizes relations among individuals and between individuals and the collective.

2.5 THE LOGIC OF THE CONTEST

It is possible to say a few more words about the nature of the dialectic and its decay evident in Nietzsche's conception of the tragic agon. In *Crossings:*

Nietzsche and the Space of Tragedy, John Sallis describes the contest between the Apollinian assertion of limits and the Dionysian breaching of those limits with excess (*Übermass*) as a "crossing of saying with unsaying."[25] He elaborates the unfolding of this crossing in terms of an "ecstatic logic"—an idea that has recently been endorsed, albeit reformulated, by James I. Porter in relation to Nietzsche's interests in materialism.[26] Although I think Nietzsche demonstrates remarkable self-awareness when he looks back on *Die Geburt der Tragödie* in the preface he adds in 1886 ("Versuch einer Selbstkritik") and notices instances of Hegelianism hostile to his true intentions, I am also inclined to agree with Sallis and others that it is helpful to recognize that the opposition of the Apollinian and the Dionysian does not represent a strict binary relation.[27] Nietzsche's fable about the development of ancient Greek art as following, seemingly necessarily, victories and counterattacks by the Apollinian and the Dionysian exaggerates their opposition. Insofar as the Apollinian and the Dionysian are *both* creative and active, insofar as they *both* seek to represent (albeit quite differently) the character of existence, and insofar as the figures who are offered as exemplars of at least certain aspects of each tendency (e.g., Homer and Socrates) contain within them (not merely accidentally) features of both tendencies, they are not diametrically opposed, and their opposition does not have a specific aim or telos.

Nietzsche appears to be struggling, even in *BT*, for some way of conceiving this conflict in terms other than Hegel's conception of *Aufhebung*, but he has a very difficult time of it. The text is replete with uses of the term in his own account of the struggle between the Apollinian and the Dionysian, and his effort to use conflict as an illustrative and *explanative* measure for understanding the development of Greek art resonates with Hegel's conception of the development of *Geist*. Still, none of this should obscure what is clearly relevant to my overall argument, namely, that Nietzsche is firmly convinced that the significance of tragic art and the source of its aesthetic pleasure issue from the *tension* of the two forces and not their resolution, as a Hegelian dialectic might suggest. Moreover, his emphases and celebrations of Dionysus aside, it is the ongoing interaction of both parties that achieves tragic effects. Thus, what precipitated tragedy's demise was the disruption of the contest of the two artistic forces and not simply the disappearance of Dionysian *Übermass*.

An ecstatic logic questions and challenges the very terms on which logic unfolds and proceeds. It contests, perhaps even "crosses," as Sallis puts it, the basic and fundamental terms on which it rests. An ecstatic logic does not simply "stand out" of logic in a flight into the irrational or illogical; rather, it is a relation in which the terms of development, conflict, and incorporation are themselves potentially transgressed, reoriented, *in play*.[28] One stands out, experiences *ekstasis* not simply by rejecting logic but by interrogating its foundations. Overcoming such challenges might result in a redefinition of the very terms on which logic progresses. I consider this to be what Nietzsche has in mind when he describes the dynamic of erecting boundaries and distinctions and then erasing, annihilating, or transgressing them. In the course of the Apollinian/Dionysian agon, measure does return—but it is refigured, reorganized, and its contingency is recognized.

The agonistic character of the engagement between the Apollinian and the Dionysian illuminates the nature of Nietzsche's dialectic in *Die Geburt der Tragödie*. Once we subject the Apollinian/Dionysian agon to an analysis of the types of contests and modes of action sketched in chapter 1 above, we more clearly see that what is happening in the tragic contest Nietzsche describes is neither a reconciliation nor a synthesis that aims at something higher. No compromise is accomplished. There is something valuable, he claims, in the *maintenance* of the tension, not its overcoming. Although it is true that he celebrates the liberating aspects of the excess characteristic of the Dionysian, it is clear he similarly admires the recovery of measure, even if it is relocated. This fact also sheds light on his characterization of what constitutes antipodes or what makes one a "good enemy" or "worthy opponent," to which I now turn.

2.6 THE "ULTIMATE AGONY": AGONISTIC ANTIPODES

Regardless of whether his account of tragedy's demise aids our appreciation of the historical development of tragic drama, it can advance our understanding of how Nietzsche thinks about the agon, its significance for art and culture, and its relevance to moral psychology. On his account, it is contest that lends art its alchemic possibilities. The transformative effects of tragedy that are so significant to him are achieved through the agonistic relation of the Apollinian and the Dionysian, a kind of interaction that he thought was rare and fragile, volatile and potentially immensely productive. Nietzsche regards the Apollinian and the Dionysian as perfect antipodes—not essentially poised to obliterate their opposition, but seeking opposing ends. He calls this the "ultimate agony" (*BT* 21), reflecting a struggle mirrored in philosophical tensions between how we conceive the particular and the universal, the apparent and the real, the phenomenal and the things-in-themselves, all issues that are treated at greater length in his subsequent works. Each opponent in the tragic agon seeks a claim to constituting the meaning of existence, what I have called an *entitlement to symbolization.* Each seeks to define the terms in which the world is ordered and organized. Each seeks to fix the points around which other things acquire their meaning. Each intends its own justification. And, in the course of these labors, each offers the participants in the drama a way to make sense of the world and imbue it with significance.

What is unique about tragedy, for Nietzsche, is that it provides a forum for expressing this tension and harnessing it for the production of art. The goal or end of this activity is not discharging ourselves of corresponding struggles we all face but rather compressing and intensifying them to some extent so that they might serve as a basis for action and be utilized in other transformative endeavors that Nietzsche later envisions as *revaluation.* He characterizes the transformation as magical because it effects a conversion of the conception of life that considers human existence as base, transforming it into one gilded with glorious possibilities. In this case, human existence is *potentially* revalued from something vile to something extraordinary, precious, desirable, *lovable.* The kind of moderation Nietzsche seeks is not the *avoidance* of extremes, as an Aristotlean model might have it, but rather the cultivation and *sustenance* of extremes as he envisions the tension of the agon of tragedy in terms of the simultaneous appropriation of both poles of artistic force.

And this provides us with some insight into what Nietzsche means when he famously heralds "worthy opponents," which I explore in greater detail in the context of discussing his principles of "war-making" as described in *Ecce Homo.* It should be clear by now that, because the Apollinian and the Dionysian antipodes are not necessarily diametrically opposed, they do not require the annihilation of their opposition as a condition of their survival. Indeed, as Nietzsche describes them, each antipode requires the presence and active force of its opposition as a condition of its thriving. What we can glean from this is that Nietzsche's antipodes have very much in common at the same time as they seek differing ends.

Elaborations and interpretations of Nietzsche's *Die Geburt der Tragödie* that focus on or emphasize one of the artistic forces over the other simply fail to capture the significance of the relation between the two and the productive possibilities that are so important to Nietzsche.[29] Both the Dionysian and the Apollinian are creative and natural; neither is merely natural or solely artificial. The Dionysian is not fundamentally pessimistic: it might indicate a recognition that life is fundamentally meaningless or without a meaning save that which is won for it. Thus, I disagree with David Allison when he writes: "The agonistic spirit recognizes that existence is meaningless, that it is doom-laden and a scene of unremitting violence."[30] As I have shown, it is precisely overcoming this that Nietzsche associates with the agonistic spirit inaugurated by Homer.

Excessive striving of any single force is, according to Nietzsche's interpretation, the source of destruction—passivity and annihilation lie at opposite ends of the same spectrum. Nietzsche claims that this happened in the case of Athens following the Persian Wars: Athenian domination diminished opportunities for robust agonistic interaction, resulting in a desire for destruction.[31] Public contests that provided creative outlets for desires to strive deteriorated into spectacle. Without the creation of a new outlet for struggle, Nietzsche imagines, the Greeks *could* have become so brutal as to have engaged in wanton destruction of each other (*BT* 15). Instead, Socratic philosophy, which appealed to the agonistic tastes of the ancient Greeks, as evident in the plethora of forums devoted to that form of interaction, emerged as a replacement. Socratic dialectic had the appearance of the old kind of struggle, but it was significantly different, on Nietzsche's account, largely because it failed to provide the openness Nietzsche linked with the productive and creative potential of agonism.[32] These ideas are elaborated in the chapter that follows, but the gist of the argument can be anticipated here on the basis of the foregoing account of distinctions Nietzsche draws between forms of contests and modes of action within them. His problem with Socrates focuses on his interpretation of dialectic as domination by an unbeatable opponent, namely, the Socratic position of unconditional truth. Moreover, he thinks the *standards of judgment* in the Socratic game are uncontestable—reason rules tyrannically in the caricature he sketches of the Socratic tendency. Another key difference between the earlier form of contest he associates with Homeric agonism and the Socratic version is that, with the new Socratic contest, struggles that constituted the public sphere are replaced by spiritual ones waged by individuals. And with that comes the withering of the opportunities for creative appropriation and the *gathering* of meaning agonistic relations provide for the community.

The tale continues to unfold as Nietzsche traces the genealogy of the spiritual contest of Socratic/Platonic philosophy to Christian morality and even to the contemporary scientific theory of organic development and health. Throughout his works, he remains attentive to forms of the struggles, the kinds of actions within them that they encouraged, and their prospects for providing the benefits of earlier forms of contest. His account depicts the contest becoming increasingly *closed* and increasingly *more violent*, even, and perhaps most especially, when aggressive actions of struggle, resistance, and challenge are judged inappropriate in the name of advancing civilization or morality. On his account, as this process continues, human beings also become less free, not because their will to be brutal is restrained, but because they have less access to creative struggle than before. This concern forms the basis of Nietzsche's skirmishes with Socrates and Paul, and it is related to his conception of willing in terms of striving or struggling in both eristic encounters and loving relations.

The contest between the Apollinian and the Dionysian forces—or, in somewhat less anthropomorphic terms, *tendencies*—constitutes a gathering of the elements for the creation of meaning and the exercise of judgment. That is to say, it provided Nietzsche with a positive account of how values can be created, shared, and transformed. Engaging Homer by trying to rise above him, Nietzsche does not necessarily surpass him, but he does begin to derive evaluative terms for various ways of producing value that are more or less effective as well as more or less affirmative. Both artistic elements play important roles in the process he investigates, and he locates the pleasure and power of aesthetic experience in the *maintenance* and *sustenance* of their tense opposition rather than its elimination or transcendence. The tragic agon sheds light on his conception of an agonistic logic of conceptual development, how he conceives the relation between antipodes, and how he stands in relation to the philosophical protagonist of his frequent nemesis Plato—themes that are explored in the next chapter.

Rising Above   vs.   ~~over~~ defeat/destroy
doing Bette   vs.   Taking out

CHAPTER THREE

Contesting Socrates:
Nietzsche's (Artful) Naturalism

Welt-Spiel, das herrische,
Mischt Sein und Schein:—
Das Ewig-Närrische
Mischt uns—hinein!

NIETZSCHE, "An Goethe"

Nietzsche attempts to revitalize not only the tragic agon but also what he sees as the agon or contest between art and science. In *Die Geburt der Tragödie*, he presents the image of "the Socrates who practices music." This figure anticipates a certain kind of union of the scientific conscience Nietzsche associates with the historical figure Socrates (i.e., neither Plato nor Plato's Socrates) and the artistic as he anticipates philosophy's future. This figure is supposed to hold a thoroughly naturalistic view shaped and informed by a variety of artistic resources human beings have at their disposal as naturally cultivated and ready for further development. This ultimately results in a conception of philosophy I will describe as *artful naturalism.* Nietzsche regards such a practice as superior to its rivals (including materialism and idealism) in at least two respects: the likelihood that it facilitates a more adequate understanding of the world and the viability and potential vitality of the value schemes it can support. He thinks a naturalistic orientation of this sort is superior because it is more likely to result in knowledge and because it supports the affirmation of life.[1] There is a third way he might argue that his naturalism might be superior: it explicitly adopts a noble perspective, which is to say that its view of the world and human life is informed by noble values. For Nietzsche, taste is at least as much a concern as it is for the Platonic Socrates in the *Republic*, who understands that a life informed by the pursuit of knowledge and justice has to be oriented on the basis of "right loves" (bk. 3) or good taste. It is just that Nietzsche does not, in this case, align his sense of righteousness with moral goodness. As a philosophical activity, artful naturalism, which I believe is at least part of what is entailed in his conception of what he calls *gay science*, is offered as superior to dialectic. This is how he considers himself to advocate and practice a form of philosophy that contends with Socrates and the Platonic legacy while still making positive contributions to contemporary inquiry. And this includes an orientation of philosophy he envisions as relevant to the natural sciences as well as other disciplines that were formalizing their methods at that time.

3.1 TOWARD A "SUPERIOR NATURALISM"

At the crux of Nietzsche's contest with Socrates is the way in which he conceives the kind of inquiry he seeks to engage, its methods, purposes, and applications. In contesting Socrates, Nietzsche seeks to go beyond simply criticizing the means and ends of his philosophy in order to provide a positive alternative. Indeed, offering a positive replacement will be crucial for Nietzsche, because, as we shall see, he contends not only the ends of the Socratic contest but also its form and the kinds of participants it produces. So, in his contest with Socrates, he will have to do more than just tear him down and win by destroying him; he will need to better him. If his contest with Socrates is to be a productive one, Nietzsche will have to find a way to exceed him, to rise above him. He will have to offer a superior alternative.

What Nietzsche sums up under the name *Socrates* lives on as a legacy he contests by envisioning a different form of philosophizing, one that makes use of the opposition of art and science very broadly conceived. As with the rivals in the tragic agon, the opposing elements *and their opposition* are to be preserved without reducing either to the other. I illustrate how Nietzsche explores this possible combination in the context of just one particular set of concerns: his ideas of development and evolution. In the course of the investigation, I attempt to shed light on two other major ideas in his philosophy: his notion of overcoming and his hypothesis of will to power.[2] Nietzsche's ideas about will to power (which take multiple forms) reflect his efforts to practice the alternative form of philosophizing he anticipates. His reengagement of a contest between art and science reflects his concern to "naturalize cheerfully."[3] *Artful naturalism*, as I shall call it, takes what is essentially a naturalistic orientation while it recognizes the value of artful activity as essential to its practice.

In elaborating this view, I focus on three primary facets: (1) what is *artful* in the kind of philosophical enterprise Nietzsche engages, (2) the extent to which it is tied to a project of naturalism, and (3) how this is relevant to his

conceptions of what he calls *gay science* and the future philosophy he anticipates in *Jenseits von Gut und Böse*. I begin with a survey of what I regard as
Nietzsche's abiding project and how it arises from his contest with Socrates,
particularly his assessment of Socrates in *Die Geburt der Tragödie*, where he
conjures the image of a "Socrates who practices music." I develop and extend
the discussion of art in the preceding chapter by focusing attention on how
he thinks about art's tendency toward and use of semblance or *Schein*. The
debasement of *Schein* is one of the legacies of Socratic rationalism as he sees
it. Artful naturalism attempts to recover some of this lost value and exploit its
resources.

Thereafter, I elaborate Nietzsche's naturalism as a guiding orientation toward inquiry that is respectful of modern science, both its methods and its
empirical findings without being compelled to simply replicate or follow either. Nietzsche's naturalism is a topic that has received considerable attention
in recent literature.[4] I generally agree that Nietzsche is a sort of naturalist, but
not in the way it is often assumed and (more rarely) argued. *Naturalism* as
applied to Nietzsche can be taken to mean little more than antisupernatural-
ism (a thesis that is neither very interesting nor very informative), scientism
(which ignores or minimizes his persistent concerns with art and the aesthetic as well as his efforts at value creation), or an endorsement of empiricism
(which he often takes as his target and a position with which he contrasts his
views). New work is emerging that will endeavor to make more robust alternative conceptions available.[5] The distinction has implications beyond Nietzsche studies since the grounds on which Nietzsche emphasizes the creative,
affective, and normative dimensions of inquiry are relevant to contemporary
concerns about the relation between philosophy and science more generally
and the basis and future possibilities of the normative force of truth.[6]

Of particular interest to Nietzsche is the relation between the findings and
methods of science and the conceptual models it utilizes in its researches.
Rather than thinking that philosophy should follow science, he thinks it can
help *further naturalize* scientific inquiry (and *Wissenschaft* more generally)
in terms both critical and productive. The critical dimension is quite familiar
to his readers since he is often observed rooting out remnants of metaphysical articles of faith that still play a role in basic assumptions and key concepts that structure the aims and methods of science. Very early in his career,
Nietzsche took an interest in a classic example of how certain ontotheological
ideas might reverberate in contemporary science, specifically in conceptions
of development and evolution in the form of teleology. I call this Nietzsche's
problem of development and examine his experiment with a solution to ac-

count for evolutionary and developmental change agonistically. His notions of will to power[7] emerge in a particular context and exemplify his philosophical practice of the *Kunst der Auslegung*, the art of interpretation. His general idea of will to power as it is characterized in his published writings (and enhanced by drawing on the evidence in his notebooks) grows out of, and is continuous with, long-standing interests that stretch back to his early publications and plans for others in which he develops his ideas about struggle and the organizing capacity of agonistic relations. This is evident in his conception of philosophical activity as incorporating both the artful and the naturalistic and thereby achieving a kind of agonistic reunion of art and science. In so doing, he provocatively stokes further contestation, one of the very features he admired in his interpretation of the Homeric legacy. Thus, his alternative account of development is not only statically descriptive but also actively transformative. In providing such an account of development, Nietzsche both describes a state of affairs or processes by which they unfold and potentially directs other forms of development insofar as the description potentially redefines what is considered desirable and valuable, worthy of pursuit, and, thus, creates new ends that might be actively pursued. The final sections of the chapter explore some of the consequences of this solution, particularly in its implications for a conception of the human subject.

3.2 THE RELATION BETWEEN VALUE AND INQUIRY

Nietzsche's contest with Socrates results in his task to revalue the meaning of human existence. Nietzsche anticipates that the terms for victory in a contest with Socrates require surpassing rather than denigrating him. Since part of what he resists in Socrates is what he regards as his ultimate judgment of the value of existence, he endeavors to envision the most affirmative of all possible stances toward life. Nietzsche explores whether and how it is possible to direct desire *toward* life and elaborates the difference it makes doing so—this becomes the project that defines the writings from *Zarathustra* at least through the *Genealogy*, and it is the centerpiece of his broader inquiry into the value of values dominating his writing for the rest of his philosophically productive life.

In this context, we can consider the beginning of the fourth book of *Die fröhliche Wissenschaft*, which opens with the image of Sanctus Januarius, whose enshrined blood evinces life and is revivified on a certain feast day. Sanctus Januarius's blood miraculously "thaws," and Nietzsche suggests he seeks a similar melting of the icy effects of "no-saying" priests and philosophers. The first section of the book is among the most beautiful in all Nietz-sche's writing and introduces the idea of *amor fati*, the love of fate:

> *For the new year*—I still live, I still think: I still have to live, for I still have to think. *Sum, ergo cogito: cogito, ergo sum.* Today everybody permits himself the expression of his wish and his dearest thought; hence I, too, shall say what it is that I wish from myself today, and what was the first thought to run across my heart this year—what thought shall be for me the reason, warranty, and sweetness of my life henceforth. I want to learn more and more to see as beautiful what is necessary in things; then I shall be one of those who make things beautiful. *Amor fati*: let that be my love henceforth! I do not want to wage war against what is ugly. I do not want to accuse; I do not even want to accuse those who accuse. *Looking away* shall be my only negation. And all in all and on the whole: some day I wish to be only a Yes-sayer. (*GS* 276)

The expression of wishes and hearts' desires is echoed and becomes a theme in the first book of *Jenseits von Gut und Böse*, namely—that the views of phi-losophers are really "most often a desire of the heart that has been filtered and made abstract [. . .] prejudices which they baptize 'truths'" rather than discoveries (*BGE* 5)—and much of that book is an effort to reveal how this is so. This is not to say that Nietzsche rejects such views because of their ori-gin. Indeed, it is difficult for him to imagine things being any other way, but he thinks philosophers are not honest or courageous enough to admit this. He expresses his new wish, the overarching wish that guides his research, thus: "I want to learn more and more to see as beautiful what is necessary in things; then I shall be one of those who make things beautiful." Seeing as beautiful and thereby becoming a creator of beauty looms large in Nietzsche's project, but the tasks of seeing in this way and discerning the most relevant point of focus—necessity—are immensely challenging. *Die fröhliche Wissen-schaft* sharpens this project and contrasts it with its opposition; *Also Sprach Zarathustra* expresses Nietzsche's own challenges with embodying a "life philosophy" that is also well disposed toward life, in contrast with the char-acter Socrates, who welcomes death as a cure for/from life.[8] And *Jenseits von Gut und Böse*—about which Nietzsche claims, "it says the same things as my *Zarathustra*, but differently, very differently—"[9]squarely focuses attention on why this matters, how and why the value of our values shapes and organizes not only what we do but also what and how we know. A value that is especially curious to Nietzsche is the value of truth: "*What* in us really wants 'truth'?"

(*BGE* 1). A partial answer to the question lies in how we regard truth, our conception of the nature of truth and how it is that we think it is good for us. One characterization of truth is especially worrisome for Nietzsche, namely, the notion that truth stands opposed to illusion or semblance. This sets up a contrast between truth-seeking and image-making, one that has deep roots in the philosophical literature, and this represents the core of Nietzsche's problem with Socrates. Nietzsche regards challenging this distinction as part of his project to both *see* what is necessary and *make* things beautiful. I elaborate those ideas before offering an illustration of how he puts this distinction into practice as he conceives knowing as a kind of *Schein*-making, rather than a form of falsification, as it has been most often interpreted in the secondary literature.

3.3 TOWARD THE "MUSIC-PRACTICING SOCRATES"

Most of this chapter is *not* about Nietzsche's agonist Socrates or even what Nietzsche writes *about* Socrates but rather what Nietzsche *does* as a result and in the course of opposing him: that is, how he expresses his opposition to Socrates in developing an alternative. But at least a portion of his lifelong agon with Socrates takes the form of engaging him directly, explicitly critiquing both the kind of struggle Socrates himself initiates and the way he goes about it. Nietzsche surely exaggerates (recall his claim that Socrates is the cause of the death of tragedy, provokes its suicide), and later in the book I return to consider whether this is indicative of a form of *Vernichtungslust*. The historic Socrates is objectionable, in part, for his effect on Plato, whom Nietzsche regards as an enemy of art despite his own artistic impulses. Plato, in his turn, is objectionable for his invention of the character Socrates, who is made a hero of sorts but one who is very different from the Homeric heroes he replaces. The new Socratic hero struggles, but instead of wrestling others he contends with parts of himself, including his so-called animal nature. Nietzsche thinks this new agon undermines the very condition of human existence. The Platonic Socrates' designation of this as good and his linkage of this with the project and value of truth have been particularly destructive, he thinks. In this way, the content of Socratic philosophy as advanced by Plato can be interpreted as life-denying and debilitating. Finally, Nietzsche objects to the form of the Platonic Socrates' project, the dialectic, which he assesses as structurally inferior to Homeric agon.

Nietzsche treats Socrates as disintegrating both of the important structural features of Homeric agon that were identified in chapter 1: the form of the contest and the kinds of action that can be taken within it. Recall that one of the distinctive features of Homeric agon as Nietzsche describes it is that it is structurally organized in such a way that it deliberately fosters a measure of openness so the contest can be sustained and thereby generate the essential communal involvement. This feature is vital for the agon to be culturally significant and relevant insofar as this sort of contest provides a channel for exercising judgment as well as grounding and sharing values. Nietzsche thought that agon, as discussed above, generated both values and valuators. And recall that another dimension of productive agonism identified earlier is the kind of action it requires and encourages as both legitimate and likely to achieve the reward of success. Oriented toward surpassing, toward exceeding the abilities of the opposition, agonism coordinates forms of social interaction and channels aggression to facilitate its creative expression.

By contrast, Nietzsche regards the Socratic dialectical contest as stultifying because it ultimately shuts down the contest as a social and cultural phenomenon insofar as Socrates succeeds in shifting the agon inward to become a psychic contest. And he regards it as fundamentally destructive because no one wins a Socratic dialectical contest by being better; instead, the character Socrates always bests his opponents, and he does so by tearing them down, not by offering his own superior views. Nietzsche's Socrates debilitates and incapacitates what he contests.[10] Although I think this ultimate assessment of the philosophical and cultural agonist Nietzsche creates is already present in *Die Geburt der Tragödie*, it is not until the agonistic framework is brought forward and fleshed out that we can fully appreciate the bases of Nietzsche's evaluation of Socrates, a perspective that is enhanced only following an examination of the legacy of these shifts as they are realized in the development of morality and values more generally.

In *Die Geburt der Tragödie*, as I have already mentioned and many others have elaborated, Socrates is defamed as having facilitated the suicide of what was widely regarded as one of the greatest artistic achievements of antiquity and an art form that arguably has been elusive ever since—tragedy. In accounting for how he did this, Nietzsche makes at least two distinct claims that are supposed to explain what happened: Socrates destroyed the basic elements of the contest at the heart of tragedy when he drove out Dionysus and transmogrified Apollo. Socratic rationalism, which Nietzsche regards as an essential precursor to modern science, attaches a supreme value to intelligibility and has no tolerance for the tendency toward the indiscernible and ambiguous that the Dionysian advances. Moreover, the beautiful illusions of the Apollinian are debased in the Socratic scheme of values, which links the true and the good. Only the facets of the Apollinian that seek to make the world more discernible, drawing clearer and sharper distinctions, are embraced. While Apollinian idolatry of imagery can make the world good by making it seem beautiful, the Socratic spirit avers that only images that are true are any good (and even they are base relative to the real, as Socrates' example of the three kinds of beds in bk. 10 of the *Republic* illustrates). It is not that Socrates' desire to know is all bad, of course. The figures Nietzsche envisions as the philosophers of the tragic age of wisdom, the pre-Platonic philosophers, were at once students of *physis* (adopting what Nietzsche describes as the theoretic attitude) and artists (tapping the creative energies of the Dionysian). What Nietzsche seems to want in a music-practicing Socrates is a figure whose life is organized around the desire to know but whose drive for knowledge is informed by the desire to create.

Much of this can be seen to turn on the status of illusion, of image making and image producing. It is the *power* of illusion that appears to be so worrisome to the Platonic Socrates and at the root of his agon with the poets, particularly Homer. Nietzsche writes in *Die Geburt der Tragödie*: "Wherever Socratism turns its searching eyes it sees lack of insight and the power of illusion; and from this lack it infers the essential perversity and reprehensibility of what exists." Nietzsche seems to think this serves as the basis of Socrates' judgment against life, against the basic character of human existence: "Basing himself on this point, Socrates conceives it to be his duty to correct existence: all alone, with an expression of irreverence and superiority, as the precursor of an altogether different culture, art, and morality, he enters a world, to touch whose hem would give us the greatest happiness" (*BT* 13). The gaze of Socrates is, for Nietzsche, one that debases, and, since it coordinates happiness with illumination, it finds grounds for dissatisfaction and calls for corrective action as it encounters every murky nook and cranny. This line of interpretation is quite familiar to readers of Nietzsche, but there are at least two less frequently examined indications in his early writing that he thinks there is something quite special about the insight of Socrates that distinguishes him from his fellow pre-Platonics.[11] Nietzsche is more ambivalent about Socrates than the passages just cited suggest.

In *BT* 15, Socrates is depicted as recognizing the nascent decadence of his own culture. Seizing on the very drives that were in decline—namely, the same agonistic impulses that were at the root of the Greeks' accomplishments—Socrates, Nietzsche suggests, turned those destructive desires inward and saved the Greeks from bringing about their own complete destruction through tremendous violence against each other:

we cannot fail to see in Socrates the one turning point and vortex of so-called world history. For if we imagine that the whole incalculable sum of energy used up for this world tendency had been used not in the service of knowledge but for the practical, i.e., egoistic aims of individuals and peoples, then we realize that in that case universal wars of annihilation [Vernichtungskämpfen] and continual migrations of peoples would probably have weakened the instinctive lust for life [Lust zum Leben] to such an extent that suicide would have become a general custom and individuals might have experienced the final remnant of a sense of duty when, like the inhabitants of the Fiji Islands, they had strangled their parents and friends [als Sohn seine Eltern, als Freund seinen Freund erdrosselt]—a practical pessimism that might even have generated a gruesome ethic of genocide [grausenhafte Ethik des Völkermordes] motivated by pity, which incidentally is, and was, present in the world wherever art did not appear in some form—especially as in religion and science—as a remedy and a preventive for this breath of pestilence.

So Socrates is supposed to have staved off an encroaching "practical pessimism" and potentially evolving "ethic of genocide." Setting aside the force of the peculiar comparison with Fiji, it is worth investigating this further. Why is it that Nietzsche thinks the ancient Greeks were on the verge of such a disaster? What was supposed to be the evidence? How is the Socratic revolution supposed to have prevented this? Nietzsche's views about the agon—the ways in which it potentially creatively channels aggression that might otherwise be expressed in violence and what he thinks is required to *sustain* the agon—are all relevant. It is particularly worth noting at this point that Nietzsche thinks the Socratic direction inward of the drives that motivated and sustained the culture of contest was advantageous insofar as it prevented these drives, which had become bent toward ruin, from destroying civilization. Of course, he is concerned to critique the long-term effects of this shift and the extent to which this adaptive strategy has outlived its utility.

There is another subtlety to be found in his contest with Socrates that leads Nietzsche to seek, at least early on, a *"Socrates who practices music"* rather than an exemplar who is altogether different from Socrates. In his lectures on the pre-Platonics, he actually identifies Socrates as the first "philosopher of life." Given what I have said above about his assessment of Socrates as a *life denier*, which reflects the common view of Nietzsche's engagement,[12] this should come as a surprise. He writes: "He is the first philosopher of life [Lebensphilosophien]. A life ruled by thought! Thinking serves life, while among all previous philosophers life had served thought and knowledge: here the proper life appears as a purpose, there proper knowledge [is seen as] the highest" (*PPP*, 145). The historic Socrates, who *precedes* Plato, is considered by Nietzsche as the first to regard philosophy as itself a way of life. Thus, the ethical dimension, broadly conceived, is a significant concern.

As Nietzsche's own ideas develop, he struggles with identifying a proper exemplar of opposition to the particular kind of Socratism he contests. Since the Socrates who practices music appears only in Nietzsche's early writing, readers might rightly wonder what the relation is between this figure and another who looms so large in Nietzsche's later writings—Zarathustra. My discussion does not turn on their being identical. I think the Socrates who practices music is intended to conjure a way of engaging philosophy as a form of living that the historic Socrates is imagined to have *initiated*; but he is also supposed to search for knowledge informed by a kind of creativity similar to what is found in the practice of music. In short, the Socrates who practices music would be one who would somehow embody the tragic agon of the Apollinian and the Dionysian and thereby produce *philosophy*.

Nietzsche's depiction of the character Zarathustra is expressive of his efforts to practice philosophy more creatively, more artfully. Thus, Zarathustra is not an ethical exemplar or model to be followed, nor does he serve as a model of one who *does* philosophy. Zarathustra is expressive of Nietzsche's philosophical views, not his mouthpiece—that is, such creative activity is illustrative, indicative of certain philosophical views Nietzsche holds. The core ideal embodied in the figure of the Socrates who practices music anticipates a certain relation between *Wissenschaft* and art. This persists in Nietzsche's philosophy, which I elaborate as indicative of his artful naturalism.

In *Die fröhliche Wissenschaft*, Nietzsche reports that he wishes the dying Socrates had remained silent rather than betray his apparent view that life is a disease (when, in the *Phaedo*, he expresses gratitude to Asclepius for his impending death). In saying this, he is claiming not that Socrates did not care about the value of life or that he considered life to be a mere secondary concern to his other pursuits but rather that, try as he might, he simply could not find the value for which he searched. Were he to practice music, this would signal a monumental change. Nietzsche considers Socrates to have the most penetrating eye into the heart of nature. If only he could have such insight *and* practice music, he would then wield the most tremendous creative power. He would be able to transform the meaning of existence by taking his fundamental insight and creatively incorporating it into a vision of what is overwhelmingly desirable. Perhaps, had he recognized that the ultimate value of life is something he would have to *create*, something that would require artistic powers rather than something to be discovered (or not) in the world, he might have been saved. If only he had been able to practice music, Nietzsche speculates, Socrates might not have so willingly chosen the hemlock.

And Nietzsche seems to think this is not just a matter of putting on a happy face or making things pretty. Two aspects of this insight stand out as particularly significant. First, he considers the artistic to be part of what should be called *wisdom*. In *Die Geburt der Tragödie*, when discussing the prospect of a musical Socrates, he mentions the report that while Socrates was in prison he was compelled in a dream to "practice music" and that he did so by writing "a prelude to Apollo" and turning "a few Aesopian fables into verse." About this Nietzsche writes: "The voice of the Socratic dream vision is the only sign of any misgivings about the limits of logic: Perhaps—thus he must have asked himself—what is not intelligible to me is not necessarily unintelligent? Perhaps there is a realm of wisdom from which the logician is exiled? Perhaps art is even a necessary correlative of, and supplement for science?" (*BT* 14). To fail to see what the artist, musician, or poet sees is to fail to gain the wisdom Socrates so desperately sought. But Socrates recognized this only too late, and then he was poorly prepared to heed the advice of the dream.

These considerations are closely related to the second aspect of Nietzsche's problem: Socrates appears to have been the instigator of his own downfall, the source of his inability to practice music; it is not just that he failed to have such an opportunity. By insisting on the criterion of intelligibility, Socrates put himself in such a position that he *could not see* what music and poetry reveal. He could not find life desirable; he could not access the potent passions that the poet taps and directs toward life. Nietzsche takes this task as his own and endeavors to strike a union between the opposing tendencies to unmask things as they are and to be the creator of images so splendid that one cares less about that which they cover if one is cognizant of the fact that they are coverings at all. Engaging in this work requires recuperating a different understanding of *semblance* (*Schein*) and the connection between art and illusion. Once it becomes clearer how Nietzsche thinks art and science stand in relation to each other and the project of truth, we will be in a better position to appreciate how he scrutinizes the particularly problematic concept of development and its relation to teleology, and how he takes an experimental approach to addressing it.

3.4 SEMBLANCE AND SCIENCE

In describing what he calls "the basic will of the spirit" ("'Grundwillen des Geistes'") in *Jenseits von Gut und Böse*, Nietzsche attributes to human existence "needs and capacities [that are] the same as those which physiologists posit for everything that lives, grows, and multiplies." He associates what he describes as fundamental powers (*Kraften*) of *appropriation* and *artful creativity* with all things that "live, grow, and multiply" (*BGE* 230). What we call *science* is, for him, a specialized and intensified exercise of these very powers. Some extensive quotation of the relevant portions of *BGE* 230 facilitates further appreciation of this point:

> The spirit's power to appropriate the foreign stands revealed in its inclination to assimilate the new to the old, to simplify the manifold, and to overlook or repulse whatever is totally contradictory—just as it involuntarily emphasizes certain features and lines in what is foreign, in every piece of the "external world," retouching and falsifying the whole to suit itself. Its intent in all of this is to incorporate new "experiences," to file new things in old files—growth, in a word—or, more precisely, the *feeling* of growth, the feeling of increased power [auf Wachsthum also; bestimmter noch, auf das Gefühl des Wachsthums, auf das Gefühl der vermehrten Kraft].
>
> An apparently opposite drive serves this same will: a suddenly erupting decision in favor of ignorance [Unwissenheit], of deliberate exclusion, a shutting of one's windows, an internal No to this or that thing, a refusal to let things approach, a kind of state of defense against much that is knowable, a satisfaction with the dark, with the limiting horizon [abschliessenden Horizonte], a Yea and Amen to ignorance—all of which is necessary in proportion to a spirit's power to appropriate [wie dies Alles nöthig ist je nach dem Grade seiner aneignenden Kraft].

And these differing, and at times opposing, drives account for (and circumscribe) our will to deceive or be deceived, which is countered by the desire or will to know: "*This* Willen zum Schein [will to semblance], to simplification, to masks, to cloaks, in short, to the surface [Oberfläche]—for every surface is a cloak—is *countered* by that sublime inclination of the seeker after knowledge who insists on profundity, multiplicity, and thoroughness [die Dinge tief, vielfach, gründlich nimmt und nehmen will], with a *will* which is a kind of cruelty of the intellectual conscience and taste [als eine Art Grausamkeit des intellektuellen Gewissens und Geschmacks]." The resemblance here to the dynamic of the artistic forces of the Apollinian and the Dionysian is obvious. Nietzsche similarly anticipates their possibilities for relations psychologically, individually, and culturally in his thinking about the relation between art and science. In embracing semblance (or, as it might be translated otherwise but more problematically, *appearances*),[13] he neither rejects *truth* (proclaiming the superiority of its opposite) nor gives up on truth altogether (celebrating *merely* the play of the apparent). The will to "simplification, to masks, to cloaks, in short, to the surface" is, for him, part of our processes of ratiocination and cognition more generally insofar as the very activities through which we investigate and acquire knowledge, such as conceptualizing, entail overlooking differences, inventing similarities, and imposing categories, regularity, and order: "delusion and error are conditions of human knowledge and sensation" (*GS* 107).[14] This is not to say that human knowledge amounts to nothing more than error and delusion; nor is this a view acknowledging that delusion and error result alongside or in competition with knowledge. I take Nietzsche to be saying that our delusions and errors, our overly rough approximations and inventions, enable us, nevertheless, to acquire knowledge. Errors, somehow, are part of the conditions for knowledge, as Nietzsche sees it.

The Socratic legacy of dissociating *semblance* and intelligibility, formerly united in the Apollinian, gave "Schein" a bad name to such an extent that semblance came to be regarded not only as epistemically deficient (e.g., the *Republic*'s Socrates who suggests that poetic images are thrice removed from the truth) but also as morally defective (corrupting). Nietzsche's contest with Socrates entails revaluing *Schein* as a major objective. If successful, this campaign would have two effects: it would provide a different conception of knowledge (shifting from the sense of it as illusion- or semblance-free, and beyond or purified of images), and it would alter the valence of illusion, diminishing the sense of guilt and decadence attached to a life that takes pleasure in consuming and producing images. A victory of this sort would inaugurate a new, more nuanced and revalued, sensibility for appearances.

Robert Rethy provides one of the most extensive discussions in English of Nietzsche's conception of *Schein*, particularly in the context of related philosophical vocabulary. He convincingly argues that early on Nietzsche, influenced by Schopenhauer, comes to see *Schein* and *Erscheinung* (the latter, for Kant, the kind of appearance that stands in opposition to the thing-in-itself) as on a *continuum* rather than in a binary relation of true or false.[15] Whereas Kant associates *Schein* with error (i.e., the mistaken belief that the apparent *is* the real) and with deception to be avoided, Nietzsche attributes a kind of innocence to it as apparent semblance, a play of appearances that can be captivating and deliberately pursued much as we do with art. Throughout Nietzsche's writings, *Schein* is associated with a form of "honest deceptiveness," itself a form or variety of truthfulness (for just a few examples in *Die fröhliche Wissenschaft*, see *GS* P:4, 54, 58, 107, 361). It is not *mere* illusion or delusion. *Schein* gives us access to the world.[16]

Nietzsche is concerned to disentangle the appearance/reality distinction from morality and interrogate the normativity of truth. In *Jenseits von Gut und Böse*, Nietzsche writes: "It is no more than a moral prejudice that truth [Wahrheit] is worth more than *Schein*; it is even the worst proved assumption there is in the world. Let at least this much be admitted: there would be no life at all if not on the basis of perspective estimates and appearances [perspektivischer Schätzungen und Scheinbarkeiten]; and if with the virtuous enthusiasm and clumsiness of some philosophers, one wanted to abolish the 'apparent world' ['scheinbare Welt'] altogether—well, supposing *you* could do that, at least nothing would be left of your 'truth' ['Wahrheit'] either" (*BGE* 34). It would be a mistake to think that Nietzsche celebrates semblance *rather than*, or *as opposed to*, truth, in which case one would maintain the opposition between *mere appearance* or *illusion* and some (presumably ontologically superior and epistemologically more faithful) *reality* whose understanding constitutes truth. He regards *Schein* as part of the enterprise of truth such that even our scientific pursuits, our quest to give naturalistic accounts of various phenomena, must have truck with *semblance*.

Just as Nietzsche calls into question the opposition of appearance and reality, so he challenges a strict binary opposition of truth and falsity. The passage from *BGE* cited above continues: "what forces us at all to suppose that there is an essential opposition of 'true' and 'false'? Is it not sufficient to assume degrees of apparentness and, as it were, lighter and darker shadows and shades of appearance [Schein]—different 'values' [verschiedene valeurs], to use the language of painters?" (*BGE* 34). In this sense, *Schein* is not *mere* but uncannily *more*—semblance is not the mere appearance of some greater reality but rather something that indicates more than itself. A quick review of some features of Nietzsche's account of tragedy offers some clues as to what constitutes this *more*. Recall that the ancient tradition maintains that behind every mask on the stage lurks Dionysus, but it is the Apollinian masking that makes the felt presence of Dionysus possible and allows him to appear. Dionysus becomes *known* through his various appearances. Nietzsche seems to think of *Schein* more generally as serving a similar function. Appearances are what allow us to see what is; they are not facsimile substitutes. What is gained for truth in embracing *Schein* is recognition of the inventiveness in the sense making that occurs in experience. It calls attention to the creative and artful, the productive dimensions of human thinking that help us sort through, organize, and communicate our experiences.

Nietzsche's music-practicing Socrates from *Die Geburt der Tragödie* and his future philosophers of *Jenseits von Gut und Böse* highlight the *Schein*-like character of experience and inquiry. *Schein*-making is inclusive of (although not exhausted by) the activities of selection, identification, coordination, and classification that are involved in naturalistic, scientific inquiry.

Nietzsche thinks that the very "harden[ing] in the discipline of science" (*BGE* 230) leads to recognition of these ideas about *Schein* and the appropriative capacities of human beings. Against the figure of Socrates he creates, he suggests that philosophy entails applying these insights about *Schein* rather than correcting existence. Human beings have among their natural capacities appropriating powers, creative and destructive, constructive and critical. Standing before the rest of nature, seeing oneself as the appropriating being that one is because one is a part of nature, because that *is* the basic text of human existence, leads, Nietzsche thinks, to this reformulated conception. In this respect, he adopts a form of naturalism, but it is crucial to understand its artful dimensions. Such insight is to be purged of its current moral content, including the moral debasement of human creativity. This is what I think Nietzsche envisions in the translation of man back into nature described in *BGE* 230, which will likely appear both "strange and insane [seltsame und tolle]" from the standpoint of metaphysics, perhaps even from the standpoint of philosophers bent toward naturalism in a narrow sense. This is what he has in mind when he seeks to "de-deif[y] nature," "to '*naturalize*' humanity in terms of a pure, newly discovered, newly redeemed nature" (*GS* 109).[17]

Inquiry guided by the spirit of what I am calling *artful naturalism* is also what Nietzsche envisions in *Die fröhliche Wissenschaft* 113 as "the higher organic system of knowledge," a system of knowledge that might further develop the multiple strengths that had to emerge in order for science to become a possibility for us. A curious thing about these different capacities, such as "the impulse to doubt, to negate, to wait, to collect, to dissolve," is that singly they could be quite detrimental, "poisons" that need to be kept "in check" by other capacities and integrated in "one organizing force within one human being." A future time might come, Nietzsche suggests, when science and art, which seem opposed and detrimental to each other, might become similarly engaged, their opposition utilized in such a way as to allow each to appropriate the resources of the other in pursuit of their ends.

Gay science advances this through its shaping and re-formation of conceptual structures and metaphoric models, and for Nietzsche this crucially requires a measure of artifice, a form of creative activity. Examples of this can be found in his effort to think through the contemporary problem of accounting for development, growth, change, and evolution. In the remainder of this chapter, I show how Nietzsche focuses his attention on matters associated with naturalistic concerns—the nature of the world in which we live, the nature of human existence, and our relations to others in nature—that he pursues and advances by way of artfully taking up conceptual forms and models that facilitate further inquiry. This is at least one of the ways in which his philosophy is naturalistic. A virtue of my account is that it allows us to see how it is intrinsically linked with his project of the revaluation of values since his criteria for what make inventive conceptual structures more suitable include whether they potentially facilitate not only knowledge (including the advancement of science) but also prospects for valuing life. The kind of naturalism I tie to Nietzsche strives to provide simultaneously a distinctive sense of nature and a new relation between knowing and valuing, which are key points of contention in Nietzsche's agon with Socrates.

3.5 ARTFUL NATURALISM

Tensions between semblance or appearance and reality are at least partially at the root of the competing views of idealism and empirical realism. Part of Nietzsche's wrestling with the legacy of Socratic philosophy takes the form of challenging what he sees as a false dilemma between these two positions. This concern motivates his *Genealogy*, where he contrasts his views with what he coins as *Reéalism*, a jab at the naturalistic approach of his former friend Paul Reé, who was at the forefront of evolutionary psychology. The same tension is persistently considered in a variety of historical contexts in Nietzsche's *Jenseits von Gut und Böse*, where he makes numerous suggestions for his anticipated alternative.[18]

The age-old philosophic argument of how to distinguish and reconcile the world as it appears and the world as it really is can, Nietzsche thinks, lead to nihilism. He mentions the debate that leads Parmenides to conclude that "all is one" and the apparent world of change (the world of our experience) is an illusion; developments of modern empiricism and idealism reflect the very same concerns that motivated the earliest Greek thinkers, Plato, the Epicureans, and the Stoics (see *BGE* 7–10). These might be compared with others whom Nietzsche describes in terms of evincing an affirmative will ("stronger and livelier thinkers who are still eager for life"); they argue for "perspective" and deny the (ultimate) reality of the sensual world. Nietzsche calls these "skeptical anti-realists and knowledge microscopists." While admiring their skepticism, a position he significantly qualifies later in the fourth part of *BGE*, he thinks they do not follow their ideas far enough, namely, to the point of questioning the value of truth and the basis of nobility, such as he anticipates possible: "A little *more* strength, flight, courage, and artistic power, and they would want to *rise*—not return!" (*BGE* 10). In other words, instead of resorting to retrograde ideas, rebels against modern philosophy might have created new conceptions of human existence and its possibilities. Nietzsche anticipates a more productive reaction against modern philosophy.

His apparent admiration for the skeptics of modern philosophy stands in contrast with his apparent praise of "sensualism" in *BGE* 15, which has been the subject of significant discussion in the Nietzsche literature, particularly as it bears on his naturalism and assessment of the aims, methods, and results of science.[19] There is a sizable body of secondary literature that relies on certain assumptions about Nietzsche's endorsement of sensualism (and, ultimately, empiricism) when he writes: "Sensualism, therefore, at least as a regulative hypothesis, if not as a heuristic principle." Some caution is warranted here because Nietzsche offers some apparently ambivalent views about "sensualism" in the same text. In *BGE* 14, he contrasts Plato's "master[y] of the senses" by dulling and limiting empirical evidence with the views of those who are captivated by what the senses relay and think such constitutes evidence and supplies the basis for explanation rather than interpretation. At this point, Nietzsche offers one of his few seemingly positive references to Plato, when he calls his philosophizing "noble," presumably in contrast with the later view, which he associates with what he calls "popular sensualism" (PS).

This popular sensualism is yet further contrasted with a different sort of imperative associated with the idea of "sensualism [. . .] as a regulative hypothesis" (SRH). In setting these views side by side, we can see there is a significant difference in what they entail:

PS: "was sich sehen und tasten lässt—bis so weit muss man jedes problem treiben" ("only what can be seen and felt—every problem has to be pursued to that point" [*BGE* 14]);

SRH: "wo der Mensch nichts mehr zu sehen un zu greifen hat, da hat er auch nichts mehr zu suchen" ("where one cannot find anything to see and to grasp he has no further business" [*BGE* 15]).

The first (PS) concerns *the extent to which* a problem is pursued by those holding the view of popular sensualism; the second (SRH) is about the *limits of problems* when guided by sensualism as a regulative hypothesis. Nietzsche is clearly not rejecting the value of sense experience, but neither is he limiting knowledge to whatever can be the subject of empirical investigation. And he is surely not patently *endorsing* scientific explanation or limiting philosophy to whatever the sciences cannot currently explain.[20] Instead, he anticipates future philosophers, among whom he might number as a philosopher whose concern *is* the future, who will reconsider the relation between invention and discovery. In this respect, philosophy invents new critical tools and frameworks—these are their distinctive artistic productions—that help shape a sense of what it is that *can be seen*, what can become objects of investigation, imaginatively projecting what might be discovered.

This relation between *erfinden* (invention) and *finden* (discovery) is a crucial dimension of Nietzsche's naturalism. It is important to not think of *erfinden* as *sheer* (trivial or capricious) invention; the creation of new soul hypotheses (*BGE* 12, discussed below) would not necessarily be pure fictions. That Nietzsche anticipates such revised concepts will be inventions rather than discoveries is consistent with what he says about truth and the limits of human knowledge, particularly as it is sought in philosophy.

Nietzsche's development of these ideas occurs in the context of contrasting his own views with those of Kant, whose allegedly "discovered" faculties are, in fact, inventions. The charge against Kant is not simply that he invented fictions but that he mistook (or misrepresented) his inventions for discoveries. And part of the reason this is problematic (besides the fact that it is dishonest, a charge Nietzsche also levies, e.g., *BGE* 5) is because it limits the development of inquiry. Having "discovered" the faculties of this or that (*BGE* 11), Kant's critical philosophy might appear more powerful, more effective in offering explanations, than it actually is, and that would bring more robust philosophical investigation to a halt. Such would limit knowledge rather than add to it.

The contrast between *erfinden* and *finden* is complemented by Nietzsche's distinction between *interpretation* and *explanation*. Even the natural sciences provide us with what are interpretations, not bald or absolute explanations of the phenomena investigated. We can acknowledge this without lapsing into a pernicious relativism that would have it that all interpretations are *the same*. Further, we can recognize that such descriptions are always organized to suit our purposes or interests without having to conclude that such interpretations simply *reduce* to nothing more than the expressions of our desires. The critical point is that we can be mindful that what are presented as explanations, in fact, *describe* and that descriptions are shaped by interests. Aware of these influences, we might more critically engage our efforts to make sense of the world around us and our place and possibilities within it.

Thus far, I have tried to argue for some distinctive aspects of Nietzsche's naturalism that make it clear it is not reducible to empiricism or scientism and it reflects his concerns about the relation between philosophy and science. What is *artful* in what I am calling Nietzsche's *artful naturalism* can be characterized partially as a form of imaginative projection by virtue of which inquiry can be *oriented*. Such creations supply guiding ideas and models that depict possible relations to be taken up experimentally in further research. What I designate as *artful* has, at least, methodological import as well as significance for interpretation and communication of results. Nietzsche's artful naturalism leads him to make use of artistic innovations to redirect and reshape vectors of inquiry, and it encourages him to look to diverse bodies and sources of knowledge for innovative models to apply to his areas of concern.

In emphasizing these features of Nietzsche's work, I am not offering an account of Nietzsche's naturalism that aims to be comprehensive. What a naturalistic philosophy entails (and rules out) was of interest to Nietzsche, but he did not develop a broad theoretical account, and I do not wish to attribute one to him. My emphasis on how the artful is evident in both *how* he pursues his investigations and *what* he attributes to nature has not gone unrecognized by those who take on philosophical projects inspired by him.[21] It is just that these features are less recognized by those focused on Nietzsche scholarship.[22] In underscoring the artful in Nietzsche's naturalism, I seek to show that this is one of the ways in which Nietzsche envisions a productive agonistic relation between what is fictive and what is true, what is invented and what is discovered. His anticipated reunion of art and science contends the separation he thinks is evident in Socratic philosophy and its enduring legacy.

3.6 NIETZSCHE'S PROBLEM OF DEVELOPMENT AND HIS HERACLITEAN SOLUTION

A union of art and science that allows for reciprocal formation of our understanding of nature is evident in Nietzsche's reflections on development. The extent to which Nietzsche contests (or affirms) Darwin and Darwinism is relevant insofar as it might be indicative of whether and the extent to which his naturalism takes the form of a kind of scientism.[23] He philosophically characterizes development in ways that are mindful of emerging and competing evolutionary theories. His engagement with these ideas reflects his views about science more generally and concerns about the nature of explanatory causes more broadly. Although my project is not about Nietzsche's Darwinism per se, the topic is relevant insofar as Nietzsche was interested in how such views might smuggle in dubious metaphysical prejudices as well as what they suggest about the aims and purposes of human existence. He had a deep and abiding interest in evolutionary and developmental histories both natural and cultural, and he followed the intense debates about these matters in his time. It is also clear from his works and notebooks that, at times, he takes sides with one particular competing view over another.[24] In so doing, he found inspiration and source material as well as evidence of lingering dubious metaphysical prejudices. Some of the results of these encounters are views about development that are reminiscent of the agonistic structures discussed in earlier chapters of this book.

This is evident in his engagement with theories of evolution and development and the emergence of his "hypothesis" of "will to power" (*BGE* 36). His writings of the 1880s reflect a relentless interest in developing a single account of change, growth, and development that would be applicable to both the realm of morality—broadly conceived and freed from its religious moorings—and that of physiology, informed by his scientific studies, particularly in the field of embryology.[25] Nietzsche wonders about the physiological effects of religious beliefs and practices as well as about how diet, nutrition, climate, disease, and health affect the mind.[26] Finding both mechanistic and teleological theories wanting, he seeks to devise an interpretation of human being that situates it within the world of becoming while remaining in dialogue with the empirical sciences and allowing for the possibility that we might also be able to raise the bar for indicating the goals for which the human might strive. In such a case, human existence would not be bound by any particular telos but would still be able to realize and possibly direct meaningful activity. Nietzsche found an exemplary model for this in (his own) Heraclitus, who serves as a precursor to the "Socrates who practices music" and a foil in his analyses of the development (and decadence) of ancient philosophy culminating in Plato.[27]

Nietzsche characterizes Heraclitus as a figure who resisted adducing teleological explanations for growth, change, and development.[28] Of particular interest is the notion of "immanent lawfulness." As Nietzsche interprets the contest at the heart of Heraclitus's world in strife, he discerns an immanent logic. Strife constitutes the cosmos like "a child playing a game, moving counters, in discord and concord" (*PPP*, 65). The overall nature of this play is nonteleological and arbitrary—"innocent." Necessity and justice abide, but they are not subject to an externally determined standard of measurement. Aims and purposes are evident, but they are not directed by some external rule, order, or goal; rather, they are internal to it. Nietzsche writes:

> only in the play of the child (or that of the artists) does there exist a Becoming and Passing Away without any moralistic calculations. He [Heraclitus] conceives of *the play of children* as that of spontaneous human beings: here is innocence and yet coming into being and destruction: not one droplet of injustice should remain in the world. The eternally living fire [Aeon], plays, builds, and knocks down: strife, this opposition of different characteristics, directed by justice, may be grasped only as an aesthetic phenomenon. We find here a purely aesthetic view of the world. We must exclude even more any moralistic tendencies to think teleologically here, for the cosmic child [Weltkind] behaves with no regard to purposes but rather only to an immanent justice: it can act only willfully and lawfully, but is does not *will* these ways (*PPP*, 70).[29]

Thus, he thinks Heraclitus supplies an artful image—the child at play—that provides him with a conceptual lead for conceiving an alternative to teleological views he finds both philosophically and scientifically problematic.[30]

Near the end of the Pre-Platonic lecture notes, Nietzsche characterizes Heraclitus's non-teleological position thus: "This playful cosmic child continuously builds and knocks down but from time to time begins his game anew: a moment of contentment followed by new needs. His continuous building and knocking down is a craving as creativity is a need for the artists; his play is a need." The play of the child has immanent purposes relative to the particularities of the play at any given moment, but its shape unfolds without any orchestrating, overarching will or design.[31] Within the play, a kind of necessity is operative, which Nietzsche characterizes as "craving as creativity is a need." But this necessity is free from conformity to some law or universal principle. He continues: "From time to time he [the child] has his fill of it [the play]—nothing other than fire exists there; that is, it engulfs all things. Not hybris but rather the newly awakened drive to play [Spieltrieb] now wills once more his *setting into order*. Rejection of any teleological view of the world reaches its zenith here: the child throws away its toy, but as soon as it plays again, it proceeds with purpose and order: necessity and play, war and justice" (*PPP*, 72–73). Heraclitus's key image demonstrates how it is possible to conceive meaningful development without imposing a teleological order.

Nietzsche's Heraclitean model allows for the intelligibility of aims, goals, and purposes—*necessity*—as immanent to the justice or law that makes a struggle or conflict possible and serves as the ground for the contest. But it also allows for *chance* as the agonistic process takes on more of the character of play than the execution of design by a supreme being or omnipotent will. Thus, Nietzsche conceptualizes phenomena of change, growth, and development in the natural world as unfolding in an evolutionary process that has no ulterior ends or purposes. Heraclitus's playing child is a poetic image of natural phenomena that metaphorically captures the becoming of physis. Nietzsche regards this view as not only artistically and aesthetically appealing but also empirically responsible insofar as it acknowledges how we experience the world and is attentive to its transformative characteristics and capabilities.[32] Change and variation are empirically observed. We do not experience things as static and identical. The poetic vision of Heraclitus grants the flux of existence while still finding ways of characterizing enduring aspects of its development. Nietzsche's hypotheses of will to power reflect his attempt to exercise similar poetic vision, to make it possible to see the world in a different way that might ultimately lead others to new discoveries within it.

Although Nietzsche does not begin to use the expression *will to power* in his published writings until *Also Sprach Zarathustra*, his earlier account of the Greek agon foreshadows the idea. The urges to strive, struggle, and overcome resistance, the "terrible drive" responsible for "fighting and the lust for victory," the irritants of *eris* and envy that plagued Themistocles and Pericles and propelled them to extraordinary accomplishments, the "monstrous desire" of Xenophanes and Plato to defame their rival Homer, the "personal struggling impulse" at the root of artistic competitions, the "base desire for revenge" experienced by Miltiades[33]—each can be read retrospectively as a manifestation of will to power. Nietzsche acknowledges as much in *Götzen-Dämmerung*. Referring to the Greeks, he writes:

> I saw their strongest instinct, the will to power [den Willen zur Macht]; I saw them tremble before the indomitable force of this drive [der unbändigen Gewalt dieses Triebs]—I saw how all their institutions grew out of preventive measures taken to protect each other against their inner explosives [um sich vor einander gegen ihren inwendigen Explosivstoff sicher zu stellen]. This tremendous inward tension [Die ungeheure Spannung im Innern] then discharged itself in terrible and ruthless hostility to the outside world [furchtbarer und rücksichtsloser Feindschaft nach Aussen]: the city-

states tore each other to pieces [die Stadtgemeinden zerfleischten sich un-
ter einander] so that the citizens of each might find peace from themselves.
(*TI*, "What I Owe the Ancients" 3)

Readers of *Jenseits von Gut und Böse* are introduced to will to power by
name in the middle of the first part, where Nietzsche writes: "Physiologists
should think before putting down the instinct of self-preservation [Selbster-
haltungstrieb] as the cardinal instinct of an organic being. A living thing seeks
above all to *discharge* its strength [Vor Allem will etwas Lebendiges seine Kraft
auslassen]—life itself is *will to power* [Wille zur Macht];[34] self-preservation
is only one of the indirect and most frequent *results*" (*BGE* 13). Part of what he
takes aim at in this passage is evolutionary theories that suggest a certain sort
of intentional teleology (the passage continues: "In short, here as everywhere
else, let us beware of *superfluous* teleological principles"), as, for example,
in the view of Paley. At the same time, he is siding with Roux's alternative
to Darwinian evolutionary theory, which he regards as having a conservative
bent. Roux argued that it is not the case that all of existence (or even existence
itself) is actively, willfully, pursuing preservation.[35] What one finds are expressions of *strength* and thereby the experience of power, as Nietzsche puts it, the
feeling of power. In some cases, but certainly not all, preservation might be the
result but not the goal of this effort.

Nietzsche goes on to explore what conclusions might follow from the hypothesis that all of these drives, which constitute "our entire instinctive life,"
ultimately spring from "the development and ramification of *one* basic form
of the will" (*BGE* 36). Ultimately, his hypotheses about will to power are experiments to test precisely such possible conclusions. If this is the case, he
suggests, it might then be possible to trace the development (*Entwicklung*)
or evolution of something—"a thing, a custom, an organ"—as unfolding from
"a succession of more or less profound, more or less mutually independent
processes of subduing, plus the resistances they encounter, the attempts at
transformation for the purpose of defense and reaction, and the results of
successful counteractions [die Aufeinanderfolge von mehr oder minder tief-
gehenden, mehr oder minder von einander unabhängigen, an ihm sich ab-
spielenden Überwältigungsprozessen, hinzugerechnet die dagegen jedes
Mal aufgewendeten Widerstände, die versuchten Form-Verwandlungen zum
Zweck der Vertheidigung und Reaktion, auch die Resultate gelungener Ge-
genaktionen]" (*GM* II:12). In short, if such is the case, then there is a developmental story of struggle to be told about everything that exists: everything
is constituted on the basis of conflict—or, in some cases, contests—in which

some facets are drawn out as the result of pressures that spring from meeting and surmounting opposition and other facets are remnants of the triumphs and overcomings of others. I take it this is also what orients Nietzsche's practice of genealogy in *Zur Genealogie der Moral* and other later writings. Thus, Nietzsche seems to think that development on the macro and micro scales can be described agonistically. He thinks an agonistic account can be nimble and subtle in its representation of the complexity of development and change without importing teleological principles or ulterior goals or aims.

Nietzsche's will to power hypothesis does not posit a simple Über-will, or a will that promises to one day overpower all others, but rather functions as a descriptive characterization of the world as composed of dynamic conflicting forces. What we call *cause* and *effect* are facets of this process: "It is a question of a struggle between two elements of unequal power: a new arrangement of forces is achieved according to the measure of power of each of them. The second condition is something fundamentally different from the first (not its effect): the essential thing is that the factions in conflict emerge with different quanta of power" (*KSA* 13:14[95]).[36] Thus, Nietzsche's naturalistic project cannot entail simply seeking causal explanations (or spelling out the terms for such) of various natural phenomena. We can compare the passage just cited from the notebooks with *GS* 112, where Nietzsche writes:

> *Cause and effect.*—[. . .] It will do to consider science as an attempt to humanize [Anmenschlichung] things as faithfully as possible; as we describe things and their one-after-another, we learn how to describe ourselves more and more precisely. Cause and effect: such a duality probably never exists; in truth we are confronted by a continuum out of which we isolate a couple of pieces [steht ein continuum vor uns, von dem wir ein paar Stücke isoliren], just as we perceive motion only as isolated points and then infer it without ever actually seeing it. The suddenness with which many effects stand out misleads us; actually, it is sudden only for us. In this moment of suddenness there is an infinite number of processes that elude us. An intellect that could see cause and effect as a continuum and a flux and not, as we do, in terms of arbitrary division and dismemberment [als willkürliches Zertheilt- und Zerstücktsein], would repudiate the concept of cause and effect and deny all conditionality [Bedingtheit].

In this passage, Nietzsche claims that reliance on causality in scientific inquiry represents the attempt to "*humanize* things as faithfully as possible" (emphasis added). This should be compared with a passage preceding it by just a few sections, cited earlier, in which he anticipates naturalizing humanity (*GS* 109). This suggests he thinks that emphasis on at least some kinds of causality and causal explanation renders the sciences *not naturalistic enough*.[37]

Returning to his account of how existence itself appears as strife, we can note that, rather than chains of causal events, Nietzsche conceives an interminable process that entails "the mutual struggle of that which becomes, often with the absorption of one's opponent; the number of developing elements not constant" (*KSA* 12:7[54]).[38] Following his hypothesis of will to power: "'Life' might be defined as an enduring form of the *process in which force is established* [Kraftfeststellungen], in which the various struggling parties grow unequally" (*KSA* 11:36[22]).[39] Accordingly, he conceives individual organisms in terms of "a struggle between parts (for food, space, etc.): its development is tied to the victory or predominance of individual parts, to an atrophy, a 'becoming an organ' of other parts" (*KSA* 12:7[25]).[40] He develops his image of will to power to describe development on a broad scale. Such description is supposed to be compatible with the best science can offer (he thinks views in psychology, zoology, and embryology support it), with science itself pushed even further to naturalize its views. And, finally, he thinks such a perspective might afford opportunities for redemption from the devaluation of the natural, which is evident in the residual Socratism in scientific inquiry. So, naturalism, for Nietzsche, entails not only a disposition toward methods of inquiry or assessment of inferences or a commitment to truth. It also involves concern for the value of what is natural as well as the evaluative scope or range it affords. What I mean by this is that it matters to him what constraints or possibilities for valuing are generated on the basis of what is posited about the world. He is concerned with both sides of the coin: how our views are expressive of certain values, what and how they reflect about what we really value, as well as what is possible for us to value given our other commitments. Nietzsche's artful naturalism is highly sensitive to this relation.

3.7 THE SUBJECT NATURALIZED: NIETZSCHE'S AGONISTIC MODEL OF THE SOUL

One of our commitments that needs reconciliation with nature is the conception of the soul and its offspring. To illustrate the difference artful naturalism might make here, we can consider Nietzsche's discussion of soul atomism (*BGE* 12). This proves to be a particularly powerful example because it crosses a variety of domains, including religion, ethics, epistemology, and science.[41] Briefly put, "soul atomism" springs from what he designates as our

Atomism

"atomistic need" to identify what is "indestructible, eternal, indivisible, as a monad, as an *atomon*" (*BGE* 12). He targets two related expressions of this need and supposition: (1) the Christian view of the everlasting soul, whose life on earth is fleeting, ephemeral, and ultimately base in comparison with its prospects in the hereafter, a view that denigrates human existence and at best leads to a kind of nihilism, and (2) the basis of the morality of intention that supposes a "doer behind the deed," whose overcoming Nietzsche anticipates, as I discuss in the next chapter.

Nietzsche begins this important section of *Jenseits von Gut und Böse* with discussion of "materialistic atomism" and the findings of Copernicus and Boscovich as "the greatest and most successful opponents of visual evidence so far" (*BGE* 12). Contrary to what the senses tell us, we now no longer believe that it is we who stand still with the rest of the heavens revolving around us, just as (and Nietzsche was not in a position to know the developments of molecular physics) we no longer believe that our world is composed of basic indivisible units of "substance" or "matter." (Boscovich, who lived in the eighteenth century, advanced the view that our world is composed of centers of force rather than atomic substances.) And he anticipates that, just as Copernicus revolutionized our view of the cosmos and Boscovich revolutionized (or made it possible to conceive such a revolution) our view of our worldly existence, it will be possible to revolutionize our conception of ourselves and our psychic world—and, moreover, that it is high time we did.

In relaying this, it is interesting to notice how Nietzsche draws on the findings of science at the same time that he emphasizes how these very findings present evidence "contrary to all the senses" and represent "the greatest triumph over the senses that has been gained on earth so far." Thus, we find him pointing to examples of scientific views, descriptive accounts that offer interpretations that came to prevail, "persuaded us to believe," without appeal to the senses and even in opposition to them. It is because such descriptions are not solely dependent on empirical observation that he can also maintain the peculiar view, which would seem at odds with a strictly scientistic picture, that, even if we are persuaded to root out and forsake the atomic need in our conception of human psychology, "one of the most ancient and venerable hypotheses," "it is not at all necessary to get rid of 'the soul'" (*BGE* 12).

Rather than giving up altogether on the soul, Nietzsche claims, we should see that now (now that atomism has been defeated in virtually every other area) "the way is open for new versions and refinements of the soul-hypothesis," and he goes on to offer some possible ways of formulating such hypotheses, including "'mortal soul,' and 'soul as subjective multiplicity,' and 'soul as social structure of the drives and affects' [Begriffe wie 'sterbliche Seele' und 'Seele als Subjekts-Vielheit' und 'Seele als Gesellschaftsbau der Triebe und Affekte']" (*BGE* 12). This presents us with a very interesting vision of Nietzsche's own naturalism and his conception of how it bears on the relation between philosophy and science. There would seem to be no basis in empirical observation for our retention and advancement of a concept of soul. Moreover, if nothing else, *soul* smacks of the very supernaturalism that any naturalistic view could not possibly abide. (To be clear, the matter does not turn on a trick of translation of the text: as evident above, Nietzsche uses the word *Seele* here, which is unambiguous in its metaphysical and supernatural implications.) So how can Nietzsche claim this if he is primarily a proponent of scientism and empiricism? He cannot, at least not in the way that we ordinarily think about these views. We can look to his list of possible alternatives, just mentioned, for some indication and then examine how he himself takes up and explores some of these possibilities.

The list above includes qualifications of the soul hypothesis that root it in a naturalistic as opposed to a supernatural conception of human beings: that we are mortal, that there are multiple phenomena for which we need to account, and that these multiple dimensions, facts, or characteristics have relational qualities and mutually affect each other. So, *soul* is nominally (but not trivially) retained at the same time as it is given natural qualities. Nonetheless, it is sure that soul itself does not atomically and independently exist; at least, Nietzsche does not make any such claim, and it would seem that the "new versions and refinements" might be regarded as inventions, not discoveries lying in wait once we are no longer blinded by the fog of atomism. Nietzsche himself goes on to take up one such hypothesis when, in *BGE* 19, he claims: "our body is but a social structure composed of many souls [unser Leib ist ja nur ein Gesellschaftsbau vieler Seelen] [. . .] in all willing it is absolutely a question of commanding and obeying, on the basis, as already said, of a social structure composed of many 'souls' [Bei allem Wollen handelt es sich schlechterdings um Befehlen und Gehorchen, auf der Grundlage, wie gesagt, eines Gesellschaftsbaus vieler 'Seelen']."

This important section sheds light on Nietzsche's conception of human subjectivity and its implications for a different conception of agency and perfectly illustrates the distinctive way in which Nietzsche might be thought to be a naturalist while nevertheless crucially relying on forms of thinking with which naturalism has been contrasted, particularly among Nietzsche scholars. It bears crucially on our conception of Nietzsche's moral psychology and our assessment of its contemporary relevance and application.[42] *Jenseits von*

Gut und Böse 19 begins with Nietzsche's observation that philosophers have a tendency to assume that the will is self-evident, "the best-known thing in the world," or, in Schopenhauer's case, the *only* thing really knowable. In this respect, Nietzsche claims, Schopenhauer committed the same error that plagues all philosophers: "he adopted a *popular prejudice* and exaggerated it." What we describe with the single word *willing* is a complex set of sensations, thoughts, and affects. If we consider the phenomenon of willing—say, the willing of raising one's arm—then we first associate it with sensations of various physical states, which seem to occur in the context of some tacit proprioceptive awareness such as "away from" my lap and "toward" the book on the shelf.

Further, there is what Nietzsche distinguishes as a "ruling thought," which he seems to suggest is the goal of whatever is willed when he writes: "let us not imagine it possible to sever this thought from the 'willing,' as if any will would then remain over!" We might consider this to be identical with what is typically discussed in the literature as "intention" or the content of the intent, the specific goal of what is willed. I elaborate both of these ideas in the following chapters, where I suggest that ruling thoughts, as Nietzsche describes them, could be more general dispositions, overarching orientations toward activity more generally, than specific intentional goals. "Amor fati" and "everything pertaining to the body is despicable" are examples of ruling thoughts conceived along these lines, and specific intentions emerge in relation to these dominant notions. Another possibility for what "ruling thoughts" might be— and these senses are not mutually exclusive—is that they are thoughts *about* ruling, about how to rule, or how to exercise and execute one's will. Regardless of whether ruling thoughts, when mentioned in *BGE* 19, have ruling as their content rather than their characteristic, Nietzsche also thinks that the organization that occurs in the context of what we designate with the single word *will* comes together as a *complex* with an abiding order, or order of rule. What allows that complex to be a distinctive organization is relative to its ability to order and organize its multiple constituents, and there are, of course, a great variety of ways in which this might occur, just as there are a great variety of political orders and forms of ruling. Conceived in this way, ruling thoughts would be those that rule or bid the action, the predominant or overarching thoughts whose contents give shape to specific intentions, or they could govern the ordering of the structure of drives that constitutes a being. Regardless of the precise nature of ruling thoughts, Nietzsche claims the most important ingredient of the complex activity that we call *willing* is the affects, specifically those experienced as the affects of commanding and obeying.

Nietzsche expresses similar ideas poetically in his *Also Sprach Zarathustra*, where he presents a model of the soul in terms of "self-overcoming." That book explores an alternative way of conceiving what a human being is, how it develops, and how such conceptions might be relevant for reflections on the aims of humanity as such. In the famous chapter entitled "On Self-Overcoming" (in *Z* II), he elaborates for the first time his idea that all existence is characterized by will to power. Zarathustra's speech is addressed to those "who are wisest" and the "lover of truth." One of the aims of the speech is to reveal what lies behind the love of wisdom, to consider the pursuit of philosophy as an expression of will to power. The desire to render intelligible what is true, good, and real is described as a manifestation of willing power. Will to power is thus conceived as the "unexhausted procreative will of life." Deploying quintessentially Heraclitean metaphors—such as the river of becoming and the play of the world—Zarathustra makes several points about life and the nature of all living creatures, claiming: "Where I found the living, there I found will to power" (*Z* II "On Self-Overcoming").

Zarathustra observes that life as will to power establishes a dynamic of commanding and obeying: all living beings strive to dominate others lest they be dominated. Even what could be considered the greatest will yield, will risk itself for the sake of power. The dynamic of commanding and obeying that constitutes life as will to power is also one of creation and re-creation. Much like the victor in a contest who aims not only to win according to the standards of judgment that are derived from the results of previous outcomes but also to serve as the standard bearer of excellence, "the greatest" must also risk its entitlement to the law. And an even greater experience of power is felt in legislating norms and all other values relative to them. The dynamic of life incorporates mutual striving, contextualized valuation, and chance—the very elements Nietzsche identifies with the contest. The process does not simply characterize discrete relations. Life itself whispers in Zarathustra's ear that it is *"that which must always overcome itself* [ich bin das, was sich immer selber überwinden muss]" (*Z* II "On Self-Overcoming"). Everything is connected in the paradigm of self-overcoming.

This goal is quite different from a model of perfection for which one is supposed to strive. What Zarathustra offers instead is an account of a "comprehensive soul [umfänglichste Seele]." In it, we can see his alternative conception of development deployed in his vision of being engaged in a process of perpetual overcoming in which "the soul that has the longest ladder and reaches down deepest [. . .] can run and stray and roam farthest within itself" (*Z* III "On Old and New Tablets" 19). It enjoys "the high body, beautiful, triumphant, refreshing, around which everything becomes a mirror" (*Z* III "On the Three Evils" 3). Everything mirrors it not because it has become thoroughly narcissistic but rather because it has become aware of itself as an overcoming-being whose own constitution organizes in an ongoing struggle of forces similar to that of the rest of life. Thus, "out of sheer joy" it "plunges itself into chance." It challenges itself; it risks itself. It is the soul "which, having being, dives into becoming; the soul which *has*, but *wants* to want and will [die seiende Seele, welche in's Werden taucht; die habende, welche in's Wollen und Verlangen will:—]; the soul which flees itself and catches up with itself in the widest circle [—die sich selber fliehende, die sich selber im weitesten Kreise einholt]; the wisest soul, which folly exhorts most sweetly [die weiseste Seele, welcher die Narrheit am süssesten zuredet:—]; the soul which loves itself most, in which all things have their sweep and counter sweep and ebb and flood [die sich selber liebendste, in der alle Dinge ihr Strömen und Wiederströmen und Ebbe und Fluth haben:—]" (*Z* III "On Old and New Tablets" 19).

Every willing being is a composite of commanding and commanded parts. What we call *willing* is not *just* the command of an atomic entity; it is the expression of what parts command other parts within the complex organization one is. Nietzsche writes: "A man who *wills* commands something within himself that renders obedience, or that he believes renders obedience" (*BGE* 19). It is not simply that we do this or experience this as springing from our "true" selves because, inasmuch as we are commanders, we are also what is *commanded*; in willing, *being commanded* is just as much *our own*; it, too, is part of our *true selves*. Nietzsche attempts to unravel the knot of sensations that emerges from this plurality: "as the obeying party we know the sensations of constraint, impulsion, pressure, resistance, and motion, which usually begin immediately after the act of will."[43] So the phenomenon of willing is not just linked with our experience of our efficacy in effecting change in the world, of ourselves as agents or actors who can be seen as the cause of such-and-such event; the phenomenon of effecting change is experienced within and among the various parts of ourselves.

But Nietzsche thinks we ordinarily "disregard this duality, and [. . .] deceive ourselves about it by means of the synthetic concept 'I' [. . .]." In other words, although willing is experienced as a dynamic of commanding and obeying (with separable and distinct features), we treat it as a singular activity and disregard half of the process. We are mistaken in at least two respects, insofar as we (1) overlook much of what occurs (that in commanding there is also obeying) and (2) associate "ourselves" with only one facet of the complex (i.e., commanding). Nietzsche claims that from this "a whole series of erroneous conclusions, and consequently of false evaluations of the will itself, has become attached to the act of willing—to such a degree that he who wills believes sincerely that willing *suffices* for action" (*BGE* 19).

Thus, regardless of what Nietzsche intended earlier in this section when he mentioned "ruling thoughts" as a component of the complex we call *willing*, there is a ruling structure at work here, in terms of both the emergence of an *organization*—a hierarchy or other configuration of ruling and ruled elements—and some particular *way* in which those parts relate and come to have the order they do, the way in which *ruling* occurs. Nietzsche seems to think that what we designate with the term *will* is more closely related to feelings generated from this interaction rather than the process itself; our sense of *will* appears to be epiphenomenal (which is not to say there is no willing), and these feelings are rather confused, as just sketched above. To compound this confusion, Nietzsche thinks we have a secondary feeling of "an increase of the sensation of power which accompanies all success" when we believe we have successfully carried out *willing*, as though we achieved some special status as its executor: "'Freedom of the will'—that is the expression for the complex state of delight [vielfachen Lust-Zustand des Wollenden] of the person exercising volition, who commands and at the same time identifies himself with the executor of the order—who, as such, enjoys also the triumph over obstacles, but thinks within himself that it was really his will itself that overcame them [aber bei sich urtheilt, sein Wille selbst sei es, der eigentlich die Widerstände überwinde]" (*BGE* 19). Even when we experience the commanded as somehow part of ourselves, we still associate willing with overcoming obstacles and our true selves as entitled to a sense of achievement of having done it. Nietzsche continues: "In this way the person exercising volition adds the feelings of delight of his successful executive instruments, the useful 'underwills' or under-souls—indeed, our body is but a social structure composed of many souls—to his feelings of delight as a commander" (*BGE* 19). But the fact that the sensations we associate with willing are epiphenomenal does not at all mean, as I think Nietzsche's discussion here makes clear, that we should abolish the notion of soul. The point is that we need a new conception, and an important question concerns how this stands in relation to his naturalism. This example precisely illustrates the need to identify the unique features of Nietzsche's naturalism, which does not simply abolish certain metaphysical notions but rather revises them on the basis of differently construing their purpose and utility.[44]

The elaborate example of Nietzsche's revision of the soul hypothesis makes clearer, I hope, how his speculation that the notion of soul might still have utility provided it can be reformulated is consistent with his naturalism, not separate and distinct from it; indeed, his experimentation with alternatives to soul atomism in the form of revisions to the soul hypothesis is not merely consistent with his naturalism but also epitomizes the way in which he intends to carry out his project "to translate man back into nature" (*BGE* 230). There is a reciprocal relation between philosophy's use of artifice and its critical engagement of science: science can be purged of the superstitious and supernatural ideas that continue to lurk in its basic concepts (as the atomistic need expressed itself there, too), and this "newly redeemed nature" can be used to further "'naturalize' humanity" (*GS* 109), not in the manner of the "clumsy naturalists who can hardly touch on 'the soul' without immediately losing it" (*BGE* 12), or through misplaced faith in causal explanations as "whoever [like natural scientists . . .] 'naturalizes' in his thinking" (*BGE* 21). Nietzsche's suggestions for new conceptualizations such as "'soul as subjective multiplicity' and 'soul as social structure of the drives and affects'" (*BGE* 12), discussed above, make it possible to pick out different features of human psychology that are obscured by the atomic model of the soul hypothesis. The conception of soul as social structure can hardly count as a *discovery*—it is surely an artificial model, an *invention* that might very well facilitate future discoveries of features that would otherwise go unnoticed because they would fail to show up as relevant objects of investigation and observation. Moreover, we should be clear that the domain of such invention is not simply everything else that is left over *after* science offers its explanations. Nietzsche thinks our scientific and empirical activities are facilitated and guided by that which we inventively produce. Engaging in this type of conceptual and theoretical innovation appears to be how he thinks about philosophy and is a significant fruit of his artful naturalism and agon with Socrates.[45] His naturalism is not a bald endorsement of empiricism or empirical research as presenting the "facts" about reality, particularly human reality. He sought to reformulate significant concepts that he regarded as created from a defective set of values, and he thought such reformulation would be relevant to a kind of naturalism that would bring philosophy and science closer together, not reductively (where philosophy is reduced to science or science to philosophical literature) but productively, in which case both areas of inquiry benefit from the application of the perspectives and investigative tools that are distinctly theirs.

Finally, this conception of philosophy also bears on Nietzsche's agon with Socrates, for, as we saw above, he criticizes both the Socratic *relocation* of the agon from the social and cultural realm to the internal psychological one and the *structure* of the contest he set up (one that pitted reason against the other parts as a domineering victor that would ultimately have the effect of shutting down any possible contest). Even if Nietzsche fails, as he likely does to replace the Platonic hero of Socrates with his own heroic (or antiheroic) model of Zarathustra, he might nevertheless still supply some fruitful ways for facilitating work formerly performed by the old concept of the soul. If so, this would have some fairly dramatic effects. It is, after all, the *effects* of the Platonic conception of soul and its relation to other values as they develop in Christianity, particularly, that so concern Nietzsche. He recognizes that those very values are unlikely to change without a change in the basic concepts that support them. He experiments with new varieties of the soul hypothesis to take aim at such thinking.

The agonistic basis of his reflection on the nature of philosophy and its future direction reveals much about how Nietzsche thinks about reality and the possibilities for human beings seeking to know more about it and appreciate its possible meanings. In the chapter that follows, I focus on the connection between agonism and his further reflections on moral psychology, particularly how reformulated conceptions of subjectivity might affect our conception of agency. The present chapter outlined how his concerns about mechanism and teleology were also bound up with concerns about the structure of belief and what constitutes knowledge. I suggested that he was concerned not only to redescribe or redefine human existence but also to potentially redirect it. But this discussion remained, of necessity, on a rather general level. In the following chapter, I focus the discussion of the relation between the agon and meaning to articulate the kinds of meanings that inform our social interactions with others. Such discussion of a possible ethos of agonism puts us in a position to develop an even more nuanced understanding of Nietzsche's conception of power, which has broad implications in contemporary philosophy, as I suggest throughout the remainder of the book.

CHAPTER FOUR

Contesting Paul:
Toward an Ethos of Agonism

4.1 ON THE POSSIBILITY OF *OVERCOMING* MORALITY

Nietzsche's reflections on forms of competition and varieties of struggle inform his views about power and organize important facets of his major philosophical projects. Nietzsche viewed the ancient Greek contest as underwriting what were primarily externally oriented enterprises, as, for example, in the communal effects of tragic art. Socrates is supposed to have shifted the orientation of Greek agon when he redirected and rehabilitated the desires to strive that threatened to destroy Greek culture, but, in doing so, Nietzsche thinks, he changed the form of the contest in ways Nietzsche finds destructive. With Christianity, he claims, spiritualized contest becomes a means of *self*-destructing its enemies and even its adherents. This is the chief reason for his anti-Christianity: the model of Christian agony, as Nietzsche sketches it, encourages a form of struggle that debilitates those who emulate it.

Using the analytic criteria for assessing contests outlined in chapter 1 and elaborated and qualified in chapters 2 and 3, we can articulate dynamics Nietzsche indicates as disabling in the Christian contest. He provides criteria for assessing contests relative to their efficacy in marshaling productive organizing cultural forces. Agonistic institutions, as he regards them, potentially facilitate the creation and re-creation of values, and this is their most attractive feature for him—he considers how and how well the Christian agon does this. Moreover, he assesses the content or character of the values thereby produced—he evaluates what forms of action are encouraged and supported in the organizational structure that constitutes the Christian agon. Following this analysis, I expand the scope to Nietzsche's considerations of the phenomenon of morality more broadly, how it construes the moral subject and a dynamic structure of agency. Finally, I return to his claim in *Ecce Homo* that, if he is successful in his analyses of morality and subjectivity, then morality will simply be *overcome*—it will no longer be a concern. I consider what this might mean for ethics construed as a way of life or a common way of living, inquiring as to whether Nietzsche's agonism implies a certain ethos that might still be relevant to action without drawing on what he regards as debilitating models of agency and judgment he associates with the "moral" period overall. Throughout the chapter, I show how his concern to reorient and reanimate possibilities for human action through the development of a different conception of agency is related to the problem of value that lies at the core of virtually all his work.

At various times, Nietzsche appears to see his own views as hastening a process that will bring about the end of morality, a result he thinks is inevitable. He outlines in *Jenseits von Gut und Böse* a three-part process that includes the appearance of the phenomenon of morality in human culture.[1] These ideas are crucial to understanding precisely why and how he is an opponent of morality "in the narrow sense" (*BGE* 32), the content and nature of his supramoralism. Drawing on distinctions in the history of philosophical ethics as well as contemporary moral philosophy and psychology, we can see that, while Nietzsche is an agonist of morality, he is not necessarily an opponent of ethics (an ethos) broadly conceived, although his views do present challenges to certain fundamental concepts that seem crucial to morality, at least as it is presently conceived.

A key development in overcoming morality, for Nietzsche, is exploring what might follow from the reconceptualization of the human subject along the lines charted in the preceding chapter. In short, he anticipates that cognitive psychology, developmental biology, and evolutionary theory will eventually undermine conceptions of agency that have been so important for moral theory, particularly the atomic subject who formulates intentions, acts as executor of those intentions, and thereby is responsible for his actions. New conceptions of agency are necessary in the wake of that destruction. As I consider Nietzsche's anticipated overcoming of morality in the final section of this chapter, I explore whether some sort of ethos might yet be retrievable from his ideas about forms of cultural production and creative action as they develop in his analyses of various forms of struggle, conflict, and contest.

The implications of Nietzsche's views of the naturalized moral subject as site of contesting forces rather than causally responsible agent are considerable. They obviously undermine certain modernist conceptions of agency and culpability that go along with them. In particular, the view of the agent as separable from and the cause of its action (and, thus, responsible, subject to praise or blame accordingly) is rendered problematic. This also challenges modern theories of autonomy as well as perspectives that place an emphasis on intentionality. I try to cash out these problematic conceptions of agency in my analysis of *Zur Genealogie der Moral* I:13 and Nietzsche's famous citation of Goethe's *Faust* that "the deed is everything" when it comes to the subject. Once a core concept of morality (the responsible and accountable subject) is superseded, the structure of values it supports is immediately threatened. Thus, Nietzsche anticipates that his abiding problem of values becomes even more pronounced and urgent in a postmoral condition. In the conclusion of this chapter and in the next chapter, I explore the prospects for developing a sense of ethos that goes beyond responsibility in the usual sense. I suggest this is one of the ways in which Nietzsche's postmoral future might take shape.

4.2 FIGHTING TO THE DEATH: THE AGONIES OF PAULINE CHRISTIANITY

If Christianity is "Platonism for 'the people'" (*BGE* P), then we can see Nietzsche's attack on Pauline Christianity as an outgrowth of his struggle with Socrates. His case against Paul is like his case against Socrates in many respects, except that Paul lacks some of Socrates' redeeming qualities. This seems to extend to Nietzsche's assessment of Paul's revaluation. As noted above, Socrates' revaluation of the contest is interpreted in both *Die Geburt der Tragödie* and *Götzen-Dämmerung* as at least saving the ancient Greeks in some respects, although its usefulness has expired and its consequences are a detriment that Nietzsche sees it as his task to fight. The same cannot be said of Paul. He is a fascinating type for Nietzsche, in part because of his tremendous revaluation, but he is ultimately an intellectual and creative inferior to Socrates. For a more explicit elaboration of this idea, consider *WS* 85–86. In section 85, Nietzsche claims that Paul *remains* Saul as a persecutor of God. By this I take it he means that the root of the revaluation that *Saint Paul* effects in the invention of Christianity is ultimately the destructive aim of the rebellion that *Saul* aimed to lead. Nietzsche does not seem to admire Paul in any way, although he is fascinated by him. We could hardly imagine him saying of Paul, as he did of Socrates, that he is "so close to me I am almost always fighting him."[2] In Paul's hands, perversion of the ends of the agon results in atrophy even more freakish than that produced in the Socratic scheme.

As modes of development, both Christianity and the model Nietzsche anticipates have their roots in the agon. Both derive value from trials of serious and painful struggle—*agonies*. Both spring from the internalized contest that results from the Socratic displacement of public contests to psychic or spiritual ones; both engage a dynamic in which the object of one's resistance is oneself. Still, Nietzsche thinks Christianity differs significantly from the agony of self-overcoming that he describes. The spiritualized contest of Christianity aims at the destruction of the opponent and, thus, is motivated by *Vernichtungslust*, but it does not even really distinguish foe from friend since it aims at the *self*-destruction of those over whom the power of faith is exercised just as much as it seeks the destruction of the enemies of Christianity.

In short, Nietzsche thinks the Christian agon encourages a form of struggle that disables, enervates, and debilitates those who emulate the exemplar of spiritual struggle that Pauline Christianity depicts. The fundamental significance of God on the cross, emphasized by Paul, results in the view that the redemption of life is possible only through the death of the flesh; it entails pursuit of the annihilation of our human qualities. Moreover, Nietzsche regards this dynamic as ultimately hostile to the contest itself since the battle to save the soul is already over, already accomplished by the death of Jesus—ultimate victory is *his*. Thus, Paul's depiction of the crucifixion and resurrection renders Christ accomplishing what was impossible for the Greek gods and distinguished them from Homer's heroes. Recall that, by risking their lives, Homer's heroes were able to give their actions maximal significance. In an evaluative economy that indexes value with risk, the significance of the accomplishments of Homer's heroes potentially exceeded even those of the gods who could not die and, thus, could not take such great risks. But, if an immortal god can risk it all and thereby determine the significance of all possible human action (redemption once and for all), then human struggles are essentially worthless. If participation in agon is one of the ways in which we are human as well as one of the ways in which we create the significance of humanity, then the elimination of the possibility of meaningful struggle (nothing could possibly compare with what Christ accomplishes) undermines the mode of value production Nietzsche thinks is potentially so creative and perpetually renewable (and, thus, redemptive in a different respect).

Recall from chapter 1 the basic analytic framework discernible in Nietzsche's works. It distinguishes *types* of contests, *modes of actions* within them, and how such activities become significant, their contributions to the *content of values* both within and without competitive institutions. In chapter 2, I elaborated how and why Nietzsche thought the Homeric achievement lay in creating a means of producing—and more importantly *reproducing*—values, including an affirmative estimation of the value of human existence as such. Moreover, he thought there was evidence that this particular mechanism was especially effective in organizing ancient Greek culture more generally by coordinating interests and directing desires toward *productive* and creative achievements and ends. It should be clear that the agon is not the only way in which values can be created, but Nietzsche takes it as a model because of its connection to creative human activity. Moreover, values derived agonistically, he thinks, have a particularly significant immediacy or tangibility: whatever comes to be valued in agonistic exchange emerges as worthy only on the condition that it is actually *manifest*. It is on this account that Nietzsche thinks there was a certain measure of added freedom for the ancient Greeks not in a modern sense of being free from restraint but rather in the sense of being free in order to act, being enabled. Tangible accomplishment and significance resulted in greater possibilities for excellence, Nietzsche seems to think. Thus, he claims: "individuals were freer in antiquity because their goals were nearer and more tangible. Modern man, however, is above all marked by infinity just like the quick-footed Achilles in the parables of the Eleatic Zeno: infinity inhibits him, he does not even once overtake the tortoise" (HC, p. 790).[3] Thus, he regards the agon as a potent means to the affirmation of life.

Nietzsche considers struggles as having either creative or destructive ends and corresponding means to reach them: at the extremes, contests can be oriented around significant achievements or excessive displays of some trivial characteristics. Moreover, the organization of contests, their terms, and the ways they structure possibilities for action can support what he considers creative action (associated with "rising above" [*erheben*]) or the negative and destructive activity of forcing back (*herabdrücken*) what poses a challenge (motivated by a kind of bloodthirstiness for the annihilation of opposition, *Vernichtungslust*). By creating channels for such activities and rewarding or punishing accordingly, the agon, Nietzsche thinks, effectively cultivates different basic motivations: for excellence or destructive violence. These ends and motivations for action he describes also affect the content of the particular values that agonistic enterprises produce. Thus, he thinks an agonistic structure oriented around the production of excellence and creative action generally results in more affirmative values, those with a higher appraisal value for human existence than those that cultivate the desire to annihilate and seek the destruction or elimination of opposition.

Nietzsche depicts Christianity as complicit in bringing about its own destruction insofar as it sets up a contest as central to the meaning of what it is to be a good Christian, but the goal (eradicating what makes one a human being) undermines the very possibility of being a legitimate contestant for vying for the meaning of human existence. Not only does the organizational structure of the contest falter, but the modes of action that otherwise would be considered virtuous in an agonistic situation (pursuit of self-interest, competitiveness, desire for victory) are hostile to the virtues allegedly sought through Christian agonies. Nietzsche's conception of self-overcoming, sketched in the previous chapter, is supposed to enhance one's capacities by encouraging a dynamic in which parts of one's self are exhausted in pursuit of surpassing them; it cultivates relations with others, and its products are (at least potentially) renewable.

To understand this better, we can compare the model of self-resistance or self-opposition that operates out of *Vernichtungslust*, or a desire for destruction, as it is presented in *Zur Genealogie der Moral*, with a model that regards the internalized opponent as something that must be overcome and in the process meets its destruction. In *Also Sprach Zarathustra*, Nietzsche often deploys organic metaphors in his account of self-overcoming. The self or the parts of the self that one overcomes are described as *going to ruin* ("zu Grunde gehen"), suggesting that they meet a natural or fitting end, connoting a kind of passing on or fading away that is appropriate in a process of becoming. The model of self-overcoming that emerges out of Nietzsche's middle and later writings utilizes the language of biology to describe the dynamic: in the process of self-overcoming, what one has been is incorporated and appropriated in the course of the *Kampf* one is: "Thus the body goes through history, a becoming [ein Werdender] and a fighting [ein Kämpfender]. And the spirit—what is that to the body? The herald of its fights [Kämpfe] and victories [Siege], companion and echo" (*Z* I "On the Gift-Giving Virtue" 1; Kaufmann's translation emended). We shall see Nietzsche describe very different models of opposition and corresponding views of the body and soul that arise in the Platonic-Christian conceptions.

Nietzsche's problem of Paul is more complex than one might initially think. It is tempting to see the case against him as synonymous with the case against Christianity or to see him as the prototypical ascetic priest so reviled in the *Genealogy*. Although these aspects are important to Nietzsche, as I have already suggested, his interest in the type Paul signifies exceeds his concerns about Christianity. I focus on two facets of the problem of Paul as he sketches it: *Saul's* conversion and *Paul's* exegesis. As the inventor of what becomes the dominant form of Christianity through his revaluation of the symbol of Jesus, Saul/Paul is interesting because Nietzsche views his feat from the perspective of what results from a specific personal struggle. Hence, he considers Saul's metamorphosis into Paul as indicative of a psychological type whose struggles are instructive, particularly when measured against the agonistic models Nietzsche advances. Saint Paul also crystallizes a perverting tendency manifest in Christianity, with whose legacy Nietzsche wrestles. Paul symbolizes for Nietzsche the consequences of the Christian valuation scheme, which reverses the transformative effects of Homer and inhibits the production of alternative values, namely, those that might contest the Christian/ascetic ideal.

Nietzsche presents and analyzes Saul's *Kampf* in *Daybreak* 68. Saul's problem is supposed to hinge on his concern with Jewish law and his standing with regard to fulfilling it. Saul seeks the highest distinction available to a human being in that context, namely, to embody and fully realize Jewish law. Nietzsche writes that Saul "was constantly combating and on the watch for transgressors and doubters, harsh and malicious towards them and with the extremest inclination for punishment" (*D* 68).[4] But Saul discovers that even he is incapable of living up to the law, and what impedes him is "his wild thirst for power [ausschweifende Herrschsucht]," intensified even more by his efforts to struggle against others in the name of the law.[5] What Nietzsche describes as Saul's "thirst" manifests *Vernichtungslust* (desire for annihilation), which he earlier linked with the destructive form of competition. Eventually, Saul comes to despise the very institution he previously sought as the means to securing his distinction of supreme piety and obedience to God: "The law was the cross to which he felt himself nailed: how he hated it! How he had to drag it along! How he sought about for a means of *destroying* it."[6] And once he finds his means—the figure of Christ—*Saul becomes Paul* as he conspires to ensure his freedom from the law. He pursues his liberation through revenge against the law.

We should consider more closely why Nietzsche binds together these two ideas: freedom and revenge. How is it that Paul seeks to be free in Nietzsche's depiction of his conversion? Why is Paul supposed to despise the law, and why is its destruction his only alternative? Paul seeks freedom from the obligations of the law not because he is essentially some sort of rebel who is too much of a free spirit to obey any law (and Nietzsche's own free spirits are obviously not free in that sense either); rather, he seeks to be free of the tyranny of the law and the institutions that enforce it. Saul revolts against impossible boundaries the law establishes. The values the law inscribes, the goals it establishes for what constitute the greatest of all possible meanings for a human life, are deemed impossible. Because he finds it hopeless to do what the law distinguishes as the only way to achieve real distinction, Saul resents it. Measured by the law, his life is worthless. That thought is unbearable, it crushes him, and he is provoked into a death struggle with the law. He revolts against the purpose of the law: "the law existed so that sins might be committed, it continually brought sin forth as a sharp juice brings forth a disease" (*D* 68). Redemption—revaluation of human existence—was thitherto possible only by fulfilling the dictates of the law. Unless it was obliterated, Saul was lost.

The logic of Saul's revenge is articulated thus—with the death of Christ to evil, the law that arbitrates sin dies: "Even if it is still possible to sin, it is no longer possible to sin against the law. [. . .] God could never have resolved on the death of Christ if a fulfillment of the law had been in any way possible without this death; now not only has all guilt been taken away, guilt as such has been destroyed; now the law is dead, now the carnality in which it dwelt is dead" (*D* 68). The abolition of the law frees Saul to seek distinction through another means, and he does so through the erection of another ideal, one that remains faithful to the destructive roots that made his creation possible.

We are now in a better position to see precisely what Nietzsche thinks is performed in the transformation of Saul into Paul; that is, we can further explore the form Paul's revenge takes and its legacy as Nietzsche sees it. If we look at the text of Luther's Bible, which we can imagine Nietzsche knew well, we find that the German words *Wettkampf* and *Kampf* appear nearly exclusively in the writings attributed to Paul. It is also notable that the Pauline writings do not include a gospel. Unlike the other apostles, Paul does not write a biography that offers an account of an exemplary life. Instead, he emphasizes the injustice of the *end* of Jesus' life and what it means for others to struggle and fight in the wake of that event. He heralds Christ's *agonies*, which Nietzsche denies are inherent in the original symbol of the figure of the Jesus of "glad tidings." And he invests those agonies with a particularly potent significance that serves to elevate his own status.

In an account Nietzsche calls "the *genuine* history of Christianity," he distinguishes Christian doctrine and dogma from the life of Christ: "in truth, there was only *one* Christian, and he died on the cross. The 'evangel' *died* on the cross. What has been called 'evangel' from that moment was actually the

[handwritten margin note: Prus' point is Lothean Bible]

opposite of that which *he* had lived: '*ill* tidings,' a *dysangel*" (*A* 39).[7] Among the "first Christians," Nietzsche most blames Paul for the destructively distorted interpretation of the significance of Jesus.

In his creation of the Christ ideal, Paul transforms the meaning of what it is to be a good (Christian) human being, and all related meanings and values are similarly unhinged. His "exegesis" is elaborated in the context of Nietzsche's investigation of the genealogy of the accretions of the meanings of the "Redeemer" at the heart of Christianity. In the fifth book of *Die fröhliche Wissenschaft*, in a section titled "On the Origin of Religions" (*GS* 353), Nietzsche describes how founders of religions posit a way of life and then offer it "an interpretation that makes it appear to be illuminated by the highest value so that this lifestyle becomes something for which one fights and under certain circumstances sacrifices one's life." Paul is described as offering "an exegesis": "he read the highest meaning and value into" "the little lives" of those in the Roman province. One could make a fruitful comparison between the *Auslegung* of Paul and the practice of *auslegen* advocated by Nietzsche in the preface to the *Genealogy*, in which Nietzsche seeks to reveal the joints of the interpretation crafted by Paul and anticipate ways of countering it.

Paul's Christ is a transmogrification of Nietzsche's Jesus. In Nietzsche's later writings, his Jesus is (loosely) conceived as a free spirit (*A* 32), in part because he is free of *ressentiment*. This is supposedly exemplified in the way he lived his life and in his free, easy death (*A* 40). He is free in the sense of being free from the limitations of "any kind of word, formula, law, faith, dogma": "the whole of reality, the whole of nature, language itself, has for him only the value of a sign, a simile" (*A* 32). In this context, Nietzsche figures Jesus as a symbolist par excellence (*A* 34). He is credited with effecting a transfiguration of all things as models of blessedness and perfection (*A* 34), an original symbolism ("ursprünglichen Symbolismus") (*A* 37) in which the concept of guilt is abolished and the "cleavage between God and man" is obliterated (*A* 41). He is thought to *live out* this unity as an affirmation much like the Israelites Nietzsche admires in his account of the early history of Judaism (*A* 25).

It is quite remarkable, given his admiration of agon, that Nietzsche appears to admire Jesus for having qualities that seem to be the *opposite* of his new agonist (and Paul is described as the opposite of Jesus in *A* 30). He characterizes Jesus' life as exhibiting a thoroughly *an*agonistic practice: "He does not resist [Er widersteht nicht], he does not defend his right [er vertheidigt nicht sein Recht], he takes no step which might ward off the worst [Äusserste]; on the contrary, he *provokes* it [er fordert es heraus] . . . And he begs, he suffers, he loves *with* those, *in* those, who do him evil . . . *Not* to resist, *not* to be angry, *not* to hold responsible [Nicht sich wehren, nicht zürnen, nicht verantwortlich-machen] [...] but to resist not even the evil one—to *love* him" (*A* 35; *KSA* 6, pp. 207–8).[8] I designate Nietzsche's characterization of Jesus as *an*agonistic to contrast it with the more common term *ant*agonistic: whereas the latter is commonly used to designate hostility toward another, the former indicates rejection of the form of opposition itself. This also differs from what might be used to describe someone who is aggressively hostile to the agonistic model, someone *anti*-agonistic. The warlike, no-saying, no-doing spirit of Christianity, Nietzsche claims in *Der Antichrist*, stands in sharp contrast to that of Jesus. The Christian form of warfare is motivated by "rebellion against the existing order [Aufruhr gegen die Ordnung]," which seeks to lay blame and assign guilt for Jesus' death (*A* 40); it is rooted in and stirred by *ressentiment*. And with *ressentiment* comes desire for revenge.

Thus, it is as an expression of this desire that the symbol of the Redeemer begins to take on the characteristics of struggle. The desired revenge is effected through the elevation and distancing of Jesus—a separation of his life from the practice of living that Nietzsche thinks it exemplifies. In so doing, Paul crafts a new sense of redemption. Salvation lies in the faith, absolute belief, in the doctrine that brings about this separation: the resurrection.

The evidence for the fundamental significance of the resurrection in Paul's conception of Christianity is offered in a loose paraphrase of 1 Cor. 15:14, 17. In *Der Antichrist* 41, Nietzsche attributes to Paul the following claim: "*If* Christ was not resurrected from the dead, then our faith is in vain" ("'wenn Christus nicht auferstanden ist von den Todten, so ist unser Glaube eitel'" [*KSA* 6, p. 215]). Luther's translation of 1 Cor. 15:14, 17, reads: "Ist aber Christus nicht auferstanden, so ist unsre Predigt vergeblich, so ist auch euer Glaube vergeblich" (14); "Ist Christus aber nicht auferstanden, so ist euer Glaube nichtig, so seid ihr noch in euren Sünden" (17). The meaning of Jesus' life, its true significance, is fully invested in the resurrection. Paul does not write a gospel because the *human* life of Jesus is practically irrelevant.[9] The foundation of the community Paul sought to establish is an absolute faith in something that denies what human experience teaches, a metaphysical miracle—the resurrection of the body of Christ. If the latter did not happen, "our belief" (i.e., for Christians)—the specific set of beliefs and values Paul sought to erect—is void and vain.

Immortality through personal salvation *overdetermines* the significance of individual human lives. Once in possession of eternal life, one trumps any and all claims to distinction some other might make. Thus, Nietzsche can claim the noble virtues are perpetually eclipsed to the point of vanishing in the light of this new ideal: "'Immortality' conceded to every Peter and Paul has so far been the greatest, the most malignant, attempt to assassinate *noble* humanity" (*A* 43). And, although he might be referring to a specific form of noble humanity in that passage—perhaps one modeled on the portrait he creates of the ancient Greeks whose deeds could become more significant even than those of the gods—I think it would be appropriate and consistent with his line of argument to further strengthen his claim by inserting the word *any* before the word *noble*: "'Immortality' conceded to every Peter and Paul has so far been the greatest, the most malignant, attempt to assassinate *any noble* humanity." At stake are the conditions that make it possible for *any* sort of nobility to emerge. Under this sign of redemption we are stripped, not only of our significance, but also of the potency to be makers of meaning.

Nietzsche claims this ultimately leads to the demise of the institutions organized to cultivate our sense of community, "gratitude for descent and ancestors" and the spirit of cooperation, trust, and promotion of the "common welfare." I think this demonstrates his concern for the social and political good, not just for personal or individual success or glory, as the heroic morality is often described. In these passages, one recognizes that Nietzsche despises Christianity precisely because of its particular kind of selfishness (not, as one might suspect, simply because of its *selflessness*): "The 'salvation of the soul'— in plain language: 'the world revolves around *me*'" ("Das 'Heil der Seele'—auf deutsch: 'die Welt dreht sich um m i c h '"). Nietzsche describes Paul's revaluation as bringing about a kind of axiological vertigo: "When one places life's center of gravity not in life but in the 'beyond'—*in nothingness*—one deprives life of its center of gravity altogether" (*A* 43).

Motivated by *ressentiment*, Nietzsche claims, the disseminators of Paul's interpretation deify Jesus so that they can use him as a weapon of revenge— and this models the Christian agon. By elevating Jesus to a supernatural status, they strip him of the ability to serve as a model for *human* emulation—no human is capable of this sort of creativity, this kind of redeeming activity; one can only passively *receive* that sort of redemption. Jesus as the almighty Son of God, as the crucified-but-resurrected Christ, becomes the lightning rod for retribution for injustice: "Precisely the most unevangelical feeling, *revenge* [R a c h e], came to the fore again. The matter could not possibly be finished with this death: 'retribution' ['Vergeltung'] was needed, 'judgment' ['Gericht'] (and yet, what could possibly be more unevangelical than 'retribution,' 'punishment' ['Strafe'], 'sitting in judgment' ['Gericht-halten']!)" (*A* 40). Considered thus, the good fight, the only one worth pursuing, is the one that seeks revenge for the injustice of the crucifixion. This pseudo-agon is a contest not *for* distinction but rather *against* evil. It is allegedly staged and engaged not by the community and individual contestants for personal distinction (as it was for Homer) or by the individual on his own behalf to better himself (as it was for Socrates) but rather by *humanity as such* against an omnipresent yet intangible nemesis (*evil in itself*) in accordance with a divine script. Moreover, to add insult to injury, Christian labors are, in the end, all for naught since the true and ultimate redemption was accomplished in the death and resurrection of Christ. With this, the destruction of the ancient agon is complete: the form of the contest, the modes of competing within it, and its ultimate aims and cultural functions are utterly deformed, dissembled, and disengaged.

Recall that, in "Homer's Wettkampf," Nietzsche begins his discussion of the significance of Homer's accomplishment by situating it as a response to a perennial problem—namely, what is the meaning of human trials and tribulations; for what do we suffer? Nietzsche writes: "The Hellenic genius had yet another answer ready to the question: 'What does a life of fighting [Kampfes] and victory [Sieges] want?' and gives this answer through the entire breadth of Greek history" (*KSA* 1, p. 784).[10] Homer is not the first to ask the question, and there are older traditions from other cultures that employ military metaphors in their accounts of the character of human existence, such as in the cults of Isis and Mithras (cf. *A* 58). Homer does not *invent* the contest that characterizes human life; he *revalues* it, transfigures it, gives it a different interpretation. As indicated in chapter 2 above, his answer to the question, "What does a life of fighting and victory want?" is "*More life*"—rather than the end of life or the good of some suprahuman being. Paul's response to this same question is "*Everything*"—the weight of all existence hangs in the balance—but his path to pursuing his end puts human beings in the position of being able to *earn* nothing, and *everything* is worthless unless miracles (e.g., the resurrection) are possible.

Nietzsche links precisely this thought to Paul's corruption of the agon. I have focused on the single most influential feature of the problem of Paul as it relates to his alteration of the agon, but Nietzsche's accounts of Christianity identify a variety of other contests that stem from the Christian worldview. A fascinating review of several of the pseudocontests engineered by Christianity to give the appearance and lure of contest can be found in *GM* III:17–21. His new concept of redemption strips the possibility for the production of any values at all. His mechanism for revaluation/redemption—a further adaptation of the contest that Socrates appropriated—operates such that everything is (and nothing can be further) redeemed in this most extraordinary act. And the act itself is precisely the complete accomplishment of what the Homeric heroes struggling for the highest glory (and any other human being seeking whatever aim of distinction) could never achieve—immortality. The death of the agon is for Nietzsche the assassination of *any* form of nobility: it obliterates distinction, difference, and the very basis of genuine respect.

4.3 CONFLICTING VALUES AND WORLDVIEWS

One of the insights Nietzsche thinks he achieves in "Homer's Wettkampf" (and repeatedly in his assessments of agonistic encounters of the sorts already described) is that values and evaluative *axes* do not simply evolve in some natural progression or trajectory but rather take hold in the context and as a result of contestation. Put simply, values are *won*. And they maintain their grip only insofar as they sustain a competitive advantage over alternatives. In this respect, Nietzsche regards the development of values in much the same way as he understood the development of art in terms of a contest of forces. This is not to say that every single value is achieved agonistically, which clearly cannot be the case—we come to love, despise, and hold dear things for a variety of reasons. Using more contemporary vocabulary, we can say that Nietzsche regards values as always relational (and this is explicitly *not* subjectively relative). This is clear in his assessment of Homer, in which he keenly emphasizes how different the Homeric view was from what preceded it. For Nietzsche, the Homeric worldview is an invention, an act of creativity, rather than a natural progression—it represents *an overcoming* of something prior; what it means to be *an overcoming* in that way is of significant interest to him.

A similar idea lies at the core of Nietzsche's *Genealogy*. The book begins by imagining a simplified situation in which the effects of conflicting worldviews are easier to ascertain. It is a strategy not unlike the exercise in Plato's *Republic* of creating the Kallipolis in order to glimpse the basic parts of the soul and understand their possible and typical relations. Nietzsche (in)famously caricatures what he calls *noble* and *slave* values and isolates them in a remote and prehistoric past that also lacks any particular place; it is *atopos—auf Deutsch*, *unheimlich*. That is, he tries to acquaint us with parts of ourselves that are nevertheless unfamiliar, uncanny, something that we *are* but from which we are estranged, and this resonates with the preface of the text, which begins by remarking how we are "strangers to ourselves" (*GM* P:1).[11]

One of the aims of the *Genealogy*, subtitled "Eine Streitschrift"—a polemic, literally "fighting writing"—is to illustrate what Nietzsche characterizes as a "deadly contradiction," a battle between "the two opposing values 'good and bad,' 'good and evil.'" A critical difference between noble and slavish modes of valuation is their conceptions of, and dispositions toward, who and what they oppose. They differ greatly in the value they place on adversity. The noble, who distinguishes the "good" from the "bad," "seeks [his] opposite only so as to affirm [him]self more gratefully and triumphantly." But the slave, who distinguishes the "good" from the "evil," is vengeful—he judges so that he can exact revenge for his own impotence. His happiness is "rest, peace, 'Sabbath,' slackening of tension and relaxing of limbs, in short passivity." The noble "desires his enemy [Feind] for himself, as his mark of distinction [Auszeichnung]; he can endure no other enemy than one in whom there is nothing to despise and *very much* to honor [sehr Viel zu ehren]." But the slave "has conceived 'the evil enemy' ['den bösen Feind'], *'the Evil One'* ['den Bösen'], and this in fact is his basic concept, from which he then evolves, as an afterthought and pendant, a 'good one' ['Guten']—himself!" (*GM* I:10). For Nietzsche, these modes of valuation are related: the slavish mode, derived from the priestly, branched off from the noble when a conflict between the two castes arose. Nietzsche contends that jealous opposition resulted in an impasse that led to the adaptation of different and opposing values by the priestly caste.

Different views of competition and struggle correspond to divergent sets of values, and we can see Nietzsche exploring modes of valuation as enactments of different types of contest, as alternative forms of opposition.[12] In the first essay of the *Genealogy*, he argues that noble value judgments "presupposed a powerful physicality, a flourishing, abundant, even overflowing health, together with that which serves to preserve it: war, adventure, hunting, dancing, war games, and in general all that involves vigorous, free, joyful activity" (*GM* I:7). The *Genealogy*'s nobles certainly appear to resemble, at least superficially, the *Wettkämpfer* of "Homer's Wettkampf," whereas the slavish clearly resemble those compelled by *Vernichtungslust*: "the priestly-noble mode of valuation" shifts the terms of evaluation because the slavish lack the physical strength requisite for victory in struggles such as war and redefine the realm of contest as a psychic space in which nonphysical strength is tested. They tap the energy of revenge to dominate that sphere. It might appear that Nietzsche tells this story from the standpoint of a defeated (would-be) master who resents being the subject of judgment of those he regards as inferior, but he is not simply condemning the slavish in assessing their revisionist appropriation and distortion of the agon, and he is not merely longing for a reinstatement of masterly, Homeric agonistic ideals. The full picture of why he thinks such retrieval is impossible will become clearer in the upcoming section on his moral psychology. The reason why it would be *undesirable* even if it were possible is that he admires the cunning slavish revaluation. *That* activity is what is significant in his account, and what he seeks to reveal and reclaim, not the supposed excellence of the nobles who lost out. It was in this "moment"— that is when this became possible—that human beings became "interesting" (*GM* I:6). For Nietzsche, this exhibits a distinctive and distinguishing possibility of human creativity in value production, in meaning-making, that was previously unrealized.

Instead of reading Nietzsche as providing us with a just-so story that cannot possibly motivate an *actual* evolutionary account of morality, I think it is worthwhile to see how he articulates and elaborates some basic characteristics of human evaluation. Nietzsche offers a *description* of features of value production rather than a factual historical account, and tied to this description is his identification of various affective states that are attendant with our moral beliefs.[13] Thus, Christopher Janaway's study of affective attachments in the *Genealogy* provides important insight: Nietzsche is concerned to investigate why it is we are drawn to certain beliefs, why we find certain beliefs so valuable.[14] In other words, the story of the contest of masters and slaves (*initiated* by the slaves, we should note—there is no prior *contest* that the masters have won) is supposed to motivate us to ask questions about how valuation *works* and what effects it has, not about when precisely this occurred or whether the account maps onto any particular historical people.[15] That the latter is obviously not Nietzsche's goal is supported by the fact that he makes no effort to tie this to any recognizable historical events. When he does link such *tendencies* with historical events (e.g., the rebellion of the Jews against the Romans), the moment of slavish revolt is presupposed to have already occurred (i.e., not too long after some prehistoric time at the emergence of social organizations resembling states), and, thus, the particular instance in question cannot possibly be the moment of historical emergence.[16]

Nietzsche's goal is to show how values are dynamic, relational, and pervasive: they radiate, and they permeate our concepts. Axes of value can differ quite substantially and can direct whole ways of life. In all the battles Nietzsche finds interesting, the stakes are ultimately struggles of values. This is as evident in his earliest writings, where the relations between the values of art and life are in play, as it is in his later writings in which he examines the relations between the values of truth and life. The question of the relation between *moral* values and the forms of life they foster and facilitate so preoccupies him that he returns to it again and again, as, for example, in a book that numbers among his last, *Der Antichrist*: "So far there has been only *this* one great war [Krieg]." He is referring here to a "war" between noble and slavish—in this case, explicitly *Christian*—values. He continues by offering the Renaissance as an example: "so far there has been no more decisive question than that of the Renaissance—*my* question is its question—nor has there ever been a more fundamental, a straighter form of *attack* in which the whole front was led more strictly against the center. Attacking in the decisive place, in the very seat of Christianity, to place the *noble* values on the throne *here*, I mean, bringing them right into the instincts, into the lowest needs and desires of those who sat there!" (*A* 61). How Nietzsche characterizes this plan of attack, and perhaps more importantly the response, illustrates the dynamic and distinction of forms of contest and opposition as they relate to valuation more generally.

Nietzsche considered the Renaissance to be the only attempt in modernity to reclaim what was lost with the victory of slavish morality as evident in the supremacy of Christian values (and, thus, we can see his projects of revaluation as opposed to modernity more generally). For him, the Renaissance was the only serious counterattack of noble values: "The *revaluation of Christian values*, the attempt, undertaken with every means, with every instinct, with all genius, to bring the *counter*values, the *noble* values to victory." But Luther, Nietzsche claims, made sure it was a failed rebellion: "This monk [Luther], with all the vengeful instincts of a shipwrecked priest [Paul] in his system, was outraged in Rome—*against* the Renaissance. Instead of understanding, with the most profound gratitude, the tremendous event that had happened here, the overcoming of Christianity in its very seat, his hatred understood only how to derive its own nourishment from this spectacle." Consequently, Protestantism is for Nietzsche "the most unclean kind of Christianity that there is, the most incurable, the most irrefutable," and the Germans bear responsibility for its invention (*A* 61).

In the final book of *Die fröhliche Wissenschaft*, Nietzsche describes two general views of the world. Each employs an understanding of the world as a site of suffering with which everything struggles. Art and philosophy, he claims, can be considered as attempted remedies for the pains of these struggles. What distinguishes these worldviews is the condition of the sufferer: "those who suffer from the *over-fullness of life* [der Ueberfülle des Lebens]" and "those who suffer from the *impoverishment of life* [der Verarmung des Lebens]." The first hold a tragic view; they yearn for tragic insight. The second "seek rest, stillness, calm seas, redemption from themselves through art and knowledge, or intoxication, convulsions, anesthesia, and madness." The differing views lead to incongruous values and conceptions of appropriate or suitable human behavior. For the first, "what is evil, absurd, and ugly seems, as it were, permissible, owing to an excess of procreating, fertilizing energies [eines Ueberschusses von zeugenden, befruchtenden Kräften] that can still turn any desert into lush farmland." The others crave "mildness, peacefulness, and goodness in thought as well as deed." They desire a god who provides alleviations for their sufferings—"a god for the sick, a healer and savior"—as well as logic, "the conceptual understandability of existence—for logic calms and gives confidence" (*GS* 370). For Nietzsche, these are ultimately driven by both specific and general aesthetic values and preferences, ones that complement, correct, relieve, and explain the experiences of those who create them. When these different worldviews meet, they clash and struggle. Rather than seeing this as a bad situation to be avoided, Nietzsche appears to think it is worthwhile: if values are relational, and if part of how they gain traction and endure is by *overcoming* alternatives, then this contentious struggle is potentially productive and fruitful, perhaps even vital. Indeed, he repeatedly suggests that reigniting such struggles is part of his task. One of his criticisms of slavish morality is that it undermines the very possibility of contestation, that it is perversely *anti*-agonistic and, as such, undermines the conditions of its existence. This at least partially accounts for Christianity's inevitable self-overcoming anticipated in the third essay of *GM*. In his last writings, Nietzsche suggests that it is the task of the free spirits, among whom he seems to include himself, to reinvigorate the conflict between Christian and noble values (see *A* 37), and this is not simply so that Christian values will be defeated.[17]

Nietzsche considers different axiological tendencies as arising from and informing different forms of life. While he links Christianity with a morality governed by the destructive desire to annihilate in contrast with an alternative mode of valuation that might exemplify creative spiritual overcoming, he does not address in the *Genealogy* the question of what is creative and what is destructive. For that, one does better returning to the fifth book of *Die fröhliche Wissenschaft*, written at nearly the same time as the *Genealogy*. In *Die fröhliche Wissenschaft*, Nietzsche claims that, when distinguishing values, he asks in each case whether it is "'hunger or superabundance that has here become creative.'" He argues that no actions are intrinsically creative or destructive; even the urge to destroy is ambivalent: "The desire for *destruction* [Zerstörung], change, and becoming can be an expression of an overflowing energy that is pregnant with future (my term for this is, as is known, 'Dionysian')." Yet that same desire can spring from "hatred of the ill-constituted, disinherited, and underprivileged." In these cases, people act destructively because they "*must* destroy, because what exists, indeed all existence, all being, outrages and provokes them" (*GS* 370).[18]

The process of ascertaining whether certain evaluative tendencies and goals are creative or destructive in specific situations can be complex, and the evaluative terms of this motivation—"hunger or superabundance"—turn on the evolutionary ideas discussed in chapter 3 above. For an example, we can draw on work from both *Die fröhliche Wissenschaft* and *Zur Genealogie der Moral*. Nietzsche isolates a particular tendency and describes how it is exemplified in the life of Schopenhauer, utilizing a strategy similar to the one he develops to link his genealogy of morality to contemporary circumstances. The "will to immortalize," to preserve "being," might seem to work unequivocally in the service of life, as a creative orientation that enhances life, but Nietzsche claims that it, too, "requires a dual interpretation." The desire to preserve an experience—whether a particular historical age or a moment of individual glory—could, he claims, be an expression of "gratitude and love; art with this origin will always be an art of apotheoses [. . .] spreading a Homeric light and glory over all things." Yet the same desire can be linked to hate-inspired destruction: "the tyrannical will of one who suffers deeply, who struggles, is tormented, and would like to turn what is most personal, singular, and narrow, the real idiosyncrasy of his suffering, into a binding law and compulsion." Under these circumstances, exercising the will to immortalize is an act of revenge: "one [. . .] revenges himself on all things by forcing his own image, the image of his torture, on them, branding them with it" (*GS* 370).[19] *Romantic pessimism* is the name that Nietzsche gives to the latter version of the will to immortalize, and he claims that Schopenhauer serves as an exemplar of that spirit.

In the *Genealogy*, Nietzsche claims: "What was especially at stake [for Schopenhauer] was the value of the 'unegoistic,' the instincts of pity, self-abnegation, self-sacrifice." These he "gilded, deified, and projected into a beyond for so long that at last they became for him 'value-in-itself,' on the basis of which he *said No* to life and to himself" (*GM* P:5). He anticipates, in contrast, a pessimism of the future, a Dionysian pessimism. The critical differences lie in the origins and goals of the two. Romantic pessimism serves the needs of those who suffer from an impoverished experience of life; it is *consolation* for misery endured so long as one's finite life lasts. The pessimism of philosophers of the future, on the other hand, springs from the unencumbered discharging of superabundant energies. At present, Nietzsche claims, the "decisive mark of a 'higher nature,' a more spiritual nature," can be discerned in those who are a battleground on which the opposing valuations of the spiritually impoverished and the spiritually overrich (the slave and the noble) are in genuine conflict and the battle is not yet decided (*GM* I:16).[20]

4.4 *SITTLICHKEIT*, *MORAL*, AND THE NATURE OF NIETZSCHE'S POSTMORALISM

Part of what would be involved in a reinvigorated conflict between such opposing valuations is a deeper understanding of the structure of motivation that supports the axes—what they ultimately seek—and what they assume. Having highlighted some such motivations in the preceding section, I am now in a position to consider the assumptions—the targets of praise or blame and what is assumed about human psychology in each case. When we recall Nietzsche's tripartite development of morality and how he thinks morality will be overcome, we bring into focus the significance of *intention* in morality and the conceptions of will and subjectivity that are bound up with the attachment of moral relevance to intent. Raising those issues leads us to further considerations of Nietzsche's moral psychology, which minimizes considerations of intention, even if it does not render them obsolete. These considerations seem to follow from his agonized conception of subjectivity and moral psychology, which he develops in opposition to (and offers as superior to) the agonized subjectivity of Pauline Christianity.

Nietzsche thinks that if his critique of morality is successful rather than *defeating* morality he will have rendered it (or it will have become) obsolete, impotent, no longer an issue (*EH* "Daybreak" 1). He writes of himself and his fellow traveling "free spirits": "we sail right *over* morality" (*BGE* 23). In some respects, we can see this as his lifelong ambition, or at least the story he tells for most of his philosophically productive life: how values emerge and change, how moral values specifically get their grip and come to dominate the scene, and how this development is linked with what might be called the *birth of the moral*, which in some respects might be thought to coincide with, if it is not identical to, the birth of the soul. In *BGE* 32, he describes a scenario in which morality could be overcome:

> During the longest part of human history—so-called prehistorical times—the value or disvalue of an action [Handlung] was derived from its consequences [Folgen]. The action itself was considered as little as its origin [Herkunft]. [. . .] Let us call this period the *pre-moral* period of mankind [. . .]. In the last ten thousand years, however, one has reached the point [. . .] where it is no longer the consequences but the origin of an action that

one allows to decide its value [. . .] the sign of a period that one may call *moral* in the narrower sense. [. . .] the origin of an action was interpreted in the most definite sense as origin in an *intention* [Absicht]; one came to agree that the value of an action lay in the value of the intention. [. . .] Don't we stand at the threshold of a period which should be designated negatively, to begin with, as *extra-moral* [aussermoralische]? [. . .] today at least we immoralists have the suspicion that the decisive value of an action lies precisely in what is *unintentional* [nicht-absichtlich] in it, while everything about it that can be seen, known, "conscious," still belongs to its surface and skin.

Nietzsche links what might be construed as "*moral* in the narrower sense" with a "reversal of perspective [Umkehrung der Perspektive]." This reversal shifts the focus of praise and blame from the consequences of an action to its origin; and, interestingly, he sees this shift as an "unconscious" effect of aristocratic values. Morality itself is described as an "achievement" of sorts that occurs "only after long struggles and vacillations" (*BGE* 32). I have sketched how Nietzsche's primary target in *GM*, Christian morality, in many respects opposes struggle or at least severely limits what constitutes a worthwhile struggle and the forms it can take. I now want to examine the agonistic milieu in which it emerges as victorious. That is, I want to consider what its overcoming entails.

In *BGE* 32, that moment of the birth of the moral, so to speak, receives only glancing attention. Nietzsche links this "great event which involves a considerable refinement of vision and standards" to "the unconscious after effect of the rule of aristocratic values and the faith in 'descent' ['Herkunft']." In effect, this sums up and is the core idea of the first essay of the *Genealogy*. What is involved in the "refinement of vision and standards [eine erhebliche Verfeinerung des Blicks und Maassstabs]" is in this case a major shift in the object of valuation in the context of an overall assessment of worth—rather than regarding the *consequence or result* of the action as decisive, as is the case in the prehistoric, premoral era, it is the origin or intention that matters. When Nietzsche suggests this is an "unconscious after effect of the rule of aristocratic values and faith in 'descent,'" he points to the fact that the focal point of evaluation shifts from the effect back to a presumed source, from which it might be thought to descend, its origin. Morality in the restricted sense becomes possible with the conception of the subject as the *cause* of action, and this conceptually motivates the notion that individuals are responsible for what they do. Since the development of morality in this specific sense is the *undoing* of customary values defined in aristocratic terms, this in effect represents the *self-overcoming* of noble *Sittlichkeit*, often translated as *morality of mores* or the *morality of custom*.[21]

The postmoral or extramoral future Nietzsche imagines is hardly simply a return to that *Sittlichkeit*. Such introspection, turning inward, the "attempt at self-knowledge" that was required to achieve the "narrowing" of perspective that yielded morality, facilitated the development of a measure of profundity in human moral psychology. What Nietzsche envisions as prompting further development is not regression but rather "another self-examination of man, another growth in profundity" (*BGE* 32). What might precipitate this, he thinks, is yet another "reversal of perspective." The focal point of this perspective is the basis or object of evaluation of worth; put another way, the reversal of perspective he anticipates calls into question and replaces what it is that *matters* or is significant in assessments of human activity. He provides just a glimpse of this in *BGE* 32 and then spends much of the remainder of that book exploring various facets and corners of "the human soul and its limits, the range of inner human experiences [that have] reached so far, the heights, depths, and distances of these experiences [. . .] 'this huge forest, this primeval forest'" (*BGE* 45), which makes the development of morality (as well as its overcoming) possible.

The advancement of this kind of psychology, Nietzsche thinks, might well prompt the reversal of perspective he anticipates, from which point of view there is "the suspicion that the decisive value of an action lies precisely in what is *unintentional* in it, while everything about it that is intentional, everything about it that can be seen, known, 'conscious,' still belongs to its surface and skin—which like every skin, betrays something but *conceals* even more." Accordingly, he thinks, what he has called "morality in the narrow sense," the "morality of intentions," is a "prejudice," one that is perhaps preparatory for some better future, "but in any case something that must be overcome" (*BGE* 32). Insights drawn from human psychology that might well lead to such development toward *postmorality* are available in Nietzsche's later writings. Of special concern is his alternative conception of the moral agent, its possibilities and its limitations.

4.5 THE (MORAL) SUBJECT NATURALIZED

In the second essay of the *Genealogy*, Nietzsche links development of the narrower sense of morality with what he calls *mnemotechnics*—practices of memory that eventually produce a responsible subject. The subject reconceived as a plurality of struggling forces, as discussed in the preceding chapter, obviously raises some problems for the conception of the subject as the single and ultimate cause of action. Nietzsche thinks a more realistic, naturalistic conception is possible. What I discuss in this section will be just part of his unfolding story since what needs further explanation is how such organizations of forces come to be what they are and whether they can change (matters not fully addressed until chapter 5 below). Nietzsche's agonism sheds light on both these concerns. In the next section, I consider how this further naturalization of the subject bears on his repeated claim and echo of Goethe in the *Genealogy*, "das Thun ist Alles"—*the deed is everything*. These combined features of his thought raise serious doubts as to whether the morality of intention is particularly instructive about the value of human activity since the conception of autonomous agency with which he wrestles appears to be incompatible with what both psychology and physiology suggest is the case about human consciousness and action. But this does not mean there is no room for a conception of agency in Nietzsche, that we must regard him as a determinist, or that his view leaves no room for the possibility of an ethos.[22]

The second essay of Nietzsche's *Genealogy* depicts the development of the human psyche in terms of a contest of forces. The opening sections focus squarely on the problem of how the power (*Kraft*) of remembering accomplished its victory, resulting in an animal capable of making (and accounting for) promises, and suggest some deleterious effects that accrue with the atrophy of forgetting in the course of human development. The upshot of this part of Nietzsche's story seems to be that the acquisition of the kind of willing that comes with promise-making had a price, the diminution of forgetting, and its withering was a detriment at the same time that it extended new possibilities for significant human activity. This idea is reinforced by Nietzsche's insistence that forgetting is not merely an absence or failure of memory but rather something that *is positively active in its own right*. Nietzsche couches the matter in organic, biological terms of nutrition and digestion: "it [forgetting] is [. . .] responsible for the fact that what we experience and absorb enters our consciousness as little while we are digesting it (one might call the process 'inpsychation' ['Einverseelung'])—as does the thousandfold process, involved in physical nourishment—so-called 'incorporation' ['Einverleibung']" (*GM* II:1). Were it not for forgetting, he suggests, we would not have a soul, a psyche, much as we would not have a body, a corpus, if we were not able to digest.[23] The theme of forgetting as an *active force* and Nietzsche's use of metaphors for digestion have not gone unnoticed. But what is less recognized is what this has to do with what he says in the very next section of *GM* II in which the reference to the sovereign individual occurs. The sovereign individual is the product of a process in which the active forces of remembering and forgetting are in contest, with the result that remembering surmounts and suppresses its opponent.[24] We should further explore precisely what the sovereign individual trumps in the course of this struggle, how the sovereign individual is a *product* of such *Kampf*, the form of this conflict and its relevant participants.

This leads us back to a deeper investigation of forgetting. Briefly, we can recall that, as Nietzsche writes in *GM* II:1, the good of forgetting issues from the effects of what Nietzsche describes as "inpsychating" consciousness; put another way, forgetting plays a role in the regulatory process that permits us to appropriate experience by taking in enough to have *an* experience and ridding ourselves of what is left behind in the relief. Thus, formation of the psyche occurs not only through processes of building up, accumulation, but also through elimination. Forgetting, it seems, is an important condition for experience—important for giving the shape, form, rhythm, texture, and depth that make the seemingly endless stream of possible objects of concern and attention *an* experience, to recall Dewey's famous distinction.[25] It does this not simply by piling experiences up or onto one another but by taking some away, encouraging some to fade, recede, fall away. Forgetting in this sense *grants* rather than evacuates or eliminates; too much remembering leaves us with experience without pause and strips possibilities for action. Nietzsche engages in more elaborate discussion of this idea in his earlier writings, particularly *BT* (in the association of the Dionysian with forgetting) and *HL* (where differentiation of the "stream of becoming" is described as necessary), and it is clear he does not think that individuals are simply monadic unitary entities. Instead, he repeatedly casts human beings as organizations of conflicting forces. We are composed of a multiplicity of forces such that "our organism is oligarchically arranged" (*GM* II:1; cf. *BGE* 6, 12, 19). In essence, Nietzsche claims that just as cultural and artistic products are the result of the agonistic tension of the Apollinian and the Dionysian so are human beings (from a particular perspective) the products of struggling forces, and he investigates at least one agon evident in the production of the human psyche—the contest between remembering and forgetting.

With this context in mind, we can further investigate the form of this contest and what it produced, the ends it serves and how. The inaugural question of the second essay of the *Genealogy* can be reformulated thus: What must have happened in order for us to be able—*for nature to have granted us the ability*—to make promises? Clearly, this is a question raised about humankind generally, one that has bedeviled philosophers for ages. It applies to the kind of being that makes us human beings. It is not asked about individual humans. Indeed, each of the essays of the *Genealogy* endeavors, from a variety of perspectives, to offer a creation story of how the human animal, generally, came to be what it is, entwined with an etiology of moral concepts. The second essay is about the development of humankind as the animal with a conscience, more precisely, one with "the bad conscience." What characterizes our species, at least as it is cast in the second essay, is the fact that some forces were strengthened over others in the course of our development. This process was *completed* (hence, it is not some tantalizing possibility for future philosophers to achieve) with the emergence of the sovereign individual. Nietzsche's preoccupation with this process in *GM* and elsewhere is tied to his concern for figuring out whether autonomy, *conceived in this way* and for all, really is the telos of humanity that modern philosophy and the emerging social sciences claimed it to be.[26] What development might take us beyond ourselves, Nietzsche asks, and what paths might we pursue if we overcame our current conceptions of humanity? Would this entail sovereign individuality *as it is described* in *GM* II:2? I think discussions of the figure of the sovereign individual, who makes a lone appearance in *GM* II:2, generally give too much weight to it and mistakenly locate the terms for discussion of it in *preserving* certain key features of morality.

There are a number of angles one might pursue in challenging the dominant interpretation of the sovereign individual as Nietzsche's ideal, including the emphasis such interpretations place on *promising* or the conception of subject that they presume.[27] What I hope to make clearer here is how Nietzsche seeks to shift the terms in which philosophers have discussed these matters, how they have framed their questions, and the stakes they see as involved. I do not think he obliterates the basis for discussions of agency, but I do think he offers accounts of multiple prospective replacement models of the subject (or soul, as discussed in the previous chapter). Our serious consideration of them would require us to significantly reconsider what we think an agent is, what it can do and how, and why it matters.

The moral ideal Nietzsche finds in the history of philosophy from Plato to Schopenhauer is one that increasingly prizes *willing* and, in so doing, ties it to responsibility, autonomy, and freedom: the greater one's exercise of will, the more complete one becomes, the more one realizes the potential of humanity, the more *being*, or actuality, one achieves. Acquiring the relevant form of willing requires the development of memory, specifically, "*memory of will* [Gedächtniss des Willens]" (*GM* II:1). Such memory is crucial for establishing what Nietzsche describes as a "long chain of will" in which the original "I will" (or the promise of some action or deed) and "the actual discharge of the will," that is, the action or actions one undertakes, remain essentially *bound* despite changes of circumstance and the emergence of other desires and acts of will. Taking this on as a goal, human beings acquired powers of memory that significantly outstrip those of forgetting, and the service of this end had dramatic secondary effects, including how one regards the past, present, and future and the expectations one has of others and oneself. In particular, what we might call the human *memory project* requires certain dispositions toward the past and the future. These stem from the necessity of securing, determining, and effecting the promised action in such a way as to be in the position to maintain the "chain of will" mentioned above. This chain links the promise made in the past with some future action. To secure the conditions that make this possible, we have sought to make human affairs as regular and predictable as possible to ward off circumstances that would interfere with the execution of the relevant actions governed by the economy of promise keeping. Nietzsche thus sees the telos of this kind of willing as inextricably bound with the development of reason, a peculiar sense of history and temporality (one that leads us to resent it, as explained below), a philosophical anthropology in which "[m]an himself must first of all have become *calculable, regular, necessary*, even in his own image of himself, if he is to be able to stand security for *his own future*, which is what one who promises does!" (*GM* II:1).

The human being who stands security for his or her own future, however, is quite different from the being with which *GM* II begins. That creature is described in terms of being an animal, and, although human beings certainly retain their animality for Nietzsche, they are nonetheless cultivated to such an extent that they are not *merely* animals or, at least, are animals that have been bred to distance themselves from those of other species.[28] In the *Genealogy*, the development of conscience more than reason distinguishes human beings, and the second essay in particular examines how such a conscience is produced and how it played a role in effecting the kind of animals modern human beings are. At the *end of this process* stands the ideal of the sovereign individual:

> If we place ourselves at the end of this tremendous process, where the tree at last brings forth fruit, where society and the morality of custom [Sittlichkeit der Sitte] at last reveal *what* they have simply been the means to: then we discover that the ripest fruit is the *sovereign individual* [s o u v e r -

aine Individuum], like only to himself, liberated again from morality of custom, autonomous and supramoral [autonome übersittliche] (for "autonomous" and "moral" are mutually exclusive), in short, the man who has his own independent, protracted will and the *capacity to make promises* [der versprechen darf]—and in him a proud consciousness, quivering in every muscle, of *what* has at length been achieved and become flesh in him, a consciousness of his own power and freedom, a sensation of mankind come to completion [Vollendungs-Gefühl]. (*GM* II:2; Kaufmann and Hollingdale's translation emended)

The ideal of the sovereign individual is the goal or the ultimate fruit of the process of moralization and refinement of conscience. It is a serious mistake to read it as *Nietzsche's* future ideal, for, when one does so, one remains blind to the fact that the sovereign individual is the ultimate product of the process of moralization whose possible overcoming Zarathustra heralds.[29]

Following the first two sections of the second essay of the *Genealogy*, Nietzsche suggests a sinister motivation for the process of moralization that is guided by the ideal of the subject as a responsible agent, including the production of *conscience* and the *bad conscience*. Conscience, he claims, became possible through torturous processes of mnemonics, which eventually[30] took the aim of instilling a sense of duty and obligation that required the extirpation of forgetting.

What do we need in order to have a conscience? Nietzsche claims it requires cultivation of special powers of memory. "'How can one create a memory for the human animal? How can one impress something upon this incarnate forgetfulness, attuned only to the passing moment, in such a way that it will stay there?'" (*GM* II:3; translation emended).[31] He offers graphic examples of how mnemotechnics have been employed in the form of human sacrifice and mutilation: "all this has its origin in the instinct that realized that pain is the most powerful aid to mnemonics" (*GM* II:3). The competitors in the contest of memory and forgetting are fierce and relentless, their tactics harsh. It is clear Nietzsche conceives quashing forgetfulness as the way in which ascetic practices achieved their fixity of standards and norms. Memory was quite literally emblazoned in the psyche, initially by means of torturing the body, to render the ideals of asceticism "inextinguishable, ever-present" and also to free "these ideas from the competition of all other ideas, so as to make them 'unforgettable'" in the sense that there could be no possible alternative to eclipse them or win out as desirable in comparison or contrast with them, thereby short-circuiting agon. Nietzsche writes: "the severity of the penal code provides an especially significant measure of the degree of effort needed to overcome forgetfulness and to impose a few primitive demands of social existence as *present realities* upon these slaves of momentary affect and desire."[32] We might note a similar degree of severity and opposition in Nietzsche's depiction of Doric art as it sought domination over Dionysian influences. In the contest of memory and forgetting, memory took as its end the domination of the competitive field. It could countenance nothing else. A goal of the ascetic practices forging memory was permanently fixing desire such that no other possible goal could even emerge on the horizon as worthy of pursuit, much less as a potential rival. Again, Nietzsche's description of the techniques employed to acquire such direction of desire is quite graphic. The penal codes and sagas detail punishments involving flaying or boiling alive, trampling by horses, ripping the criminal body to shreds, piercing the body and cutting out the vital organs while the criminal is alive, stoning, crushing the skull on the wheel, and so on—and all this in full public view. Memory sought to extinguish its opponent as well as the very possibility of opposition. These practices have the purpose of producing a memory that contains "five or six 'I will not's' in regard to which one had given one's *promise* so as to participate in the advantages of society." This is the brutal basis of promising Nietzsche highlights, and he thinks it also serves as the primal basis of reasoning: "it was indeed with the aid of this kind of memory that one at last came 'to reason'!" (*GM* II:3).

Some who are wont to emphasize sovereign individuality as Nietzsche's central counterimage and ideal in the *Genealogy* underscore *promising* as its signature feature.[33] I worry that such accounts sneak in a moral prejudice. Promising is one of the favorite examples of moral theorists, and our ability to make promises, keep them, and hold others to them lies at the core of social contract theory.[34] Those who highlight promising as a defining characteristic of Nietzsche's ideal appear to continue to advance the view that our ability to promise is somehow essential to the very possibility of any morality (and possibly civility). I think it is a mistake to assume this, to continue to hold without question the unconditional value of promising. Nietzsche envisions the very moral view that places such emphasis on promising will be overcome. As suggested in *BGE* 32 and elsewhere, such overcoming entails superseding the values and a good number of the basic concepts that are essential to that way of thinking.[35] This is not to say there is nothing retained in this process, that promising could have *no* place or value at all; it is only to suggest it might not be as crucial as many contemporary readers seem to have it.

A task of the second essay of the *Genealogy* is to describe how it is the current human condition to not be able "to be done" with our experiences, and that essay seeks to envision a way of bringing about an increased, if not restored, health. Nietzsche calls our inability to be done with experience *ressentiment*, which differs from revenge against others in response to specific acts. Ressentiment is a revolt against the temporal-historical character of human existence as such, the revenge against *time* and all "it was" (*Z* II "On Redemption"). To resent the fact that things are not otherwise than what they might have been keeps us stuck with a past we resent we cannot change. It thus differs from vengeance we might feel toward others or their specific acts of harm against us. The news is not all bad, for Nietzsche: this very same strengthening of memory also produced creatures that possess an uncanny capacity for willing. Such capacity has tremendously creative possibilities, which is what makes humankind so interesting (*GM* I:6). By the end of *GM* II, Nietzsche essentially asks, *What now?*—How can we recover from the psychic dyspepsia we acquired along the way in our moralization? Might we be able to deploy the capacity for willing it simultaneously produced? The answer seems to be linked with development or the advancement of this form of will, not simply a revolution in its valuation. And this potentially affects how we act and how we understand and interact with others. I return to this matter in the next section.

The lure of such power as the sovereign individual *thinks* he possesses is certainly tremendous; that is precisely the point of the *Genealogy*. The values we *already* hold lead us to think that the sovereign individual, quivering as he does at the very thought of all the power he thinks he has (but has he, really?), is desirable. His thought (something that might strike us as desirable for ourselves, too) that he is "mankind come to completion" seems to us, to those who hold the values that we do, that being a sovereign individual, if it were possible, would be rather (really) good. But I suggest that what is being displayed in *GM* II:2 is not an ideal type for us to pursue but rather an image of ourselves that follows from values we currently hold not because *we are already* sovereign individuals but rather because the allure of the sovereign individual instructs us about the nature of our true desires. Deep down, though we might have sympathized with the poor little lambs of *GM* I, we (and apparently a good number of Nietzsche scholars) *want* to be sovereigns.

What makes the life of the sovereign individual desirable, and how it attracts those inspired to pursue it, is that there is an aesthesis of power that courses throughout the entire economy of promise-making—making promises, breaking them, and punishing others who are unable or unwilling to keep them, which the rest of *GM* II elaborates in graphic detail. The anticipated rewards are so great that humans have even instigated their own further deformity in the form of diminishing their powers of forgetting in order to pursue that feeling. The sovereign individual is a peculiar conceptual accretion formed by the gravitational pull of the sensation of power that accumulates through the processes of cultivating memory and will, to the degree that promising becomes, not only desirable, but also possible. What began as this *feeling* has become conceptualized as an ideal orienting the development of morality, finally culminating in modern rationalistic accounts of human subjectivity. The postmoral future Nietzsche envisions lies beyond, not within, this scope.[36]

Overcoming humanity at the very least involves overcoming, by reconsidering and reconceiving, our *conception* of humanity—the one we presently have eclipses any possibility of genuine self-knowledge, clouded as it is by various psychological errors identified and described throughout Nietzsche's writings and particularly in *GM*, though we might want to be more careful about just what we mean by *self-knowledge*. (Is this knowledge about *our own* selves or knowledge about what *selves* are?) Our failure to appreciate our psychological nature and the errors to which it is prone has led us to embrace a morality that is not only false (incongruent with most of the human and physical sciences) but also limiting and debilitating. This occurs not simply by redescribing or renaming the human or by reaffirming the old concepts to thereby make them new and lively again, for it is not possible to have such concepts (e.g., *human*) without the influence of some value. The values make a difference: if and when we overcome morality, it will come along with a different conception of humanity. But, for all Nietzsche's shouting and hand-wringing about the enormity of the task, we do not get much in the way of a specific answer as to how it will acquire such a conceptualization. The argument of this book thus far has been that Nietzsche's lifelong project included a study of how values get produced and reproduced (and all the various ways in which values influence and relate to virtually every dimension of human existence and our experience with and knowledge of the natural world). One answer to the question, *What next?* available to Nietzsche is to consider the viability of an agonistic engagement in which the terms of conflict give new meaning to human existence. This is what I regard as the project of *Also Sprach Zarathustra*, one that fails, or has yet to be successful if one thinks it is a viable option, because it was an individual project. Given what Nietzsche knows full well about the origin and force of value creation and production, such work cannot be done by a lone individual. Whatever it is Nietzsche envisions for the future, it cannot be islands of quivering self-legislators. This raises again the question of where, tempohistorically, we might place the sovereign individual so that we can better assess where we (and any possible future beings) stand in relation to it, particularly in light of how Nietzsche undermines the conception of the agent as doer or cause of its deeds, discussed below.

If we situate the figure of the sovereign individual in the context of his interest in and accounts of the postmoral future of humanity, we can recognize along with Nietzsche that there are benefits that come with acquiring capacities at earlier stages of development but they may also come with a price. Just as what might be called the *memory project* (the process that produced human capabilities for remembering and sought to exterminate forgetting) had the good consequence of making us more rational, what might be called the *autonomy project* (which gives us the sovereign individual) could have had a good consequence, perhaps benefits on which we have yet to capitalize.[37] This at least remains a possibility, and such a view would be consistent with Nietzsche's text and a postmoral future that we could imagine in which the autonomy project inadvertently primed us, not for thinking of ourselves as dominating ourselves, but rather for conceptions of agency and action in which we think of ourselves as in our deeds rather than *behind* our deeds as freewheeling masters.

4.6 "DAS THUN IST ALLES"

I now wish to return to Nietzsche's conception of the subject to see how it congeals with a view of human beings that would lead to the conclusion that the "intention" is not the ultimate object of moral evaluation, that "the decisive value of an action lies precisely in what is *unintentional* in it, while everything about it that is intentional, everything about it that can be seen, known, 'conscious,' still belongs to its surface and skin—which like every skin, betrays something but *conceals* even more" (*BGE* 32). I argued in the preceding chapter that Nietzsche's artful naturalism is evident in his experimentation with alternatives to what he calls the *soul hypothesis*, leading him to consider replacing belief in the existence of atomic individuals with a conception of the human being as a social structure, a complex of forces. We can consider whether and how such revised notions of the subject might affect conceptions of human willing as primarily and ultimately causally responsible for action. If the moral subject as it has hitherto been conceived is no longer tenable following a more rigorous naturalistic account, then must morality ("in the narrow sense") similarly be undermined? We have already seen that Nietzsche thinks philosophy *might* nevertheless retain a notion of soul reconceived; in this section and the next chapter, I explore a future possibility for orienting further thinking about this kind of subject.

To further glimpse what might be an image of humanity beyond morality and what might become of old moral concepts we might treasure so dearly, we can begin by examining Nietzsche's conception of the relation between action and human existence as suggested in his repeated claim, "das Thun ist Alles" (the deed is everything). One of the goals of *Zur Genealogie der Moral* is to demonstrate the genealogy of human psychology, of the conception of the person as agent. In *GM* I:13, Nietzsche uses an image of the "lightning flash" as a metaphor for conceptualizing human subjectivity that is potentially devastating in its consequences. The familiar passage runs as follows:

> To demand of strength that it should *not* express itself as strength, that it should *not* be a desire to overcome, a desire to throw down, a desire to become master, a thirst for enemies and resistances and triumphs, is just as absurd as to demand of weakness that it should express itself as strength. A quantum of force is equivalent to a quantum of drive, will, effect—more, it is nothing other than precisely this very driving, willing, effecting, and only owing to the seduction of language (and of the fundamental errors of reason that are petrified in it) which conceives and misconceives all effects as conditioned by something that causes effects, by a "subject" can it appear otherwise. For just as the popular mind separates the lightning from its flash and takes the latter for an *action*, for the operation of a subject called lightning, so popular morality also separates strength from expressions of strength, as if there were a neutral substratum behind the strong man, which was *free* to express strength or not to do so. But there is no such substratum; there is no "being" behind doing, effecting, becoming; "the doer" is merely a fiction added to the deed—the deed is everything.

> Von der Stärke verlangen, dass sie sich nicht als Stärke äussere, dass sie nicht ein Überwältigen-Wollen, ein Niederwerfen-Wollen, ein Herr-werden-Wollen, ein Durst nach Feinden und Widerständen und Triumphen sei, ist gerade so widersinnig als von der Schwäche verlangen, dass sie sich als Stärke äussere. Ein Quantum Kraft ist ein eben solches Quantum Trieb, Wille, Wirken—vielmehr, es ist gar nichts anderes als eben dieses Treiben, Wollen, Wirken selbst, und nur unter der Verführung der Sprache (und der in ihr versteinerten Grundirrthümer der Vernunft), welche alles Wirken als bedingt durch ein Wirkendes, durch ein "Subjekt" versteht und

missversteht, kann es anders erscheinen. Ebenso nämlich, wie das Volk den Blitz von seinem Leuchten trennt und letzteres als Th u n, als Wirkung eines Subjekts nimmt, das Blitz heisst, so trennt die Volks-Moral auch die Stärke von den Äusserungen der Stärke ab, wie als ob es hinter dem Starken ein indifferentes Substrat gäbe, dem es freistünde, Stärke zu äussern oder auch nicht. Aber es giebt kein solches Substrat; es giebt kein "Sein" hinter dem Thun, Wirken, Werden; "der Thäter" ist zum Thun bloss hinzugedichtet,—das Thun ist Alles.

If the lightning flash is a metaphor for conceptualizing human subjectivity, it is potentially overwhelming in its consequences for morality since such would undermine a significant source of pride as well as conditions for self-assessment and aspiration, namely, our sense of responsibility for our deeds. Such responsibility is related not only to a moral framework that makes our actions worthy of praise or blame but also to our picture of agency and what it means to be the original (or, at the very least, the *primary*) source of our actions.

There are at least three ways of approaching this concern. One would be to simply claim that Nietzsche obliterates any possibility of agency with this passage, to assert that he thinks human beings are just as determined in their activity as the lightning flashing. Lightning flashes, humans act according to the type of being they are: there is simply nothing else behind human deeds. Another approach is to distinguish *doers* behind deeds; this would qualify, if not *modify*, Nietzsche's claim such that he would be supposed to hold the view that not every deed has a doer behind it because not everyone is *a real* agent. And a third view could involve scrutinizing the kind of relation Nietzsche thinks abides between doer and deed; perhaps doers are not *behind* deeds but nevertheless exist and are still intimately connected with them. The first view is consistent with those views maintaining that Nietzsche is a determinist of sorts, a position I engage in the next chapter. In discussing Nietzsche's conception of free will, Ken Gemes has taken the second path of distinguishing varieties of willing, identifying which of these Nietzsche appears to praise. And I find the third view evident in Robert Pippin's expressivist reading of this passage.

Gemes argues that Nietzsche distinguishes between "deserts free will" and "agency free will," rejecting the former and affirming the latter. The sense of *responsibility* invoked in these distinct conceptualizations is nonetheless similar: both regard the agent as cause, and both find something *praiseworthy* in the will's proper (or particular) exercise, though the terms of evaluation differ. Deserts free will focuses on moral praise and blame and requires that one could have done otherwise; agency free will is supposed to be "an achievement" in which one reaches the status of agent (presumably from out of some condition in which one is more or less *not* yet an agent, though the process of such achievement is not clear). We can be grateful to Gemes for refining this conceptual distinction, although there still needs to be an account of how agency can be achieved since it appears to require an immense store of creative resources to accomplish—precisely those of the sort associated with one who is *already an agent.*[38]

Robert Pippin takes up the lightning-flash passage in the course of investigating Nietzsche's "picture arguments" in *Nietzsche, Psychology, and First Philosophy*, extending his well-known work on expressivist conceptions of agency and prior analyses of this particular passage.[39] Pippin claims that Nietzsche "appears to be relying on a notion of expression, rather than intentional causality, to understand how the doer is in the deed."[40] Elsewhere, he elaborates what follows from this: "What principles or motive seem consciously of great moment to you are not 'up to you,' but reflect or express who you have become given the family, community, and tradition within which you 'got to be you.'" He underscores how the image strikes at the heart of our faith in *our own* subjectivity because our deeds "reflect or express who [we] have become."[41] More recently, Pippin emphasizes that this image does not undermine our picture of responsible agency as such: "Nietzsche is not denying that *there is* a subject of the deed. He is just asserting that it is not *separate*, distinct from the activity itself; it is 'in' the deed. [. . .] He does not say, 'There are just strength-events.'" What this means, he continues, is this: "We cannot say 'there are only deeds,' not agents, just as we cannot say that the flash is *just* an electrical discharge in the air. Clearly, a certain *sort* of meteorological event is 'expressed,' and so a phenomenally identical 'flash' might not be lightning, but could be artificially produced. It would be a phenomenally identical event, but not lightning."[42] Pippin emphasizes the need to distinguish "deeds" from "mere events."[43] He focuses on what we, as philosophers and interpreters of Nietzsche, should conclude about his picture and the analogy it draws:[44] "what he thinks *giving up such a commitment* would amount to [. . .] and how we ought to picture a life without such a commitment."[45] The image shatters our sense of ourselves as freewheeling causes of our actions, as though we are their authors (this is what Pippin emphasizes in his earlier treatments), but it might also shelter a sense of responsible agency that is otherwise conceived.

The first approach to interpreting *GM* I:13, identified above, might gather steam from what it claims as indicated by Nietzsche's naturalism, where this is taken to mean that he "holds that there are only material objects in space and time (perhaps just the entities and properties referred to by the most advanced modern sciences)" and, thus, is essentially just denying the existence of a "separate soul" and along with it "'free will,'" at least of the sort typically conceived as requiring a "metaphysically free subject behind the deed." But Pippin maintains this misses the broader scope of Nietzsche's characterizations of what we believe and why: "He denies that whole model of behavior, 'root and branch.'"[46] If the simile holds, we must grant there is nothing *behind* the deed, neither soul nor material brain states. In other words, Nietzsche is not just seeking to replace metaphysical objects with physical ones, preserving the basic framework for causation and explanation. The picture challenged in his lightning flash "picture argument," as Pippin puts it, includes both postulation of a metaphysical subject-agent (the soul) and the account of "act descriptions" that turn on causation by some prior substratum. It is not just the concept of soul that is under attack here but also attendant conceptions of action, agency, and free will that might still be retained in a substitution of a collection of brain states for soul.

Pippin is eager to avoid another conclusion that might follow from this: namely, that, in the crumbling of the metaphysical picture that supports the account of agency as caused by a substratum, Nietzsche dissolves the distinction between deeds and events: "There would be little reason to take Nietzsche seriously if he were out to make what Bernard Williams has called the 'uninviting' claim that 'we never really do anything, that no events are actions.'"[47] Thus, he works to draw out what Nietzsche *does not say* when he compares human subjectivity to lightning flashing: "He is not denying, in other words, that there is a deed, and that it must be distinguishable from any mere event."[48] In directing readers to an alternative to the conception of the agent as author, creator, or root cause of its actions, Pippin cites *Also Sprach Zarathustra* (*Z* II "On the Virtuous"), in which Zarathustra advises his disciples to give up their attachment to their "virtues": "I wish *your* self were in the deed as the mother is in the child. Let that be *your* word concerning virtue."[49] He concludes: "This suggests a very different relation between self and deed than cause and effect, but we would still have to know first *how*, for Nietzsche, a mother can be said to be 'in' her child before we can appreciate what is being suggested, and that is not initially clear."[50] But he does not pursue an interpretation of the related image of the deed in the person like the mother in the child or what precisely *it* depicts as the relation between self and deed. Instead, he explores what *expression* means in this context, namely, expression *of* something in particular. I wish to consider whether elaborating the basis of expression sufficiently recasts Nietzsche's challenge to the concept of a substratum behind our actions as well as speculate about why one might be so reluctant to give up this notion and why the very thought of doing so is "uninviting" to many.

We can explore how the lightning-flash picture case might show Nietzsche's concern with *expression* rather than *intention* in his depiction of human action. This is a promising line of inquiry for glimpsing what might be entailed in overcoming the emphasis on intent and its locus of value as Nietzsche expects to occur in the overcoming of morality (*BGE* 32; cf. *BGE* 3, 6, 12). Recall that Pippin is concerned to show that Nietzsche's depiction is not reductive: "We cannot say 'there are only deeds,' not agents, just as we cannot say that the flash is *just* an electrical discharge in the air. [. . .] Its distinctness depends on *what* it is expressing."[51] Distinctness of deeds, it might seem, turns on what is being expressed. So, although they are phenomenally identical, my arm just going up and my willing my arm to go up would be distinguished on account of one being the expression of nerve damage that results in confused signals to the brain, say, and the other being the expression of my will, whatever that might be.

Pippin claims that when Nietzsche writes "the deed is everything" there is still a *doer* but that it is *in* rather than *behind* the deed;[52] thus, a doer remains. What distinguishes the expression in the second case (that of the doer rather than lightning flashing) is that it is done by a doer (presumably, an agent) rather than something else. But it is unclear that this amounts to an explanation of the distinction rather than just an assertion. Pippin's conceptual addition of the preposition *in* is intriguing. We might consider whether, when Nietzsche writes "das Thun ist Alles," we have a statement of *identity* or a statement of *predication*. The latter might be construed as the assertion, "Everything is (in) the deed," which is Pippin's view. The former (identity) interprets it as the claim, "The deed is everything"—that is, the deed, the *doing*, is all there is. While sympathetic toward Pippin's view and his expressivist picture, I am not certain we have fully understood Nietzsche here. If "the deed is everything" is a claim of identity, it would seem the deed—the *doing*—is all there is. Moreover, if Pippin grants that both occurrences (phenomena, events) such as lightning flashing and human acting can be expressive, then it is not clear to me how he has shown the distinctness of acts and events other than to assert that acts are the expressions of doers whereas events are not. We still need to know more about the *doing*, why it needs a *doer*, and the particular nature of such doers and how they stand in relation to their activities.

One might respond that surely the lightning is not *just* the flash and, thus, following the analogy, the doer is not *just* or *only* the deed. A conceptual distinction is clearly possible while it is the case that lightning-and-flash, doer-and-deed, are not actually separable. But what is wanted is a subjective distinction in the act that would make it genetically different from an event. Sticking with the metaphoric analogy, we might say with greater precision that it is not the case that *lightning flashes*. There is simply *lightning flashing*, and that is one of the ways in which a particular meteorological event is expressed. Nietzsche draws the analogy of human action as like an event, both of which can be construed as expressive. It would seem that what needs explanation or exploration are the possibilities for expression that distinguish human actions from others (beyond saying the distinction rests on human actions as being the expressions of agents—nothing is gained in such a claim, at least not without a transformation of the concept of the agent). The passage suggests it is Nietzsche's view that *strength expresses itself in action*, or that *strength is expression in action*, not that strong agents express themselves in action. If it cannot be said that an agent can be strong in any meaningful sense without expressing strength, then why bother with the superfluous distinction between the deeds and the doer in such cases? Agents are strong by virtue of expressions/acts/deeds of strength. Why suppose there is an agent, who is already strong, expressing strength?

One can see why one might want to hold onto the concept of the agent as distinct, if not separable, from the deed. We have significant attachments to this idea. But thinking of oneself as in one's deed like a mother is in the child has the effect of transforming our attachment: it at once creates some distance (distinct from identification) and affirms a sort of genetic continuity. Mothers and their children are not related by virtue of the mothers' intentions. For one's children, one has *hopes* but not intentions—one has a longing, desiring *for*, a wanting something for the child, and this can succeed or fail, it can turn out well or not. Guided by the image in this analogy, we could still formulate assessment criteria. Yet, in such cases, our focus of attention, our discrimination of what is most relevant, might shift. If retribution and reward were no longer primary objects of moral concern, the problems of responsibility and accountability that drive much discussion in the secondary literature on Nietzsche's alternative to morality in the narrow sense might more or less dissolve, or at least they would be refocused. Nietzsche anticipates this in his discussion of punishment in *GM*, particularly in *GM* II:10, where he imagines a society strong enough that it does not need to punish:

> It is not unthinkable that a society might attain such a *consciousness of power* [Machtbewusstsein] that it could allow itself the noblest luxury

possible to it—letting those who harm it go *unpunished* [ihren Schädiger straflos zu lassen]. "What are parasites to me?" it might say. "May they live and prosper: I am strong enough for that!" The justice that began with, "everything is dischargeable [Alles ist abzahlbar], everything must be discharged," ends by winking and letting those incapable of discharging their debt go free: it ends, as does every good thing on earth, by *overcoming itself* [sich selbst aufhebend]. This self-overcoming of justice [Selbstaufhebung der Gerechtigkeit]: one knows the beautiful name it has given itself—*mercy* [Gnade]; it goes without saying that mercy remains the privilege of the most powerful man [das Vorrecht des Mächtigsten], or better, his—beyond the law [sein Jenseits des Rechts].⁵³

The self-overcoming of justice Nietzsche envisions here is not an embrace of lawlessness or anarchy. His playful use of *Recht* and the difference between being *vor*—suggesting *before*, a sense of *prior to*—and *Jenseits*—beyond, above and beyond—make it clear that he anticipates that the merciful society would have a different relation to the law. How it thinks about itself and what it needs from the law would be different from the views of the society that *needs* to punish, to discharge debts. This is an economy of value organized in terms of abundance rather than scarcity, and in this respect it resembles the circulation of value described in the section on Pindar in chapter 1. The development of such a society would represent the overcoming of Christian morality, which originated in Saul's inability to reconcile himself to the law, which is why he sought its destruction. Overcoming Pauline Christian morality for Nietzsche entails neither reinstating the law Saint Paul annihilated for the price of taking on crushing, undischargable, irremediable debt in the form of guilt. The remedy Nietzsche envisions addresses the felt *need* for such an economy, and he anticipates the realization of a form of creative power that would transform our sense of ourselves, our prerogatives, and what we expect of each other.

We can outline how a sense of creative power akin to the creation of life that mothering entails might well attend a revised conception of agency *available* in the lightning-flash passage as well as the one Pippin himself flags from *Also Sprach Zarathustra*. In such a case, little might be gained by sustaining attachment to a distinct doer (rather than attending to *doing*), regardless of whether it is *behind* or *in* the deed; preserving such attachment might well be indicative of our abiding attachment to morality, which Nietzsche aims to loosen. Souls, in the sense relevant to Nietzsche's experiment described in the preceding chapter, express their constitutive relations; their possibilities for expression are related to the kinds of organizations they are, much as meteorological expressions issue from the complex sets of conditions that temporarily organize when lightning is expressed. The difference between lightning and human action, then, turns on the kinds of organizations they are, not a genetic difference in their kinds of *expression*.

As to how subjects are *in* expressions, Pippin offers "the inseparability thesis": the subject, while not identical to its expression, is nevertheless inseparable from it.[54] This certainly seems to follow analytically from our use of the term he selects to describe the deed—how could one have expression without *something* expressing? Pippin grants that even the lightning flash is an expression (of a certain meteorological event) and that it does not need anything more *in* the event. What leads him to suppose that the case is otherwise in human action is that he wants to distinguish acts from events. But there is nothing in the passage cited that suggests this concerns *Nietzsche*. (The concern might be *ours*, I have suggested, because *we* might want a more robust notion of morally relevant agency and appraisal, which I address at further length in the next chapter.) Additionally, we can question whether we can conclude from the fact that we can achieve *conceptual* separation between doer and deed that such a distinction is real to the extent that the extension of responsibility should apply. Pippin expresses the concern this way: "Should not Nietzsche be aware that, by eliminating as nonsensical the idea that appears to be a necessary condition for a deed being a deed [as opposed to a *mere* event]—a subject's individual causal responsibility for the deed occurring—he has eliminated any way of properly understanding the notion of *responsibility*, or that he has eliminated even a place for criticism of an agent?"[55] If *causal* responsibility is not the only way in which one can be responsible, *or* if our ways of valuing actions and persons somehow shifted such that *responsibility* was somehow less significant in our deliberations and estimations, then it might not be so bad if it should happen to be that, in fact, Nietzsche is fully aware that causal and moral responsibility would be undermined by his depiction, and that is at least part of his point (as *BGE* 32 suggests). These are two distinct alternatives, and we should explore and consider how he could plausibly hold either such view. (There is at least a third alternative: Nietzsche could be offering us a view that undermines responsibility in a sense that we might want to retain. Assuming we have other reasons for retaining it, we should reject his views on these grounds, rather than finding ways to accommodate ourselves within his position.)

That causal responsibility is not the only form of responsibility is clear from the mother-child image. Whereas causal responsibility (particularly for the purposes of accountability and the attribution of praise and blame) looks back to the past, a mother's sense of responsibility for her child is nearly entirely future oriented (setting aside tantrums in public places, boasting one does among family and friends, and the shame and regret one might suffer when one's child does some monumental harm to others). In other words, the abiding sense of responsibility that a mother has for a child primarily and for the most part stems not from the fact that she caused the child in contributing genetic material and giving birth or in providing the material and cultural conditions that nurture and sustain the child, but from a form of love (and terror) that is given shape in the promise for the future of that child and his or her ultimate independence. It is in caring for the future of the child that a mother's (any parent's) sense of responsibility is typically and for the most part motivated. This is not to say that causal responsibility is wholly alien to how we think about parental responsibility, as the exceptional cases attest, and we have such a sense of responsibility written into laws, particularly those that pertain to obligations and expectations for providing for the material needs and physical welfare of the child. What is important to note is that another sense of responsibility (the one not linked with causality and not codified in law) motivates both the mundane and the extraordinary acts and sacrifices parents make for their children; it is driven by love, affective attachment to the child, not causal responsibility.

Even if it should be the case that causal responsibility is the primary form of responsibility relevant for moral evaluation, it need not be the exclusive consideration. It seems possible to imagine, and Pippin's discussions elsewhere of what would follow from such alternative conceptions of the relation between oneself and one's deed provide some specific suggestions. If we were drawn toward different goals, organized ourselves in different terms, acquired reordered priorities, and thought of ourselves differently, it seems entirely possible that we might not be so concerned with fixing responsibility and critiquing others or even ourselves in the terms of intentional morality.[56] An alternative view of agency could make a dramatic difference. Pippin envisions this along with Nietzsche in an earlier analysis of the lightning-flash passage and surrounding text in which he emphasizes precisely the *lack* of causal responsibility (or at least its diffusion): "The central assumption in this contrasting picture is strength or a strong character expressing itself in (*sich aüssern*) an action, rather than some intention or motive causing the deed." Giving "an account of oneself" as a form of responsibility would still be possible and might entail the very hard, sobering work of articulating that "within which you 'got to be you'" without relying on a story that highlights one's own (self-)causal responsibility.[57] The future philosophers conjured in *BGE* 210 are still able to give an account of themselves concerning that and how they express what they do (and in such a respect refer back to what they have done), but such accounting need not focus on themselves as causal agents (rather than organizations with a variety of expressive possibilities or capacities for expression). And this would significantly change our perspective on ourselves with respect to responsibility and regret. When something goes awry, rather than feeling "'I ought not to have done that'" (*GM* II:15), we face "disappointment that I was not who I thought I was[;] sadness at what was expressed 'in' the deed, replaces guilt or the sort of guilt that depends on the claim that I could have done otherwise," as Pippin writes.[58] Nietzsche's movement away from a sense of responsibility linked with recompense and toward one defined in terms of capabilities and domains of activity is relevant to an alternative account of justice, one whose terms are potentially "beyond good and evil." I regard this distinction between different forms of responsibility to be crucial to understanding possibilities that Nietzsche attempts to introduce to his readers and relevant to different economies of power, which are at stake in Nietzsche's agon with Paul.

Nietzsche might motivate us to reconsider why an attachment to causal responsibility is so important to preserve and retain. We might wonder whether such a sense of ourselves stems from attachment to a fundamentally *moral* concept such that we would have to have a new conception of agency in the overcoming of morality. None of this is to say that Nietzsche obliterates the possibility of any picture of agency, that he "leaps into the abyss" of "existential, groundless choices,"[59] but this need not—as both Nietzsche and Pippin have shown—depend on a sense of causal responsibility as its primary characteristic or implication. I think Pippin's sense of expressivist agency might be compatible with Nietzsche's experimental soul hypothesis, as described in the preceding chapter, and his view that beyond morality in the narrow sense the decisive value of an action would not be linked with intent. If we shifted concern *away* from intention, self-consciousness, and responsibility and moved *toward* a conception of agency that emphasizes that we are what we do, then *who* we are would not be somehow separate from what we have done. There would be no existential gap, although there obviously would be a conceptual one, between who we are and what we do. At every moment, we sum up our lives in terms of what we are by virtue of what we do; we *are not* that which we have not done but wish we had.

What the story of the sovereign individual from *GM* II:2 helps Nietzsche's readers appreciate, once we acknowledge its connection with the developmental process I have called the *memory project*, is a relation of desire and human ends—in short, it focuses attention on exploring a theory of action and future possibilities, which is precisely what Zarathustra anticipates at the end of *GM* II. Nietzsche's anticipated overcoming of the image of humanity consolidated in Paul's invention of Christian morality is an overcoming of the model of self-conception and -relation built on a basis of torture and cruelty. Nietzsche's replacement seeks to render obsolete the Socratic and Christian models that reengineered the agonistic form of Homer. In this respect, replacement of the ideal of the sovereign subject not only signals a kind of liberation from a potentially harmful and destructive project (motivated by *Vernichtungslust*, eliminating parts of oneself) but also potentially makes it possible for us to relate to ourselves and others in a different way. This is what is at stake in Nietzsche's pursuit of the realization of agonized subjectivity: a new conception of ourselves would transform our moral concepts affecting the orientation of our goals and means of achieving them. Thus, his agonism is not limited to various kinds of mind games but rather gives shape to matters of common concern and the prospect for a shared future. How such agents become what they are is a subject Nietzsche repeatedly takes up, and this animates his lifelong struggle with Wagner and his understanding of how that struggle informed who he was.

CHAPTER FIVE

Contesting Wagner:
How One Becomes What One Is

Nietzsche's contest with Paul pushes him not only to articulate precisely what he finds problematic with the form of life Pauline Christianity cultivates but also to develop his own positive alternative. I have argued that Nietzsche's reflections on the agon bring forward important features of both his critical and his constructive projects, but significant questions and concerns linger, particularly about his alternatives. In the preceding chapter, I sketched dimensions of a possible positive project from a somewhat cryptic angle insofar as they are evident in scattered remarks related to action and agency. I suggested such views might possibly be compatible with some core concerns in moral psychology, including possible bases for responsibility; this chapter explores such prospects in greater detail. Specifically, it is possible to provide a more elaborate account of the organization of forces linked with Nietzsche's alternative soul hypothesis. How such organizations come about and are maintained bears on contemporary debates about his conception of freedom. Finally, it remains a question as to just how central and thoroughgoing his agonism is. I have argued that Nietzsche considers the agon to be immensely productive for organizing both cultures and individuals and for mediating the relations between individuals and the broader society. But these ideas and some conclusions I will draw from them are in tension with certain other concerns that seem especially important to Nietzsche and (perhaps even more so to) his readers. This is particularly evident in his account of himself, his own becoming, in which he highlights both his "practice of war" and what he presents as a complete lack of struggle.

Moreover, it might seem that Nietzsche's self-imposed imperative to re-deem or revalue existence on the basis of *love* might stand at odds with the aggressive hostility implied in war-making. At the risk of taming the agon, I have sought to indirectly alleviate this tension by highlighting the many ways in which productive agonism is a distinctive form of stylized struggle and is distinguished from its violent relatives much as the twin Eris goddesses are. But this alone does not dissolve the problem: if Nietzsche truly thought struggle was vital for development (or crucial for a form of *vitality*), then why, in his presentation of himself as well turned out ("clever," "wise," a writer of "good books," "a destiny"), does he claim that *he never struggled*? What does he mean by this, and why does he emphasize it? I think we find significant clues relevant to each of these concerns in his later writings, particularly in his reflections on his relationship with Wagner and his own effort to become himself *through* struggle with him.

It is not an overstatement to claim that Wagner influenced Nietzsche from the beginning to the very end of his career, and he appears by name or in the guise of a "type" in each and every work he wrote. While Nietzsche is immensely interested in the lives and works of other persons he thinks are greatly important (for better and for worse)—such as Homer, Socrates, Paul, Goethe, Beethoven, and Napoléon, to name just a few—only Wagner is ana-lyzed in such detail in terms of his development.[1] Wagner becomes increas-ingly important to Nietzsche after his death, at which time Nietzsche both writes his harshest criticisms of and professes his deepest affection for Wag-ner. In *Ecce Homo*, against the backdrop of the earlier account of Wagner's exemplary evolution, he depicts his own development in terms of a tense op-position between fighting and loving, which he respectively links to his wis-dom and his cleverness.

Nietzsche's reflections on his own becoming also advance some puzzling ideas he has about the human constitution and its possibilities, specifically, how relations among drives emerge, organize, and are sustained. As he dis-penses guidance or insight into "how one becomes what one is,"[2] he consid-ers it in relation to accounts (both early and late) he provides of Wagner's becoming. His wrestling with Wagner—his significance, legacy, *type*—reflects his efforts not only to understand but also to orient and effect himself. In his agon with Wagner, Nietzsche became Nietzsche, and he did so not simply as his rival (as with Homer and perhaps Socrates) or his opposite (as with Paul). His virtually lifelong quest to account for (and manipulate) Wagner's type ultimately leads him to consider his agonism in the context of a dynamic of love and hate that coordinates the various drives that constitute him. Consideration of how this is so allows us to further explore Nietzsche's conception of persons as organizations that evince orders of rank among their constitutive parts, characterized by various ruling orders.

5.1 BECOMING WHAT ONE IS

Nietzsche's allusion to Pindar in the subtitle to *Ecce Homo* raises a host of questions. In the form it appears there—"Wie man wird, was man ist"—no paradox need be evident: we could expect that the book might have kinship with bildungsroman literature, providing us with that sort of account of Nietzsche's maturation. But, as Nietzsche uses the expression in the text and elsewhere in his writings, as, for example, in *Die fröhliche Wissenschaft*, it becomes less clear what he intends. About himself and kindred spirits, he writes: "We want to become those we are" (*GS* 335). And in *GS* 270 we find an imperative: "you should become the one you are." Zarathustra, we are told, "once counseled himself, not for nothing, 'Become who you are'" (*Z* IV "The Honey Sacrifice"). It is unclear how we could *become* what we *already* are in any ordinary sense of those terms. Perhaps Nietzsche refers simply to what we (already) have the *potential* to become but have yet to realize or make manifest.[3] If we already *are* such selves, then it is difficult to see how we could *want* to become them, at least if wants follow from lack or need. Moreover, if we already *are* such selves, it is unclear how it could possibly be that things could turn out otherwise, that is, that we might *become* in any other way. Moreover, Nietzsche's curious imperative seems in tension with other ideas he holds, including the notion of self as subjective multiplicity and the repeated prioritizing of *becoming* over being.

To gain insight into what it means to become what one is and why and how it is necessary, we can consider an earlier account of the same that Nietzsche provides. Published nearly two decades prior, its subject was Wagner rather than Nietzsche.[4] In *Richard Wagner in Bayreuth*, Nietzsche endeavors to account for Wagner's development, his evolution: "wie er wurde, was er ist, was er sein wird" (*RWB* 1).[5] He depicts Wagner's "powerful striving" (*RWB* 2), his great struggles to identify his life's task and reconcile multiple parts of himself that were in tension (*RWB* 8). It seems clear that, on Nietzsche's account, Wagner's struggle with and against himself is a significant part of what Nietzsche thinks constitutes his achievement and serves as an indication of his greatness; it is largely what Nietzsche discusses and what he ultimately praises in his early work. Here, Wagner is depicted as a spiritual hero of sorts, one whose struggles might be exemplary. As we shall see, a curious feature of Nietzsche's ultimate account of his own development will be that *he* is *not* heroic in the way in which he depicts Wagner. Although he describes his own development similarly in terms of unifying multiple, opposing drives, his ultimate view focuses more on the process than on the ends.[6]

In his earlier work, Nietzsche sums up the story of Wagner's development as follows: "The struggles that [his life's story] depicts are simplifications of the real struggles of life; its problems are abbreviations of the endlessly complicated reckoning of human action and aspiration" (*RWB* 4). This gap between aspiration and action and the necessary adjustment of aspiration to achieve reconciliation mark an interesting contrast between his account of Wagner's development and the story he later tells himself about himself (*EH* interleaf). His own story has at least two features distinguishing it from Wagner's: he claims he "never struggled," as previously mentioned, and, in contrast to Wagner's development, which was organized around his various ideas about cultural revolution and himself as its instigator, *becoming* (*Werden*) of the sort Nietzsche finds interesting requires that one *not have the slightest idea what one is*. This opens a complicated set of concerns about how Nietzsche thinks about what constitutes becoming and how one goes about it or how it occurs. It is also relevant to a significant disagreement in the scholarly literature as to whether he is a fatalist or an advocate of self-creation.[7] Examining his later account of himself, particularly in light of his agon with Wagner, we find crucial clues about what Nietzsche has in mind, for becoming what one is appears to turn, at least in part, on *making oneself necessary*. Becoming what one is involves becoming "not just a piece of chance but rather a necessity" (*EH* "Why I Am So Clever" 8). This is precisely what, according to the youthful Nietzsche, Wagner is supposed to have done in his heroic struggles (*RWB* 6), and in this respect he is exemplary. But, by the time Nietzsche writes *Ecce Homo*, he sees himself as quite different from the man he clearly loved and admired, perhaps above all others (*EH* "Why I Am So Wise" 3, "Why I Am So Clever" 5), even as he remained his harshest critic (e.g., *The Case of Wagner*). In understanding how his self-presentation of his own development differs from his presentation of Wagner, we also catch a glimpse of how Nietzsche endeavors, as he puts it, to become "powerful *through* Wagner *against* Wagner" (*RWB* 7). But, before considering his ultimate presentation of himself, I consider how he characterizes both what he saw as real promise in the appearance of Wagner and the problems Wagner illuminated.

5.2 THE PROMISE AND PROBLEM OF WAGNER

Among Nietzsche's extensive discussions of Wagner are the very familiar account in *Die Geburt der Tragödie* and the less frequently examined treatment in the penultimate chapter of *Jenseits von Gut und Böse*, "On Peoples and Fatherlands."[8] Part of what Nietzsche struggles with in the latter text is the problem of modern taste and the need and challenge of synthesizing without destroying the many that "want to become one." The feat requires harnessing productive cultural resources from the rich diversity of European cultures to create a stronger, more resourceful, more resilient *new* form of human organization, which is more specifically anticipated in the final part of the book and inquires into the possibility of a new nobility.[9]

Nietzsche sees Wagner drawing on an immense wealth of resources, a great variety of possible tastes and expressive capabilities. Moreover, in his efforts to create the artwork of the future, Wagner engaged (though ultimately failed to resolve) the very problem Nietzsche thinks moderns, particularly, face: he attempted to draw on the collective forces of the arts and organize them into a significant whole.[10] Appreciating the nature of this challenge and its possibilities requires us to draw on several other important discussions of Wagner. That Nietzsche had difficulty understanding his problem of Wagner, why and how Wagner failed to deliver, and why it matters *that* he failed are evident in Nietzsche's relentless efforts to articulate and reframe the problem in his later writings, each of which has significant sections devoted to Wagner and his type.

In the second half of *Die Geburt der Tragödie*, Nietzsche extends the hope that Wagner's operas might achieve for modern Europeans what tragedy did for the ancient Greeks, which he regarded not merely as a *product* of a culture already vibrant, as we have seen, but rather as a vehicle for *producing* culture. He considered the ancient Greeks *as becoming Greeks*—as *becoming what they are*—in and through their creation of and participation in the tragedies. The tragedies were not simply representations of views about the significance of human beings and their relation to the gods; instead, participation in the tragic festivals *forged* those relations. And, ultimately, Nietzsche thought these were maximally affirmative in terms of their judgments of the value of human existence despite all the pain and suffering it entails.

The evidence of this affirmation is a particular taste he thought the tragedies evinced—in short, they expressed a *taste for life* in rendering beautiful (through the tragedy as a whole) what was otherwise unbearable: the senseless sufferings of human beings. Nietzsche conceived this as redemptive—human existence was positively revalued—and in sharp contrast to the moral, particularly Christian, model of redemption that locates the meaning and significance of human existence in relation to a supreme *otherworldly* giver of meaning. *Die Geburt der Tragödie* sought to comprehend the logic of redemption that gave tragedies their culturally formative powers and the relation between those effects and the individuals who experienced them. And, as we have seen, Nietzsche linked this with an agonistic form of engagement and expression. The relation between the opposing tendencies of the Apollinian and the Dionysian is similar but not identical to how he describes the agonistic tension between what he calls the *will to knowledge* and the *will to ignorance* in *Jenseits von Gut und Böse* 230, in which these opposing tendencies *potentially* further each other's ends rather than cancel or overcome them. In *Jenseits von Gut und Böse*, he couches this productive tension in terms analogous to digestion. Were it not for the fact that the will to ignorance "shuts its doors" and "says no," it would not be possible for the will to knowledge to have anything in particular to cling to, to distinguish out of the flow of what is perceived; there could be no proper experience as distinct from this flow. Thus, the will to ignorance has a "pruning effect" on the reaches of the will to knowledge and makes it possible for what is known, appropriated, and synthesized to stand out as something specific—this allows for a genuine unity distinguished from the chaotic multiplicity of which its components were once a part.

In both *Die Geburt der Tragödie* and *Jenseits von Gut und Böse*, we see Nietzsche inquiring into how a multiplicity—of cultural characteristics (French, German, English) or creative possibilities—becomes united and potent rather than dysfunctional. He sees his fellow Germans (and English and French, but particularly his German compatriots) asking the question, *How do we become what we are?* He thinks there are better and worse ways to set about ultimately answering this question and for the most part his contemporaries have failed, quite miserably. Right from the start, he thinks the Germans have failed to understand how such a question is fundamentally oriented toward the *future*. The answer does not lie wholly in past origins; there is no specific and necessary historical destiny: it requires a measure of invention and is not simply a matter of discovery. As invention, it will necessarily be a creative product that requires artistic resources (which might include *making a claim* to a particular destiny as a way of setting a goal) and, just as significantly, a particular sense of taste. Yet the available resources for such becoming are a matter of inheritance. How they become *bound up* in fate, how they realize a kind of destiny, is what is at stake. One way of describing this that Nietzsche sometimes has recourse to is in terms of *style*.[11] Insofar as the question *What is German?*

is about ways of living that follow from shared ideals and goals, conceptions of distinctive and definitive characteristics or types, it is fundamentally a matter of taste; thus, *becoming German* will turn on questions of style. But there is more, for one does not create ex nihilo, and projects of becoming and establishing those distinguishing qualities occur in a variety of ways. From early on, particularly in *Die Geburt der Tragödie*, where he is specifically concerned with the fate of Germany rather than all of Europe, as he is in *Jenseits von Gut und Böse*, Nietzsche is critical of the project of establishing excellence simply on the basis of the achievement of military superiority (e.g., *DS*). Successful demonstration of force alone does not establish *nobility*, and we clearly see him return to this concern when he considers both the cultural resources and the creative (as well as the decadent) inheritances of European peoples. In both these cases, Wagner stands at the center of Nietzsche's questioning of what *makes* a people (how a social and cultural entity is formed, on what basis *one* becomes) and how it possibly becomes great—or, more precisely, how, in its formation, it takes on the goal of pursuing greatness.

In both early and later writings, Wagner represents for Nietzsche great potential as a transitional figure, though he certainly expresses rather different impressions of this prospect early and late; yet it is important to notice that the core challenge remains. In short, Nietzsche thinks Wagner nearly but ultimately failed to achieve a dynamic and productive synthesis harnessing and preserving the variety of human cultural and physiological inheritances. His Wagner exemplifies a mixture characteristic of modern humanity that *nearly* became synthetic and consummatory: "What flavors and forces, what seasons and climes are not mixed here! It strikes us now as archaic, now as strange, tart, and too young, it is just as capricious as it is pompous-traditional, it is not infrequently saucy, still more often coarse and rude." It "has the pride of presupposing two centuries of music as still living, if it is to be understood" (*BGE* 240). Yet his ultimate judgment is that Wagner failed to achieve this synthesis or produce an artwork that would embody such unity. Instead, Wagner remains in his eyes primarily an actor rather than a musician, his artistic effects largely dramatic—Nietzsche thinks the kind of unity his works exhibit is achieved artificially through the technical use of the leitmotiv, resulting in a superficial organization that resolves in a decadent, ultimately pessimistic form of redemption. The latter is particularly problematic because of the deformed conception of love it advances.

We can gain further insight into Nietzsche's problem with Wagner by considering his juxtaposition of Bizet's Carmen and Wagner's Kundry in his later writings, where Nietzsche draws on ideas about sexual agonistics (the ultimate battle of the sexes) and sexual reproduction as paradigmatic of creative fecundity. Carmen's consuming love of life exudes what Nietzsche later calls a "burnt sensibility" [verbrannteren Sensibilität] in language that recalls the end of his *Jenseits von Gut und Böse*. Bizet's *Carmen* expresses "love translated back into nature" [in die Natur zurückübersetzte]: "love as *fatum*, as fatality, cynical, innocent, cruel—and precisely in this a piece of nature. That love which is war in its means, and at the bottom deadly hatred of the sexes!" (*CW* 2).[12] Nietzsche associates this form of passion with "the south" and the "Mediterraneanization" of music that he anticipates in *BGE* 255 and elaborates in *CW* 3.[13] He goes on to contrast this form of passion, which he also associates with a form of elevating pathos needed for philosophy (*CW* 2), with the notion of love as selfless. While love as *fatality* is fecund, love as selflessness is sterile, "chaste." Wagner's Kundry, he writes in *BGE* 47, is a flesh and blood personification of the *type* "das religiöse Wesen." She dies in her moment of redemption, which was accomplished by Parsifal, whose powers stem from the chastity he achieved through renunciation and compassion. What Nietzsche writes of Wagner's heroines generally is doubly true of her: "Wagner's heroines never have children? *They can't.—*" (*CW* 9). Kundry fails to tempt Parsifal even when she lures him with mother's love—she neither gives birth nor succeeds in becoming a surrogate. She becomes free, free as a bird, in fact, only through the redemptive act of Parsifal's compassion, and only in release from human life. We shall see how these ideas about fatality and reproduction animate Nietzsche's account of his own type, his ruminations on how types develop, and his suggestions for an alternative conception of agency.

5.3 NIETZSCHE'S INHERITANCE

Nietzsche begins his self-presentation in *Ecce Homo* with reference to his "fatality" ("Verhängniss"), how his life is bound together in becoming *his*, and he concludes *EH* with a section claiming his title as "a destiny" ("Warum ich ein Schicksal bin"). He uses this as an entry to explore his descent or ancestry ("Herkunft"), which includes what is both "highest and lowest," common and noble. Specifically, he focuses on what he inherited from his parents, his "dual descent"; he describes his life as both ascendant and decadent (*EH* "Why I Am So Wise" 1). This accounts for the fact that he is a "Doppelgänger" (*EH* "Why I Am So Wise" 3).[14] His interest in inheritance includes consideration of acquired resources, capabilities, and capacities and the intensification or diminution of powers, temperament, and inclinations. It includes intellectual, cultural, historical, psychological, and physiological considerations relevant to his reception and criticisms of evolutionary theory as well as his interest in atavism. At the same time that he focuses on the resources and liabilities he inherited from his parents, he diminishes their role in determining him when he writes: "to be related to one's parents is the most typical sign of commonality. Higher types have their origins infinitely further back, on which at long last, an atavism must be unified, retained. Great individuals are the most ancient individuals."[15] This suggests that, as Nietzsche conceives it, a higher type is someone who somehow accesses and taps other, ancient characteristics and is perhaps distinguished by virtue of the depth and reach of ancestral resources. Indeed, this is how Nietzsche describes himself earlier in the same section when he writes: "But as a Pole I am also an uncanny atavism. One must go back centuries to discover in this noblest race of men pure instincts to the degree that I represent them."[16] The same idea is evident in *RWB*, in which he links Wagner with Alexander, much as he suggests in *EH* that "Julius Caesar could be my father—*or* Alexander, that Dionysus incarnate" (*EH* "Why I Am So Wise" 3). This inheritance provides him with a vast multiplicity of perspectives (*EH* "Why I Am So Wise" 1), resources that *could* be utilized; it does not simply *make* him great. What distinguishes the "well-turned-out person" is this: "He instinctively gathers *his* totality from everything he sees, hears, experiences: he is a principle of selection [Er sammelt instinktiv aus Allem, was er sieht, hört, erlebt, s e i n e Summe: er ist ein auswählendes Princip, er lässt Viel durchfallen]" (*EH* "Why I Am So Wise" 2).[17] We might consider just what this multiplicity is and how it becomes something that approximates something singular, something capable of being choosy in the way he describes someone who is, as he puts it, "basically healthy" (*EH* "Why I Am So Wise" 2); and we need to know more about what serves as the "principle of selection" in order to understand how there is some abiding principle at work holding together this manifold. It is not just sheer multiplicity that makes a person rich on his account. Having certain kinds of resources, particularly those that characterize opposing tendencies so that the strength of their opposition might itself become a resource, seems to be important. His notion of subjective multiplicity includes distinctions of *orders of rank* and *orders of rule*, and those ideas can help us appreciate how he thinks his various parts organized to make possible the productive life he presents.

5.4 ORDERS OF RANK, TYPES, AND RULING THOUGHTS

As we have seen, Nietzsche repeatedly advances the view that individuals are composites or conglomerates of multiple, competing drives, affects, and thoughts. These parts become organized, on his view, in terms of "orders of rank." He discusses at length several types of such orders, including the types of the "master," the "slave," and the "priest."[18] The "last man" might also be thought a type, and the *Übermensch* could be construed as an as-yet-unachieved type (human, transhuman, or more than human). We can consider types as distinguished by the general orders of rank constituting them. What are ranked, as Nietzsche considers such cases, are "drives" (*Triebe*), and the rank ordering reflects the *relations* of the drives: which predominate, which serve the others, etc.

Orders of rank *characterize* individual human beings (*BGE* 6), on his hypothesis, such that Nietzsche thinks who or what one is, strictly speaking, is this collection of drives in the particular order or relation they are in. Because there is no self either *behind* the ordering or *doing* the ordering (*GM* I:13), the distinguishing character of what one is lies in the order, or perhaps put another way the order expressed in action. But, if this is what human beings are, then it is hard to see how there can be anyone to appeal to in Nietzsche's Pindaric imperative to "become who you are": there should be *no one there* to answer a call to action, if indeed that is what Nietzsche's imperative is. I have already suggested there is another way to make sense of Nietzsche's insistence that there is nothing to *us* other than the competing drives of which we are constituted while he repeatedly appeals to some sense of agency. We can gain even further insight by examining his accounts of how such drives are organized because he thinks we are not merely a collection, group, or bundle of drives but drives *organized in a certain way*, characterized by a political arrangement, and that such arrangements can change and take on different characteristics.

Steven D. Hales and Rex Welshon offer an account of what they call Nietzsche's bundle theory of both objects and selves in which they claim that Nietzsche's views are similar to those found in such diverse sources as Buddhism, the moral psychology of Amelie Rorty, and views on selfhood advanced by Derek Parfit. They also emphasize and document his "organizational" model and highlight the problem of unification, claiming that types are distinguished on the basis of the type of drive that dominates (e.g. [though these are generic], there is an aesthetic drive, a scientific drive, etc.).[19] Moreover, they discuss Nietzsche's strategies for disciplining drives, which they argue "does *not* entail a subject distinct from the drives because the task the subject is supposed to perform is shouldered by each and every drive or set of drives that go into composing the self." They also highlight a feature discussed at greater length by Richardson, namely, that there are first-order and second-order drives in which "every drive attempts to dominate all others and [. . .] some drives take as their object other drives or sets of them rather than an external object."[20]

Orders of rank can be examined from at least two related perspectives: in terms of the specific order, hierarchy, or relative rankings of the drives and in terms of the way in which ruling or dominant drives relate to other drives. That is, such orders have a political character, and this allows us to consider *what* rules, *how* it rules, and how it *came to rule*. Indeed, in virtually all his writings, we find Nietzsche exploring the nature and further implications of a conception of soul that follows from a notion of a "social structure of the drives and affects" (*BGE* 12).[21] I argue below that types are distinguished on the basis of the prevailing form or order of rule of the whole rather than the particularities of any ruling drive(s); moreover, I think Nietzsche's explorations of the very different ways in which power can be expressed, as evident in his analyses of the agon and its deformations, show that domination is not the only form of power drives might seek, or at least that domination can take a variety of forms, not all of which are necessarily exploitative. Compare, for example, the great difference between the domination of Homer and that of Paul as Nietzsche characterizes such in his agones with them. He speculates, like Plato, that there is an isomorphism between forms of social, cultural, and political power and the organizations that constitute the "household of the soul." This comparison has been observed by others who generally claim that, like Plato's Socrates, Nietzsche prefers the aristocratic (or sometimes the tyrannical or even the democratic) form of organization on the grounds that it is the most effective form of psychic power. In this book, I have tried to make the case that he thinks agonistic economies of power are particularly effective for coordinating and organizing various elements because they potentially produce values and provide imminent occasions for the development and exercise of judgment and such activities potentially orient organizations toward productive ends.

What philosophers have designated as *will* is (minimally), for Nietzsche, a complicated and multidimensional process of interacting sensations, thoughts, and affects (*BGE* 19) that includes awareness of various states ("away from which," "toward which," and "from" and "toward" more generally), thinking ("a ruling thought"), and affect (particularly "the affect of the command" insofar as "a man who *wills* commands something within himself that renders obedience, or that he believes renders obedience"). Another way of accounting for *willing* as Nietzsche depicts it is as shorthand for the *processes of or-*

ganization of an entity: what it senses as significant, its orientation, and the structure of ordering it achieves (*BGE* 19).

Nietzsche thinks suppositions about the status of human freedom more generally are unwarranted on the basis of this experience because what is perceived here is not so much the condition of the whole organism in the world (an individual *agent* of activity) as an aspect or dimension of the interactions of the organism itself: "'Freedom of the will'—that is the expression for the complex state of delight of the person exercising volition, who commands and at the same time identifies himself with the executor of the order—who, as such enjoys also the triumph over obstacles, but thinks within himself that it was really his will itself that overcame them" (*BGE* 19).[22] Yet we neither simply nor solely command or obey. Willing is complex. We experience ourselves as individual, atomic willing agents when actually we are a composite structure of wills and "under-wills," which is another way of speaking of drives seeking to master other drives: "we are at the same time the commanding *and* the obeying parties, and as the obeying party we know the sensations of constraint, impulsion, pressure, resistance, and motion. [. . .] *we are accustomed to disregard this duality, and to deceive ourselves about it by means of the synthetic concept 'I'*" (*BGE* 19; emphasis added). Thus, our best evidence of our freedom—the felt perception of freedom, our sense of ourselves as agents—is indexed not to our metaphysical or ontological status but rather to the perception of one aspect of a complex process of organization: "our body is but a social structure composed of many souls" in which some obey and others command (*BGE* 19).[23] These structures of *orders of rank* and their discernible patterns are one significant, but not exhaustive, aspect of what might be regarded as Nietzsche's interest in types.

What constitutes a *type* in the sense discussed here is not only the particular drives that make up the social structure distinguishing an individual but also *how* those drives are ordered and how their organization develops and is maintained. There is a dynamic relation, a form of rule that achieves and preserves that arrangement or ordering of drives. For example, strictly speaking, the master and the slave in *Zur Genealogie der Moral* reflect *different ways of ruling* and not simply different types of people. What Leiter calls *type facts*[24] do not themselves *determine* what one does; rather, type facts are descriptions, *determinations* of the rank order of drives. Leiter's type facts might be better understood as statements about conditions of a rank ordering (rather than particular features of such an ordering). Each individual is a myriad of type facts, which are perhaps innumerable. They are fixed or determined insofar as they are *in relation to* the order of rank one is, but not necessarily fixed or determined for the entire duration of the life of the organism. Such orderings are the result of the abiding organization and order of rule: type facts themselves do not determine but rather are themselves *determinations* of this ordering.

Orders of rank are neither absolutely fixed nor absolutely determined, and this is precisely what worries Nietzsche. Drives appear to be there from the start, and they seem to be inherited and shaped historically. These can vary among different people and constitutions. Constitutive elements and inheritances might be fixed, but their relative strengths and orderings are not. How, then, do they acquire their ordering? Nietzsche's account of himself as both a lover and a fighter offers some indications of how ordering occurs and how in the process (and in some cases) one becomes what one is by becoming a "necessity" rather than "a piece of chance" (*EH* "Why I Am So Clever" 8).

5.5 NIETZSCHE AS A LOVER: SELFISHNESS VERSUS SELFLESSNESS

In the chapter of *Ecce Homo* titled "Why I Am So Clever," Nietzsche, finally, directly provides "the real answer to the question, *how one becomes what one is*": it entails what he calls "the masterpiece of the art of self-preservation [Selbsterhaltung] or *selfishness* [S e l b s t s u c h t]." But his account raises more questions than it answers because it does not include deliberate, conscious, active creation in the way in which self-creation might be thought to require: "to become what one is," "one must not have the faintest notion *what* one is." How can we become what we are if we do not even know what that is, if we *have not the faintest notion* what that is? This clearly seems to support the fatalist interpretation that we simply become what we *already* are—there is no conscious *planning* or *creating* at work, and, thus, there can be no imperative to action of self-creation, no special *kudos* to accrue if and when one happens to turn out well.[25] There is, according to Nietzsche, an "organizing idea" that is "destined to rule," one that "keeps growing deep down—it begins to command; slowly it leads us *back* from side roads and wrong roads; it prepares *single* qualities and fitnesses that will one day prove to be indispensable as means toward a whole—one by one, it trains all *subservient* capacities before giving any hint of the dominant task, 'goal,' 'aim,' or 'meaning' [Inzwischen wächst und wächst die organisirende, die zur Herrschaft berufne 'Idee' in der Tiefe,—sie beginnt zu befehlen, sie leitet langsam aus Nebenwegen und Abwegen z u r ü c k, sie bereitet e i n z e l n e Qualitäten und Tüchtigkeiten vor, die einmal als Mittel zum Ganzen sich unentbehrlich erweisen werden,—sie bildet der Reihe nach alle d i e n e n d e n Vermögen aus, bevor sie irgend Etwas von der dominirenden Aufgabe, von 'Ziel,' 'Zweck,' 'Sinn' verlauten lässt]" (*EH* "Why I Am So Clever" 9).

One way of understanding what is meant by *destined* here is to see it in light of Nietzsche's proposition of will to power (*BGE* 36), which supposes that all things seek the full expression of their capacities, the full measure of their powers. In this sense, what is destined to rule is simply whatever proves strongest, whatever succeeds in enabling the multifarious drives to be effectively coordinated in a single entity. There is no separate faculty of will in itself that stands independent of the drives that constitute us, no independent will that adjudicates the inevitable conflict and contest of drives we are such that it could be said to be within our power to have things turn out otherwise. *Destined*, then, in this sense does not mean "predetermined," that is, decided already in advance of our becoming the particular organization of drives we are; nor does it necessarily mean that things are fixed and must always remain exactly the same. Thus, in the particular instance in question, *destined* is a loose way of speaking about eventual outcomes and does not refer to any particular outcome that necessarily should come to pass (other than the general idea that what is strongest determines the order of the others since that is just how strength is expressed).

But Nietzsche invokes stronger senses of destiny elsewhere in his writings, including in *Also Sprach Zarathustra*, which he makes so central to his presentation in recounting of his life. In that context and others, he makes reference to *fate* and links his philosophical practice and axiological project of revaluation with *loving fate, amor fati*.[26] In *Ecce Homo*, Nietzsche writes: "My formula for greatness in a human being is *amor fati*: that one wants nothing to be different, not forward, not backward, not in all eternity. Not merely bear what is necessary, still less conceal it—all idealism is mendaciousness in the face of what is necessary—but *love* it . . ." (*EH* "Why I Am So Clever" 10).[27] This idea that is so important to him receives a variety of treatments in the scholarly literature, but I wish to focus here on just one sense of love as a form of care, which complements the general consensus in the scholarly literature that *amor fati* entails a certain kind of affirmation. In this case, *love* and *fate* are united in his conception of selfishness, which, as noted above, Nietzsche explicitly links with self-conservation (*Selbsterhaltung*)[28] and its role in his own development. As we shall see, he also characterizes his selfishness in terms of self-cultivation (in *EH* "Why I Am So Clever" 9 and *EH* "Untimely Meditations" 1, he plays on the relation between *Selbstsucht* and *Selbstzucht*) and self-restoration (see "Selbst-Wiederherstellung" in *EH* "Why I Am So Wise" 2). This way of describing his selfishness, I argue below, is consistent with his anticipation of an alternative to the conception of self as the locus of intentional willing evident in Christian morality and the reformulated sense of responsibility that might follow its overcoming. Love has a binding rather than a dividing effect, yet we shall later see that love and war (as he sometimes characterizes it) might not be as distant as we might presuppose. To clarify the relation in Nietzsche's view, we can return to comparison of his account of his own becoming with that of Wagner.

A major point of difference between Nietzsche's earlier account of Wagner's development and his own later self-presentation of the type he *is* is found in his account of his own selfishness, or self-seeking: *Selbstsucht*.[29] Rather than engaging in heroic struggles, as he describes Wagner early on, Nietzsche claims he was particularly adept at self-preservation (*Selbsterhaltung*), in the sense of "selfishness" or "self-seeking" rather than simply "self-perpetuation." This is the ruling thought he proposes in *Ecce Homo* as an alternative to the ruling thought of morality and the ruling thought of Wagner, whom he saw as advocating *selflessness*. Later, Nietzsche repeatedly expresses the view that hostility toward *Selbstsucht* leads to decadence, declining life: "The best is lacking when self-interest [Selbstsucht] begins to be lacking. Instinctively to choose what is harmful for *oneself*, to feel attracted by 'disinterested' ['uninteressirte'] motives, that is virtually the formula for decadence [décadence]." "'I no longer know how to *find* my own advantage.' Disgregation of the instincts! Man is finished when he becomes altruistic [Disgregation der Instinkte!—Es ist zu Ende mit ihm, wenn der Mensch altruistisch wird]" (*TI* "Skirmishes of an Untimely Man" 35).[30] In *Richard Wagner in Bayreuth*, Nietzsche depicts Wagner as seeking *fidelity* (*Treue*) above all else. This loyalty was directed toward both the multitude (to be united as a "people" [*RWB* 8]) and the multiple and opposing parts of himself. It regards unity as a higher value than any individual needs or desires.

The objections to morality in the narrow sense include its promotion of selflessness, which Nietzsche thinks is ultimately life denying and a symptom of decadence.[31] He attacks the general idea repeatedly, as when he expresses his suspicions against the "so-called 'selfless' drives ['selbstlosen' Triebe]": "It always seems a weakness to me, a particular case of being incapable of resisting stimuli [Widerstands-Unfähigkeit gegen Reize]: *pity* [Mitleiden] is considered a virtue only among decadents [...] and sometimes pitying hands can interfere in a downright destructive manner in a great destiny [Schicksal]" (*EH* "Why I Am So Wise" 4).[32] But, in his presentation of Wagner's evolution in *RWB*, the realization of selflessness marks the pinnacle of his development:

> we sense how the man Wagner evolved: [. . .] how the whole current of the man plunged into first one valley, then another, how it plummeted down the darkest ravines. Then, in the night of this half-subterranean frenzy, high overhead appeared a star of melancholy luster. As soon as he saw it, he named it *Fidelity, selfless Fidelity!* [Treue, selbstlose Treue!] [. . .] Investing it with the utmost splendor he possesses and can realize—that marvelous knowledge and experience by which one sphere of his being remained faithful to another. Through free, utterly selfless love, it preserved fidelity. The creative sphere, luminous and innocent, remained faithful to the dark, indomitable, and tyrannical sphere [aus freier selbstlosester Liebe Treue wahrte, die schöpferische schuldlose lichtere Sphäre, der dunkelen, unbändigen und tyrannischen]. (*RWB* 2)

This is echoed later when he writes: "For Wagner himself the event is a dark cloud of toil, worry, brooding, and grief; a renewed outbreak of conflicting elements [feindseligen Elemente], but all irradiated by the star of *selfless fidelity* [selbstlosen Treue] and, in this light, transformed into unspeakable joy" (*RWB* 8). The kind of love he praises in his early text on Wagner is one that involves completely relinquishing oneself (*Selbstentäusserung*) (*RWB* 7). In the "soul of the dithyrambic dramatist" (which Nietzsche claims for Wagner in *RWB* and then for himself in *EH*), "the creative moments of his art" occur

> when this conflict of feelings is taut, when his gloomy arrogance and horrified distaste for the world fuse with his passionate urgency to approach the world as a lover. When he now casts his eyes on earth and life, his eyes are like the rays of the sun which "draw up the water," collect mist, and accumulate towering thunderheads. *Cautiously lucid and selflessly loving* at the same time, his gazing eyes touch earth, and everything illuminated by this binocular vision is compelled by Nature with frightful rapidity to discharge all its powers, and to reveal its most hidden secrets. (*RWB* 7)

> wenn er in diese Kreuzung der Empfindungen gespannt ist, und sich jene unheimlich-übermüthige Befremdung und Verwunderung über die Welt mit dem sehnsüchtigen Drange paart, derselben Welt als Liebender zu

nahen. Was er dann auch für Blicke auf Erde und Leben wirft, es sind immer Sonnenstrahlen, die "Wasser ziehen," Nebel ballen, Gewitterdünste umher lagern. Hellsichtig-besonnen und liebend-selbstlos zugleich fällt sein Blick hernieder: und Alles, was er jetzt mit dieser doppelten Leuchtkraft seines Blickes sich erhellt, treibt die Natur mit furchtbarer Schnelligkeit zur Entladung aller ihrer Kräfte, zur Offenbarung ihrer verborgensten Geheimnisse: und zwar durch S c h a m.

It is interesting to note the impersonal nature of Nietzsche's description of Wagner here. Wagner is in his own right active, but he is also subject to what is at work *in* him. Nietzsche also conjectures about how Wagner himself experiences this. Here, there is clearly a constellation of activities, but they are not Wagner's lone creation or orchestration. He *suffers* rather than organizes the great work in him. Of course, Nietzsche takes a very different view of Wagner in his later works. In *Der Fall Wagner*, for example, he accuses him of "disgregation," of being fundamentally unable to bring unity to anything, of offering only the superficial appearance of development and form (e.g., *CW* 7, 10). And Wagner not only exhibits such a condition himself but also brings it about in others insofar as he merely stokes up passions and emotions to achieve "effects" and overpower his audience; in short, Nietzsche later claims that Wagner ultimately *seduces* rather than *creates* (*CW* Postscript 1). But we cannot simply trust Nietzsche in *Ecce Homo* when he implies that we might resolve the vast differences between his accounts of Wagner in *Richard Wagner in Bayreuth* and *Der Fall Wagner* by substituting the name *Nietzsche* where the reader finds *Wagner* in the earlier work. He offers readers a very different presentation of himself in *Ecce Homo*, and it largely depends on the differences he identifies in *how* one evolves, *what* it amounts to, and what it entails.

In contrast to his earlier portrait of Wagner, Nietzsche presents himself as cleverly *selfish*, a theme he treats repeatedly in works published after *RWB*. He highlights his "instinct" and "art" of "self-preservation [*Selbsterhaltung*]": "In all these matters—in the choice of nutrition, of place and climate, of recreation—an instinct of self-preservation [Selbsterhaltung] issues its commandments, and it gains its most unambiguous expression as an instinct of *self-defense* [Selbstverteidigung]" (*EH* "Why I Am So Clever" 8). This is affected by and engaged with seemingly insignificant matters of nutrition, place, climate, and recreation:

these small things—nutrition, place, climate, recreation, the whole casuistry of selfishness [Selbstsucht]—are inconceivably more important than

everything one has taken to be important so far. Precisely here one must begin to *relearn*. What mankind has so far considered seriously have not even
been realities but mere imaginings—more strictly speaking, *lies* prompted
by the bad instincts of sick natures that were harmful in the most profound
sense. [. . .] All the problems of politics, of social organization, and of education have been falsified through and through because one mistook the
most harmful men for great men—because one learned to despise "little"
things, which means the basic concerns of life itself. (*EH* "Why I Am So
Clever" 10)

Looking after "basic concerns of life" turns out to be crucially important because we otherwise find ourselves expending immense amounts of energy
fighting off harmful conditions. Any ruling thought that directed our attention away from such concerns, denigrated them as unimportant or inconse-
quential, would have potentially quite harmful effects.[33] Thus, an important
dimension of how one becomes what one is is by nurturing oneself, looking
after what nourishes and facilitates self-recovery and avoiding counterpro-
ductive resistance. Though our constitutions may be determined to a certain
extent by the drives we happen to have—and this is qualified below in important ways—self-cultivation, *Selbstzucht*, development, is nevertheless possible
by virtue of taking care of ourselves in very basic ways. These greatly affect
our capacities to maximize our resources and become integrated rather than
suffering disgregation. Nietzsche's later writings offer examples of a variety
of relations and associations that are informative of the types we are, including: inheritance; sensory experiences of smells, touches, and tastes; tempo;
experiences with art; diet and nutrition; biorhythms and times of day; conditions of climate, seasons, and weather; geography and topography; national-
ity; physiological constitutions and states of health; characteristics of dwelling
places and domiciles; friendships and enemies; sexual relations; and forms of
recreation. All are aspects that contribute to becoming what Nietzsche calls
choosy, having a principle of selection.[34]

The kind of selfishness Nietzsche praises and seeks to revalue does not
aim at or depend on exploiting others. What he links with his cleverness and
good fortune is much like what he describes as "*ideal selfishness* [idealische
Selbstsucht]" in *D* 552, where he likens it to pregnancy and ripening. And
this marks an important contrast between the kind of conservation he associates with *selfishness* as self-seeking and the motivation toward conservation
that he finds suspicious in his interpretation of Darwinian evolutionary accounts of development, discussed in chapter 3 above. It is useful to draw out

this distinction here as it allows us to further explore the alternative model of
agency that is the product of his agon Paul and becomes crystallized in his
ultimate struggle with Wagner.

The passage on *Selbstsucht* from *Morgenröthe* also sheds further light on why
Nietzsche thinks it is important not to have the slightest idea what one is, and
it is related to an alternative picture of agency after the morality of intention:
"In this condition we avoid many things without having to force ourselves
very hard! We know nothing of what is taking place, we wait and try to be
ready. At the same time, a pure and purifying feeling of profound irresponsibility [Unverantwortlichkeit] reigns in us almost like that of the spectator
before the curtain has gone up—*it* is growing, *it* is coming to light: *we* have
nothing at hand by which to determine either its value or the hour of its coming. All the influence we can exert lies in keeping it safe." Nietzsche associates
this with "a state of consecration" such that "if what is expected is an idea,
a deed—towards every bringing forth [Vollbringen] we have essentially no
other relationship than that of pregnancy and ought to blow to the winds all
presumptuous talk of 'willing' and 'creating.' This is *ideal selfishness*: continually to watch over and care for [sorgen] and to keep our soul still, so that our
fruitfulness [Fruchtbarkeit] shall *come to a happy fulfillment*." Such happy
fulfillment, however, is not an end in itself; the process is not merely self-
serving and self-satisfying. It benefits others, as Nietzsche imagines it: "Thus,
as intermediaries, we watch over and care for to the *benefit of all* [für den
Nutzen Aller]; and the mood in which we live, this mood of pride and
gentleness, is a balm which spreads far around us and on to restless souls too"
(*D* 552). This marks at least two distinguishing features of Nietzsche's alternative image to the ascetic ideal—*pregnancy* and *giving birth* or overflowing—
and they are the basis of an alternative ethos he envisions as possible beyond
the morality of intention, which might include reformulated conceptions of
care and *responsibility*. But, to bring this into sharper focus, it is helpful to
remind ourselves how Nietzsche thinks about human motivation and action
so that we can better understand the orientation of the relations he describes,
and this will ultimately be relevant to distinguishing the place of his agonism
in his conception of a possible future development.

5.6 THE FEELING OF POWER

We have already seen that Nietzsche thinks about human beings as organizations of striving drives. What organizes them? In the third essay of the *Ge-*

nealogy, he marvels at the engine that leverages ascetic ideals to produce a binding force on the basis of maximal tension. Ascetic ideals generate such intensity because they turn on, play, and prey on the discordant character of human existence as such. Considered simply in this respect, ascetic ideals are not problematic; indeed, they might be seen as immensely powerful forces of organization that are potentially creative. In determining the value and meaning of ascetic ideals, one of the most relevant considerations for Nietzsche is whether the ambiguous, "unstable equilibrium" that constitutes our lives seduces us to life or undermines us.

The third essay of the *Genealogy* begins with the question *What is the meaning of ascetic ideals?* There are at least two ways to interpret the question. Nietzsche could be asking about the meaning of ascetic ideals generally, that is, what it means that they exist. Or he could be asking about what they *are*—the various forms they can take in light of what they mean in various contexts. I think his study takes up both dimensions. One facet of his answer includes examination of how ascetic ideals stand with regard to meaning, how it is that they effectively produce meanings generally, and then how they generate the specific meanings they do. At least one thing seems clear to him: ascetic ideals are particularly effective for producing the feeling of power, and he believes all beings seek precisely that. In *GM* III:7, he reiterates this view when he writes:

> Every animal—therefore *la bête philosophe*, too—instinctively strives for an optimum of favorable conditions under which it can expend all its strength and achieve its maximal feeling of power [sein Maximum im Machtgefühl erreicht]; every animal abhors, just as instinctively and with a subtlety of discernment that is "higher than all reason," every kind of intrusion or hindrance that obstructs or could obstruct this path to power (I am *not* speaking of its path to happiness, but its path to power, to action, to the most powerful activity [sein Weg zur Macht, zur That, zum mächtigsten Thun], and in most cases actually its path to unhappiness).

Thus, it is not happiness in the sense of satisfaction (or, following the Darwinians, self-preservation in the form of simply prolonging the *duration* of life) that ultimately motivates human activity, as Nietzsche sees it. What follows from his assumption that all beings are composites of striving forces is the view that all beings seek and strive for the *expansion* of power. And, as we have seen, he regards this as particularly expressive—organizations of forces ultimately seek their *expression* rather than *sheer* conservation. Thus, a considerable motivation for human action arises from pursuit of the *feeling of power—Machtgefühl*. The attraction of this sensation at least partially accounts for the lure and efficacy of the ascetic ideal.[35]

Nietzsche regards the pursuit of *Machtgefühl* as basic, and it appears to be produced in a context that is relational and expressive. An ascetic ideal is a way of generating and intensifying meaning that relies on a logic of opposition. It entails "a radical reversal of sense [radikale Sinnes-Umschlag]" in which one "leaps over into his opposite [in seinen Gegensatz umspringt]" a kind of antithesis (*GM* III:2). He explores the nature of this form of opposition, the structure of the antithesis, and considers whether and how the ascetic ideal might have an opponent. Ascetic ideals can take the form of a "tragic antithesis [tragischer Gegensatz]." An example of this is Wagner's *Parsifal*, in which chastity and sensuality are opposed with deadly results (Amfortas is redeemed only by Kundry's death, and Parsifal acquires his healing powers, it is suggested, by virtue of the force he marshals in resisting the advances of Kundry).

The new tragic antithesis is contrasted with one in which opposition serves as a "stimulant [Lebensreiz]," which "seduce[s] one to existence [Solche 'Widersprüche' gerade verführen zum Dasein]," much as contest acts as a cultural stimulant in Nietzsche's account of ancient Greece as described in "Homer's Wettkampf." To further illustrate this feeling, Nietzsche offers the example of Schopenhauer's need for enemies:

> Schopenhauer, who treated sexuality as a personal enemy (including its tool, woman, that *"instrumentum diaboli"*), *needed* enemies in order to keep in good spirits; that he loved bilious, black-green words, that he scolded for the sake of scolding, out of passion; that he would have become ill, become a *pessimist* (for he was not one, however much he desired it), if deprived of his enemies, of Hegel, of woman, of sensuality and the whole will to existence, to persistence [den ganzen Willen zum Dasein, Dableiben]. [. . .] his enemies held him fast, his enemies seduced him ever again to existence [seine Feinde aber hielten ihn fest, seine Feinde verführten ihn immer wieder zum Dasein]; his anger was, just as in the case of the Cynics of antiquity, his balm, his refreshment, his reward, his specific against disgust, his *happiness*. (*GM* III:7)[36]

Machtgefühl can be produced in relation to resistances, obstacles, or challenges. And this process can function as a stimulant and propellant toward overcoming, as the example above illustrates. Elsewhere, Nietzsche explores how *Machtgefühl* can also emanate from overfullness—a plenitude, a spirit of generosity linked with the power of gift-giving, as Zarathustra might be thought to express. Moreover, it seems the quest for this feeling can be energized by and organized in terms of a kind of tension that leads one to become ever more invested in existence—that is, engaged in opposition that motivates one's activity and generates a kind of *passion* for life—or by a form of tension that leads one to endeavor to escape or avoid opposition by displacing it to a different realm (i.e., to "flee existence," as Nietzsche puts it). These ideas overlap with the analysis of contest drawn in chapter 1 above. Pursuit of *Machtgefühl* in the manner Nietzsche associates with investment in existence suggests the form of engagement realized in *Wettkampf*, a stimulus that entices one to *overcome* what one opposes. Pursuit of *Machtgefühl* through a tragic antithesis appears to engage the desire to destroy one's opposition, *Vernichtungslust*, since its resolution seems to require destruction of one of the opposed elements; the tension cannot be borne. In his discussion of the ascetic ideal, Nietzsche considers how different forms of opposition generate the feeling of power, *Machtgefühl*, in different ways. How this feeling is produced, he claims, is related to what motivates each, their investment in existence, and whether they regard human existence as worth pursuing or ultimately to be fled.

5.7 NIETZSCHE'S RESPONSIBILITY

Can an organization motivated and arranged so as to squander itself also be responsible? And how is such responsibility compatible with the selfishness highlighted above? As discussed above, selfishness can be construed as a form of conservation in which the goal is to not engage in enervating self-expenditure. This notion is potentially compatible with a form of generosity in which one gathers resources sufficient to be overflowing, as argued above, and we can see how *Machtgefühl* might accompany such expenditures and expressions. Building on this, we might also consider how contemporary discussions of responsibility that do not require a thick sense of agency are helpful for understanding at least one distinctive sense of responsibility Nietzsche describes in positive terms. (Such views can nevertheless be compatible with more metaphysically and psychologically freighted accounts of agency.) First, we can distinguish senses of responsibility in terms of *accountability* and *attribution*.[37] Responsibility as accountability is familiar enough and assumes culpability of the sort we find in moral responsibility. Responsibility as attribution is linked with actions, particularly those chosen, although the specific outcome need not be explicitly chosen; when we use *responsibility* in this sense, we attribute an action to someone or take her as linked by virtue of her activity with a happening or an event. For Nietzsche, both of these forms of responsibility lie at the base of morality (*BGE* 21), ground claims to entitlement, and provide conditions for assessment.

Some have sought to elaborate nonintentionalist accounts of responsibility so as to justify claims of responsibility for unintentional behaviors, characteristics, and qualities that make one who one is, specifically those that reflect or are expressive of judgments that guide or explain the actions. On such accounts, and with the latter qualification of the connection with the exercise of judgment, one is not responsible for things such as bodily movements or mental states that could not possibly be informed by or spring from judgments, but one would be responsible for a host of other characteristics less typically regarded as relevant in determinations of responsibility, including "most of our desires, emotions, beliefs, and other attitudes, despite the fact that they do not arise from conscious choice or decision and are not normally under our immediate voluntary control."[38] On this view, we are responsible for expressive value judgments, which include but are not limited to actions. We can have this with or without a robust notion of free will; it is linked with expressive being and with acting conceived as a way of being. Defenders of this view argue they still provide grounds for assessment since the expressive value judgments are open to analytic critique.[39]

This form of responsibility blends both attribution and accountability notions—one is accountable for an expansive scope of what is attributable to *what one is*, in which case one is what one does. This is compatible with a sense of agency modeled on capacities or capabilities rather than causation. Capacities might well (perhaps, should) be constitutionally determined with a causal relation abiding between having those capacities and engaging in activity. But one need not suppose that there is some doer orchestrating things behind the scenes, one whose choices are entirely unrestricted, for they will be limited by their abiding capabilities, attitudes, beliefs, etc., many of which are not freely chosen or even immediately consciously available. Angela Smith, a proponent of such a view, puts it this way: "Our patterns of awareness—e.g., what we notice and neglect, and what occurs to us—can also be said to reflect our judgments about what things are important or significant, so these responses, too, will count as things for which we are responsible on the rational relations view. What matters, on this account, is whether an action or attitude is normatively connected to a person's underlying judgments in such a way that she can, in principle, be called upon to defend it with reasons and to acknowledge fault if an adequate defense cannot be provided."[40]

Nietzsche could hold a similar view but arguably without Smith's rational judgment criterion. Instead of rational critique as a basis for assessment, he might offer a genealogical account to examine connections between what we can do, how we think, what we want, and how we act as well as the ways in which we attempt to justify our actions. This strikes me as a helpful way to think about responsibility in relation to what is *unintentional*—the situation Nietzsche anticipates in *BGE* 32. In such a case, considerations of responsibility need not focus on intention, conceived as an executable order that requires a commander/doer, the very sort of agential entities and resources Nietzsche disavows, and it is congenial with a sense of self as constituted by evaluative judgments.

Critics of this sort of view, such as Susan Wolf, worry that it is too thin, leaving us with a "'superficial' kind of responsibility, a kind of responsibility that is merely causal and can be applied to '[e]arthquakes, defective tires, and broken machines . . . [as well as] dogs and children and adults with various physical and mental handicaps,"[41] although the emphasis on responsibility for what follows from one's *judgments* would seem to rule out earthquakes, tires, and the like. We can find a similar worry reflected even within expressivist readings, as identified above in Pippin's legitimate concern that the lightning-flash passage of the *Genealogy* still leaves us with the need to find a way to distinguish a *doing* from a *mere event*. But we might recall that Nietzsche's analogy for human action in the passage in question *is* by comparison with *an event*. While perhaps not identical to an event (as some forms of determinism have it), the lightning-flash depiction of a replacement for intentional agency must share some similarities with events; otherwise, the analogy makes no sense and serves no purpose. Moreover, the notion that there is no doer behind the deed is one Nietzsche repeats; it is not a casual or passing observation, and it is not limited only to those (many, perhaps) who think that they are agents when they really are not.

If Nietzsche's replacement picture of agency abides, then it seems possible to develop a sense of responsibility that allows for assessment and attribution on the basis of *expressed values* rather than *intentional choices*. Such an approach might focus on what the nature of the deed is such that its emergence would not require a doer lurking behind it; deeds, then, could be particular kinds of expressions, not somewhat independent products. We could tie all this to a view of agency in Nietzsche that is consistent with what he writes about giving style to one's character, becoming who one is, and so on. Such might even sufficiently broaden conceptions of agential responsibility such that responsibility in the sense Gemes describes becomes a genuine possibility.[42]

Without discounting the alternative just sketched, I also wish to point out that there is at least another sense of responsibility that does not receive much attention in the literature, perhaps because it is not regarded as immediately relevant to the moral cases, though I think it is, and I do not think discussion of responsibility should be limited to the domain of morality. To views of responsibility as *accountability* and responsibility as *attribution* (and blended formulations, as above), we can add responsibility as *authority*, in the sense of what identifies or defines a domain of activity or scope of powers. Some common uses of this sense of the term *responsibility* can guide our thought and provoke reflection on whether this sense is also compatible with what Nietzsche envisions.

Positions of employment, assignment of other professional or government duties, and legal contracts are defined and distinguished in terms of *responsibilities*. These are specific and tangible, yet they can rarely be spelled out in a way that is exhaustive or formulaic. For example, in the statement "General Petraeus is responsible for military operations in Afghanistan," *responsible* refers minimally to a state of affairs, a definition of a scope of powers, a measure of authority, and a sphere of activity. What follows from this is not so much that the subject deserves praise or blame for all activities that occur within that sphere, although what occurs in such domains, even when it issues from the actions of others, is not irrelevant to judgments of how well subjects have met and exercised their responsibilities. Furthermore, we surely do not mean that a person responsible in this way, even indirectly, will be the *cause* of all actions that occur there. Instead, when we say that one has *responsibility for* something in this way, we are picking out or identifying a certain scope of powers, a domain in which the subject can act, and this is not necessarily or exclusively moral, although it can be.[43] I think that is somewhat different from the attribution notion since it is future oriented and outwardly, expressively directed. Thinking about responsibility in this sense also has interesting implications for the organizational model of self sketched above, and I think it is compatible with the earlier discussion of thinking of oneself as in the deed as the mother is in the child.

In Nietzsche's works, we see this sense of responsibility quite clearly in *BGE* 212, in which the philosopher is regarded as a question mark and the bad conscience of his time: "Facing a world of 'modern ideas' that would banish everybody into a corner and 'specialty,' a philosopher—if today there could be philosophers—would be compelled to find the greatness of man, the concept of 'greatness' [die Grösse des Menschen, den Begriff 'Grösse'], precisely in his range and multiplicity [Umfänglichkeit und Vielfältigkeit], in his wholeness in manifoldness [Ganzheit im Vielen]. He would even determine value and rank [Werth und Rang] in accordance with how much and how many things one could bear and take upon himself [wie viel und vielerlei Einer tragen und auf sich nehmen], how *far* one could extend his responsibility [wie w e i t Einer seine Verantwortlichkeit spannen könnte]." This particular sense of responsibility neither fixates on a notion of causal agency nor retreats to an ethics of self in which responsibility is primarily understood in terms of perfecting oneself. Focus on a scope of powers in the context of thinking about *responsibility* also implies a domain of care, regard, concern, that is mindful of our social and historical nature. I think this is consistent with the ultimate affective orientation of *love* that becomes Nietzsche's concern in *amor fati* and affirmation modeled on the *love of life*. Furthermore, I think it provides insight into the compatibility of this view with the *unintentional* cited in *BGE* 32.

We can now return to *D* 552 to see how Nietzsche contrasts the sense of responsibility attached to causation with the sense of responsibility linked with care. His image of pregnancy is apt, for it is quite clear that while a mother has responsibility for *caring for*—in the sense of safeguarding, sheltering, anticipating, and hoping—she is not strictly the cause or creator of the child she carries. She bears the activity of the developing fetus (and there are surely some things she can do to support or interfere), but she is not "at work" in creating it. In this respect, there is "a pure and purifying feeling of profound irresponsibility [ein reines und reinigendes Gefühl tiefer Unverantwortlichkeit]." When we look at the passage in whole, we find a much greater sense of responsibility implied, and the imagery used conjures the very same form of relation of self and deed developed in the passage from *Also Sprach Zarathustra* discussed in chapter 4. We can now take a fuller scope on the passage:

Ideal selfishness.—Is there a more holy condition than that of pregnancy [Schwangerschaft]? To do all we do in the unspoken belief that it has somehow to benefit that which is coming to be [dem Werdenden] within us! This has to *enhance* its mysterious value [geheimnissvollen Werth], upon which we think with delight! One thus avoids a great deal without having to force oneself too hard. One thus suppresses a violent word, one offers a conciliatory hand: the child must emerge from the mildest and best of conditions. We are horrified if we are sharp or abrupt: suppose it should pour a drop of calamity into the dear unknown's cup of life! Everything is veiled, ominous, we know nothing of what is taking place, we wait and try to be *ready* [man wartet ab und sucht bereit zu sein]. At the same time, a pure and purifying feeling of profound irresponsibility reigns in us almost like that of the spectator before the curtain has gone up—*it* is growing, *it* is coming to light; *we* have nothing at hand to determine either its value or the hour of its coming. We are thrown back solely on that mediate influence of protecting. [Einzig auf jeden mittelbaren segnenden und wehrenden Einfluss sind wir angewiesen.] "What is growing here is something greater than we are" is our most secret hope: we are preparing everything for it so that it will come into the world thriving: not only everything beneficial but also the joyfulness eand laurel wreaths of our soul [die Herzlichkeiten und Kränze unserer Seele].—One ought to live in this state of consecration! One can live in it! [In dieser Weihe soll man leben! Kann man leben!] And if what is expected is an idea, a deed [ein Gedanke, eine That]— toward all that we bring forth we have essentially no other relationship than that of pregnancy and ought to let blow in the wind all presumptuous talk of "willing" and "creating"! [wir haben zu allem wesentlichen Vollbringen kein anderes Verhältniss, als das der Schwangerschaft und sollten das an- maassliche Reden von "Wollen" und "Schaffen" in den Wind blasen!] This is proper *ideal selfishness*: continually to watch over and care for and to keep our souls still, so that our fruitfulness shall *come to a happy fulfillment!* [immer zu sorgen und zu wachen und die Seele still zu halten, dass unsere Fruchtbarkeit schön zu Ende gehe!] Thus, in this mediate way, we care and watch over for the *benefit of all* [So, in dieser mittelbaren Art sor- gen und wachen wir für den Nutzen Aller] and the mood in which we live, this mood of pride and gentleness, is a balm which spreads far around us and on to restless souls too.—But the pregnant are *strange* [wun- derlich]! So let us be strange, too, and let us not hold it against others if they too have to be so! And even if the outcome is bad and dangerous [Schlimme und Gefährliche], let us not, in our reverence for what is com- ing to be [Ehrfurcht vor dem Werdenden], lag behind worldly justice [der weltlichen Gerechtigkeit], which does not permit a judge or an executioner to lay hands on one who is pregnant![44]

Safekeeping, watching over, and taking care are what define responsibility here, a relation between mother and child. This form of creativity is rather different from other artistic varieties Nietzsche discusses. In this case, one is responsible for what grows within, not because one is its master, because one caused it by dint of one's will, but rather because one *shelters* it with the hope that "it will come into the world thriving." We can also note that the underlying affect that appears to support this sense of responsibility is that combination of love and terror, mentioned above in the example of the relation between the mother and child, whose expression is found in breeding, rearing, nurturing, and watching grow. Nietzsche's image of selfishness as like pregnancy is relevant to his later suggestion in *Zarathustra* that we think of our relations to our deeds as like the ways in which mothers are in children, only here we find them in vitro rather than out in the world. Moreover, his account of what it is like to experience this from the perspective of the mother is noteworthy: one can *have* responsibility in the sense of being in a relationship requiring extraordinary care without being able to directly determine the outcome and in this respect completely *irresponsible*. This bears resemblance to how he describes Wagner's *becoming who he is* (as subject to a process rather than orchestrating it) and Nietzsche's later account of such a process more generally in terms of not having the faintest notion about eventual outcomes yet having responsibility for a certain kind of active vigilance, watching and waiting.

Nietzsche criticizes the reigning picture of moral responsibility as too *limited*, too restrictive (rather than just too demanding). Comparing our current sense of responsibility with that of the past, he writes: "Today one feels responsible only for one's will and actions and one finds one's pride in oneself. [. . .] To be a self and to esteem oneself according to one's own weight and measure—that offended taste in those days. An inclination to do this would have been considered madness; for being alone was associated with every misery and fear. In those days, 'free will' was very closely associated with a bad conscience; and the more unfree one's actions were and the more the herd instinct rather than any personal sense found expression in an action, the more moral one felt. Whatever harmed the herd, whether the individual had wanted it or not wanted it, prompted the sting of conscience in the individual—and in his neighbor, too, and even in the whole herd.—There is no point on which we have learned to think and feel more differently" (*GS* 117). And we can compare this with the frequently cited passage from *D* 103, where Nietzsche writes: "It goes without saying that I do not deny—unless I am a fool—that many actions called immoral ought to be avoided and resisted, or that many called moral ought to be done and encouraged—but I think the one should be encouraged and the other avoided *for other reasons than hitherto*. We have to *learn to think differently*—in order at last, perhaps very late on, to attain even more: *to feel differently* [Wir haben umzulernen,—um endlich, vielleicht sehr spät, noch mehr zu erreichen: umzufühlen]." A different way of thinking about the subject, about the agent, a revision of the soul hypothesis, might provide us with opportunities to feel differently about ourselves, our actions, and our responsibilities and thereby facilitate a variety of sentiments that differ from what morality instructs. I think this is the sense of redemption Nietzsche envisions: *redeeming being* by acknowledging the innocence of becoming (*TI* "The Four Great Errors" 8) rather than by setting up procedures to account for its (and our) guilt. Such perspectives might make it possible to embrace guiltlessness while still retaining some important senses of responsibility.

In the passage cited above from *Die fröhliche Wissenschaft*, Nietzsche challenges the view that our current conceptions of responsibility are superior and represent progress with respect to those evident in the distant past. Bernard Williams shares Nietzsche's skepticism about such progress. He provides an interesting examination of whether the notion of *intention* is evident in Homeric literature, arguing that while there is no noun in ancient Greek directly corresponding to the word the basic idea is there. Moreover, he further claims that the lack of such a *thing* as intentions issuing from wills that themselves have distinctive causal relations to actions is a virtue rather than simply evidence of naïveté.[45] The invention of an intentional will in the sense lacking in Homer produces a host of unnecessary philosophical problems we would do well to avoid: "All that Homer seems to have left out is the idea of another mental action that is supposed necessarily to lie between coming to a conclusion and acting on it: and he did well in leaving it out, since there is no such action, and the idea of it is the invention of bad philosophy."[46] Among some of the unfortunate results of the grip of this later idea is the moralization of our theory of action and human psychology more generally.[47] How this affects a sense of responsibility is also taken up by Williams.

For Williams, causality is essential to a conception of responsibility. He writes: "Cause, is primary: the other issues can arise only in relation to the fact that some agent is the cause of what has come about. Without this, there is no concept of responsibility at all."[48] But he claims *intentional causality* is not the exclusive concern or even reflective of the most refined and robust sense of responsibility. He writes: "Progressivist writers refer to a concept of moral responsibility that we supposedly enjoy and the Greeks lacked, but it is unclear what they have in mind. Their thought seems most typically to be that the Greeks, or at least archaic Greeks, blamed and sanctioned people for things that they did unintentionally, or again—though this distinction is often neglected—for things that, like Agamemnon, they did intentionally but in a strange state of mind. We are thought not to do this, or at least to regard it as unjust. But if this means that the Greeks paid no attention to intentions, while we make everything turn on the issue of intentions, or at least think that we should, this is doubly false."[49] Some of the apparent differences are not conceptual but spring from differing ideas about the state's role in *holding responsible* and prosecuting accountability, but this is not all.

Williams goes on to draw some distinctions between what he regards as *metaphysical depth* of views about what is voluntary and how this bears on our notions of responsibility.[50] We, too, have a sense that one can be responsible for many things, even those that we did not intend but that result from our decisions and actions. As evidence of this, Williams writes: "The whole of the *Oedipus Tyrannus*, that dreadful machine, moves to the discovery of just one thing, that *he did it*. Do we understand the terror of that discovery only because we residually share magical beliefs in blood-guilt, or archaic notions of responsibility? Certainly not: we understand it because we know that in the story of one's life there is an authority exercised by what one has done, and not merely by what one has intentionally done."[51] I think this abiding sense of authority is akin to the *scope of powers* sense of responsibility I sketched. It refers us to a field of possible action that includes much that we might have done without an explicit intent tied to some isolated act, and it involves, *in part* (though not entirely), the sense of sheltering that is evident in Nietzsche's description of ideal selfishness and the profound *irresponsibility* that accompanies it. We can now see more clearly that *irresponsibility* in *D* 552 flags a divorce from intent. This need not diminish our sense of responsibility; we need not conclude that shifting focus away from exclusively fixing on intent would somehow weaken or erode what we think of as deeper or more robust. If anything, it potentially broadens and enlivens it. As Williams concludes: "When the response is demanded by someone else and there are claims for damages, this itself reaches beyond the intentions of the responsible agent. As the Greeks understood, the responsibilities we have to recognize extend in many ways beyond our normal purposes and what we intentionally do."[52] To Williams's sense of authority evident in the story of Oedipus I would add not only the exercise of what one has done but also what one *has not done*, which includes the active vigilance and anticipation suggested in Nietzsche's image of pregnancy.

It is important to notice that both asceticism and agonism draw one into activity, but, between these, only one sort of activity might be thought to enhance responsibility in the sense explored above. We might wonder whether there might be some imperative that could follow, whether it might be good to take on more responsibility, whether it should be sought. In the abstract, and as a general rule, it would seem that Nietzsche must think it should not. Indeed, we would not want others to take responsibility where they are incapable. That could be disastrous. But responsibility could be recognized as a good, as something one wants (and not something to which one is entitled or for which one is obliged, although one who is responsible surely has a more expansive scope of authority and obligation). Responsibility then becomes something one strives to attain, something for which one hopes to be capable and worthy. Nietzsche's replacement concept here cannot strictly be agonism for its own sake because one does not want to be a worthy opponent for and against one's children (even though it might at times seem that the child strives for such). Worthwhile opposition, much like the sexual tension to which Nietzsche repeatedly refers, has its end in—*birth*. This notion of birth and its connection with responsibility obviously leads us back to the image of the mother and child from *Zarathustra*, the very same text that so vividly offers the image of self-squandering introduced in chapter 3.

The broad context of the section that evokes the image of thinking of one-self as in the deed as the mother is in the child is that Zarathustra is talking to his disciples, having returned to them after growing concerned that his teaching was in jeopardy (because his enemies are gathering) and that he was not particularly successful as a teacher—he taught them to say *overman* but not to create (or to prepare for those who *could* act in this way). And it is in relation to this second concern and the nature of creation that he first draws the picture of the relation between mother and child in that part of the book: "To be the child who is newly born, the creator must also want to be the mother who gives birth and the pangs of the birth-giver" (*Z* II "Upon the Blessed Isles").[53]

At least part of what follows from this, from Zarathustra's perspective, is that one perishes (in Zarathustra's case, "a hundred" times or more) in realizing the creative capacities he envisions. He reaches this conclusion after linking "creation [Schaffen]" and "redemption from suffering [Erlösung vom Leiden]": "Creation—that is the great redemption from suffering, and life's growing light. But that the creator may be, suffering is needed and much change. Indeed, there must be much bitter dying in your life, you creators. Thus you are the advocates and justifiers of all impermanence [Vergänglichkeit]." The soul is impermanent: in renewing itself and thereby redeeming itself from suffering, it perishes, "passing through a hundred cradles and birth pangs" (*Z* II "Upon the Blessed Isles"). What Zarathustra has in mind appears to be a kind of self as aspect or dimension of a larger creative process rather than enduring entity or substance; somehow, mysteriously, it suggests that one gives birth to oneself repeatedly and perpetually.[54] This certainly strains the imagination, and how it differs significantly from Münchhausen's effort "to pull oneself up into existence by the hair, out of the swamps of nothingness" (*BGE* 21), I leave for others to attempt to explain. I do not think that Zarathustra or Nietzsche sufficiently sorted this out. Nevertheless, if we connect this with the idea of being in our deeds as mothers are in their children, then one might be thought to *live on* to some extent to carry on or extend one's domain of activity through one's children in some limited sense, but each child is at the same time the beginning of something new, a new creation, which is not simply reducible to a product or replica of what gave it birth.

We might also notice what Zarathustra thinks about how this image will be received by his disciples, how even *he* thinks about this view of perpetual birth and passing: "Many a farewell have I taken; I know the heart-rending last hours" (*Z* II "Upon the Blessed Isles"). He acknowledges attachments to these selves; their passing is significant, not something frivolously dismissed or passed over. In his image, redemption turns on dying, but it also has the prospect of love if we can see ourselves in terms of becoming the next generation and loving it, *caring for it* as a mother would. In highlighting this theme, of course, I am not reducing Nietzsche's agonism to tender motherly love, but I am arguing that he at least regards such possibilities as compatible with his depiction of existence as characterized by inherent exploitation, violence, and incorporation of otherness.

The multiple personalities that appear in this image of the mother and child, however, might seem to suggest that, instead of one doer behind the deed, there are scores in a lifetime and perhaps even more than one at a time (both mother *and* child) *behind* each. But Zarathustra undercuts that second possibility in the statement immediately following his acknowledgment of the sense of loss in such a process: "But thus my creative will, my destiny, wills it. Or, to say it more honestly: this very destiny—my will wills" (*Z* II "Upon the Blessed Isles"; "Aber so will's mein schaffender Wille, mein Schicksal. Oder, dass ich's euch redlicher sage: solches Schicksal gerade—will mein Wille" [*KSA* 4, p. 111]). When he corrects his grammatical habit of inserting a separate verbal subject to provide an agent of willing, he limits the activity to willing itself. It is not as though he stands behind a creative act that results in his destiny but rather that it is this very destiny ("thus it shall be")—willing—that he is. The relevant distinction to notice is that his will is an *affirmation*, not a source of origination or causation.[55]

Zarathustra continues to elaborate what he envisions his disciples would have to give up, how they would have to think differently if they truly take in what he has offered them. He recognizes that they have significant investments in these ideas and that they would experience forsaking them as a loss. In this context, he turns to the mother-child image in *Z* II "On the Virtuous." Prior to the instance in which Zarathustra suggests that one should be in the deed as the mother is in the child, discussed in the previous chapter, Zarathustra invokes a similar image when he tells his disciples: "You love your virtue as a mother her child" (*Z* II "On the Virtuous"). In this case, he underscores how precious virtue is to his disciples and how this is indicative of a certain purity, sincerity, and earnestness, which make them "too good" for "the filth of the words: revenge, punishment, reward, retribution" (the primary topics of the process of the slave revolt in morality that resulted in the creation of the bad conscience in *GM* I–II). And, since they are appropriately disposed thus, Zarathustra claims, they should give up expectations they have and ideas they hold about the value of their virtues: "what mother ever wished to be paid for her love?" (*Z* II "On the Virtuous"; *KSA* 4, p. 121).

Zarathustra evokes yet another image to stand in the stead of thinking of virtue as something that deserves reward (even as itself a reward). It is the light of a dying star: "like a dying star is every work of your virtue: its light is always still on its way even when the work has been done. Though it be forgotten and dead, the ray of its light still lives and wanders." "Your virtue," he says, "is your most loved self" ("Es ist euer liebstes Selbst, eure Tugend"; *Z* II "On the Virtuous").[56] So, when he later counsels his disciples "that your self be in your deed as the mother is in her child—let that be *your* word concerning virtue," I think we are meant to recall the idea of the regenerating self linked earlier with destiny (and its attendant conception of willing as affirmation rather than cause) as well as this image of what happens to the "dead" ones thereafter: their light continues to shine, to give the appearance of the star it was before even though *it* is gone. This shining light, it seems to me, is related to the lightning flash in *GM* I:13 and what we are to glean from it about how Nietzsche thinks about agency and alternative conceptions of the soul hypothesis we might develop.

As discussed in the previous chapter, the notion of the agent as distinct, if not separable, from the deed has some clear utility for the moral picture of action and responsible agency. Moreover, we have a significant investment in the idea in terms of how it provides us with a sense of self, as indicated above. Thinking of oneself as in one's deed as a mother is in a child challenges not only our imaginations but also our estimation of our own powers and worth. While I think that Nietzsche did not do much more than scout the terrain (or unsettled waters) beyond morality, I do think he anticipates conceptual and theoretical resources for envisioning a kind of ethos beyond morality that make it possible to see that, if we reformulated the soul hypothesis and retribution and reward were no longer desirable ends, the problems of responsibility and accountability would take on a much different cast. While popular culture might at times cultivate the ideal image of the mother as selfless (and Nietzsche sometimes casts *real* mothers as slavish), we can further see how this image is compatible with the image of selfishness discussed above.

The kind of self-preservation Nietzsche describes aims not at preserving sheer existence or mere survival (so it is not conservative in the sense he rejects) but rather at achieving a certain "self-sufficiency that overflows and gives to men and things" (*GS* 55). Thus, *Selbstsucht* is not simply self-absorption or withdrawal but rather a form of storing up for the purpose of enhancing expressive capacities and sharing them with others. Throughout his texts, Nietzsche provides insight into what might result as something that could be regarded as great. For example, in *GS* 143, he claims the impulse "to posit [one's] own ideal and to derive from it his own law, joy, and rights" becomes creative rather than destructive, as in the case of polytheism: "The wonderful art and gift of creating gods—polytheism—was the medium through which this impulse could discharge, purify, perfect, and ennoble itself; for originally it was a very undistinguished impulse, related to stubbornness, disobedience, and envy." Morality is opposed to it, but the "invention of gods, heroes, and overmen of all kinds, as well as near-men and undermen, dwarfs, fairies, centaurs, satyrs, demons, and devils was the inestimable preliminary exercise for the justification of selfishness and self-rule of the individual."[57] He links this with freedom: "the freedom that one conceded to a god in his relation to other gods—one eventually also granted to oneself in relation to laws, customs, and neighbors." And, in this respect, self-creation is possible, not by making ourselves whole, but rather by cultivating and maximally expressing our creative powers, which allow us to project ourselves beyond what we presently are: "In polytheism the free-spiriting and many-spiriting of man [die Freigeisterei und Vielgeisterei des Menschen] attained its first preliminary form—the strength to create for ourselves our own new eyes—and ever again new eyes that are even more our own: hence man alone among all the animals has no eternal horizons and perspectives." Thus, Nietzsche regards selfishness as a means to free- and full-spiritedness. In this respect, self-preservation is a form of nurturance.[58]

Where Nietzsche further links selfishness with destiny in the concluding chapter of *Ecce Homo*, he claims that the most "*severe* self-love [Selbstsucht]" is "what is most profoundly necessary for growth" but that morality instead valorizes "the 'selfless,' the loss of a center of gravity, 'depersonalization' and 'neighbor love' (*addiction* to the neighbor)" ("im 'Selbstlosen,' im Verlust an Schwergewicht, in der 'Entpersönlichung' und 'Nächstenliebe' [—Nächstensucht!]"). Indeed, he thinks that morality has so highly valued the opposite of selfishness that self*less*ness has become the "*absolute value*." He claims that the only morality known so far has been "Entselbstungs-Moral"—awkwardly translated, this is *unselfing morality*,[59] which constitutes "a will to an end" ("einen Willen zum Ende") and undermines the basis of life ("Grunde das Leben") (*EH* "Why I Am a Destiny" 7).[60] The evidence he offers for this in *Ecce Homo* is that Christian morality teaches that the basic conditions of life—"nourishment, abode, spiritual diet, treatment of the sick, cleanliness, and weather"—are "small things," trivial matters, rather than the most important. For him, again, they are the most important because, when we find ourselves in unsuitable states of affairs (unsuitable relative to our constitutions), we are forced to expend great energy simply in *fighting off* what threatens our very existence rather than being able to *fight for* something else (*EH* "Why I Am So Clever" 8). The nature of this *fighting for* and how and why it might matter are elaborated in Nietzsche's account of his *Kriegs-Praxis* in which he presents himself as a kind of fighter.

Nietzsche proposes to revalue the meaning of selfishness and present an account of its fruits in his self-presentation. Self-seeking is proposed as a ruling thought that might have an organizing feature that could counter the ruling thought of morality. Orders of rule emerge in moralities in terms of the kinds of struggles they link with the ways of life they advance, their interpretation of the struggles of human existence and their purposes, and the ways in which they encourage or discourage struggling more generally, including what they designate as *worthy* struggles. As we have seen, both the *forms of struggle* and the contests they promote and how they promote *action* within those contexts are relevant, and Nietzsche distinguishes struggles that are enervating—"when defensive expenditures, be they ever so small, become the rule and a habit, they entail an extraordinary and entirely superfluous impoverishment [eine ausserordentliche und vollkommen überflüssige Verarmung] [. . .] energy *wasted* on negative ends [zu negativen Zwecken verschwendete]" (*EH* "Why I Am So Clever" 8)—from those that are invigorating. In reading his account of himself as a fighter as he presents his *Kriegs-Praxis*, we come to appreciate how he thinks about productive expenditures as well as how he thinks about our active participation in becoming who we are.

5.8 FIGHTING WRITING: NIETZSCHE'S *KRIEGS-PRAXIS*

Nietzsche's *Kriegs-Praxis* is an expression of the organization he is. It issues from an *order of rule* expressed in his engagements with others and their ideas. In articulating his *Kriegs-Praxis*, he identifies *what* rules in him as well as *how* it does so. This makes an interesting comparison and contrast with the kind of opposition he identifies as seducing Schopenhauer to life and that provides him with a measure of *Machtgefühl*, and it provides a window on *how one becomes what one is*. One does not simply realize some potency already there, fully formed, from the start; nor does one make oneself into something other than what one already is. Rather, *becoming what one is* is realized through an interactive process in which the constitutive rank ordering of drives is achieved by virtue of a form of ruling expressed in engaging others.

Nietzsche's *Kriegs-Praxis* is a particular manifestation of his views about the development of organisms (more properly, organizations) as primarily oriented toward expansion rather than conservation, the notion that every "living thing seeks above all to *discharge* [auslassen] its strength" (*BGE* 13).[61] In this particular case, it entails "[b]eing *able* to be an enemy—that is, being prepared to resist and engage combat and *in a certain way*—and "*being* an enemy"—seeking out arenas in which such engagements can occur and participating in them (*EH* "Why I Am So Wise" 7). Repeatedly, Nietzsche links this with *Natur*, which might suggest he thinks it is strictly the result of a particular type he already is. But that is not the whole story, for it was not necessary that he turn out to be a fighter; he became one only because he sufficiently sought himself, sufficiently loved himself, realized his ideal selfishness.

In *Ecce Homo*, Nietzsche describes a strong nature as one that "needs objects of resistance," suggesting a relation between strength and its expression. In such cases, what is wanted is "what requires us to stake all our strength, suppleness, and fighting skill" (*EH* "Why I Am So Wise" 7). The right sorts of fights provide conditions in which one potentially gathers strength in the course of its expression (i.e., one's battles are occasions to *produce* strength; one does not first muster strength in the absence of challenge and *then* express it). Claiming that he is "warlike by nature,"[62] Nietzsche suggests his wisdom is tied to his need to find resistance and exercise it. He goes on to elaborate the grounds on which his practice is founded and the fruits of those labors. To achieve the conditions most conducive to this sort of activity, he claims he applies four principles of engagement. A brief survey of these provides a more complex portrait of his practice of war and how it constituted him as an author who produced the works he did: (1) he attacks causes or ideas and not individuals; (2) those ideas or causes have to be regarded as "victorious" such that the struggle against them is significant; (3) he attacks only when he lacks any personal grudges; and (4) his attacks are his alone and not something done as part of some mass movement.[63]

This gives some insight into what he thinks are healthy or invigorating kinds of fighting in contrast to sources of resistance that are merely destructive and enervating. What is at stake in these battles, allegedly, is, not who is a better person, or even who has better fighting skills, but rather whatever their common concerns might be, their vision of a good life, for example, or some characterization of the nature of human existence and its possible aspirations. His battles, Nietzsche would have us believe, are modeled more after the gadfly aiming to waken rather than the duelist seeking personal honor or glory. The purpose of the engagement is to draw attention to what actually is already a crisis (e.g., the failure of a particular commonplace way of conceiving the world to adequately address the contemporary challenges), although it is not yet fully recognizable as a threatening predicament.

The second principle indicates the importance of taking on a worthy competitor. The engagement must truly test him if it is to bring out the best in him. It is important that he strives to surpass what he engages rather than simply destroy or denigrate it. This latter point is further advanced by the third principle, which prohibits utilizing these struggles to settle personal grudges. The fourth principle, concerning his individual pursuit, might be regarded as also contributing to the form of personal cultivation possible in agonistic encounters. Mass movements do not necessarily require the same sort of personal investment.

Concerning the first and third principles, we might question whether Nietzsche, in fact, actually applied them. It is hard to see how his attacks on Strauss and Wagner are not directed at those individuals, despite his claim in *Ecce Homo* that he uses the names of persons as indicative of types, as magnifying glasses for broader concerns. And it is hard to see how his lifelong and repeated engagement with Wagner does not take on the character of trying to settle a score. Nevertheless, in *Ecce Homo* as well as *Der Fall Wagner*, Nietzsche clearly states that he is supremely grateful for Wagner, cherishes his relation with him above all others, and considers him a "windfall" for philosophy insofar as he provides an exemplary psychological type that crystallizes what is problematic about modern human beings (*CW* Epilogue), and I have tried to indicate above some of the larger concerns he thought were at stake in his wrestling with the promise and problem of Wagner.

Each of his agones attest to how it is the case that, challenging "problems [. . .] to single combat [fordert auch Probleme zum Zweikampf heraus]" (*EH* "Why I Am So Wise" 7), Nietzsche became the philosopher he was and had the thoughts he did. This is precisely how he *presents* himself in the context of elaborating his *Kriegs-Praxis*. In defining his problems, he establishes mammoth challenges that he sets out to surmount. He endeavors to show how these engagements brought forth his skills and summoned all his abilities. These struggles not only test qualities and capacities he already has but also facilitate the development of new or enhanced powers he would not have otherwise. It is hard to imagine how his views on the task of the creative affirmation of life, for example, could form without the contrast evident in his analyses of the moralization and denigration of human existence he finds in Platonic metaphysics, for example. Virtually all his positive views are inseparable from the positions he battles such that his *Kriegs-Praxis* plays a significant role in shaping both *what* ideas he expresses and *how* he does so.

Nietzsche seeks to exclude malice, petty jealousy, and revenge as motives for action in the contest. He thinks he preserves the possibility that his resistance might even be considered a kind of reverence, and this condition also underscores the practical dimension of his work. Such engagement entails drawing out his opposition's distinctive accomplishments for the purpose of challenging them. Competition thereby honors ("ehren") in creating an occasion for distinguishing the opponent's prior accomplishments and worthy qualities. In the course of such struggles, Nietzsche appears to believe, we do not simply vanquish or overcome our opposition; rather, we become bound ("verbinden") to what we oppose. Indeed, "Homer's Wettkampf" is, as discussed above, notable for its emphasis on investigating how the agon not only produces individuals but also creates communities. Nietzsche hails the contest specifically and repeatedly as a mechanism for the production of value through which individuals and communities become *bound to*, not *liberated from*, the claims of values of others.[64] He cites his practice of war against Christianity in a similar context, claiming it is justified because he has no personal grudge against it or against Christians themselves; rather, his war is with "Christianity de rigueur." In other words, he chooses battles that are far-reaching in importance and address themselves to the concerns of others generally rather than isolating idiosyncratic grudges.

Throughout *Ecce Homo*, Nietzsche clarifies and qualifies these principles as he repeatedly makes reference to how his agonistic practice unfolds and is evident in his writings. He locates "the real opposition" he generates in *Die Geburt der Tragödie* in his effort to fight "the degenerating instinct that turns life against life," which he contrasts with "a formula for the highest affirmation, born of fullness, of overfullness, a Yes-saying without reservation" (*EH* "The Birth of Tragedy" 2). He describes his *Unzeitgemäße Betrachtungen* as "warlike [kriegerisch]" (*EH* "Untimely Meditations" 1) and makes frequent use of martial metaphors, describing himself as "quick on the draw," taking "pleasure in fencing," making "attempts at assassination" in which "paradise lies in the shadow of my sword" (*EH* "Untimely Meditations" 2). He links *Menschliches, Allzumenschliches* with war, but he qualifies and distinguishes it as "war without powder and smoke, without warlike poses, without pathos and strained limbs" (*EH* "Human All-Too-Human" 1). He flags his "campaign against morality," but we see further evidence of his agonistic ethos as he emphasizes his affirmative motivations and intentions when he claims he accomplishes his mission with "no negative word, no attack, no spite—that it lies in the sun, round, happy, like some sea animal basking among rocks" (*EH* "Daybreak" 1).

As we have repeatedly seen, Nietzsche thinks it is possible to vanquish opposition by superseding it rather than by destroying or committing violence against it, and this is what he thinks he does in his writings: "morality is not attacked, it is merely no longer in the picture" (*EH* "Daybreak" 1). Concerning his *Zarathustra*, he explains that, while it inaugurates a "revaluation of values," which he also calls "the great war [der grosse Krieg]" (*EH* "Beyond Good and Evil" 1), his goal is not simply defeating his opponent but rather creating a new entity, one in which "all opposites are blended into a new unity [sind alle Gegensätze zu einer neuen Einheit gebunden]" (*EH* "Thus Spoke Zarathustra" 6). In other words, Nietzsche's practice of his philosophical martial art aims to incorporate his opposition and not simply to destroy or incapacitate it. Yet, despite what he represents as the overall affirmative project of his writings, he acknowledges that it is not solely creative and certainly not passive: "I know the pleasure in destroying to a degree that accords with my powers to destroy—in both respects I obey my Dionysian nature which does not know how to separate doing No from saying Yes. I am the first immoralist: that makes me the annihilator *par excellence* [Ich bin der erste Immoralist: damit bin ich der Vernichter par excellence.—]" (*EH* "Why I Am a Destiny" 2). Thus, it would seem that Nietzsche thinks destruction is an inevitable dimension and consequence, if not a primary aim, of his agonistic practice. This is so not merely as a by-product, as his remarks about the overcoming of morality suggest, but as a necessary condition: "negating and destroying are conditions of saying Yes [im Jasagen ist Verneinen und Vernichten Bedingung]" (*EH* "Why I Am a Destiny" 4). This makes it challenging to assess his *Kriegs-Praxis* both in terms of how well he applied his principles as he specified them and in terms of how they square with his long-term project to analyze and assess oppositional structures and forms of organization, such as those evident in types.

In addition to elaborating his agonistic principles and their evidence in practice in his writings, Nietzsche tries to account for the fitness necessary to engage his *Kriegs-Praxis*. He emphasizes he is resistant without being reactive. Thus, he thinks his exposure to German decadence has the effect of strengthening him insofar as he resists it (*EH* "Why I Am So Clever" 6), but he claims that he is not merely oppositional and defiant, and he repeatedly describes himself as "the opposite of a no-saying spirit" (*EH* "Why I Am a Destiny" 1; see also *BGE* 31). He describes himself as "full" of opposites and believes that a source of his strength can be found in what it takes to coordinate the expression of (rather than simply unifying) such great diversity; he repeatedly champions his diversity rather than singularity of type.[65] To be sure, this is not sheer diversity, and individuality does not disappear. Nietzsche emphasizes how his diversity constitutes a plentitude by virtue of his *sublimation* of differing tastes (*EH* "Beyond Good and Evil"). This sense of unity is more like a manifold than a synthesis, and this helps us better understand how he offers somewhat more than a bundle theory in his conception of individuals as organizations of conflicting drives.[66] Individuals are distinguished on the basis of their constituent drives *and* their constitutional organization, that is, what I have called the *order of rule* that organizes the drives.

In what precedes the often-cited four principles of his war-making, Nietzsche indicates the ultimate significance of his endeavors. A type of measure ("eine Art Maass") of strength is found in opposition required in an encounter with resistance. The structure resistance provides is the ground out of which measure or rule emerges, but it does not specify or prescribe the particular measure or norm itself. Establishing a norm and what will constitute judgment is itself something *produced* in the interaction between the contestants— relative to their performances and capabilities. Measure, contextualized and thus conceived, is an emergent product connected directly with the experiences of the community in which it abides. In the course of participating in the agon he envisions for himself by means of his *Kriegs-Praxis*, Nietzsche does not strive to establish a single ideal measure. He writes that becoming master of what resists is not really the objective but rather "*becoming one who has pressed out of himself all of his strength* [seine ganze Kraft], flexibility [Geschmeidigkeit], and mastery of weapons [Waffen-Meisterschaft]—over an equal opponent [über gleiche Gegner . . .]" (*EH* "Why I Am So Wise" 7; emphasis added in translation). I take it that this passage is also crucial for considering whether Nietzsche is an advocate of the view espoused by Thrasymachus in Plato's *Republic* and would form the basis of a response to the typical indictment of the agonistic model, namely, that its chief aim is, at best, winning at all costs or, at worst, legitimating the subjugation and exploitation of others.[67] Through his *Kriegs-Praxis*, Nietzsche strives to maximize human activity and enable it to find creative expression: he aims to draw out—press out, *ex*press ("einzusetzen")—all his vigor, suppleness, and capacity for resistance, not for the purposes of subjugating others, but rather with the goal of transforming himself. His agones represent his efforts to engineer, harness, and direct in the future the efficient force that is the will to power that he *is*. They realize his "art of transfiguration," which he identifies with philosophy in the second preface to *GS*, and I think that part of this project entails a renewed emphasis on practical philosophy in which he sees opportunities for philosophy to play a role in orienting life.

Thus, through his *Kriegs-Praxis*, Nietzsche directly links the potency he acquires with enhanced capacities:

> For the task of a *revaluation of all values* more capacities may have been needed than have ever dwelt together in a single individual—above all, even contrary capacities that had to be kept from disturbing, destroying one another [vielleicht mehr Vermögen nöthig, als je in einem Einzelnen bei einander gewohnt haben, vor Allem auch Gegensätze von Vermögen, ohne dass diese sich stören, zerstören durften]. An order of rank among these capacities; distance; the art of separating without setting against one another; to mix nothing, to "reconcile" nothing; a tremendous variety that is nevertheless the opposite of chaos—this was the precondition, the long secret work and artistry of my instinct [Rangordnung der Vermögen; Distanz; die Kunst zu trennen, ohne zu verfeinden; Nichts vermischen, Nichts "versöhnen"; eine ungeheure Vielheit, die trotzdem das Gegenstück des Chaos ist—dies war die Vorbedingung, die lange geheime Arbeit und Künstlerschaft meines Instinkts].

Yet he claims that there is "no trace of struggle," no difficult challenge he sought to surmount ("I cannot remember that I ever tried hard"). In this activity, he refers to himself as "the opposite of a heroic nature"; "there is no ripple of desire." But this is because he successfully sought himself, preserved and defended himself through his practice of selfishness and self-protection. Thus, his account of his own *becoming* suggests that it did not entail becoming something other than what he already was, or at least that such was not his intent: "I do not want in the least that anything should become different than it is; I myself do not want to become different" (*EH* "Why I Am So Clever" 9). Thus, in his presentation of himself, we can come to appreciate that the swell of interest in his writings for agonism includes currents of nonagonistic elements that he appears to regard as complementary, not opposed.

5.9 *HOW* ONE BECOMES WHAT ONE IS

Nietzsche's presentation of himself as both a lover and a fighter suggests that *becoming what one is* is a process involving both more and less action on our parts than what accounts of his philosophy sometimes suggest. It is *less* because it is not a matter of us having a definite plan, a fixed notion of what we might become, or even sufficient will to bring about an alignment between our ambitions and our actions, as Nietzsche seems to have previously thought in his account of Wagner's development. It is *more* because, even though we can neither change the particular set of drives that constitute us nor deliberately arrange them as we might flowers in a vase, oil on a canvas, or words and ideas in poetry and literature, we can nevertheless influence whether our constitutive parts take a form capable of powerfully expressing the organization it becomes or whether we waste ourselves away through various forms of trivial and fruitless resistance, remaining nothing more than bits of chance.[68] Becoming what one is involves becoming a necessity, and this is how Nietzsche depicts himself in his work.

How does one become a necessity rather than a piece of chance? And what light does this shed on Nietzsche's views about the human subject and its possibilities for freedom? It seems odd to think that necessity is somehow optional or at least contingent. How could necessity be anything other than—*necessary*? As discussed above, Nietzsche repeatedly describes his development in terms of self-preservation rather than pure self-creation, and he characterizes the former as a way of harnessing energy so that it might be used for extraordinary tasks of the sort we find in his *Kriegs-Praxis* and the self-overflowing picture advanced by his Zarathustra. Self-preservation consists in cultivating oneself to avoid what is enervating; it involves care, sheltering, waiting, as discussed above. Becoming necessary, for Nietzsche, is a form of freedom, perhaps the highest form achievable by human beings, because it entails becoming capable, becoming enabled, activated, and enlivened. This conception of freedom as being capable allows us to see how Nietzsche's views about self-preservation and selfishness concern not sheer survival but rather a way of tapping creative powers. Thus, both fatalistic and existential dimensions are evident in his works even though they are incomplete without their complement.[69]

We have seen that Nietzsche thinks individuals are characterized by both orders of rank and ruling orders that maintain them. Orders of rank are more than fixed arrangements because there are also *abiding relations* (i.e., various ways of holding together and maintaining such arrangements) that characterize organizations. Constitutions are distinguished by the relative strength of the drive or drives that are dominant *and* their expressive efficacy and efficiency—that is how and how well constitutions are able to order the other drives to pursue and achieve their ends.[70] Organizations form on the basis of the nature of their constituent parts (drives) and the kinds of possible relations that are thereby circumscribed. They are also constituted in and through their external relations.

Nietzsche's presentation of his *Kriegs-Praxis* shows that he not only *organizes* fights, but also, by virtue of that activity *becomes organized*; he becomes what he is.[71] His practice of war is both *expressive* of the order of rank he is and *effective* in rendering that ordering so that in the course of such activity he becomes ordered in a certain way. The discussion above of the binding force of the agon is relevant here insofar as his fighting practices are complementary to his emphasis on love, and this provides further insight into to how it is possible to bind the multiple forces that constitute a person—how from *many* things one becomes *one*. Agonistics is but one (powerful) way of facilitating the union or binding of "the most multifarious drives," those vast ancestral inheritances, so as to make them resources and bases of strength rather than draining, distracting, misleading. This is not, however, the only relation that has this sort of constitutional character, and Nietzsche identifies and refers to a variety of relations that are similarly (if not more so) constitutive, including nutrition, climate, geography, topography, friendship, and a variety of other associations and experiences. He thinks that philosophical (particularly moral and religious) ideas can *literally* make us sick, physically decadent, and it is on this basis that he anticipates a revaluation of the body and all related dimensions of what is "this-worldly" (as opposed to *otherworldly*) might be reinvigorating, revitalizing. This is evident in his discussions of a wide range of physical and sensory experiences and how they bear on psychophysiological orders or constitutions, how orders of rank emerge, develop, and change.[72]

For example, when describing "why he writes such good books," Nietzsche nearly always mentions the *places* where they were written (e.g., St. Moritz, Naumburg, Genoa), and he frequently comments on the conditions of lighting and topography.[73] He mentions specific locations where ideas "come" to him, such as his famous declaration about the origin of the idea of eternal recurrence "6000 feet beyond man and time" in Silvaplana near Surlei (*EH* "Thus Spoke Zarathustra" 1).[74] His Mediterranean experiences are virtually inseparable from his writing *Zarathustra*: the climate; the proximity to sea and mountains; the lifeways of the inhabitants, especially the fishermen; means of locomotion, health, vitality, particularly in terms of constitutional fitness; and the topography, which provided sweeping and vast "vistas" (*EH* "Thus Spoke Zarathustra" 2). He associates these physiological and cultural experiences with his development of a capacity for *feeling*, which he describes as the *pathos of distance*: feeling something below or beneath as part of a process of heightening that is characteristic of the pathos of distance, for example, Christianity as beneath, "altogether unheard-of psychological depth and profundity" (*EH* "Why I Am a Destiny" 6). He claims this feeling gave him a particularly sharp sense of difference that facilitates rank ordering; it provides the conditions that make possible the exercise of judgment concerning what is higher and lower, nearer and further, and that allow one, at least potentially, to achieve a new order of relation "within" and "without" (e.g., *BGE* 57).

Nietzsche appears to hold that there is a wealth of human resources, a trove belonging to humanity as such, to the "household of the soul" (*BGE* 20), that one can tap, educe, activate, and bring to life in the order one is. One of the ways we draw out these resources, facilitate their development and organization, is through seeking out a variety of experiences and other relations that can make it possible to cultivate what early in his writings he calls a "second nature" (*HL* 3). He presents himself as doing precisely this in his account of the dual (even triple) nature he heralds in *EH* ("Why I Am So Wise" 3). What is significant to notice is that he does not claim distinction to *having* such a dual nature, much less willing it or simply creating or fashioning it for himself; he *acquires* it through experiences that access and cultivate resources that emerged through larger related historical, cultural, and physiological evolutionary and developmental processes.[75]

In his *Vom Nutzen und Nachtheil der Historie für das Leben*, Nietzsche describes a process of change in which we "plant in ourselves a new habit, a new instinct, a second nature, so that the first nature withers" (*HL* 3). This suggests that a deep level of change is possible, but we should inquire into *how* it is possible, particularly given that we do not have recourse to a true self or orchestrating agent behind the scenes who could be responsible for such cultivation. Moreover, any desire for a second nature, for a reordering of the drives that we are, can be nothing other than the expression of yet another drive that longs to be dominant, and thus we might wonder whether *deeper* is really the right way to think of it.[76] Would the dominant drive not simply seek to reproduce itself, albeit perhaps in a somewhat different pattern or taking on a somewhat different form of expression of what is essentially the same drive? If *nature* here refers simply to the nature of the dominant drive, then it does not seem to be the case that the second nature is a distinction that makes a difference. But, if a being's nature is characterized by both the order of rank one is *and* the ruling order that abides in its constitution and preservation, then perhaps a genuine difference can be possible, not just because one wills it, and not simply by force of accident or chance.

Acquiring a second nature or undergoing some sort of change in one's constitutive rank order is, we might imagine, something quite rare and not easily accomplished. In the first place, rank orders are inclined to preserve themselves; they tend toward *Selbsterhaltung*, as noted above. Moreover, that to which one is drawn to interact reflects preferences that accord with desires one *already* has on account of the order one *already* is. Yet it does seem possible to change what it is that one typically wants, to develop new desires as well as new tastes, and thereby to be drawn into new relations—were this not possible, the various forms of training and discipline in which we engage simply would not be possible. While the orientations of the drives might well be self-preserving, the effect of new relations among them is not entirely within any single drive's or collection's control. Organizations are constituted by their activities *in relation*, both internally and externally, and these relations potentially affect the ordering one is.

There are things we do that affect or influence the rank ordering we are, and these are deliberate without being deterministic: we select climates, foods, natural and constructed environments, friends, lovers, books, music, etc., experiment with new and different relations, try to develop new tastes and new loves, and stubbornly and relentlessly cling to others. In sum, we *are* amid a whole host of attachments, some of which can change, expand, or whither.[77] But the *we* here should be regarded as shorthand for *the order of drives that constitutes us as agents and the ruling order that abides therein.*[78] That *we* that selects and experiments is itself an order that has come to rule and be powerful enough to do the selecting, and it will select in ways compatible with the orientation of the drive or drives that prevail. It is the result of a process in which some parts strengthen relative to others, and that ruling order henceforth interacts with others and potentially seeks to refine or refigure *the order one is.*

In this respect, we can see that change is possible, indeed, that it is likely given the complexity of the constitutive elements, which Nietzsche characterizes as involved in a perpetual struggle for superiority over other drives and supremacy over the whole. In this respect, I think it is appropriate to regard his view of types as dynamic and fluid, with considerable possibilities for change. This does not mean that any individual drive or the whole itself deliberately seeks fundamental change; rather, the individual drives pursue only their further enhancement, though this is always in relation to the other drives. The order is characterized by a certain *manner of ruling*: its organization is maintained in a certain sort of way. Like Socrates in Plato's *Republic*, where we find the famous discussion of the different constitutions, Nietzsche is preoccupied with exploring how constitutional changes are possible and the role philosophy might play in bringing about such. In this context, he finds *necessity*, which is not inextricably linked with either essentialism or sheer affirmation.

It is through and within networks of interrelations that the particular perspectives and sets of orientations reflective of constitutive orders of rank come to be. As relations among drives change, relative to the strengthening or weakening of others, so too change the orders of rank relative to their more general *orientations* or how more powerful drives maintain their strength. What we call *I* is constituted, takes on a specific character and form, and becomes individual rather than a diffuse mix of competing forces in these contexts. One can, Nietzsche thinks, amplify, heighten, and pique such relations through a variety of physiological, historical, and psychological experiences and relationships. Some people appear to do this more readily and more ably than others. Predisposition to seeking out such relations appears to contribute to the process while not determining it. In other words, whether one *becomes* in a certain way is not simply a matter of whether one was (really, already) such a type from the start.

An explicit appreciation for both orders of rank and means of achieving and maintaining such ruling orders is essential to understanding how Nietzsche thinks about moral psychology and related philosophical concerns. Fatalistic views conceived solely in terms of types are too rigid and too simplistic: we are both orders of rank and ruling orders. Self-creationist models can too easily dismiss the *durability* of orders of rank and too readily overlook the fact that Nietzsche undermines the very conceptual resources needed for the kinds of projects they envision. The activity of ordering is dependent not only on acts of will but also on the variety of relations of which we are a part, including "small things" that nurture us and the actions we are thereby able to take.

Thus, we can see that becoming what one is also involves becoming able to act as some *one* entity that draws resources and gathers strength from having a great variety of dimensions. Becoming what one is, then, also entails from many things becoming one. This is a form of sovereignty, which for Nietzsche, at least in some contexts, refers to the form, efficiency, and efficacy of the activity of ruling that characterizes the organization of the constitutive drives, the order of rank *one is*. At the same time that he undermines the conception of the unitary, atomic, metaphysical substratum *I* (and in so doing emphasizes the multiplicity of drives and the potency of their *expression*), he nevertheless envisions orders or forms of ruling that give any particular organization integrity, durability, and expansive capabilities. A form of organization that he extensively examines and compares and contrasts with other forms is modeled on the agon. But, as we have also seen, in the end, this is not the complete story of his anticipated alternative to the ethics and metaphysics of morality in the narrow sense.

One becomes—is organized, becomes what one is—through relations of opposition and resistance as well as love, and this is what I think Nietzsche takes away from his agon with Wagner. Thus, the self is more than a mere collection of multiple parts that might be properly called an individual. Nietzsche makes it clear he thinks persons are many things, that rather than a singular agent there are many agencies at work in expressions of activity, but in great individuals, particularly, they are able to achieve a certain form of coordination of such multiplicity so as to maximize the expression of its diversity. Nietzsche expends great effort in examining effective and potent structures of ruling as well as various possible ways of educating the drives and effecting new possibilities for relations. It is an expressive activity that refers to the effective ruling of the order of rank that constitutes a person and allows one to "become what one is."

Nietzsche's sustained interest in agon involves much more than clinging to an idealized past. In the agon, he finds an engine for meaningful evaluation, a possible route to affirmation. This does more than build great individuals: it has a binding force, one that potentially supports a sense of responsibility, mutual indebtedness, and gratitude. The very same mechanism that distinguishes individuals, allows them to take their measure, also potentially increases the sense of achievement, the feeling of power, of all those who participate, even if indirectly, as Pindar's "Olympian 10" suggests. Throughout his writings, Nietzsche explores forms of struggle and opposition—those creative and destructive, those that seem to serve life, enhance it, and those that seem to diminish life, pursue its end or release—in order to understand how such forms of relation cultivate human organizations both individually and collectively. He seeks to identify features that are enabling, those that gather resources for expressive power, and tries to understand what makes such relations vulnerable to decay, how they disintegrate and become less effective.

In the course of his investigations, Nietzsche identifies various sorts of limits and conditions, possibilities and fragilities, that distinguish and qualify agonistic interactions. In his own philosophizing, itself agonistically oriented, he strives to realize what he calls his "Kriterium des rechten Handelns," or criteria for fair play (*EH* "Why I Am So Wise" 1): whether he succeeds or fails, he wants to fight at the right time and in the right way. Such practices demand what he claims as agonal wisdom—knowing when *not* to fight and what to avoid, what relations to refuse to be drawn into, so that he might have the resources for what could be fruitfully pursued. His goal is not, as some challengers describe it, merely "incessant contestation,"[1] contesting just for the sake of it. The contest, as evident in his analyses and applications, offers an engine for producing and reproducing values, which is crucial for combating nihilism, one of the greatest challenges he thinks modern human beings face.

Part of what is at stake in agonistic interaction, for Nietzsche and evident in each of the agones investigated here, is something like the *entitlement to symbolization* over which the Apollinian and the Dionysian are depicted as battling in his first work—that is, the right to determine the meaning and significance of things, the authorization or legitimation of values, setting the course for affirmative, creative expression. Agonistic engagements afford occasions to define what will count as excellent on the basis of what is actually expressed and evident in particular contests. Thus, it allows those who compete and those who gather to *stand by* and thereby share in making *manifest* such excellence, however it be defined. Such *standing by*, in the way Pindar depicts it, elaborated in the first chapter, contributes to making it real, tangible, true.

The organizing and orienting features of agon were important to Nietzsche and led him to consider whether such a relation might provide an apt characterization of the dynamic processes of development, growth, and change, more generally. Whether the agon is appropriately or fruitfully applied to all the concerns he imagined and just how useful it might be for contemporary readers surely merit even further exploration, but it should be clear from the cases considered here that his view of agon unfolds in an attempt at offering a comprehensive description of life, one that potentially enhances rather than diminishes its meaning and broadens opportunities for others to affirm it as valuable and worthwhile.

One result of agonistic exchange is that what is contestable becomes increasingly desirable, alluring, enticing. As one element vies for victory over its opponent, it stretches itself to maximally bring forth the quality that is tested, thereby making itself and its aims more attractive, more wanted. Thus, in agonistic exchange, two social currents are at work simultaneously—one eristic, oppositional, and the other erotic, drawing together—and they seem to be interdependent. Nietzsche's appreciation of the contest stems from his admiration for how the agon affords a dynamic gathering of elements that acquire meaning and give shape to forms of life that its participants and witnesses find attractive, worthwhile, and compelling. Such is a community bound together by both eris and eros.[2]

Agonistic engagement, considered in this way, not only reproduces or reevaluates current values but also supports the creation of new ones, new "wishes of the heart" (*BGE* 5) that make new forms of life possible.[3] What this amounts to is setting new interpretative paths for others to explore, exciting and drawing out and thereby strengthening some drives such that others simply die out or fade away. And it is in this respect that I think the ideas of will to power and eternal return are both supposed to have a therapeutic effect as they are valued as ideas to be incorporated in lives, as ways of organizing desires and their aims.

Such ignition of desire is of special interest to Nietzsche. He strives to create a new affective stance that makes it possible for us to *want* again,[4] to find something worthy of commitment, something *worth fighting for*. This affective stance is supposed to combat nihilism by making it possible to be drawn into the fight. So, in addition to fighting in order to become who he is, he endeavors to draw us into the fray, as he describes the alluring power of tragedy; this is precisely what he pursues as a promising possibility. This is not to say that the seduction of images is an unqualified good. He also recognizes the need for limits, and the agon model helps make more readily graspable the relation between erotic excess and the demands of justice. The maintenance of that boundary involves both ignition of desire and some sense of its *measure*. An ethos of agonism plays a role in this economy of desire that seems to be at the heart of most, if not all, of his projects.

Desire is certainly antecedent to committing oneself to an agonistic enterprise, but it is important to appreciate with Nietzsche how it is intensified, shaped, and refined through participation in such activity. It is not fully formed in advance and static. Those who compete often find that in the course of taking on such goals desire itself is perpetually tested and challenged such that the *maintenance of desire* itself becomes part of the struggle. This is true not only for sustaining the specific desire or desire for the particular goal but also the sustenance of any desire. Combating such desire fatigue can result in not only strengthening desire but also its redirection and reorientation.

Consider the example of the person who commits herself completely to some challenging activity such as running a marathon. The desire initially manifests as one to reach a specific end: running the 26.2-mile course. First-time marathoners soon learn, however, that the particular end in itself hardly seems to justify the months of training, physical discomfort, and time commitment. Unless one abandons one's goal, the desire must take on a different form, a transformation, a reorientation: one desires to become more physically able, one desires to maintain the community of friends one develops in the training process, or one comes to desire running simply for its own sake, no longer seeing it as a means to an end. And, because the training, and not only the activity of running the race itself, is the most difficult part, sustaining a desire conducive to *readiness* to complete the event becomes vital. This can be a life-altering experience because plugging into or connecting with such circuits of desire reorganizes and reorients one's priorities in such a way as to affect many basic decisions about how one lives, works, and plays. In the process, the overarching organization of one's life, the ways in which one directs one's actions, the aspirations to which one is attuned, all change. At times when this desire is challenged, compromised, or diminished, one finds not so much that one simply has a desire to do something else, say, paint or go rock climbing; rather, it seems that desire itself fades. A diminution of the meaning of the end, loosening the grip of desire for that end and all it takes to achieve it, can result in one not wanting anything at all. But, when such desire is abundant, vital, and robust, it can animate all other aspects of one's life. Goals of many varieties appear worthwhile and significant, not only those in the service of the one that ignited desire from the start. I think Nietzsche's analysis of the poignancy of the ascetic ideal and the internal opposition that drives it is tied to this matter of desire and the problems of its maintenance and direction. Much as he thinks the pleasure of tragedy issues from experience of the feeling of power that mounts in the tension of the contest of the Apollinian and the Dionysian, Nietzsche speculates we are drawn, at times going to extraordinary lengths, by the ascetic ideal and its practices of self-cruelty, seduced by the feeling of power that accrues in that dynamic. He considers whether agonism just might be a contender against asceticism or whether it is one particular form of it.

Agonistic engagement, I have argued, is a form of opposition that *produces* values in two significant respects, and these are worth underscoring as what distinguishes Nietzsche's attempt to overcome the nihilism inherent in the modern condition. In subjecting oneself to the test of engagement with others and the ultimate judgment by the standards that define the contest in the first place, one is compelled to manifest the distinction that is supposed to be measured in the decision of superiority. In the kinds of contests Nietzsche thinks are most productive, one does not win simply by tearing down one's opposition or by merely presenting oneself as morally superior or superior in any respect other than what one actually manifests in the engagement. One is a victor because of what one *does*, not what one *intends*, or what one has done in the past. So agonistic engagement can be thought of as productive in the sense that it instigates expression and motivates action.

Opponents should *want to win*. Nietzsche never casts his conception of the agon in any way that commits him to the facile view that "it isn't whether you win or lose but how you play the game." For those participating in the contest, for those subjecting themselves to the scrutiny of the community that provides the condition for the possibility of contestation, winning is surely the primary aim and the greatest source of motivation, although, as I have discussed above, this does not necessarily commit participants to holding the view that they must seek to win at any cost. Clearly, desiring to compete well is compatible with desiring to win, and one might prudently strive to compete well as a means toward greater success. But truly great competitors have an interest in *competing well*, in whatever way that becomes defined by the community or institution that makes competition possible, and not merely as a means to the end of victory. In this respect, we can also see how trivial ways of making one's struggles more arduous add nothing to victories—*simply struggling* is not the point.

What great victors want are *legitimate* (and legitimizing) wins. Great victors are those whose accomplishments acquire maximal meaning in their communal context. There can be little doubt that what such competitors seek for themselves is a victory that is definitive and, in its particular context, complete. That is, they want what secures their entitlement to the distinction of not only surmounting opposition but also serving as the standard bearers of what constitutes excellence in the context of those particular kinds of agonistic exchange. In this sense, it is perfectly reasonable to say that victors want *mastery*, that victors do not wish to be subjected to ostracism, that victors might rightly consider ostracism a violation of the terms of fair play. But that does not mean that the community seeking its own regulation through agonistic interaction must be similarly disposed. Nietzsche is quite mindful of this difference. Some might object that there is an apparent conflict between respect for the agon and the competitors' desire to win.[5] It is surely the case that playing a game has a telos of victory that requires wanting to win (though some games have no such terms), but playing to win and playing well are not mutually exclusive goals. If it were really the case that competitors played exclusively and only to win, we might imagine that the best competitors would be those who would refuse to compete against those potentially superior to them, that they would agree to engage their opposition only when their opponents were dwindling in their powers, and that cheating would be rampant even among, perhaps especially among, the top competitors. This is not the case precisely for the reason that competitors recognize—indeed, actively seek out and subject themselves to—the *legitimizing function* of institutionalized agon. What they seek is not only winning or recognition: winners want *meaningful* accomplishment.

Struggles can take various forms, obviously—agones or contests are just one. It should be clear from the foregoing analysis that Nietzsche's interest is not simply in the might or power of winners; rather, he is concerned with the whole process of agonistic exchange as well as the context in which it occurs. So, for example, in his contest with Homer, Nietzsche is concerned with the *dynamic* relations of the Apollinian and Dionysian—the whole process of their engagement—and not simply the emergence of the Dionysian (as is sometimes emphasized in the interpretative literature) or the tragic end. Nietzsche's interest is something different from just the fact that some strong(er) participant *wins* any particular engagement—he explores *how* victors emerge, considered both from the standpoint of the actions of the vying parties and from the viewpoint of those responsible for the decision. This interest is clear throughout and especially in his engagements with Socrates, whom he regards as winning by default when he tears down his opponents dialectically, and with Paul, whom he regards as aiming to obliterate his opposition. Moreover, Nietzsche's early considerations of how the relations between the individual and the community are mediated in agonistic exchange also draw our attention to the significance of the exercise of judgment and the activity of esteeming that agonistic institutions provide.[6] This was clear in his discussion of ostracism as indicative of the importance of perpetuating contest and his account of the tangibility of what emerges as victorious. Victors in contests do not typically just seize their victories; they are beholden to rules that define and make possible any exchange in the first place and the community of judges (or the tradition of judgment) that determines what constitutes superlative performance. This kind of interaction binds together one's own performance and excellence with that of another as well as the community of judges that makes it possible and those who memorialize it, as Pindar so beautifully describes. Our appreciation of these significant qualifications for what Nietzsche regards as victorious strength should give us a more subtle appreciation of how he conceives power and what *will to power* means.

Another major point of emphasis in this book is how agonism is evident in Nietzsche's notion of self-overcoming. It responds to needs that follow from what he describes as the Socratic/Platonic and Pauline/Christian relocations and perversions of contest. Instigating what might be characterized as a deepening of soul, Socrates is depicted as shifting the site of agon from the Homeric public sphere to the psychic realm. At the same time, he reorganizes it so as to encourage incapacitating opposition, with the result that participation is enervating rather than invigorating. Paul capitalizes on this model of organizing psychic power, intensifying the *Vernichtungslust* that animates the activity, and he develops it further for use as a weapon against others in order to dominate them. Nietzsche associates these models of opposition with the ascetic ideal insofar as they foster practices of self-opposition that generate particularly intense forms of power and are ultimately bent toward self-destruction. Such forms achieve and maintain supremacy by annihilating legitimate opposition and thwarting any possible challenge. His vision of self-overcoming recasts the nature of the subject in terms of conflicting natural drives that can be creatively oriented in their strivings, prospectively (but not at all necessarily) motivated by rising above (*Erhebung*) and oriented toward some form of excellence. Put bluntly, I argue that Nietzsche appears to be trying to reformulate the psychic agon and he explores the necessary conceptual resources (including his revision of the soul hypothesis) as well as consequences that follow from this shift in thought as evident in his self-presentation and his contrasting portrait of Wagner. One important consequence is especially relevant for discussion of competing images of subjectivity and the forms of life they might realize. The self-overcoming subject has a different sensibility about power and the means of achieving it. One critical difference between the ascetic ideal and Nietzsche's model of self-overcoming is the way in which they generate the feeling of power, *Machtgefühl*. This significantly affects both their self-relations and their possible relations with others. In the self-giving model, one seeks to expand one's scope of responsibility, and this provides a basis for a certain kind of social agency that Nietzsche heralds but never explores in considerable depth, perhaps because he did not think it worthwhile, but that we might.

The basic idea of existence as struggle informs Nietzsche's interests in the relation between art and culture as well as the science of his day; it guides his engagement of questions relating to development and evolution and his conception of philosophy's role in reformulating, directing, and critiquing both the structure and the assumptions of various kinds of inquiry. Everything strives for power, broadly construed, and the means of doing so can vary considerably (e.g., as interpretation, appropriation, as well as exploitation). The agonistic framework provides Nietzsche with an analytic tool for understanding how such striving takes place as well as an assessment measure of its efficacy and benefits.

Enmity can be a *potentially* positive and creative motivating force, a propellant toward overcoming. Of course, it can also be an enervating situation from which one seeks peace, rest, the dissolution of tension, "sleep," as Nietzsche describes repeatedly in his works and with intensive focus in the third essay of the *Genealogy*. In the preface to *Jenseits von Gut und Böse*, he notes that there have been at least two attempts to relax or unbend the bow, to cut the string that produces such tension: among the Jesuits and with the democratic Enlightenment. What he highlights as a distinguishing characteristic of the community that his book aims to draw together—those he summons as "we *good Europeans* and free, *very* free spirits"—is that they "still feel it," that is, still feel this tension. Part of his task throughout his writings is to bring this out and potentially generate such feeling in others. Thus, his contest with Socrates might also be considered an attempt to reinvigorate or revitalize a tremendous struggle, not necessarily—indeed, if I am right, explicitly *not*—for the purpose of deciding it; that is, in contesting Socrates, Nietzsche strives to put competing values seriously *in play*, revitalizing the contest for his readers and others and not just bringing it to a different end in which he claims victory. Nietzsche's early figure of the music-making Socrates might embody this magnificent tension rather than dissolving or resolving it one way or the other. What hangs in the balance of this contest, the prize that is sought, is entitlement to determine the significance of human existence.

Consideration of these stakes also sheds light on why Nietzsche at times (increasingly as he was approaching the end of his productive career) refers to his activities in terms of *war* rather than *play*, even though I have argued that his agonism seeks to temper or at least qualify his martial and belligerent stances. Both the force or *magnitude* of the opposition (e.g., "Christianity") and the *stakes* (e.g., forms of life) suggest use of such language. Others have also explored instances of Nietzsche's war practices and his sense of *gegen* or opposition in terms of the form of opposition he takes, contrasting it with the kind of opposition he repeatedly criticizes.[7] I have elaborated how Nietzsche is critical of forms of anti-agonistic actions and aims throughout his writings. The primary basis of his critique of exemplars of world-historic value creators (or redirectors) rests on the basis of his assessment of their agonistic fitness. But Nietzsche faces the challenge of how to oppose them without simply committing himself to the very practices and ends he criticizes. Put another way, if Homer, Socrates, Paul, and Wagner emerge in a world-historic agon for values in which they seek to vanquish their predecessors and become the ultimate victors in a contest of determining values and the forms of life they animate, then there is a question about how Nietzsche can join the fray and what it is he should aim to achieve, particularly if he does not want to be guilty of the very same tendencies he criticizes. It might seem contradictory to hold simultaneously the perspectives of wanting to win and wanting the field of contestation to remain open, but I do not think such a conflict is absolutely necessary. Our best examples of sports, political, and cultural exemplars all show a deep recognition of and respect for the institutions that make their accomplishments and victories possible. They can both want to win, even dominate their field, have legitimate authority in their relevant sphere of activity, *and* recognize that a necessary condition is sustenance of the institution that enables them to act at all, that is, what defines the arena in which they act. They can both love the institution that provides the condition for their expression (and so affirm and strive to preserve it) and resist with all their might challenges to their own title.

In some respects, we might judge Nietzsche's contest with Wagner the most successful. It might be the only one that actually gains some traction in terms of truly pushing him to formulate a positive alternative. The other contests, to varying degrees, elicit strong oppositional force but generally fail to produce a positive alternative. Nietzsche vies to exceed Homer, but he certainly does not achieve that in his lifetime and arguably still has not done so in his legacy. He struggles desperately to envision an alternative to Socratic philosophy yet rarely, if at all, advances beyond his earlier condition of being so close to him that he constantly resists him. The contest with Paul is very difficult to recognize as exemplifying the positive terms Nietzsche identifies and much more closely resembles the *Vernichtungslust* he accuses Paul of intensifying. But in the case of Wagner Nietzsche appears, in the end, motivated to formulate a positive alternative (setting aside the strengths and weakness of the art he sought to produce in his *Also Sprach Zarathustra*). There are genuinely provocative insights and suggestions for alternative conceptions of agency that Nietzsche advances in his struggles with and against Wagner. I have suggested how these are particularly relevant to discussions of moral psychology today.

Agonistic engagements potentially facilitate development of shared bases for values, a sense of community, what is "ours" both because it is the outcome of public decision and because it refers to activity that has been produced within and emerges out of the community itself. This is a form of social identity different from what is conjured in theories of recognition. It is not just that one feels validated when subjected to the evaluation of someone else whose opinion one respects. Worthy enemies are good because they *motivate us to certain kinds of action*, they spur us to do the particular deeds that will define us; they move us to *become what we are* and not just because they make us feel good about ourselves or because our value is contingent on the *idea* another holds of us. Thus, the agon is potentially a bridge to love, as Nietzsche describes it in the passage from the *Genealogy* that serves as this book's epigraph, and not merely an engine for churning destructive jealousy.

Each of Nietzsche's agonists serves as a standard bearer for value, resetting and reestablishing the terms of measure that garner the respect and adoption of others. In this way, we can see the stakes of agonistic exchange as *one route* toward achieving greater responsibility in the sense sketched in the final chapter. It is also reminiscent of the sense of responsibility and indebtedness evident in Pindar as discussed in chapter 1. Participation in agonistic exchange involves staking a claim to achievement and in some cases to becoming a standard bearer. It provides access to new and more expansive domains of activity, spheres of expressive power, and opportunities to realize and manifest capabilities. One might have desires and preferences individually, but values capable of *organizing a life* have to be shared, or at least be sufficiently overlapping, so as to allow for social action. Nietzsche thought that the agon was a particularly effective way, though not necessarily the only one, to sustain such actionable commitments to shared values.

What such actionable commitment entails is explored throughout this book in a variety of ways and contexts. It requires direction and motivation, which Nietzsche finds expressed in the figure of the good Eris, who whets ambitious appetites and steers human beings to excel. It requires an institutional organization that gathers the community to witness and sanction decisions about the outcomes. This is evident in the vast community Pindar summons in praising Hagesidamos, which includes not only the boy and his trainer but also his fellow challengers, his past competitors, those who make his home and share his city, and the deities and intermediaries in whose honor the games are held. The community is essential not only for the exercise of judgment but also because it is needed to cultivate the habits and dispositions that are conducive to productive participation.

Nietzsche construed many, if not all, of his inquiries (and objects of inquiry themselves) as struggles and often, more specifically, as *contests*. To illuminate the impetus to art and creative activity, he presents the contest of Apollo and Dionysus. Exploring the relation between art and culture, he pits Homer against Hesiod and the "forest wisdom" of Silenus more generally. He characterizes inquiry itself, particularly philosophy and science, as a contest between wills to truth and ignorance. He presents the development of values generally as monumental struggles between conflicting worldviews that tend to diminish or affirm the significance of life, what one might characterize as a contest between affirmation and negation. And he conceives individual and collective human development in terms of processes in which contestation plays an important role—it can help define us not merely in terms of what "survives" such conflict but also in terms of that to which such engagements thereby *bind* us, making it possible to organize and access the great diversity that constitutes life.

NOTES

INTRODUCTION

1. John Richardson, *Nietzsche's System* (New York: Oxford University Press, 1996); Robert B. Pippin, *Nietzsche, Psychology, and First Philosophy* (Chicago: University of Chicago Press, 2010).

2. See Alexander Nehamas, *Nietzsche: Life as Literature* (Cambridge, MA: Harvard University Press, 1985), chap. 1; and *KSA* 11:27[59].

3. I am also indebted to the account of such organizations in terms of *soul* in Graham Parkes, *Composing the Soul: Reaches of Nietzsche's Depth Psychology* (Chicago: University of Chicago Press, 1994), esp. 106–20. I engage Parkes's work in chapter 5.

4. Nehamas, *Nietzsche: Life as Literature*.

5. See esp. Richardson, *Nietzsche's System*, 156–58, 161–63, 186–89.

6. For established critiques of the use of *The Will to Power* in the scholarly literature, see Bernd Magnus, "The Use and Abuse of *The Will to Power*," in *Reading Nietzsche*, ed. Robert C. Solomon and Kathleen Marie Higgins (New York: Oxford University Press, 1988), 218–36; and Wayne Klein, "Nietzsche's Apocrypha: *The Will to Power* and Contemporary Scholarship," *New Nietzsche Studies* 1, nos. 1/2 (Fall/Winter 1996): 102–25.

7. Kaufmann does Nietzsche a disservice when he claims that "Homer's Wettkampf" is a fragment, for this suggests that it was merely one of the many rough and unfinished pieces left in the notebooks. See Walter Kaufmann, *Nietzsche: Philosopher, Psychologist, Antichrist* (Princeton, NJ: Princeton University Press, 1974), 193. He overlooks Nietzsche's own remarks about the work and the circumstances in which it came to be shared with others.

8. Their dedication reads: "Für Frau Cosima Wagner in herzlicher Verehrung und als Antwort auf mündliche und briefliche Fragen, vergnügten Sinnes niedergeschrieben in den Weihnachtstagen 1872." *KSA* 1, p. 754.

9. For a few examples of plans, see *KSA* 7:1[23], 2[7], 2[8], 9[18], virtually all of fragment 16, 19[327], 20[1], 21[5], 21[22], 23[5], 26[23], 29[169], 29[173], 8:22[10].

10. See, e.g., *HH* 158–59, 170, 259, 261; *AOM* 222, 379; *WS* 29–31, 33, 99, 226. See also *D* 38, 69; *GS* 168; *Z* I "On Enjoying and Suffering Passions," "On War and Warriors," "On the Friend"; *BGE* 23; and *A* 16.

11. Owing to the writings of William Connolly and, more recently, of Lawrence J. Hatab, David Owen, Alan Schrift, Herman Siemens, Paul van Tongeren, Joe Ward, and others. To appreciate the range of applications of Nietzsche's agonism, see a special issue devoted to the topic: *Journal of Nietzsche Studies* 24 (Fall 2002). See also Lawrence J. Hatab, "Prospects for a Democratic Agon: Why We Can Still Be Nietzscheans," *Journal of Nietzsche Studies* 24 (Fall 2002): 132–47; David Owen, "Equality, Democracy, and Self-Respect: Reflections on Nietzsche's Agonal Perfectionism," *Journal of Nietzsche Studies* 24 (Fall 2002): 113–31; Herman Siemens, "Agonal Communities of Taste: Law and Community in Nietzsche's Philosophy of Transvaluation," *Journal of Nietzsche Studies* 24 (Fall 2002): 83–112; Paul van Tongeren, "Nietzsche's Greek Measure," *Journal of Nietzsche Studies* 24 (Fall 2002): 5–24; and Janet Lungstrum Ward, "Nietzsche's Transvaluation of Jewish Parasitism," *Journal of Nietzsche Studies* 24 (Fall 2002): 54–82.

12. Thus, I agree with Bernard Reginster's general claim that the affirmation of life is a central concern for Nietzsche and that struggle plays a very important role in how such is possible. See Bernard Reginster, *The Affirmation of Life: Nietzsche on Overcoming Nihilism* (Cambridge, MA: Harvard University Press, 2006). I see my work as offering a more elaborate and detailed account of the relation between struggle and affirmation. I engage some of Reginster's specific claims below.

13. Others have described this as an *ecstatic logic*. John Sallis is notable among Anglophone writers for discussing this idea. See his *Crossings: Nietzsche and the Space of Tragedy* (Chicago: University of Chicago Press, 1991), discussed in chapter 2 below.

14. See Richard Patterson, "'Philosophos Agonistes': Imagery and Moral Psychology in Plato's 'Republic,'" *Journal of the History of Philosophy* 35, no. 3 (1997): 327–54.

15. The affective dimensions of Nietzsche's work are especially important. Helpful treatments of this include Christopher Janaway, *Beyond Selflessness: Reading Nietzsche's Genealogy* (Oxford: Oxford University Press, 2007); Reginster, *The Affirmation of Life*; and Parkes, *Composing the Soul*.

CHAPTER ONE

1. "Wenn man von Humanität redet, so liegt die Vorstellung zu Grunde, es möge das sein, was den Menschen von der Natur abscheidet und auszeichnet. Aber eine solche Abscheidung giebt es in Wirklichkeit nicht: die "natürlichen" Eigenschaften und die eigentlich "menschlich" genannten sind untrennbar verwachsen. Der Mensch, in seinen höchsten und edelsten Kräften, ist ganz Natur und trägt ihren unheimlichen Doppelcharakter an sich." Friedrich Nietzsche, "Homer's Wettkampf" (HC), in *KSA* 1, pp. 783–92. All translations of this text are my own, slightly revised from my translation published in "Re/Introducing 'Homer's Contest': A New Translation with Notes and Commentary," *Nietzscheana* 5 (Fall 1996): i–iv, 1–8.

2. In recent years, some extensive research has explored both Nietzsche's knowledge of contemporary science as well as his assessment of it. See esp. Gregory Moore, *Nietzsche, Biology and Metaphor* (Cambridge: Cambridge University Press, 2002); Gregory Moore and Thomas H.

Brobjer, eds., *Nietzsche and Science* (Aldershot: Ashgate, 2004); Robin Small, *Nietzsche in Context* (Aldershot: Ashgate, 2001); and Thomas H. Brobjer, *Nietzsche's Philosophical Context: An Intellectual Biography* (Urbana: University of Illinois Press, 2007). For an extensive meditation on Nietzsche's views of science and how they inform his conception of philosophy, see Babette Babich, *Nietzsche's Philosophy of Science: Reflecting Science on the Ground of Art and Life* (Albany: State University of New York Press, 1994).

3. This is not to say that human beings are unique in valuing. Others have discussed how Nietzsche regards all perspective taking as laden with values and how there are places in his works suggesting that all existence (even the inorganic world) can be said to have a perspective. My claim here is simply that he has a keen interest in the *particular way in which* human beings value; as *valuing animals* he finds them most interesting.

4. For helpful discussion of precisely this concern and a variety of forms of teleology, see John Richardson, *Nietzsche's New Darwinism* (New York: Oxford University Press, 2004), 26ff. See also his *Nietzsche's System*, 21.

5. Included among them, though neither English nor chiefly a psychologist, is Paul Rée. See his "The Origin of Moral Sensations," in *Basic Writings*, trans. and ed. Robin Small (Urbana: University of Illinois Press, 2003), 85–164.

6. See, e.g., Stephen Stich, John Doris, and Erica Roedder, "Altruism," in *The Moral Psychology Handbook*, ed. J. M. Doris and the Moral Psychology Research Group (Oxford: Oxford University Press, 2010), 147–205.

7. See Jacob Burckhardt, *The History of Greek Culture*, trans. Sheila Stern, ed. with an introduction by Oswyn Murray (New York: St. Martin's, 1998), passim, esp. "The Agonal Age." Although most commentators have claimed that Nietzsche derived his views about the agon from Burckhardt, Murray corrects this view in his introduction. It is clear from examining his *Nachlass* that Nietzsche was thinking about the subject well before he became personally acquainted with Burckhardt or attended his lectures in Basel, as I detailed for Mr. Murray in a personal communication in 1996. Burckhardt's lectures on ancient Greece were not published until after his death, and, although Nietzsche did have a transcript, prepared by a student, it was acquired well after he had begun to think about the significance of the agon. More likely sources for his ideas are George Grote's *Geschichte Griechenlands* (1859–65), translated as *History of Greece*, 12 vols. (New York: Harper & Bros., 1859–65), which includes discussions about Greek competitions, and Ernst Curtius's "Der Wettkampf" (1856), in *Göttinger Festreden* (Berlin: Wilhelm Herz, 1864), 1–22.

8. See Pausanias 9.31.4.

9. There is no evidence that the second Eris goddess played a significant role in Greek mythology. However, two modern studies suggest that the conceptual distinction Hesiod personifies might have played a significant role in ancient Greek society, specifically, the distinction between *zelos* (commonly translated *jealousy*) and *phthonos* (commonly translated *envy*). *Zelos* was generally a positive word, indicating a desire to imitate or emulate, while *phthonos* was used to indicate dangerous and hostile antagonism of the sort that might arise in sibling rivalry or sexual jealousy. See Peter Walcot, *Envy and the Greeks* (Warminster: Aris & Phillips, 1978); and Patricia Bulman, *Phthonos in Pindar*, Classical Studies, vol. 35 (Berkeley and Los Angeles: University of California Press, 1995).

10. My translation. Compare *HH* 300: "*Two kinds of equality.*—The thirst for equality can

express itself either as a desire to draw everyone down to oneself (through diminishing them, spying on them, tripping them up) or to raise oneself and everyone else up (through recognizing their virtues, helping them, rejoicing in their success)" (Hollingdale, trans.).

11. See, e.g., Don Dombowsky, *Nietzsche's Machiavellian Politics* (Basingstoke: Palgrave, 2004), 39.

12. For a somewhat different account of Socrates as a philosophical agonist, see Patterson, "'Philosophos Agonistes.'"

13. Roger Caillois's famous study of games provides a helpful taxonomy. See *Man, Play, and Games*, trans. Meyer Barash (New York: Free Press, 1961).

14. Hatab's and Richardson's discussions of this are especially helpful. See Lawrence Hatab, *A Nietzschean Defense of Democracy: An Experiment in Postmodern Politics* (Chicago: Open Court, 1995); and Richardson, *Nietzsche's System.*

15. Diogenes Laertius 9.1 recounts the incident. See also Heraclitus, frag. 121.

16. Thus anyone who attempts to utilize *Nietzsche's* views specifically for democratic political theory needs to show how the resultant views meet the challenges to democracy that he makes. The most elaborate attempt to do just that is Hatab's *A Nietzschean Defense of Democracy.* See also Herman Siemens and Vasti Roodt, eds., *Nietzsche, Power and Politics: Rethinking Nietzsche's Legacy for Political Thought* (Berlin: Walter de Gruyter, 2008).

17. This is the basis of the critique of contemporary political agonism in my *"Demos Agonistes Redux*: Reflections on the *Streit* of Political Agonism," *Nietzsche-Studien* 32 (2003): 373–89.

18. See the *Oxford English Dictionary*, 2nd ed. (1998). See also J. D. Ellsworth, *"Agon*: Studies in the Use of a Word" (Ph.D. diss., University of California, Berkeley, 1971).

19. My understanding of the nature and influence of agonistic relations in ancient Greek culture has been shaped by many works not cited here, although I include them in the bibliography. I am also indebted to my colleagues and teachers, particularly Jay Bregman, Adele Haft, Nickolas Pappas, Richard Patterson, and Steven Strange, for recommendations for sources and nourishing my curiosity.

20. Pindar, "Olympian 10," in *Pindar's Victory Songs*, trans. Frank J. Nisetich (Baltimore: Johns Hopkins University Press, 1980), 131–35. Unless otherwise noted, my citations of Pindar are drawn from this translation. I have also benefited from Nisetich's commentary.

21. This etymological account is not free of contention, although it has many followers. It is possible to affirm the etymological connections without committing to the history of the concept of truth or the ontological implications that Heidegger draws from it.

22. Pindar, "Olympian 10," lines 19–21: "With a god's favoring hand, one man may whet another's ambition, inspire him to prodigious feats, if glory's in his birthright."

23. In preparing my analysis, I have consulted multiple translations of Pindar. For clarification, I occasionally provide additional translations drawn from Pindar, *Complete Odes*, trans. Anthony Verity and Stephen Instone (Oxford: Oxford University Press, 2007), as noted below.

24. These are the Molionidai, the twins Kteatos and Eurytos, who played important roles in the successful effort to beat back Herakles in his first attack against Augeas.

25. Pindar, "Olympian 10," lines 34–42.

26. Ibid., lines 43-48, 43-54.

27. I highlight this point because the sense of agency evident in ancient Greek literature, particularly that of the archaic period, has been a source of contention in the scholarship. See the discussion in Bernard Williams, *Shame and Necessity* (Berkeley and Los Angeles: University of California Press, 1993), chap. 2 ("Centres of Agency").

28. "Olympian 10," lines, 55-63, 13. The most elaborate account of Herakles' battle with Kyknos is found in a text traditionally attributed to Hesiod, "The Shield of Herakles." The inference I suggest might have a basis in the account at lines 338-49. This battle was a favorite subject of painters throughout ancient Greece. Modern scholars generally agree that "The Shield of Herakles" was *not* written by Hesiod, although it is widely acknowledged to be a very early text. For discussion, see R. Janko, "The Shield of Heracles and the Legend of Cycnus," *Classical Quarterly* 36, no. 1 (1986): 38-59; and H. A. Shapiro, "Herakles and Kyknos," *American Journal of Archaeology* 88, no. 4 (1984): 523-29. "The Shield of Heracles" is collected in *Hesiod: The Homeric Hymns and Homerica*, trans. Hugh Evelyn-White, Loeb Classical Library (Cambridge, MA: Harvard University Press, 1914).

29. "Olympian 10," lines 49-53.

30. The Moirai play a significant role in the Myth of Er, mentioned below, which concludes Plato's *Republic* (620d-621d).

31. "Olympian 10," lines 76-84, 97-105.

32. Ibid., lines 91-96.

33. Dana L. Burgess, "Pindar's Olympian 10: Praise for the Poet, Praise for the Victor," *Hermes* 118, no. 3 (1990): 273-81.

34. Burgess writes: "He [Pindar] has used praise of himself to intensify the praise of the *laudandus*. He has finessed the problem of reciprocal relations which devolve into a coarse battle for superiority" (ibid., 277-78). I agree with Burgess (who builds on an argument by E. Bundy) that there is a "crucial paedogogy" at work here. I simply think there is more to be offered as explanation for how this was achieved by virtue of the broader economy that made it possible for Pindar to stake his claim to an *achievement*.

35. Ibid., 278.

36. Bernard Williams, *Truth and Truthfulness: An Essay in Genealogy* (Princeton, NJ: Princeton University Press, 2002), esp. 271-77.

37. Leslie Kurke, "The Economy of Kudos," in *Cultural Poetics in Archaic Greece: Cult, Performance, Politics*, ed. Carol Dougherty and Leslie Kurke (New York: Cambridge University Press, 1993), 141, 132.

38. See Herodotus 6.133-37. See also my "Nietzsche's Problem of Homer," *Nietzscheforschung: Jahrbuch der Nietzsche-Gesellschaft* 5/6 (Spring 2000): 553-74.

39. "Und dieser göttliche Neid entzündet sich, wenn er den Menschen ohne jeden Wettkämpfer gegnerlos auf einsamer Ruhmeshöhe erblickt."

40. Compare: "At present, all [cultural] bases, the mythical and sociopolitical, have changed; our pretended culture has no stability because it's been built on shaky, indeed already crumbling, conditions and beliefs.—So, if we fully understand Greek culture, we see that it's gone for good" ("Jetzt haben sich nun alle Fundamente, die mythischen und die politisch-socialen verändert; unsere angebliche Cultur hat keinen Bestand, weil sie sich auf unhaltbare, fast schon

verschwundene Zustände und Meinungen aufbaut.—Die griechische Cultur vollständig be-greifend sehen wir also ein, dass es vorbei ist"; *KSA* 8:3[76]). "To be noted: how *prevalent* degeneration is, even in Hellas; how rare and transient greatness is, how inadequately (on the false side) evaluated" ("Zu zeigen, wie überwiegend auch in Hellas die Entartung ist, wie selten und kurz das Grosse, wie mangelhaft (von der falschen Seite) geschätzt"; *KSA* 8:5[146]). Both translations are William Arrowsmith's from the compilation of passages he gathered un-der the title "We Classicists" in *Unmodern Observations* (New Haven, CT: Yale University Press, 1990), 345, 375.

41. See Herodotus 9.120.

42. Burckhardt (*The Greeks and Greek Civilization* [1872]) makes frequent observations about the connection between the agonistic culture of the ancient Greeks and warfare. For more contemporary discussion, see Jean-Pierre Vernant, *Myth and Society in Ancient Greece*, trans. Janet Lloyd (New York: Zone, 1988), esp. 29–53.

43. The term *agonistic respect* is William Connolly's. See his *Identity/Difference: Demo-cratic Negotiations of Political Paradox* (Ithaca, NY: Cornell University Press, 1991), and *The Ethos of Pluralism* (Minneapolis: University of Minnesota Press, 1995).

44. "Bemerken wir wohl daß so wie Miltiades untergeht, auch die edelsten griechischen Staaten untergehen, als sie, durch Verdienst und Glück, aus der Rennbahn zum Tempel der Nike gelangt waren."

45. N. R. E. Fisher analyzes contexts for use of the word *hybris* and traces the similarities of its use from Homer to the New Comedy in *Hybris: A Study in the Values of Honour and Shame in Ancient Greece* (Warminster: Aris & Phillips, 1992).

46. "Das Agonale ist auch die Gefahr bei aller Entwicklung; es überreizt den Trieb zum Schaffen.—Der glücklichste Fall in der Entwicklung, wenn sich mehrere Genie's gegenseitig in Schranken halten."

47. I emphasize the cultural value of history in my analysis. Christian J. Emden argues that such cultural interest is inherently politically oriented. While I am uncertain about the primacy of this motivation, I think Emden is right to emphasize the social dimensions of Nietzsche's conception of history. He provides a valuable account of the context in which Nietzsche's ideas about history emerge, specific connections between the development of historiography and modern politics, and a nuanced reading of Nietzsche's *HL*, among other topics, in *Friedrich Nietzsche and the Politics of History* (Cambridge: Cambridge University Press, 2008).

48. Compare *GS* 143, where Nietzsche considers varieties of normative possibilities stem-ming from the adoption of multiple, even opposing, perspectives. Such reflections suggest that subjective agonism might facilitate individual activity and development, as Nietzsche describes his own case in *Ecce Homo*.

49. Or, more properly speaking, as exemplified in the Homeric worldview. Nietzsche is interested in the classic Homeric question—Who was Homer? Did such a person exist and was he the author of what became the Homeric texts?—but he has a different approach to this de-fining problem in philology. See my "The Contest between Nietzsche and Homer: Revaluing the 'Homeric Question,'" in *Nietzsche and the German Tradition*, ed. Nicholas Martin (Berne: Peter Lang, 2003), 83–109.

50. Of course, it is not at all a good thing to be envied by the gods. It is, however, quite an accomplishment to reach such a position.

51. This is why I suggested above that Nietzsche might be regarded as sympathetic to Thrasymachus's charge against Socrates in the *Republic* that he is interested only in tearing down his opponents rather than demonstrating that his own views are superior.

52. Thus, although there are numerous other contestants one might wish to consider (e.g., Luther, Darwin, etc.) the selection of Homer, Socrates, Paul, and Wagner is not accidental. In Nietzsche's eyes, these particular contests are intrinsically linked in the manner just described.

CHAPTER TWO

1. See, e.g., *Z* II "On Self-Overcoming"; and Nietzsche's characterization of the ascetic ideal in *GM* III.

2. This expression occurs in several sources, including Sophocles, "Oedipus at Colonus," lines 1224–25, cited and discussed in *BT* 3; Aristotle's fragmentary dialogue *Eudemos*; and Schopenhauer's citation of Calderón's reference to the view. Opinions differ about the source of Nietzsche's evidence for an older pessimistic view that he thinks Homer overcomes. I think the most likely influence comes from Theognis, the focus of Nietzsche's intensive research at Leipzig. In his *Elegies*, Theognis writes: "For man the best thing is never to be born, / Never to look upon the hot sun's rays, / Next best, to speed at once through Hades' gates / And lie beneath a piled-up heap of earth" (*Hesiod and Theognis*, trans. Dorothea Wender [New York: Penguin, 1973], 111 [lines 425–28]). While Schopenhauer favorably cites Calderón, it is clear in *BT* that Nietzsche cheers for the overcoming of such a view. This suggests that, even from the start, he renounced some of his intellectual mentor's central ideas while at the same time retaining deep admiration for his work.

3. But *who is Homer?* This concern is one among several questions defining the discipline of philology, which sought to identify the authenticity of ancient texts, determine authorship, and track transmission. Like virtually all budding philologists, Nietzsche was expected to take a position on what is called the Homeric Question. I discuss this in my "The Contest between Nietzsche and Homer." My focus there is to show how Nietzsche attempted to recast the Homeric Question in such a way as to make it *philosophical* by virtue of focusing on the rise and fall of Homeric values.

4. A version of the decline of humankind from its original moral ideal is described by Hesiod in *Works and Days* (lines 156–73). M. I. Finley contrasts Greek versions of the myth, similar to those in other cultures, with an earlier Zoroastrian version in his *The World of Odysseus*, 2nd rev. ed. (1978; reprint, New York: Penguin, 1991), 26–27.

5. Ibid., 28.

6. James Redfield, "Homo Domesticus," in *The Greeks*, ed. Jean-Pierre Vernant, trans. Charles Lambert and Teresa Lavender Fagan (Chicago: University of Chicago Press, 1995), 164–65.

7. A particularly interesting account of the relation between the Apollinian and the Dionysian, one highlighting the importance of both elements in tragedy, is offered in David Allison's *Reading the New Nietzsche* (Lanham, MD: Rowman & Littlefield, 2001).

8. Elsewhere, Nietzsche writes of Hesiod that "he knew of no way of handling the contradiction presented by the glorious but at the same time terrible and violent world of Homer ex-

cept by dividing one epoch into two epochs, which he then placed one behind the other—first the epoch of the heroes and demigods of Troy and Thebes, the form in which that world had survived in the memory of the noble races who were those heroes' true descendants; then the bronze epoch, the form in which that same world appeared to the descendants of the down trodden, pillaged, mistreated, abducted, enslaved: and epoch of bronze, as aforesaid, hard, cold, cruel, devoid of feeling or conscience, destructive and bloody" (*GM* I:11).

9. Compare: "auf einander folgenden Geburten" (*BT* 4).

10. For interesting discussions of this phenomenon in the context of *GM*, see Wolfgang Müller-Lauter, "Nihilism as Will to Nothingness," in *Critical Essays on Nietzsche's On the Genealogy of Morals*, ed. Christa Davis Acampora (Lanham, MD: Rowman & Littlefield, 2006), 209–19; and Tracy Strong, "Genealogy, the Will to Power, and the Problem of a Past," in ibid., 93–106. Müller-Lauter's treatment of how the reversal of values becomes *bound* to what it reverses resembles, although it occurs in a very different analytic framework, the discussion of bad conscience in Judith Butler, *The Psychic Life of Power: Theories in Subjection* (Stanford, CA: Stanford University Press, 1997), 63–82.

11. The most elaborate account (in English) of Nietzsche's pessimism in *BT* is Julian Young's *Nietzsche's Philosophy of Art* (Cambridge: Cambridge University Press, 1992).

12. For example, see Martha Nussbaum, "The Transfiguration of Intoxication: Nietzsche, Schopenhauer, and Dionysus," *Arion* 1, no. 2 (Spring 1991): 75–111; and James I. Porter, *The Invention of Dionysus: An Essay on The Birth of Tragedy* (Stanford, CA: Stanford University Press, 2000).

13. I am in basic agreement with Nussbaum on all these points. She draws all this from the description of the Apollinian and the Dionysian in *BT* 1–2. See her conclusion in "The Transfiguration of Intoxication," 349.

14. See, e.g., Christoph Menke and James Swindal, "Tragedy and the Free Spirits: On Nietzsche's Theory of Aesthetic Freedom," *Philosophy and Social Criticism* 22, no. 1 (1996): 1–12, esp. 3–6; and Sallis, *Crossings*, passim.

15. As well as awe inspiring. These ideas might be compared with Freud's discussions of the feelings of the boundaries and limitations of the ego. See "Negation" (1925), in *The Standard Edition of the Complete Psychological Works of Sigmund Freud* (24 vols.), ed. and trans. James Strachey (London: Hogarth, 1956–74), vol. 19, "The Ego and the Id and Other Works" (1923), in ibid., vol. 19, esp. pp. 233–40, and *Civilization and Its Discontents* (1930), in ibid., vol. 21, esp. chap. 1. I am grateful to an anonymous reviewer for this reference.

16. This idea is famously elaborated by Nehamas in *Nietzsche: Life as Literature*.

17. On this point, see Martha Nussbaum, introduction to *The Bacchae of Euripides*, trans. C. K. Williams (New York: Farrar Straus Giroux, 1990), and "The Transfigurations of Intoxication." Sallis (*Crossings*) traces the roots of Nietzsche's judgment of Euripides in writings that precede *BT*. Generally, commentators follow Nietzsche's explanation that the *Bacchae* represents Euripides' (belated) recapitulation, i.e., that he reluctantly gives in to Dionysus in the *Bacchae*, but I suggest another way of interpreting Euripides' conception of the Dionysian as it is depicted in the work in question.

18. *KSA* 1, p. 789: "die sich gegenseitig zur That reizen, wie sie sich auch gegenseitig in der Grenze des Maaßes halten."

19. "Der glücklichste Fall in der Entwickelung einer Kunst ist der, dass mehrere Genie's sich gegenseitig in Schranken halten; bei diesem Kampfe wird gewöhnlich den schwächeren und zarteren Naturen auch Luft und Licht gegönnt." Compare *KSA* 8:5[146] in a section titled "Critique of Development": "Der glücklichste Fall in der Entwicklung, wenn sich mehrere Genie's gegenseitig in Schranken halten."

20. Thus, the purpose of this chapter is to draw out from *BT* features of Nietzsche's agonism rather than defending his aesthetics or offering a novel interpretation of it.

21. Helpful discussions of Nietzsche's ideas in relation to Schopenhauer's are found in Janaway, *Beyond Selflessness*; and Reginster, *The Affirmation of Life*. Reginster briefly mentions Nietzsche's agonistic conception of human existence and the significance of overcoming resistance in his reflections on suffering, but those ideas are not elaborated at length. See also Christopher Janaway, ed., *Willing and Nothingness: Schopenhauer as Nietzsche's Educator* (Oxford: Oxford University Press, 1998).

22. See James I. Porter, *Nietzsche and the Philology of the Future* (Stanford, CA: Stanford University Press, 2000).

23. This particular sense of revaluation is consistent with what Aaron Ridley emphasizes in terms of the *re*evaluation of values in Nietzsche's works. See "Nietzsche and the Re-Evaluation of Values," *Proceedings of the Aristotelian Society* 105 (2005): 171–91. *Reevaluation* in this sense reaffirms or finds new grounds for reaffirming what is already esteemed. There is, of course, another sense of *revaluation*, which involves transforming and replacing existing values.

24. Recent work in this vein that includes substantial discussion of Nietzsche can be found in Roberto Esposito, *Bíos: Biopolitics and Philosophy*, trans. Timothy Campbell (Minneapolis: University of Minnesota Press, 2008). For discussion of the related concept of sovereignty, see my "Agonistic Politics and the 'War on Terror,'" *Insights* (Institute of Advanced Study, Durham University) 2, no. 11 (2009): 1–21.

25. Sallis, *Crossings*, 55.

26. Porter, *The Invention of Dionysus*.

27. Sallis (*Crossings*) endeavors to describe this relation, playfully, in terms of what one might call a *double crossing*. Since the Dionysian does not merely represent a disruptive figure who breaches limits in order to remake or reestablish them at another point but is rather *Übermass* itself and therefore represents the end of limits as such, the Dionysian also obliterates the possibility of recognizing any limit at all. See also the characterization of the Apollinian and the Dionysian as antipodes in Porter, *The Invention of Dionysus*; and my discussion of Nietzsche's characterization of antipodes in *BT* below.

28. This notion is also somewhat similar to what Schiller describes as the *reciprocal formation* of the two drives. Further elaboration of the similarities and differences between Nietzsche's views and Schiller's can be found in Nicholas Martin, *Nietzsche and Schiller: Untimely Aesthetics* (Oxford: Clarendon; New York: Oxford University Press, 1996).

29. David Allison's account (*Reading the New Nietzsche*, 40–42) is exceptional in this regard, particularly as it describes how tragedy affords opportunities for both individuation and identification.

30. Ibid., 60–61.

31. Nietzsche tells this fable of Greek history in several different contexts: in "Homer's

Wettkampf," in his notebooks from the 1870s, particularly in the notes for an untimely meditation on philology, and in *Die Geburt der Tragödie* when he tries to account for the influence of
Socratism and its relation to the end of tragedy. See *BT* 15.

32. Nietzsche tells this part of the story twice, and a comparison is interesting. See (the
early) *BT* 15; and (the late) *TI* "The Problem of Socrates."

CHAPTER THREE

1. More on *superior naturalism* is forthcoming from Keith Ansell-Pearson (for now, see
his "Naturalism and Immoralism: Nietzsche and Guyau" [University of Warwick, n.d., type-
script]), to whom I am indebted for this expression. On Nietzsche and taste as a form of judgment with epistemic import, see my and Keith Ansell-Pearson's *Nietzsche's Beyond Good and
Evil: A Reader's Guide* (New York: Continuum, 2011), chap. 11; and Richardson, *Nietzsche's
New Darwinism*, chap. 4.

2. My choice of the term *overcoming* is intended to include both the idea of *self-overcoming*
and that of the *overman* (*Übermensch*), sometimes translated as *superman* or *superhuman*. Although I tend to find the latter terms too distracting given their popular associations with a
comic book character, such translations of *Übermensch* might be preferable in the context I
am investigating. I shall try to link a more nuanced understanding of these important ideas to
Nietzsche's reception of evolutionary theory and his endeavors to "naturalize cheerfully" above
and beyond the materialists of his day. In a developmental context, *super*—connoting also *superseding* and perhaps *surpassing*—might, in fact, be more suggestive than *over*. Because I do
not think this matter can be satisfactorily resolved through translation, I shall simply leave the
term in its original German as often as possible.

3. My thoughts on this topic over the years have been influenced by Richard Schacht's
work on Nietzsche's naturalism. See esp. "Nietzsche's *Gay Science*: How to Naturalize Cheerfully," in Solomon and Higgins, eds., *Reading Nietzsche*, 68–86. Schacht offers an interesting
analysis of *GS* 109, where Nietzsche famously wonders about the future possibility of *naturalizing* humanity. For Schacht, this entails at least two movements: "reading" human beings back
into nature once it is purified of its supernaturalism and then "reading" them *back out*, i.e., "as
something no longer *merely* natural in consequence of its transformation" (ibid., 71), though
much turns on what counts as "more" or "other" than "*merely* natural." For Schacht, this is
how Nietzsche attends to both "*what we are*" and "*what we might become*," which is the theme
of chapter 5 below.

4. For very different approaches, cf. Brian Leiter, *Routledge Philosophy GuideBook to Nietzsche on Morality* (New York: Routledge, 2002); and Robert B. Pippin, "Lightning and Flash,
Agent and Deed (*GM* I:6–17)," in Acampora, ed., *Critical Essays on Nietzsche's On the Genealogy of Morals*, 131–46.

5. See Christian J. Emden, "Nietzsche's Naturalism: Philosophy and the Life Sciences in
the Nineteenth Century" (Rice University, n.d., typescript).

6. For a contemporary perspective on similar issues in a form that differs greatly from Nietzsche's work, see Joseph Rouse, *How Scientific Practices Matter: Reclaiming Philosophical
Naturalism* (Chicago: University of Chicago Press, 2002).

7. My use of *will to power* here indicates it as emerging and is not meant to suggest that

Nietzsche had any single, definite sense in which he used the phrase or that he had a full-blown *theory* in which will to power would play a central role. Rather, I agree with those who remind readers that his ideas about will to power changed over time, that he never wrote a work in which will to power appeared as the central thesis (indeed, that he abandoned at least one plan to execute such a project), and that any account of will to power that rests solely on evidence drawn from his unpublished (including even *discarded*) writings is suspect at best.

8. This struggle is perhaps most evident (and often discussed in the secondary literature) in the conclusion of the fourth book of *Die fröhliche Wissenschaft*, and it is a dynamic that I think is pervasive in the book as a whole. For a taste, see *GS* 337–42, where the notion of a new form of humanity (later to become *superhumanity* or *overhumanity*) is introduced, leading up to the section introducing Zarathustra.

9. Letter to Jacob Burckhardt, September 22, 1886, cited in Kaufmann's preface to *BGE*, p. x.

10. This is precisely Thrasymachus's objection to Socrates in the first book of the *Republic*, and it is the reason why Thrasymachus shrinks from the discussion.

11. Nietzsche's lecture notes for his courses on the pre-Platonics have been published as *The Pre-Platonic Philosophers*, trans. and ed. with an introduction and commentary by Greg Whitlock (Urbana: University of Illinois Press, 2001).

12. Alexander Nehamas is exceptional among Nietzsche scholars in this regard, although I suspect that he might not grant my suggestion here that Nietzsche's early work, including *Die Geburt der Tragödie*, reflects a deep admiration and accreditation of Socrates for bringing about a *positive* change in the course of human history. Nehamas has argued that Nietzsche changes his mind about Socrates at least twice: he was initially ill disposed toward Socrates, as is evident in his comments in *BT*; then he struck a kind of truce with him during his so-called middle period; and, finally, the enmity was renewed in his later writings, as is evident in Nietzsche's scathing comments on Socrates in *TI*. A search for an explanation of the latter, particularly his famous remark about Socrates' face and his ugliness, motivates Nehamas's investigation in *The Art of Living: Socratic Reflections from Plato to Foucault* (Berkeley and Los Angeles: University of California Press, 1998), esp. 128–56. Ultimately, Nehamas thinks that Nietzsche perceives a great threat in the character of Socrates, namely, a threat to his own project of making himself an individual. Compare Pierre Hadot, *Philosophy as a Way of Life: Spiritual Exercise from Socrates to Foucault*, ed. Arnold Davidson, trans. Michael Chase (New York: Blackwell, 1995).

13. Kaufmann actually compounds the philosophical problem of the opposition of the real and the apparent worlds when he translates this as "*mere* appearance" (emphasis added).

14. Similar points are made repeatedly throughout *GS* and *BGE*, as, e.g., in *GS* 110. I take Nietzsche's claim that the will to semblance plays an important and formative role in our making sense of the world to be somewhat different from what Maudemarie Clark designates as *the falsification thesis*: the view that consciousness necessarily falsifies. Clark famously argues that, while Nietzsche holds such in his earlier writings, he abandons it in his mature work. See *Nietzsche on Truth and Philosophy* (Cambridge: Cambridge University Press, 1991), with important clarifications in Maudemarie Clark and David Dudrick, "Nietzsche's Post-Positivism," *European Journal of Philosophy* 12, no. 3 (2004): 369–85.

15. Robert Rethy, "Schein in Nietzsche's Philosophy," in *Nietzsche and Modern German Thought*, ed. Keith Ansell-Pearson (London: Routledge, 1991), 59–87.

16. It is not just that Nietzsche wishes to revalue *Schein*; he does so on the basis of opposition to *Erscheinungen*: "Es giebt verhängnißvolle Worte, welche eine Erkenntniß auszudrücken scheinen und in Wahrheit eine Erkenntniß verhindern; zu ihnen gehört das Wort 'Erscheinungen.' Welches Wirrsal die 'Erscheinungen' anrichten, mögen diese Sätze verrathen, welche ich verschiedenen neueren Philosophen entlehne. [/] gegen das Wort 'Erscheinungen'" (*KSA* 11:40[52]). In the next section he writes: "NB. Schein wie ich es verstehe, ist die wirkliche und einzige Realität der Dinge [. . .] Ich setze also nicht 'Schein' in Gegensatz zur 'Realität' sondern nehme umgekehrt Schein als die Realität, welche sich der Verwandlung in eine imaginative 'Wahrheits-Welt' widersetzt. Ein bestimmter Name für diese Realität wäre 'der Wille zur Macht,' nämlich von innen her bezeichnet und nicht von seiner unfaßbaren flüssigen Proteus-Natur aus" (*KSA* 11:40[53]). Later in this chapter, I suggest that Nietzsche's hypothesis of will to power is an expression of his affirmation of *Schein*.

17. *GS* 109 concludes: "Wann werden wir anfangen dürfen, uns Menschen mit der reinen, neu gefundenen, neu erlösten Natur zu vernatürlichen!" Kaufmann replaces Nietzsche's exclamation point with a question mark.

18. I discuss these views in two other publications: Christa Davis Acampora, "Naturalism and Nietzsche's Moral Psychology," in *The Blackwell Companion to Nietzsche*, ed. Keith Ansell-Pearson (Malden, MA: Blackwell, 2006), 314–33; and Acampora and Ansell-Pearson, *Nietzsche's Beyond Good and Evil: A Reader's Guide*. Both include earlier formulations of ideas found in this section and the next.

19. See, e.g., Nadeem Hussain, "Nietzsche's Positivism," *European Journal of Philosophy* 12, no. 3 (2004): 326–68; and Clark and Dudrick, "Nietzsche's Post-Positivism."

20. Compare Maudemarie Clark and David Dudrick, "The Naturalisms of *Beyond Good and Evil*," in *A Companion to Nietzsche*, ed. Keith Ansell-Pearson (Oxford: Blackwell, 2006), 148–68.

21. Two very different examples can be found in works by Williams and by Prinz. See, e.g., Williams, *Truth and Truthfulness*, esp. chaps. 1–3; and Jesse Prinz, "Where Do Morals Come From?" in *Philosophical Implications of Empirically Informed Ethics*, ed. M. Christen (New York: Springer, forthcoming). For Williams: "A genealogy is a narrative that tries to explain a cultural phenomenon by describing a way in which it came about, or could have come about, or might be imagined to have come about. Some of the narrative will consist of real history, which to some extent must aim to be, as Foucault put it, 'gray, meticulous, and patiently documentary'" (20). But some of it will be fiction: "an imagined developmental story, which helps to explain a concept or value or institution by showing ways in which it could have come about in a simplified environment containing certain kinds of human interests or capacities, which, relative to the story, are taken as given" (21). Prinz, who describes himself as a methodological antinativist about morality draws inspiration from Nietzsche in advocating a genealogical approach (which "may appear to be unscientific in an important sense") to develop "a cultural science of moral norms."

22. I engage some of these in my "Naturalism and Nietzsche's Moral Psychology."

23. Compare Richardson, *Nietzsche's New Darwinism*; and Dirk R. Johnson, *Nietzsche's Anti-Darwinism* (Cambridge: Cambridge University Press, 2010).

24. So, e.g., although it is common today to think of Darwin as the founder of the evolu-

tionary theory now regarded as having the greatest explanatory power, it is important to note that there were many competing views in Nietzsche's day and that certain aspects of those views have been integrated in modern evolutionary approaches and might even hold some promise for future development. On the history of evolutionary theory, see Stephen Jay Gould, *The Structure of Evolutionary Theory* (Cambridge, MA: Belknap Press of Harvard University Press, 2002). Some limited discussion of which side Nietzsche takes and on what points appears above. More thorough discussion is found in Moore, *Nietzsche, Biology and Metaphor*.

25. I discuss earlier expressions of these interests in my "Between Mechanism and Teleology: Will to Power and Nietzsche's 'Gay' Science," in Moore and Brobjer, eds., *Nietzsche and Science*, 171–88.

26. See, e.g., *GS* 39. For a discussion of a concept of health that is allied with Nietzsche's agonism, see Alfred I. Tauber, "A Typology of Nietzsche's Biology," *Biology and Philosophy* 9 (1994): 25–44.

27. I qualify the exemplar as *his own Heraclitus* because, as in his discussions of Homer, Socrates, Paul, and Wagner, there is much that is invented by Nietzsche in his characterization of Heraclitus.

28. Both Christoph Cox and Wolfgang Müller-Lauter have recognized that Nietzsche's alternative account of development is indebted to his study of Heraclitus. Both also acknowledge that his proposed solution rests on his claim that struggle is the most immediate and pervasive phenomenon of existence. Cox even goes so far as to tie such views to Nietzsche's interest in the agon, although his treatment is brief. See Christoph Cox, *Nietzsche: Naturalism and Interpretation* (Berkeley and Los Angeles: University of California Press, 1999), 233ff.; and Wolfgang Müller-Lauter, "On Judging in a World of Becoming: A Reflection on the 'Great Change' in Nietzsche's Philosophy," in *Nietzsche, Theories of Knowledge, and Critical Theory*, ed. Babette E. Babich and Robert S. Cohen (Boston: Kluwer, 1999), 168–71.

29. Compare *PTAG* 7.

30. Nietzsche contrasts Heraclitus's view with Anaxagoras's "teleological insight" that "construes the order of the world as a determinant will with intentions, conceived after the fashion of human beings." This notion was picked up by Aristotle, according to Nietzsche's philosophical genealogy, and it then reverberated throughout the history of philosophy in the conception of the opposition of soul and matter: "a force that knows and sets goals but also wills, moves, and so on and yet is rigid matter. It is strange how long Greek philosophy struggled against this theory" (*PPP*, 72).

31. In *BT* 24, Nietzsche associates Heraclitus's characterization of the "world-building force as like a playing child" with what is Dionysian.

32. By contrast, consider what Nietzsche writes about the development of the concept of substance at *GS* 111: "In order that the concept of substance could originate—which is indispensable for logic although in the strictest sense nothing real corresponds to it—it was likewise necessary that for a long time one did not see nor perceive the changes in things."

33. All in "Homer's Wettkampf," *KSA* 1, pp. 783, 785, 786, 788, 790, and 791, respectively.

34. Emphasis here added by Kaufmann.

35. William Paley famously argued that the teleological order of nature constitutes proof of an intelligent designer (see his *Natural Theology* [1802]). Wilhelm Roux was a proponent of

evolutionary mechanics. Wolfgang Müller-Lauter has documented Nietzsche's exploration of Roux's work. See Wolfgang Müller-Lauter, *Nietzsche: His Philosophy of Contradictions and the Contradictions of His Philosophy*, chap. 9 ("The Organism as Inner Struggle: Wilhelm Roux's Influence on Nietzsche"). Helpful elaboration of these ideas in their context of other scientific developments is found in Moore's *Nietzsche, Biology, and Metaphor*, esp. chap. 1 ("The Physiology of Power").

36. The full note reads:

Zwei aufeinander folgende Zustände: der eine Ursache, der andere Wirkung

: ist falsch.

der erste Zustand hat nichts zu bewirken
den zweiten hat nichts bewirkt.

: es handelt sich um einen Kampf zweier an Macht ungleichen Elemente: es wird ein Neu-arrangement der Kräfte erreicht, je nach dem Maß von Macht eines jeden.

der zweite Zustand ist etwas Grundverschiedenes vom ersten (nicht dessen "Wirkung"): das Wesentliche ist, daß die im Kampf befindlichen Faktoren mit anderen Machtquanten herauskommen.

37. Further discussion of the relation between conceptions of causality and naturalism as this bears on the resemblance between the views of Nietzsche and Hume can be found in P. J. E. Kail, "Nietzsche and Hume: Naturalism and Explanation," *Journal of Nietzsche Studies* 37 (Spring 2009): 5–22.

38. The influence of Roux is evident here.

39. "Leben wäre zu definiren als eine dauernde Form von Prozeß der Kraftfeststellungen, wo die verschiedenen Kämpfenden ihrerseits ungleich wachsen."

40. "Das Individuum selbst als Kampf der Theile (um Nahrung, Raum usw.): seine Entwicklung geknüpft an ein Siegen, Vorherrschen einzelner Theile, an ein Verkümmern, 'Organwerden' anderer Theile."

41. Further exploration of this particular example would also allow one to develop an account of the Kantian legacy that extends from Nietzsche's critical analysis. While Nietzsche criticizes Kant in the ways I have mentioned above, he also develops a good number of Kantian ideas, including applying some of Kant's own critical insights to Kant's positive alternatives. But this is not the focus of my chapter. Detailed treatment along these lines can be found in R. Kevin Hill, *Nietzsche's Critiques: The Kantian Foundations of His Thought* (Oxford: Oxford University Press, 2003), esp. 180–95 (on topics discussed here). And, I contend, this very example also presents some challenges for contemporary interpretations of Nietzsche's naturalism, particularly for those mining his thought in the context of pushing philosophy toward empirical research in the form of experimental philosophy.

42. Two recent accounts apparently diverge on the extent to which *BGE* 19 illustrates an application of Nietzsche's naturalism or shows his assessment of its limitations, advancing a metaphysical agenda (Brian Leiter, "Nietzsche's Theory of the Will," in *Nietzsche on Freedom and Autonomy*, ed. Ken Gemes and Simon May [Oxford: Oxford University Press, 2009], 107–26; and Maudemarie Clark and David Dudrick, "Nietzsche on the Will: An Analysis of BGE 19," in ibid., 247–68). For further discussion along the lines of what I am resisting as the exclusive or

important sense in which Nietzsche is a naturalist, see Leiter, *Routledge Philosophy GuideBook to Nietzsche on Morality*. Leiter advances the view that Nietzsche is a methodological naturalist, which is supposed to mean that he thinks philosophy should follow the methods of the natural sciences. This includes maintaining a commitment to empiricism and explanation in causal terms. Clark and Dudrick argue that Nietzsche has a *limited* naturalistic perspective in which he maintains: "The best explanation for everything that is not rational or sense-making activity is the kind of causal or mechanistic explanation that natural science provides. Of course, beings that engage in sense-making activities are part of nature, according to Nietzsche and therefore much about them is explicable in scientific terms. But although human beings are part of nature, Nietzsche's version of naturalism insists that science doesn't tell us all there is to know about their doings. Nietzsche's view doesn't have us postulating any extra *things* (e.g., immaterial, immortal souls); rather, it says that fully natural beings have developed in such a way as to admit of true descriptions that cannot be had from an empirical perspective" (Clark and Dudrick, "The Naturalisms of *Beyond Good and Evil*," 165).

43. "als Gehorchende die Gefühle des Zwingens, Drängens, Drückens, Widerstehens, Bewegens kennen, welche sofort nach dem Akte des Willens zu beginnen pflegen [. . .] ."

44. Leiter seems to think that *BGE* 19 demonstrates that Nietzsche abandons the idea of freedom of the will in favor of a fatalist conception of human existence and human psychology, which I discuss further in chapter 5. Clark and Dudrick claim that "BGE 19 aims to rehabilitate *the traditional notion of the will* in the face of the tendency of naturalism to simply dismiss it" (Clark and Dudrick, "Nietzsche on the Will," 248 [emphasis added]). I think *BGE* 19 shows how a different kind of naturalism can better support the aims of science and revitalize inventive philosophical thinking. This does not carve out a separate niche for philosophy and distinguish naturalism from metaphysics, as Clark and Dudrick, among others, suggest. Clark and Dudrick write: "Although Nietzsche is a naturalist in an important sense, and certainly rejects all forms of supernaturalism, there is an important sense in which he is not a naturalist, for he holds that human thought and action can be understood only from a perspective constituted by norms that have no role to play in our understanding of the natural world" (ibid.). However, I maintain that Nietzsche does not believe that science or any other area of inquiry offers a value-free perspective, and thus there cannot be a "pure" naturalism as they and others seem to suggest.

45. It should now be clear that I do not think Nietzsche is arguing that art should *replace* science or even that it *supplements* it. Nor am I claiming that art's role is to make science itself more beautiful or elegant, more appealing. I am not advocating that we should prioritize his aestheticism since I do not think he ultimately claims that the best we can do is to regard the world and especially ourselves as works of art. However, I also do not think that those who emphasize Nietzsche's aestheticism are necessarily *reducing* his views to just these claims in the way in which such positions are often caricatured.

CHAPTER FOUR

1. He provides a similar account earlier in *Morgenröthe*, as I discuss below.

2. From "The Struggle between Science and Wisdom," translated in *Philosophy and Truth*, p. 121 = *KSA* 8, p. 97.

3. "Deshalb waren die Individuen im Alterthume freier, weil ihre Ziele näher und greifbarer waren. Der moderne Mensch ist dagegen überall gekreuzt von der Unendlichkeit, wie der schnellfüßige Achill im Gleichnisse des Eleaten Zeno: die Unendlichkeit hemmt ihn, er holt nicht einmal die Schildkröte ein."

4. In general, I rely on Hollingdale's translation here; however, I have consulted other translations and emend Hollingdale in some places, so I also provide the German original for comparison. This passage is found at *KSA* 3, p. 65: "fortwährend im Kampfe und auf der Lauer gegen die Übertreter und Anzweifler desselben, hart und böse gegen sie und zum Äussersten der Strafen geneigt."

5. Nietzsche explains Luther's actions in similar terms, thus linking him with the modus operandi and spiritual dynamic of Pauline Christianity.

6. *KSA* 3, p. 66: "Das Gesetz war das Kreuz, an welches er sich geschlagen fühlte: wie hasste er es! wie trug er es ihm nach! wie suchte er herum, um ein Mittel zu finden, es zu v e r n i c h t e n."

7. In general, I rely on Kaufmann's translation, but I emend the text in several places and include phrases from the original that Kaufmann omitted, as noted below.

8. Kaufmann's translation amended to include Nietzsche's punctuation. Kaufmann also omits the following passage in this section: "Die Worte zum S c h ä c h e r am Kreuz enthalten das ganze Evangelium. 'Das ist wahrlich ein g ö t t l i c h e r Mensch gewesen, ein "Kind Gottes"' sagt der Schächer. 'Wenn du dies fühlst—antwortet der Erlöser—so b i s t d u i m P a r a d i e s e, so bist auch du ein Kind Gottes.'"

9. Of course, none of the apostles are thought to have actually authored the Gospels. Nietzsche's analysis turns on what is associated with the perspective that is gathered in the name *Paul* and its influence on the development of the Christian church.

10. "Der hellenische Genius hatte noch eine andere Antwort auf die Frage bereit 'was will ein Leben des Kampfes und des Sieges?' und giebt diese Antwort in der ganzen Breite der griechischen Geschichte."

11. For further analysis of how it is that Nietzsche thinks we are strangers to ourselves and what this has to do with genealogy, see Ken Gemes, "'We Remain of Necessity Strangers to Ourselves': The Key Message of Nietzsche's *Genealogy*," in Acampora, ed., *Critical Essays on Nietzsche's On the Genealogy of Morals*, 191–208. While I agree with Gemes that one of the central goals of *GM* is to show its audience that and how modern humanity is the embodiment of the ascetic ideal, I think this is no cleverly disguised secret revealed only at the end. Indeed, evidence that we have deceived ourselves about having overcome this ideal is found in our affirmation of the ideal of the sovereign individual, discussed in *GM* II:2, which I discuss below, in strong opposition to the swelling tide of literature on the figure.

12. In a dubious etymology, Nietzsche links the Latin word *bonus* (good) with the Latin *duellum* (the warrior). He then announces: "*bonus* as the man of strife, of dissension (*duo*), as the man of war: one sees what constituted the 'goodness' of a man in ancient Rome. Our German *gut* [good] even: does it not signify 'the godlike,' the man of 'godlike race'?" (*GM* I:5).

13. In this book, I focus on Nietzsche's analysis of different forms of evaluation and the terms on which they turn and are organized in order to show how conflict and contest provide means for their definition and generation. Elsewhere, I consider how these ideas are relevant to

other work in the areas of political ontology (which examines the nature of political entities and the power relations that create and sustain them) and political semantics (which analyzes the language of politics and political theory to understand how such terms are meaningful and their potential to create new relations). See my "Nietzsche's Political Agonism" (n.d., typescript), "*Demos Agonistes Redux*," and "Agonistic Politics and the 'War on Terror.'"

14. See Janaway, *Beyond Selflessness*. As an example of the difference that this perspective makes, consider Janaway's commentary on *BGE* 21, in which he claims that Nietzsche is "at his usual genealogical business flushing out an underlying affective state—'longing for "freedom of the will" in the superlative metaphysical sense'—and hypothesizing an explanation for its genesis and persistence" (ibid., 115) and, thus, not making positive claims *for* or *against* the idea of human freedom. I return to matters pertaining to freedom of the will below. Where I disagree with Janaway is, as should become clear below, his account of Nietzsche's alternative.

15. Robert Pippin puts it this way: "When we ask ourselves questions like: what were Christians actually doing in promoting the practices of self-denial, what were they after, or what was the point of Socrates' promotion of dialectic, definition, and logos, we are not asking for any fact of the matter but for some compelling and persuasive re-description, some reading as if we were to ask why Emma Bovary was so dissatisfied in marriage . . . we are not concerned simply with a psychological individual, or in Nietzsche's case a historical event, but with general questions of significance, history, what has become possible for us, and we have no method or formal approach that will resolve disputes about these issues" (Robert B. Pippin, *Modernism as a Philosophical Problem* [Cambridge, MA: Blackwell, 1991], 86).

16. On the use of fiction, particularly in the form of a state of nature story, in pursuit of true accounts of human nature and possibilities, see Williams, *Truth and Truthfulness*.

17. See also *A* 45, where Nietzsche notes his own contribution to distinguishing "noble morality" from "chandala morality." See also the end of *GM* I.

18. "Das Verlangen nach Z e r s t ö r u n g, Wechsel, Werden kann der Ausdruck der übervollen, zukunftsschwangeren Kraft sein (mein terminus ist dafür, wie man weiss, das Wort "dionysisch"), aber es kann auch der Hass des Missrathenen, Entbehrenden, Schlechtweggekommenen sein, der zerstört, zerstören m u s s, weil ihn das Bestehende, ja alles Bestehn, alles Sein selbst empört und aufreizt—man sehe sich, um diesen Affekt zu verstehn, unsre Anarchisten aus der Nähe an."

19. "Er kann aber auch jener tyrannische Wille eines Schwerleidenden, Kämpfenden, Torturirten sein, welcher das Persönlichste, Einzelnste, Engste, die eigentliche Idiosynkrasie seines Leidens noch zum verbindlichen Gesetz und Zwang stempeln möchte und der an allen Dingen gleichsam Rache nimmt, dadurch, dass er ihnen s e i n Bild, das Bild s e i n e r Tortur, aufdrückt, einzwängt, einbrennt." In *Der Antichrist*, Nietzsche offers a similar interpretation of lying. Lying in and of itself is not to be condemned; it can be destructive or creative: "Indeed, it makes a difference to what end one lies: whether one preserves or *destroys* [. . .] . Christianity found its mission in putting an end to precisely such an organization [of society in the times of Manu] *because life prospered in it*" (*A* 58).

20. "so dass es heute vielleicht kein entscheidenderes Abzeichen der 'h ö h e r e n Natur,' der geistigeren Natur giebt, als zwiespältig in jenem Sinne und wirklich noch ein Kampfplatz für jene Gegensätze zu sein."

21. In the preface to *GM*, Nietzsche directs the reader to his earlier discussions germane to the topic of the origin of morality, especially his *Menschliches, Allzumenschliches*, which had *its* genesis, in part, as a response to a work by his friend Paul Reé. A group of sections he flags is *HH* 96 and 99 and *AOM* 89, which treat the "Sittlichkeit der Sitte." In the preface, he describes this as "that much older and more primitive species of morality which differs *toto caelo* from the altruistic mode of evaluation (in which Dr. Rée, like all English moral genealogists, sees moral evaluation *as such*)," and later, in *GM* II:2, as I discuss below, he characterizes it as "the tremendous labor [. . .] performed by man upon himself during the greater part of the existence of the human race, his entire *prehistoric* labor" (and at this point he also directs readers to earlier discussions, this time to *D* 9, 14, 16). Finally, in the third essay of *GM*, in a section discussing how "all good things were formerly bad things" (a notion underscoring the relation and interdependency of values and their overcoming), he cites *D* 18, where he describes the "morality of mores" as "that vast era [. . .] which preceded 'world history' as the truly decisive history that determined the character of mankind: when suffering was everywhere counted as a virtue, cruelty as a virtue, dissembling as a virtue, revenge as a virtue, slander of reason as a virtue, and when on the other hand well-being was counted as a danger, thirst for knowledge as a danger, peace as a danger, pity as a danger, being pitied as a disgrace, work as a disgrace, madness as divine, *change* as the very essence of immorality and pregnant with disaster" (*GM* III:9).

22. A conclusion that follows from my study, though it is not the main object, is that the current focus of debate over whether Nietzsche is a determinist or a fatalist is somewhat misguided, asking the wrong question. I also suggest that what motivates much of that discussion is attachment to current moral values, particularly, the very sense of responsibility that Nietzsche associates with what is definitive about morality "in the narrow sense" in which we regard it now (*BGE* 32). Ken Gemes distinguishes moral responsibility from what he calls *agent responsibility* ("Nietzsche on Free Will, Autonomy and the Sovereign Individual," *Proceedings of the Aristotelian Society Supplementary Volume* 80 [2006]: 321–38). I engage those ideas below.

23. A recent extensive reflection on forgetting in Nietzsche is found in Vanessa Lemm, *Nietzsche's Animal Philosophy* (New York: Fordham University Press, 2009). The classic discussion of forgetting as an active force is found in Gilles Deleuze, *Nietzsche and Philosophy*, trans. Hugh Tomlinson (New York: Columbia University Press, 1983). Deleuze argues that Nietzsche distinguishes active and reactive forces with respect to whether they obey or command in relation to each other (e.g., ibid., 39–40). In such a case, consciousness is at least partially the product of reactive force. On the "eternal return" conceived as the overcoming of forgetting, see Paul S. Loeb, "Finding the Übermensch in Nietzsche's *Genealogy of Morality*," *Journal of Nietzsche Studies* 30 (Autumn 2005): 70–101.

24. Richardson explores this from the perspective of evolutionary theory in *Nietzsche's New Darwinism*.

25. See John Dewey, *Experience and Nature* (Chicago: Open Court, 1925).

26. Scholarly literature on the sovereign individual has turned toward articulating Nietzsche's sense of autonomy in terms of an *achievement* rather than an entitlement (e.g., Gemes, "Nietzsche on Free Will, Autonomy and the Sovereign Individual"; and Janaway, *Beyond Selflessness*, chap. 7).

27. I have pursued both approaches, including a polemical article in which I first took up these ideas ("On Sovereignty and Overhumanity: Why It Matters How We Read Nietzsche's

Genealogy II:2," *International Studies in Philosophy* 36, no. 3 [Fall 2004]: 127–45) and a chapter on Nietzsche's moral psychology ("Naturalism and Nietzsche's Moral Psychology").

28. This idea is developed in a variety of ways in Christa Davis Acampora and Ralph R. Acampora, eds., *A Nietzschean Bestiary: Becoming Animal Beyond Docile and Brutal* (Lanham, MD: Rowman & Littlefield, 2004).

29. Further argument that the sovereign individual is the ideal of current morality and not anticipated as the ideal of a postmoral future is advanced in Lawrence J. Hatab, *Nietzsche's On the Genealogy of Morality: An Introduction* (Cambridge: Cambridge University Press, 2008). Hatab also notes the similarities between the sovereign individual and "the modern construction of rational morality" as elaborated by Kant (ibid., esp. 76–78).

30. The process originated in economic debtor/creditor relations, as Nietzsche tells the story.

31. *GM* II:3: "'Wie macht man dem Menschen-Thiere ein Gedächtniss? Wie prägt man diesem theils stumpfen, theils faseligen Augenblicks-Verstande, dieser leibhaften Vergesslichkeit Etwas so ein, dass es gegenwärtig bleibt?'" Kaufmann and Hollingdale's translation amended.

32. Interesting discussion of the extension and development of these and related ideas in the works of Kafka and Foucault can be found in Judith Butler, "Foucault and the Paradox of Bodily Inscriptions," *Journal of Philosophy* 86, no. 11 (1989): 601–7. I am grateful to an anonymous reviewer for this suggestion.

33. See, e.g., Owen, "Equality, Democracy, and Self-Respect"; and Randall Havas, *Nietzsche's Genealogy: Nihilism and the Will to Knowledge* (Ithaca, NY: Cornell University Press, 1995), esp. 193ff., and "Nietzsche's Idealism," *Journal of Nietzsche Studies* 20 (2000): 90–99.

34. Hatab elaborates the connection between social contract theory and promising in *Nietzsche's On the Genealogy of Morality: An Introduction*. His earlier interpretation of the sovereign individual in *GM* II.2 as bound up with Nietzsche's condemnation of the moral tradition predates mine, and I am indebted to his earlier account.

35. Janaway emphasizes Nietzsche's analyses of our affective attachments to "the morality of selflessness," which shift and orient our concepts, presumably including promising, though that particular attachment is not explored. Nietzsche is attempting to loosen such ties so that we might be able to think differently. See Janaway, *Beyond Selflessness*, 121–22.

36. If I am right, then this presents a clue as to the temporal order that Nietzsche describes here. The sovereign individual likely stands at the end of the morality of custom (as both Janaway [*Beyond Selflessness*, 116–20] and Hatab [*Nietzsche's On the Genealogy of Morality: An Introduction*, 75–82] point out) and not in some distant future. Previously, in "Sovereignty and Overhumanity" (2004), I claimed that the sovereign individual was the culminating ideal of the modern, and I now think that this is not quite right. It is an orienting ideal that guides the development of the modern subject; its emergence, as a goal full of promise, was prior, a distinguishing point of origination of the moral. See also the discussion in Daniel Conway, *Nietzsche's On the Genealogy of Morals: A Reader's Guide* (New York: Continuum, 2008).

37. Here, *project* does not refer to the actions or plans of any human agent or agents. It refers to a series of related events, activities, and orientations that had this result.

38. Gemes, "Nietzsche on Free Will, Autonomy and the Sovereign Individual."

39. See also Robert B. Pippin, *Idealism as Modernism: Hegelian Variations* (Cambridge: Cambridge University Press, 1997), 351–71 (chap. 14, which has "Das Thun ist Alles" as its epigraph), and "Lightning and Flash, Doer and Deed."

40. Pippin, *Nietzsche, Psychology, and First Philosophy*, 75–76.

41. Pippin, *Idealism as Modernism*, 367.

42. Pippin, *Nietzsche, Psychology, and First Philosophy*, 75–77.

43. Pippin claims that what is needed here are the conditions that "in Wittgenstein's famous words would distinguish my arm going up from my raising my arm" (ibid., 72n5).

44. In previous treatments of this passage, cited above, Pippin elaborates some of the mistaken and unwarranted assumptions in the "common-sense psychological view" toward which we are drawn on the basis of our supposition that *intentions we freely and spontaneously form (which we produce independently) are the causes of our deeds*. My own analysis is greatly influenced by Pippin's questioning of the lure of such notions.

45. Pippin, *Nietzsche, Psychology, and First Philosophy*, 68.

46. Ibid., 73–74.

47. Ibid., 75. Pippin is citing Bernard Williams, "Nietzsche's Minimalist Moral Psychology," in *Nietzsche, Genealogy, Morality: Essays on Nietzsche's On the Genealogy of Morals*, ed. Richard Schacht (Berkeley and Los Angeles: University of California Press, 1994), 241.

48. Pippin, *Nietzsche, Psychology, and First Philosophy*, 76.

49. Ibid. *KSA* 4, p. 122: "Dass e u e r Selbst in der Handlung sei, wie die Mutter im Kinde ist: das sei mir e u e r Wort von Tugend!" Pippin cites the translation in Friedrich Nietzsche, *Thus Spoke Zarathustra*, trans. Adrian Del Caro, ed. Adrian Del Caro and Robert B. Pippin, Cambridge Texts in the History of Philosophy (Cambridge: Cambridge University Press, 2006).

50. Pippin, *Nietzsche, Psychology, and First Philosophy*, 76. See also Nehamas's discussion of this passage in *Nietzsche: Life as Literature*, esp. 72, 88, 162, 176.

51. Pippin, *Nietzsche, Psychology, and First Philosophy*, 76–77.

52. Ibid., 77.

53. This can be contrasted with the society too weak to punish as described in *BGE* 201: "There is a point in the history of society when it becomes so pathologically soft and tender that among other things it sides even with those who harm it, criminals, and does this quite seriously and honestly. Punishing somehow seems unfair to it, and it is certain that imagining 'punishment' and 'being supposed to punish' hurts it, arouses fear in it. . . . [Thus,] the morality of timidity draws its ultimate consequence. Supposing that one could altogether abolish danger, the reason for fear, this morality would be abolished, too, *eo ipso*: it would no longer be needed, it would no longer *consider itself* necessary."

54. Pippin, *Nietzsche, Psychology, and First Philosophy*, 77.

55. Ibid., 80n15.

56. See also Alan Schrift, "Rethinking Exchange: Logics of the Gift in Cixous and Nietzsche," *Philosophy Today* 40, no. 1 (Spring 1996): 197–205. While I cannot explore these broader implications here, I think that the reformulated sense of responsibility that Nietzsche suggests and his reasons for introducing it are compatible with what Schrift finds in Cixous. If I am right about this, I think it also suggests that the agonistic ethos Nietzsche anticipates might retain important oppositional relations that nevertheless do not require "assumptions of scarcity and reciprocal commodity exchange" (ibid., 203) in order to be successful.

57. Pippin, *Idealism as Modernism*, 367.

58. Pippin, *Nietzsche, Psychology, and First Philosophy*, 83.

59. Ibid., 84.

CHAPTER FIVE

1. Joe Ward's discussion of Nietzsche's account of Goethe's development is illuminating. See "Nietzsche's Value Conflict: Culture, Individual, Synthesis," *Journal of Nietzsche Studies* 41 (Spring 2011): 4–25, esp. 13–14.

2. His project is surely primarily descriptive rather than normative, but Nietzsche does occasionally use the Pindaric expression as an imperative, as mentioned below.

3. Nehamas (*Nietzsche: Life as Literature*, 175) discusses problems with this interpretation.

4. Nietzsche might be thought to minimize Wagner's significance when he writes in *Ecce Homo* that *Richard Wagner in Bayreuth* is really about himself rather than Wagner (*EH* "Birth of Tragedy" 4), but it is nevertheless illuminating to explore the similarities and differences in these two works because they provide insight into the process Nietzsche envisions as well as its (and his) task.

5. This is not simply a casual remark in the essay; rather, it serves as its guiding and organizing theme. See, e.g., Nietzsche's drafts, which use the phrases *wie er wurde, was er ist*, and *was er sein wird* as subheads (e.g., *KSA* 8, 14[8]).

6. Drawing on Deleuze, Alan Schrift makes important distinctions between evolution and becoming in Nietzsche's thought: "Evolutionary language focuses our attention on the beginning and endpoint of a process in a way that obscures the passage between them. The language of compound becoming, in contrast, draws our attention to what happens *between* these ever-receding endpoints. Becomings take place *between* poles; they are the in-betweens that pass only and always along a middle without origin or destination" ("Rethinking the Subject; or, How One Becomes-Other Than What One Is," in *Nietzsche's Postmoralism: Reassessments of Nietzsche's Philosophy*, ed. Richard Schacht [Cambridge: Cambridge University Press, 2001], 56.)

7. Brian Leiter ("The Paradox of Fatalism and Self-Creation in Nietzsche," in Janaway, ed., *Willing and Nothingness*, 217–57) reads Nietzsche's antimetaphysical comments about the soul and concludes that "there is [. . .] no 'self' in 'self-mastery,'" whereas Nehamas (*Nietzsche: Life as Literature*) regards the self as something that *becomes* by virtue of some special activity in which one engages that allows for self-transformation and transfiguration, self-becoming. Though these views seem at odds, perhaps it is a mistake to think that we must embrace only one or the other. A third option might grant subjective multiplicity while locating agency in the various powers of the contributors, claiming *multiple agencies*, as one finds in Parkes, who claims that Nietzsche presents a "a multiplicity [of subjective entities] behind which it is not necessary to posit a unity: it suffices to conceive the multiplicity as a regency" (*Composing the Soul*, 354 [see also 320, 325]; cf. *KSA* 11:40[38]). I find Parkes's account illuminating and supported by the text, but I think the *pattern* of the organization of the drives, which he claims is fated, is not fixed, and I think there is potentially greater unity than what his ultimate claim of the "play of masks" suggests, even though I recognize that he thinks this occurs on the basis of what he calls *enlightened spontaneity* (*Composing the Soul*, 459n74).

8. I am particularly grateful to Gary Shapiro ("Beyond Peoples and Fatherlands: Nietzsche's Geophilosophy and the Direction of the Earth," *Journal of Nietzsche Studies* 35/36 [2008]: 9–27, and "Nietzsche's Unmodern Thinking: Globalization, the End of History, and 'Great Events,'" *American Catholic Philosophical Quarterly* 84, no. 2 [Spring 2010]: 205–30)

and Burnham (*Reading Nietzsche: An Analysis of Beyond Good and Evil* [Montreal: McGill-Queen's University Press, 2007]) for encouraging me to think more carefully and more seriously about *BGE* VIII "On Peoples and Fatherlands."

9. Nietzsche's efforts to scout (although they fail to identify) a new nobility are discussed in my and Ansell-Pearson's *Nietzsche's Beyond Good and Evil*.

10. For discussions of Nietzsche's first effort to pinpoint this as Wagner's problem, see Julian Young, "Richard Wagner and the Birth of *The Birth of Tragedy*," *International Journal of Philosophical Studies* 16, no. 2 (2008): 217–45; and Shapiro, "Nietzsche's Unmodern Thinking."

11. In different ways, both Nehamas (*Nietzsche: Life as Literature*) and Pippin (*Nietzsche, Psychology, and First Philosophy*) explore this dimension of Nietzsche's account of how one becomes what one is.

12. "Sondern die Liebe als Fatum, als Fatalität, cynisch, unschuldig, grausam—und eben darin Natur! Die Liebe, die in ihren Mitteln der Krieg, in ihrem Grunde der Todhass der Geschlechter ist!"

13. Interestingly, Nietzsche is more specific in *CW* about what he intends by the geographic locator "south" in *BGE* 255: it is "African"; thus, what he anticipates in "the good European" is "*supra*-European" insofar as it intensifies and maximizes diversity and hybridity rather than simplifying and eradicating what would be regarded as foreign by his contemporaries.

14. Here, Nietzsche scouts ancestral resources (and liabilities) similar to those he ascribes to the modern European inheritance in bk. 8 of *Jenseits von Gut und Böse*, "On Peoples and Fatherlands" (see esp. *BGE* 264, 268).

15. "Man ist am wenigsten mit seinen Eltern verwandt: es wäre das äusserste Zeichen von Gemeinheit, seinen Eltern verwandt zu sein. Die höheren Naturen haben ihren Ursprung unendlich weiter zurück, auf sie hin hat am längsten gesammelt, gespart, gehäuft werden müssen. Die grossen Individuen sind die ältesten[. . .]." Translated in Mazzino Montinari, *Reading Nietzsche*, trans. Greg Whitlock (Urbana: University of Illinois Press, 2003), 105. The passage cited is part of a replacement text that Nietzsche submitted for *EH* "Why I Am So Wise" 3 when he returned the first and second signatures of the book to the publisher on December 18, 1888. It does not appear in the Kaufmann translation, on which I most often rely. This passage is somewhat at odds with *BGE* 264, mentioned above, which underscores that it is "absolutely impossible" not to embody the "qualities and preferences" of one's parents. These can be reconciled if one grants that Nietzsche holds that one is not *merely* what one inherits most immediately and that in so-called higher types the ancient inheritances are enhanced and more pronounced.

16. Translated in Montinari, *Reading Nietzsche*, 105. "Aber auch als Pole bin ich ein ungeheurer Atavismus. Man würde Jahrhunderte zurückzugehn haben, um diese vornehmste Rasse, die es auf Erden gab, in dem Masse instinktrein zu finden, wie ich sie darstelle" (*KSA* 6, p. 268; cf. *GS* 10, 127; *BGE* 20, 149, 261).

17. Compare the discussion of Goethe's totality in *TI* "Skirmishes of an Untimely Man" 49 in Ward, "Nietzsche's Value Conflict," 13. Ward emphasizes how the passage on Goethe is decidedly not agonistic, nonrelational, and evident of purely intrinsic value. I do not see this strict separation. I suspect that part of my disagreement turns on the matter of what Nietzsche

can mean when he says that such a person "instinctively gathers" and what it means to be a "principle of selection." If there is *no one* doing the gathering, if such individuals *are* gatherings, then we still need to know more about how such gathering occurs, the conditions that make it possible.

18. For discussion of types as orders of drives, see John Richardson, "Nietzsche's Freedoms," in Gemes and May, eds., *Nietzsche on Freedom and Autonomy*, 127–49, and *Nietzsche's New Darwinism*.

19. Steven D. Hales and Rex Welshon, *Nietzsche's Perspectivism* (Urbana: University of Illinois Press, 2000), 174.

20. Ibid., 181. See also Richardson, *Nietzsche's New Darwinism*.

21. Ward ("Nietzsche's Value Conflict") explores how Nietzsche's conception of values is related to his views about constitutions, orders of rank, and orders of rule in ways similar to how I discuss them here and in my "Beholding Nietzsche: *Ecce Homo*, Fate, and Freedom," in *Oxford Handbook on Nietzsche*, ed. John Richardson and Kenneth Gemes (Oxford: Oxford University Press, forthcoming). I am not yet convinced that Nietzsche's preference for (or valuation of) a particular order of rule is as clear as Ward seems to think.

22. See the interesting debate about whether Nietzsche's discussion of the will in *BGE* 19 is an account of the *phenomenology* of willing (and linked with dismissal of the efficiency of the will) or an alternative account of what constitutes willing and the circumstances in which it occurs in Leiter, "Nietzsche's Theory of the Will"; and Clark and Dudrick, "Nietzsche on the Will." See also sec. 3.7 above.

23. For further comments by Nietzsche on the aptness of political organizations as metaphors for the subject, see, e.g., *KSA* 11:40[21], which is discussed briefly in Nehamas, *Nietzsche: Life as Literature*, 181–82 (as *WP* 492).

24. Leiter (*Routledge Philosophy GuideBook to Nietzsche on Morality*, and "Nietzsche's Theory of the Will") attributes a "doctrine of types" to Nietzsche.

25. One might also place the emphasis on an implied restraint against our tendency to *want* to know and to fabricate such answers that seek to unify conflicting and contrasting traits and characteristics. This is explored at length in Gary Shapiro, *Nietzschean Narratives* (Bloomington: Indiana University Press, 1989), chap. 6 (on *Ecce Homo*), which emphasizes the importance of the dopplegänger in Nietzsche.

26. Contrasting positions on Nietzsche's views about fate are evident in the different accounts given by Leiter ("The Paradox of Fatalism and Self-Creation in Nietzsche," and "Nietzsche's Theory of the Will") and Robert C. Solomon (*Living with Nietzsche: What the Great "Immoralist" Has to Teach Us* [Oxford: Oxford University Press, 2003]). For Leiter, what he calls *type facts* play a "crucial role [. . .] in determining what one does, even what morality one accepts" ("Nietzsche's Theory of the Will," 118). While events are not determined in advance for Leiter—and, thus, there is no predestination in that sense—"facts" about a person, which limit and determine a range of possibilities, *are*. Thus, Leiter regards his view as attributing a form of "causal essentialism" to Nietzsche ("The Paradox of Fatalism and Self-Creation in Nietzsche," 225). Solomon emphasizes distinctions between fatalism and determinism, whereby determinism is focused on necessary causal connections and fatalism emphasizes the necessity of eventual outcomes without commitment to any specific causes that lead to such

outcomes. Solomon thinks Nietzsche's fatalism is most closely related to ancient views and that it is decidedly not a form of determinism in the contemporary sense.

27. Compare *GS* 276, discussed above. Siemens doubts that Nietzsche can realize this and still maintain his *Kriegs-Praxis*, but, as I argue below, I see them as compatible. See Herman Siemens, "Umwertung: Nietzsche's 'War-Praxis' and the Problem of Yes-Saying in *Ecce Homo*," *Nietzsche-Studien* 38 (2009): 182-206.

28. As discussed below and in chapter 3 above, Nietzsche is surely opposed to the notion of self-conservation advanced in what he understands as Darwinian accounts of evolution. Günter Abel discusses this in detail in "Nietzsche contra 'Selbsterhaltung': Steigerung der Macht und Ewige Wiederkehr," *Nietzsche-Studien* 10 (1982): 367-407. Curiously, however, at least in that work, Abel does not explore Nietzsche's positive association of *Selbsterhaltung* with selfishness.

29. Kaufmann and others translate *Selbstsucht* quite reasonably as *selfishness*, but I think that *self-seeking*, conceived as part of a process of self-formation, is also appropriate. It resonates with the opening of *Zur Genealogie der Moral*, where Nietzsche writes: "Wir sind uns unbekannt, wir Erkennenden, wir selbst uns selbst: das hat seinen guten Grund. Wir haben nie nach uns gesucht,—wie sollte es geschehn, dass wir eines Tags uns fänden?" (*GM* P:1).

30. Compare *NCW* 7; and *TI* "Errors" 2. For discussion, see Müller-Lauter, "Nihilism as Will to Nothingness."

31. Extensive discussion of Nietzsche's wrestling with and ultimate rejection of selflessness is found in Janaway, *Beyond Selflessness*. Interestingly, Nietzsche does not mention *Selbstsucht* in *GM* even though he discusses it in works prior to and after it.

32. Part of what is so problematic about pity is that it can motivate us to conserve what ought to perish, and in *Ecce Homo* Nietzsche presents himself as a physiologist who is experienced in understanding organic degeneration and can apply those insights to psychological health. He writes: "When the least organ in an organism fails, however slightly, to enforce with complete assurance its self-preservation [Selbsterhaltung], its 'egoism,' restitution of its energies [vollkommner Sicherheit durchzusetzen]—the whole degenerates [entartet]. The physiologist demands *excision* of the degenerating part; he denies all solidarity with what degenerates [Entartenden]; he is worlds removed from pity [Mitleiden] for it. But the priest desires precisely the degeneration of the whole, of humanity: for that reason he *conserves* what degenerates [c o n s e r v i r t er das Entartende]—at this price he rules" (*EH* "Daybreak" 2).

33. Although avoiding unnecessary fights is important, for Nietzsche, it is also a marker of strength to be capable of bearing much, as his discussion of parasites in *GM* II:10 suggests.

34. The kinds of things that concern Nietzsche here might be compared with his reflections on independence as "not remaining stuck" in *BGE* 41. *Independence* in this sense is not being *free* of any and all attachments; rather, it is being able to form a variety of attachments because none is so binding as to limit one's connections with others. This is discussed in chap. 10 of my and Ansell-Pearson's *Nietzsche's Beyond Good and Evil*.

35. See also *GS* 13 ("das Verlangen nach Zerstörung" [the desire for destruction]) *GS* 370.

36. This echoes a point mentioned in chapter 2 above, namely, that Nietzsche thought that Schopenhauer failed to take his pessimism far enough, a view that he expresses in *Jenseits von Gut und Böse* when introducing his own notion of eternal recurrence as a form of

self-overcoming pessimism. Thus, we cannot see Nietzsche as simply succumbing to *Schopenhauer's* pessimism because for him Schopenhauer is not pessimistic enough.

37. These are distinguished in Gary Watson, "Two Faces of Responsibility," *Philosophical Topics* 24 (1996): 227–48, which is discussed by Gemes ("Nietzsche on Free Will, Autonomy and the Sovereign Individual," 2006).

38. Angela M. Smith, "Control, Responsibility, and Moral Assessment," *Philosophical Studies* 138 (2008): 367–92, 370.

39. For Smith (ibid.), these are essentially rational.

40. Ibid., 370.

41. Susan Wolf, *Freedom within Reason* (New York: Oxford University Press, 1993), 40, cited in Smith, "Control, Responsibility, and Moral Assessment," 372.

42. Gemes, "Nietzsche on Free Will, Autonomy and the Sovereign Individual." See the discussion in sec. 4.6 above.

43. What I am describing here is not the same as the notion of legal liability that accompanies senses of responsibility that define a scope of accountability in contexts that do not require direct causal attribution. Bernard Williams takes up this sense of responsibility. See *Shame and Necessity*, chap. 3.

44. This quotation relies on the translations of both Hollingdale and Smith, with slight emendations.

45. Williams, *Shame and Necessity*, 35–36.

46. Ibid., 36.

47. Ibid., 43–44.

48. Williams does consider the cases of liability where the responsible party is in no way the cause of the act in question, but he considers these rare and that they nevertheless turn on some voluntary prior act of accepting responsibility.

49. Williams, *Shame and Necessity*, 64.

50. Ibid., 68.

51. Ibid., 69.

52. Ibid., 74.

53. *KSA* 4, p. 111: "Dass der Schaffende selber das Kind sei, das neu geboren werde, dazu muss er auch die Gebärerin sein wollen und der Schmerz der Gebärerin." The translation is my own.

54. Nietzsche's "psychical polycentrism" is focus of Graham Parkes's *Composing the Soul*.

55. In this respect, we might see Zarathustra as drawing on the idea of *amor fati*. Pippin helpfully and repeatedly draws his readers' attention to the importance of love in Nietzsche's works, and this image of the redemptive possibilities of love (in the here and now) might be relevant. See esp. Pippin, *Idealism as Modernism*, 360–64.

56. My translation. Compare further on in the same passage: "Dass eure Tugend euer Selbst sei. . . ."

57. Kaufmann's translation amended: "Die wundervolle Kunst und Kraft, Götter zu schaffen—der Polytheismus—war es, in der dieser Trieb sich entladen durfte, in der er sich reinigte, vervollkommnete, veredelte: denn ursprünglich war es ein gemeiner und unansehnlicher Trieb, verwandt dem Eigensinn, dem Ungehorsame und dem Neide. [. . .] Die Erfindung von

Göttern, Heroen und Übermenschen aller Art, sowie von Neben- und Untermenschen, von Zwergen, Feen, Centauren, Satyrn, Dämonen und Teufeln, war die unschätzbare Vorübung zur Rechtfertigung der Selbstsucht und Selbstherrlichkeit des Einzelnen [. . .]" (*GS* 143).

58. See also earlier draft of the concept for *EH* (1888), which focuses on the "problem of nutrition [Ernährung]" (*KSA* 13.24[1]). Compare *BGE* 36; *D* 171; and *GS* 347.

59. Note the similarity to the word Nietzsche uses (positively) to describe Wagner in *RWB* 7, cited above, when he highlights his self-relinquishing: *Selbstentäusserung*.

60. It is also interesting to compare here how Nietzsche thinks that unselfing morality makes an imperative of "zu Grunde gehen," which I discuss in chapter 4 above. But, whereas Zarathustra advises his disciplines to "go to ruin" in seeking to overcome themselves, in seeking to surpass themselves, Nietzsche thinks that *unselfing morality* takes destroying oneself as a primary goal: "Die Entselbstungs-Moral ist die Niedergangs-Moral par excellence, die Thatsache 'ich gehe zu Grunde' in den Imperativ übersetzt: 'ihr sollt alle zu Grunde gehn'—und nicht nur in den Imperativ! . . . Diese einzige Moral, die bisher gelehrt worden ist, die Entselbstungs-Moral, verräth einen Willen zum Ende, sie verneint im untersten Grunde das Leben."

61. This is the same passage in which Nietzsche criticizes the concept of *Selbsterhaltungstrieb* advanced by "physiologists." For discussion, see Abel, "Nietzsche contra 'Selbsterhaltung.'"

62. *KSA* 6, p. 274: "Ich bin meiner Art nach kriegerisch."

63. I have listed these in an order that differs from Nietzsche's because I do not think his sequence indicates any particular priority. Whether Nietzsche *actually* put these principles into action is another matter, as I suggest below and in the afterword. See also the discussion in my "Nietzsche's Agonal Wisdom," *International Studies in Philosophy* 35, no. 3 (Fall 2003): 205–25.

64. And this recalls Nietzsche's conception of the entwinement of friendship and enmity, which he expresses repeatedly in his writings, perhaps best known in Zarathustra's remarks in *Z* I "On the Friend." This dual aspect of agonism—that it both *divides* or distinguishes and *binds*—helps resolve a conflict between Nietzsche's self-imposed imperative of affirmation and the inherently negative dimensions of his thought that especially trouble Herman Siemens, who similarly highlights the binding function of the agon. See Siemens, "Umwertung."

65. Nietzsche also regards Wagner as a great mixture of types (*EH* "Why I Am So Clever" 7). See also discussion of mixture and hybridity in *BGE* "On Peoples and Fatherlands." The discussion in the latter text, particularly, shows that he has ambivalent views about such a condition. On the one hand, he thinks it is a quintessential condition of modern human beings that they are great mixtures of types and tastes and this is generally deforming and incapacitating. On the other hand, he seems to think such a condition might be potentially enhancing provided there is some way of yoking the multifarious tastes in a way that allows them to be individually preserved and intensified. I elaborate his views about such hybridity in my and Ansell-Pearson's *Nietzsche's Beyond Good and Evil*.

66. For a plausible account of how Nietzsche holds a kind of bundle theory and its resemblance to some contemporary varieties of the same, see Hales and Welshon, *Nietzsche's Perspectivism*, chap. 7.

67. Fredrick Appel claims that Nietzsche's agonism champions a "castelike society" led by "high-spirited aristocrats" who are "constrained only by a sense of respect for and gratitude toward their peers and focused on the contests and challenges at hand they think nothing of

using the mass as fodder for their creative enterprises. They also accept with equanimity the prospect of widespread destruction and loss of life that occur as a by-product of their innocent experimentation" (*Nietzsche Contra Democracy* [Ithaca, NY: Cornell University Press, 1999]), 160. I obviously disagree with this characterization of a Nietzschean agonistic ethos (Appel does endorse what he construes as an Aristotelian conception of agonism).

68. Compare *EH* "Books" 4: "multiplicity of inward states is exceptionally large in my case, I have many stylistic possibilities—the most multifarious art of style that has ever been at the disposal of one man."

69. See Nehamas, *Nietzsche: Life as Literature*, esp. 177–86; and Leiter, "The Paradox of Fatalism and Self-Creation in Nietzsche," 255.

70. Clark and Dudrick ("Nietzsche on the Will") emphasize without elaborating the significance of what they call *political authority* in organizations of drives. They write: "The viewpoint of the person who experiences willing is constituted by, in the sense that it simply *is*, the viewpoint of the drives who use the trappings of political authority to get their way in conflicts with the other drives" (256). I agree that "political authority" is an appropriate way in which to understand how Nietzsche conceives the relations of the drives, but I suggest it is more than "us[ing] [. . .] trappings." The drives *are* successful on the basis of their participation in the political arrangements. This means that no drive gets its way by sheer strength alone; it is (and, thus, *we* are) inherently social and political, all the way down, so to speak.

71. For discussion of Nietzsche's "sociophysiology," see Herman Siemens, "Nietzsche contra Liberalism on Freedom," in *A Companion to Nietzsche*, ed. K. Ansell-Pearson (Oxford: Blackwell, 2006), 437–54, which explores how agonistic social relations can be constitutive.

72. For other discussions of how small things potentially influence and affect orders of relations such that we can see individuals as constituted *in relation* to their environments, see Brian Domino, "The Casuistry of the Little Things," *Journal of Nietzsche Studies* 23 (2002): 51–62; Horst Hutter, *Shaping the Future: Nietzsche's New Regime of the Soul and Its Ascetic Practices* (Lanham, MD: Lexington, 2006); and, in Nietzsche's own case, David Farrell Krell and Donald Bates, *The Good European: Nietzsche's Work Sites in Word and Image* (Chicago: University of Chicago Press, 1997).

73. Rich detail of Nietzsche's travels can be found in Krell and Bates, *The Good European*.

74. Other examples in *EH* include the reference to the facts that "Songs of Prince Free Bird" was written in Sicily, *HH* in Sorrento, and *D* in Genoa.

75. Nietzsche's works are replete with references to "what has been achieved in us," not by the dint of our own will, but rather "by nature."

76. This idea is most clearly reflected in *D* 109, which numerous commentators cite. See, e.g., Parkes, *Composing the Soul*, 290–92.

77. I discuss Nietzsche's ideas about the relation between attachments and our sense of ourselves as free and independent in my "In What Senses Are Free Spirits *Free*?" (paper presented at the conference "Nietzsche at Warwick: The Philosophy of the Free Spirit," March 2012).

78. In a discussion of the sort of unity that is possible for the assemblages Nietzsche thinks human beings are, Nehamas explores whether he has in mind unity as coherence or unity as numerical identity. He sees a much greater fluidity in what *rules* in such orders, with the effect that they might be thought to roughly constitute some specific or distinctive collectivity, at least more than what I would grant. Here is where Leiter's emphasis on types could be instructive

if modified to pertain, not exclusively or even primarily to type facts, but rather to orders of rank that consider both what is ordered and what rules so as to preserve that order. The reason I find both accounts partial is because I think there needs to be an emphasis on the nature of the ruling that abides in the composite under consideration. See Nehamas, *Nietzsche: Life as Literature*, esp. 181–82; and Leiter, "The Paradox of Fatalism and Self-Creation in Nietzsche," *Routledge Philosophy GuideBook to Nietzsche on Morality*, and "Nietzsche's Theory of the Will." There is also significant difference between the two concerning how unity is achieved in this multiplicity. For Nehamas, literature supplies an artistic creative model for producing the unity of the self. For Leiter, it is simply given. Also instructive is Richardson on unity as "that synthesis of a stable power-system of drives [...] accomplished by a single drive taking control, and imposing its single command" ("Nietzsche's Freedoms," 135), though I do not see why it must be a single drive that does this rather than a regency or an oligarchy. The political and agonistic character of the soul indicates greater possibilities.

AFTERWORD

1. Dana R. Villa, "Democratizing the *Agon*: Nietzsche, Arendt, and the Agonistic Tendency in Recent Political Theory," in *Why Nietzsche Still? Reflections on Drama, Culture, and Politics*, ed. Alan D. Schrift (Berkeley and Los Angeles: University of California Press, 2000), 225.

2. For a wide-ranging set of meditations on the relation between eris and eros, see Paul van Tongeren, Paul Sars, Chris Bremmers, and Koen Boey, eds., *Eros and Eris: Contributions to a Hermeneutical Phenomenology: Liber Amicorum for Adrian Peperzak* (Dordrecht: Kluwer Academic, 1992).

3. On the connection between Nietzsche's naturalism and forms of life, see Richard Schacht, "Nietzsche's Naturalism," *Journal of Nietzsche Studies* 43 (forthcoming).

4. A fine account of this is offered in Robert B. Pippin, "Gay Science and Corporeal Knowledge," *Nietzsche-Studien* 29 (2000): 136–52.

5. See Herman Siemens, "Nietzsche's Political Philosophy: A Review of Recent Literature," *Nietzsche-Studien* 30 (2001): 521n78: "One cannot play a game unless one wants to win; and one cannot play to win if one is playing for the sake of the game itself. See also van Tongeren, P., *Die Moral von Nietzsche's Moralkritik* [Bonn: Bouvier, 1989], on 'Nietzsche's impraktikable Moral.'"

6. See the discussion of the "medial sense of the agon" and immanent judgment in Siemens, "Nietzsche's Political Philosophy," esp. 521–22, 516–18. On the same topic, Siemens discusses V. Gerhardt, "Das 'Prinzip des Gleichgewichts,'" *Nietzsche-Studien* 12 (1983): 111–33. See also Siemens, "Agonal Communities of Taste," esp. 102–6.

7. See Siemens, "Umwertung"; and Gerd Schank, *Dionysos gegen den Gekreuzigten: Eine philologische und philosophische Studie* (New York: Peter Lang, 1993).

BIBLIOGRAPHY

PRIMARY SOURCES

Unless otherwise noted, I use the following translations of Nietzsche's works. In cases where more than one translation is listed, I use the first except when otherwise noted in the text. Translations of materials from Nietzsche's notebooks are generally my own; however, I also consult Walter Kaufmann's translations of unpublished selected notes from the period 1883–88 in *The Will to Power*, ed. Walter Kaufmann, trans. Walter Kaufmann and R. J. Hollingdale (New York: Vintage, 1967).

The Antichrist (1888). In *The Portable Nietzsche*, ed. and trans. Walter Kaufmann. New York: Viking, 1968.

Assorted Opinions and Maxims (1879). Vol. 2, pt. 1, of *Human, All Too Human*, trans. R. J. Hollingdale. Cambridge: Cambridge University Press, 1986.

Beyond Good and Evil: Prelude to a Philosophy of the Future (1886). Translated by Walter Kaufmann. New York: Vintage, 1966.

The Birth of Tragedy; or, Hellenism and Pessimism (1872, 1886). In *The Birth of Tragedy and The Case of Wagner*, trans. Walter Kaufmann. New York: Vintage, 1967.

David Strauss: The Writer and the Confessor (1873). Translated by R. J. Hollingdale. Cambridge: Cambridge University Press, 1983.

Daybreak: Thoughts on the Prejudices of Morality (1881). Translated by R. J. Hollingdale. Cambridge: Cambridge University Press, 1982.

Dawn. Translated by Brittain Smith, with afterword by Keith Ansell-Pearson. In *The Complete Works of Friedrich Nietzsche*, vol. 5, *Dawn: Thoughts on the Presumptions of Morality*. Stanford, CA: Stanford University Press, 2011.

Ecce Homo: How One Becomes What One Is (1889). In *On the Genealogy of Morals* and *Ecce Homo*, trans. Walter Kaufmann. New York: Vintage, 1969.

The Gay Science: With a Prelude in German Rhymes and an Appendix of Songs (1882 and 1887 [fifth book and new preface added]). Translated by Walter Kaufmann. New York: Vintage, 1974.

"Homer's Contest" (1871 [unpublished]). Translated by Christa Davis Acampora. *Nietzscheana* 5 (Fall 1996): i–iv, 1–8.

"Homer's Contest" (excerpts). In *The Portable Nietzsche*, ed. and trans. Walter Kaufmann. New York: Viking, 1968.

Human, All Too Human: A Book for Free Spirits, vol. 1 (1878). Translated by R. J. Hollingdale. Cambridge: Cambridge University Press, 1986.

On the Genealogy of Morals (1887). In *On the Genealogy of Morals and Ecce Homo*, trans. Walter Kaufmann and R. J. Hollingdale. New York: Vintage, 1969.

On the Genealogy of Morality. Translated by Carol Diethe. In *On the Genealogy of Morality*, ed. Keith Ansell-Pearson. Cambridge: Cambridge University Press, 1994; rev. ed., Cambridge: Cambridge University Press, 2006.

On the Genealogy of Morality. Translated by Maudemarie Clark and Alan J. Swensen. In *On the Genealogy of Morality*. Indianapolis: Hackett, 1998.

On the Use and Disadvantage of History for Life (1874). In *Untimely Meditations*, trans. R. J. Hollingdale. Cambridge: Cambridge University Press, 1983.

The Pre-Platonic Philosophers. Translated and edited with an introduction and commentary by Greg Whitlock. Urbana: University of Illinois Press, 2001.

Richard Wagner in Bayreuth (1875). In *Untimely Meditations*, trans. R. J. Hollingdale. Cambridge: Cambridge University Press, 1983.

Schopenhauer as Educator (1874). In *Untimely Meditations*, trans. R. J. Hollingdale. Cambridge: Cambridge University Press, 1983.

Thus Spoke Zarathustra (1883 [pts. 1–2]; 1884 [pt. 3]; 1885 [pt. 4]). In *The Portable Nietzsche*, ed. and trans. Walter Kaufmann. New York: Viking, 1968.

Twilight of the Idols (1888). In *The Portable Nietzsche*, ed. and trans. Walter Kaufmann. New York: Viking, 1968.

The Wanderer and His Shadow (1880). Vol. 2, pt. 2, of *Human, All Too Human*. Translated by R. J. Hollingdale. Cambridge: Cambridge University Press, 1986.

Wir Philologen; "We Classicists." In *Unmodern Observations*, ed. and trans. William Arrowsmith, 321–87. New Haven, CT: Yale University Press, 1990.

SECONDARY SOURCES

Abel, Günter. "Nietzsche contra 'Selbsterhaltung': Steigerung der Macht und Ewige Wiederkehr." *Nietzsche-Studien* 10 (1982): 367–407.

Acampora, Christa Davis. "Re/Introducing 'Homer's Contest': A New Translation with Notes and Commentary." *Nietzscheana* 5 (Fall 1996): i–iv, 1–8.

———. "Nietzsche's Problem of Homer." *Nietzscheforschung: Jahrbuch der Nietzsche-Gesellschaft* 5/6 (Spring 2000): 553–74.

———. "Of Dangerous Games and Dastardly Deeds: A Typology of Nietzsche's Contests." *International Studies in Philosophy* 34, no. 3 (Fall 2002): 135–51.

———. "Nietzsche contra Homer, Socrates, and Paul." *Journal of Nietzsche Studies* 24 (Fall 2002): 25–53.

———. "The Contest between Nietzsche and Homer: Revaluing the 'Homeric Question.'" In *Nietzsche and the German Tradition*, ed. Nicholas Martin, 83–109. Berne: Peter Lang, 2003.

———. "*Demos Agonistes Redux*: Reflections on the *Streit* of Political Agonism." *Nietzsche-Studien* 32 (2003): 373–89.

———. "Nietzsche's Agonal Wisdom." *International Studies in Philosophy* 35, no. 3 (Fall 2003): 205–25.

———. "Between Mechanism and Teleology: Will to Power and Nietzsche's 'Gay' Science." In *Nietzsche and Science*, ed. Gregory Moore and Thomas H. Brobjer, 171–88. Adlershot: Ashgate, 2004.

———. On Sovereignty and Overhumanity: Why It Matters How We Read Nietzsche's *Genealogy* II:2." *International Studies in Philosophy* 36, no. 3 (Fall 2004): 127–45.

———. "Naturalism and Nietzsche's Moral Psychology." In *The Blackwell Companion to Nietzsche*, ed. Keith Ansell-Pearson, 314–33. Malden, MA: Blackwell, 2006.

———. "On Sovereignty and Overhumanity: Why It Matters How We Read Nietzsche's *Genealogy* II:2." In *Critical Essays on Nietzsche's On the Genealogy of Morals*, ed. Christa Davis Acampora, 147–62. Lanham, MD: Rowman & Littlefield, 2006.

———. "Unlikely Illuminations: Nietzsche and Frederick Douglass on Slavery, Power, and Freedom." In *Critical Affinities: Reflections on the Convergence of Nietzsche and African-American Thought*, ed. Todd Franklin and Jacqueline Scott, 175–202. Albany: State University of New York Press, 2006.

———. "Forgetting the Subject." In *Reading Nietzsche at the Margins*, ed. Steven V. Hicks and Alan Rosenberg, 34–56. West Lafayette, IN: Purdue University Press, 2008.

———. "Agonistic Politics and the 'War on Terror.'" *Insights* (Institute of Advanced Study, Durham University) 2, no. 11 (2009): 1–21.

———. "Beholding Nietzsche: *Ecce Homo*, Fate, and Freedom." In *Oxford Handbook on Nietzsche*, ed. John Richardson and Kenneth Gemes. Oxford: Oxford University Press, forthcoming.

———. "Nietzsche's Responsibility." In *Nietzsche's Postmoralism*, ed. Christopher Janaway and Ken Gemes. Oxford: Oxford University Press, forthcoming.

———. "Nietzsche's Political Agonism." n.d., typescript.

Acampora, Christa Davis, and Ralph R. Acampora, eds. *A Nietzschean Bestiary: Becoming Animal beyond Docile and Brutal*. Lanham, MD: Rowman & Littlefield, 2004.

Acampora, Christa Davis, and Keith Ansell-Pearson. *Nietzsche's Beyond Good and Evil: A Reader's Guide*. New York: Continuum, 2011.

Allison, David. *Reading the New Nietzsche*. Lanham, MD: Rowman & Littlefield, 2001.

Ames, Roger T., Wimal Dissanayake, and Thomas P. Kasulis, eds. *Self as Body in Asian Theory and Practice*. Albany: State University of New York Press, 1992.

Anders, Anni, and Karl Schlechta. *Von den vorborgenen Anfängen seines Philosophierens*. Stuttgart: Fromann, 1962.

Ansell-Pearson, Keith, ed. "Nietzsche and the Problem of the Will in Modernity." In *Nietzsche and Modern German Thought*, ed. Keith Ansell-Pearson, 165–91. London: Routledge, 1991.

———. "Nietzsche's Brave New World of Force: On Nietzsche's 'Time-Atom Theory' Fragment and the Matter of Boscovich's Influence on Nietzsche." *Journal of Nietzsche Studies* 20 (2000): 5–33.

———. *A Companion to Nietzsche*. Malden, MA: Blackwell, 2006.

———. "Naturalism and Immoralism: Nietzsche and Guyau." University of Warwick, n.d., typescript.

Appel, Frederick. *Nietzsche Contra Democracy*. Ithaca, NY: Cornell University Press, 1999.

Arrowsmith, William, ed. and trans. *Unmodern Observations*. New Haven, CT: Yale University Press, 1990.

Aydin, Ciano. "Nietzsche on Reality as Will to Power: Toward an 'Organization-Struggle' Model." *Journal of Nietzsche Studies* 34 (2007): 25–48.

Babich, Babette E. *Nietzsche's Philosophy of Science: Reflecting Science on the Ground of Art and Life*. Albany: State University of New York Press, 1994.

———. "Nietzsche's Imperative as a Friend's Encomium: On Becoming the One You Are, Ethics and Blessing." *Nietzsche-Studien* 33 (2003): 29–58.

Baer, Karl Ernst von. *Festrede zur Eröffnung der russischen entomologische Gesellschaft in Mai 1860*. Berlin, 1862.

Bieber, M. *The History of the Greek and Roman Theatre*. Princeton, NJ: Princeton University Press, 1961.

Brobjer, Thomas. *Nietzsche's Philosophical Context: An Intellectual Biography*. Urbana: University of Illinois Press, 2007.

Brown, Truesdell S. "Herodotus' Views on Athletics." *The Ancient World: Athletics in Antiquity* 7, nos. 1–2 (1983): 17–29.

Bulman, Patricia. *Phthonos in Pindar*. Classical Studies, vol. 35. Berkeley and Los Angeles: University of California Press, 1995.

Burckhardt, Jacob. *The History of Greek Culture*. Translated by Sheila Stern. Edited with an introduction by Oswyn Murray. New York: St. Martin's, 1998.

Burgess, Dana L. "Pindar's Olympian 10: Praise for the Poet, Praise for the Victor." *Hermes* 118, no. 3 (1990): 273–81.

Burnham, Douglas. *Reading Nietzsche: An Analysis of Beyond Good and Evil*. Montreal: McGill-Queen's University Press, 2007.

Butler, Judith. "Foucault and the Paradox of Bodily Inscriptions." *Journal of Philosophy* 86, no. 11 (1989): 601–7.

———. *The Psychic Life of Power: Theories in Subjection*. Stanford, CA: Stanford University Press, 1997.

Caillois, Roger. *Man, Play, and Games*. Translated by Meyer Barash. New York: Free Press, 1961.

Clark, Maudemarie. *Nietzsche on Truth and Philosophy*. Cambridge: Cambridge University Press, 1991.

Clark, Maudemarie, and David Dudrick. "Nietzsche's Post-Positivism." *European Journal of Philosophy* 12, no. 3 (2004): 369–85.

————. "The Naturalisms of *Beyond Good and Evil.*" In *A Companion to Nietzsche*, ed. Keith Ansell-Pearson, 148–68. Oxford: Blackwell, 2006.

————. "Nietzsche on the Will: An Analysis of BGE 19." In *Nietzsche on Freedom and Autonomy*, ed. Ken Gemes and Simon May, 247–68. Oxford: Oxford University Press, 2009.

Connolly, William. *Identity/Difference: Democratic Negotiations of Political Paradox.* Ithaca, NY: Cornell University Press, 1991.

————. *The Ethos of Pluralism.* Minneapolis: University of Minnesota Press, 1995.

The Contest between Homer and Hesiod. In *Hesiod, the Homeric Hymns, and Homerica*, 318–53. Loeb Classical Library. Cambridge, MA: Harvard University Press, 1978.

Conway, Daniel W. *Nietzsche's Dangerous Game: Philosophy in the Twilight of the Idols.* Cambridge: Cambridge University Press, 1997.

————. *Nietzsche's On the Genealogy of Morals: A Reader's Guide.* New York: Continuum, 2008.

Conway, Daniel W., and Rudolf Rehn. *Nietzsche und die antike Philosophie.* Trier: WVT Wissenschaftlicher Verlag Trier, 1992.

Cornford, Francis MacDonald. *The Origin of Attic Comedy.* 1914. Reprint, Ann Arbor: University of Michigan Press, 1993.

Cox, Christoph. *Nietzsche: Naturalism and Interpretation.* Berkeley and Los Angeles: University of California Press, 1999.

Curtin, Deane W. "Food/Body/Person." In *Cooking Eating Thinking: Transformative Philosophies of Food*, ed. Deane W. Curtin and Lisa M. Heldke, 3–22. Bloomington: Indiana University Press, 1992.

Curtius, Ernst. "Der Wettkampf" (1856). In *Göttinger Festreden*, 1–22. Berlin: Wilhelm Herz, 1864.

Deleuze, Gilles. *Nietzsche and Philosophy.* Translated by Hugh Tomlinson. New York: Columbia University Press. 1983.

Deleuze, Gilles, and Felix Guattari. *Anti-Oedipus: Capitalism and Schizophrenia.* Translated by R. Hurley, M. Seem, and H. Lane. Minneapolis: University of Minnesota Press, 1983.

Dodds, E. R. *The Greeks and the Irrational.* Berkeley: University of California Press, 1951.

Dombowsky, Don. *Nietzsche's Machiavellian Politics.* Basingstoke: Palgrave, 2004.

Domino, Brian. "The Casuistry of the Little Things." *Journal of Nietzsche Studies* 23 (2002): 51–62.

Ellsworth, J. D. "*Agon*: Studies in the Use of a Word." Ph.D. diss., University of California, Berkeley, 1971.

Else, G. F. *The Origin and Early Form of Greek Tragedy.* Cambridge, MA: Harvard University Press, 1965.

Emden, Christian J. *Nietzsche on Language, Consciousness, and the Body.* Urbana: University of Illinois Press, 2005.

————. *Friedrich Nietzsche and the Politics of History.* Cambridge: Cambridge University Press, 2008.

————. "Nietzsche's Naturalism: Philosophy and the Life Sciences in the Nineteenth Century." Rice University, n.d., typescript.

Esposito, Roberto. *Bíos: Biopolitics and Philosophy*. Translated by Timothy Campbell. Minneapolis: University of Minnesota Press, 2008.

Finley, M. I. *The World of Odysseus*. 2nd rev. ed. 1978. Reprint, New York: Penguin, 1991.

Finley, M. I., and H. W. Pleket. *The Olympic Games: The First Thousand Years*. New York: Viking, 1976.

Fisher, N. R. E. *Hybris: A Study in the Values of Honour and Shame in Ancient Greece*. Warminster: Aris & Phillips, 1992.

Fitzgerald, William. *Agonistic Poetry: The Pindaric Mode in Pindar, Horace, Hölderlin, and the English Ode*. Berkeley and Los Angeles: University of California Press, 1987.

Fontenrose, Joseph. "The Cult of Apollo and the Games at Delphi." In *The Archaeology of the Olympics: The Olympics and Other Festivals in Antiquity*, ed. Wendy Raschke. Madison: University of Wisconsin Press, 1988.

Fuks, Alexander. *Social Conflict in Ancient Greece*. Leiden: E. J. Brill, 1984.

Furness, Raymond. "Nietzsche and Empedocles." *Journal of the British Society for Phenomenology* 2 (May 1971): 91–94.

Gardiner, E. Norman. *Greek Athletic Sports and Festivals*. London: Macmillan, 1910.

Gemes, Ken. "Nietzsche on Free Will, Autonomy and the Sovereign Individual." *Proceedings of the Aristotelian Society Supplementary Volume* 80 (2006): 321–38.

———. "'We Remain of Necessity Strangers to Ourselves': The Key Message of Nietzsche's *Genealogy*." In *Critical Essays on Nietzsche's On the Genealogy of Morals*, ed. Christa Davis Acampora, 191–208. Lanham, MD: Rowman & Littlefield, 2006.

Gemes, Ken, and Simon May, eds., *Nietzsche on Freedom and Autonomy*. Oxford: Oxford University Press, 2009.

Gerhardt, V. "Das 'Prinzip des Gleichgewichts.'" *Nietzsche-Studien* 12 (1983): 111–33.

Gould, Stephen Jay. *The Structure of Evolutionary Theory*. Cambridge, MA: Belknap Press of Harvard University Press, 2002.

Gouldner, Alvin W. *Enter Plato: Classical Greece and the Origins of Social Theory*. New York: Basic, 1965.

Grote, George. *Geschichte Griechenlands*. 1859–65. Translated as *History of Greece*. 12 vols. New York: Harper & Bros., 1859–65.

Gründer, Karlfried, ed. *Der Streit um Nietzsches' Geburt der Tragödie*. Hildesheim: Georg Olms, 1969.

Hadot, Pierre. *Philosophy as a Way of Life: Spiritual Exercise from Socrates to Foucault*. Edited by Arnold Davidson. Translated by Michael Chase. New York: Blackwell, 1995.

Hales, Steven D., and Rex Welshon. *Nietzsche's Perspectivism*. Urbana: University of Illinois Press, 2000.

Hatab, Lawrence J. *A Nietzschean Defense of Democracy: An Experiment in Postmodern Politics*. Chicago: Open Court, 1995.

———. "Prospects for a Democratic Agon: Why We Can Still Be Nietzscheans." *Journal of Nietzsche Studies* 24 (Fall 2002): 132–47.

———. *Nietzsche's On the Genealogy of Morality: An Introduction*. Cambridge: Cambridge University Press, 2008.

Havas, Randall. *Nietzsche's Genealogy: Nihilism and the Will to Knowledge*. Ithaca, NY: Cornell University Press, 1995.

——. "Nietzsche's Idealism." *Journal of Nietzsche Studies* 20 (2000): 90–99.

Herman, Gabriel. *Ritualised Friendship and the Greek City.* Cambridge: Cambridge University Press, 1987.

Herodotus. *The Histories.* Translated by Aubrey De Sélincourt and John Marincola. New York: Penguin, 1996.

Hershbell, J. P., and S. A. Nimis. "Nietzsche and Heraclitus." *Nietzsche-Studien* 8 (1979): 17–38.

Hesiod and Theognis. Translated by Dorothea Wender. New York: Penguin, 1973.

Hildebrandt, Kurt. *Nietzsches Wettkampf mit Sokrates und Plato.* Dresden: Sybillen, 1922.

Hill, R. Kevin. *Nietzsche's Critiques: The Kantian Foundations of His Thought.* Oxford: Oxford University Press, 2003.

Hillesheim, James W. "Nietzsche Agonistes." *Educational Theory* 23 (Fall 1973): 343–53.

Homer. *The Odyssey.* 2 vols. Loeb Classical Library. Cambridge, MA: Harvard University Press, 1919.

Homer. *The Iliad.* 2 vols. Loeb Classical Library. Cambridge, MA: Harvard University Press, 1924.

Hoy, David. "Two Conflicting Conceptions of How to Naturalize Philosophy: Foucault vs. Habermas." In *Metaphysik nach Kant?* ed. D. Heinrich and R. Horstmann, 743–66. Stuttgart: Klett-Cotta, 1988.

Huizinga, J. *Homo Ludens: A Study of the Play-Element in Culture.* 1949. Reprint, Boston: Beacon, 1955.

Humphreys, Milton. "The Agon of the Old Comedy." *American Journal of Philology* 8, no. 30 (1882): 179–206.

Hussain, Nadeem. "Nietzsche's Positivism." *European Journal of Philosophy* 12, no. 3 (2004): 326–68.

Hutter, Horst. *Shaping the Future: Nietzsche's New Regime of the Soul and Its Ascetic Practices.* Lanham, MD: Lexington, 2006.

Jaeger, Werner. *Paideia: The Ideals of Greek Culture.* Translated by Gilbert Highet. 4 vols. 1944. Reprint, Oxford: Blackwell, 1957.

Janaway, Christopher. *Beyond Selflessness: Reading Nietzsche's Genealogy.* Oxford: Oxford University Press, 2007.

——, ed. *Willing and Nothingness: Schopenhauer as Nietzsche's Educator.* Oxford: Oxford University Press, 1998.

Janko, R. "The Shield of Heracles and the Legend of Cycnus." *Classical Quarterly* 36, no. 1 (1986): 38–59.

Johnson, Dirk R. *Nietzsche's Anti-Darwinism.* Cambridge: Cambridge University Press, 2010.

Jovanovski, Thomas. "Critique of Walter Kaufmann's 'Nietzsche's Attitude toward Socrates.'" *Nietzsche-Studien* 20 (1991): 329–58.

Kahn, Charles H. *The Art and Thought of Heraclitus: An Edition of the Fragments with Translation and Commentary.* Cambridge: Cambridge University Press, 1979.

Kail, P. J. E. "Nietzsche and Hume: Naturalism and Explanation." *Journal of Nietzsche Studies* 37 (Spring 2009): 5–22.

Kaufmann, Walter. *Tragedy and Philosophy.* Princeton, NJ: Princeton University Press, 1968.

————. *Nietzsche: Philosopher, Psychologist, Antichrist.* 4th ed. Princeton, NJ: Princeton University Press, 1974.

Kemal, Salim. "Nietzsche's Genealogy: Of Beauty and Community." *Journal of the British Society for Phenomenology* 21 (October 1990): 234–49.

Kerferd, G. B. *The Sophistic Movement.* New York: Cambridge University Press, 1981.

Klein, Wayne. "Nietzsche's Apocrypha: *The Will to Power* and Contemporary Scholarship." *New Nietzsche Studies* 1, nos. 1/2 (Fall/Winter 1996): 102–25.

Kofman, Sarah. *Nietzsche and Metaphor.* Translated by Duncan Large. Stanford, CA: Stanford University Press, 1993.

Kohn, Alfie. *No Contest: The Case against Competition.* Boston: Houghton Mifflin, 1986.

Krell, David Farrell, and Donald Bates. *The Good European: Nietzsche's Work Sites in Word and Image.* Chicago: University of Chicago Press, 1997.

Kurke, Leslie. "The Economy of Kudos." In *Cultural Poetics in Archaic Greece: Cult, Performance, Politics*, ed. Carol Dougherty and Leslie Kurke, 131–63. New York: Cambridge University Press, 1993.

Lachterman, David R. "Die Ewige Wiederkehr der Griechen: Nietzsche and the Homeric Question." *International Studies in Philosophy* 23, no. 2 (1991): 83–101.

Lampert, Laurence. *Nietzsche's Teaching: An Interpretation of Thus Spoke Zarathustra.* New Haven, CT: Yale University Press, 1986.

Lange, F. A. *History of Materialism: And Criticism of Its Present Importance.* With an introduction by Bertrand Russell. 3 vols. Reprint, New York: Routledge, 2000.

Lecky, William Edward Hartpole. *History of European Morals.* 2 vols. Reprint, New York: D. Appleton, 1908.

Lee, Hugh M. "Athletic Arete in Pindar." *The Ancient World: Athletics in Antiquity* 7, nos. 1–2 (1983): 31–37.

————. "The 'First' Olympic Games of 776 B.C." In *The Archaeology of the Olympics: The Olympics and Other Festivals in Antiquity*, ed. Wendy Raschke, 110–18. Madison: University of Wisconsin Press, 1988.

Leiter, Brian. "The Paradox of Fatalism and Self-Creation in Nietzsche." In *Willing and Nothingness: Schopenhauer as Nietzsche's Educator*, ed. Christopher Janaway, 217–57. Oxford: Oxford University Press, 1998.

————. *Routledge Philosophy GuideBook to Nietzsche on Morality.* New York: Routledge, 2002.

————. "Nietzsche's Theory of the Will." In *Nietzsche on Freedom and Autonomy*, ed. Ken Gemes and Simon May, 107–26. Oxford: Oxford University Press, 2009.

Lemm, Vanessa. *Nietzsche's Animal Philosophy.* New York: Fordham University Press, 2009.

Lloyd, G. E. R. *Polarity and Analogy: Two Types of Argumentation in Early Greek Thought.* New York: Cambridge University Press, 1966.

Lloyd, Michael. *The Agon in Euripides.* Oxford: Clarendon, 1992.

Loeb, Paul S. "Finding the Übermensch in Nietzsche's *Genealogy of Morality*." *Journal of Nietzsche Studies* 30 (Autumn 2005): 70–101.

Longinus. *On the Sublime.* Translated with commentary by James A. Arieti and John M. Crossett. New York: E. Mellen, 1984.

Magnus, Bernd. "The Use and Abuse of *The Will to Power*." In *Reading Nietzsche*, ed. Robert C. Solomon and Kathleen Marie Higgins, 218–36. New York: Oxford University Press, 1988.

Marrou, H. I. *A History of Education in Antiquity*. Translated by George Lamb. New York: Sheed & Ward, 1956.

Martin, Nicholas. *Nietzsche and Schiller: Untimely Aesthetics*. Oxford: Clarendon; New York: Oxford University Press, 1996.

May, Simon. *Nietzsche's Ethics and His "War" on Morality*. Cambridge: Cambridge University Press, 2000.

Meier, Christian. *The Political Art of Greek Tragedy*. Translated by Andrew Webber. Baltimore: Johns Hopkins University Press, 1993.

Menke, Christoph, and James Swindal. "Tragedy and the Free Spirits: On Nietzsche's Theory of Aesthetic Freedom." *Philosophy and Social Criticism* 22, no. 1 (1996): 1–12.

Meyer, Matthew. "Menschliches, Allzumenschliches und der musiktreibende Sokrates." *Nietzscheforschung: Jahrbuch der Nietzsche-Gesellschaft* 10 (2003): 129–37.

Miller, Stephen G. *Arete*. Chicago: Ares, 1979.

Moles, Alistair. *Nietzsche's Philosophy of Nature and Cosmology*. New York: Peter Lang, 1990.

Momigliano, Arnaldo. *Essays in Ancient and Modern Historiography*. Middletown, CT: Wesleyan University Press, 1977.

Montinari, Mazzino. *Reading Nietzsche*. Translated by Greg Whitlock. Urbana: University of Illinois Press, 2003.

Moore, Gregory. *Nietzsche, Biology and Metaphor*. Cambridge: Cambridge University Press, 2002.

———. "Nietzsche, Spencer, and the Ethics of Evolution." *Journal of Nietzsche Studies* 23 (Spring 2002): 1–20.

Morgan, Catherine. *Atheletes and Oracles: the Transformation of Olympia and Delphi in the Eighth Century B.C.* New York: Cambridge University Press, 1990.

Müller-Lauter, Wolfgang. "On Judging in a World of Becoming: A Reflection on the 'Great Change' in Nietzsche's Philosophy." In *Nietzsche, Theories of Knowledge, and Critical Theory*, ed. Babette E. Babich and Robert S. Cohen, 168–71. Boston: Kluwer, 1999.

———. *Nietzsche: His Philosophy of Contradictions and the Contradictions of His Philosophy*. Translated by David Parent. Urbana: University of Illinois Press, 1999.

———. "Nihilism as Will to Nothingness." In *Critical Essays on Nietzsche's On the Genealogy of Morals*, ed. Christa Davis Acampora, 209–19. Lanham, MD: Rowman & Littlefield, 2006.

Nehamas, Alexander. *Nietzsche: Life as Literature*. Cambridge, MA: Harvard University Press, 1985.

———. "Who Are the Philosophers of the Future?" In *Reading Nietzsche*, ed. Robert C. Solomon and Kathleen Marie Higgins, 46–67. New York: Oxford University Press, 1988.

———. "What Did Socrates Teach and To Whom Did He Teach It?" *Review of Metaphysics* 46 (December 1992): 279–306.

———. *The Art of Living: Socratic Reflections from Plato to Foucault*. Berkeley and Los Angeles: University of California Press, 1998.

Nisetich, Frank J., trans. *Pindar's Victory Songs*. Baltimore: Johns Hopkins University Press, 1980.

Nussbaum, Martha C. Introduction to *The Bacchae of Euripides*, trans. C. K. Williams. New York: Farrar Straus Giroux, 1990.

———. *The Fragility of Goodness: Luck and Ethics in Greek Tragedy and Philosophy*. New York: Cambridge University Press, 1994.

———. "The Transfiguration of Intoxication: Nietzsche, Schopenhauer, and Dionysus." *Arion* 1, no. 2 (Spring 1991): 75–111. Reprinted in *Nietzsche: Critical Assessments* (4 vols.), ed. Daniel W. Conway and Peter S. Groff, 1:331–59. London: Routledge, 1998.

O'Flaherty, James C., Thmothy F. Sellner, and Robert M. Helm, eds. *Studies in Nietzsche and the Classical Tradition*. Chapel Hill: University of North Carolina Press, 1976.

Ong, Walter J. *Fighting for Life: Contest, Sexuality, and Consciousness*. Ithaca, NY: Cornell University Press, 1980.

Ovid. *Metamorphoses*. Translated by Frank Justus Miller. 3rd ed. Loeb Classical Library 42. Cambridge, MA: Harvard University Press, 1984.

Owen, David. "Science, Value, and the Ascetic Ideal." In *Nietzsche, Epistemology, and Philosophy of Science*, ed. Babette E. Babich and Robert S. Cohen, 168–78. Boston: Kluwer, 1999.

———. "Equality, Democracy, and Self-Respect: Reflections on Nietzsche's Agonal Perfectionism." *Journal of Nietzsche Studies* 24 (Fall 2002): 113–31.

———. *Nietzsche's Genealogy of Morality*. Stocksfield: Acumen, 2007.

———. "Autonomy, Self-Respect and Self-Love: Nietzsche on Ethical Agency." In *Nietzsche on Freedom and Autonomy*, ed. Ken Gemes and Simon May, 197–221. Oxford: Oxford University Press, 2010.

Pangle, Thomas L. "The 'Warrior Spirit' as an Inlet to the Political Philosophy." *Nietzsche-Studien* 15 (1986): 140–79.

Parkes, Graham. *Composing the Soul: Reaches of Nietzsche's Psychology*. Chicago: University of Chicago Press, 1994.

Patterson, Richard. "'Philosophos Agonistes': Imagery and Moral Psychology in Plato's 'Republic.'" *Journal of the History of Philosophy* 35, no. 3 (1997): 327–54.

Pausanias. *Description of Greece*. Translated by W. H. S. Jones, Henry Arderne Ormerod, and R. E. Wycherley. Loeb Classical Library. Cambridge, MA: Harvard University Press, 1978.

Pfeiffer, Rudolf. *History of Classical Scholarship from 1300 to 1850*. Oxford: Clarendon, 1976.

Pfitzner, Victor C. *Paul and the Agon Motif: Traditional Athletic Imagery in the Pauline Literature*. Leiden: E. J. Brill, 1967.

Pindar. *Pindar's Victory Songs*. Translated by Frank J. Nisetich. Baltimore: Johns Hopkins University Press, 1980.

———. *Complete Odes*. Translated by Anthony Verity and Stephen Instone. Oxford: Oxford University Press, 2007.

Pippin, Robert B. *Modernism as a Philosophical Problem*. Cambridge, MA: Blackwell, 1991.

———. *Idealism as Modernism: Hegelian Variations*. Cambridge: Cambridge University Press, 1997.

———. "Gay Science and Corporeal Knowledge." *Nietzsche-Studien* 29 (2000): 136–52.

———. "Lightning and Flash, Agent and Deed." In *Critical Essays on Nietzsche's On the Genealogy of Morals*, ed. Christa Davis Acampora, 131–46. Lanham, MD: Rowman & Littlefield, 2006.

———. *Nietzsche, Psychology, and First Philosophy*. Chicago: University of Chicago Press, 2010.

Plato. *Republic*. Translated by P. Shorey. In *Plato in Twelve Volumes*, vols. 5–6. Cambridge, MA: Harvard University Press, 1969.

Pleket, H. W. "Zur Soziologie des antiken Sports." *Mededelingen van het Nederlands Instituut te Rome* 36 (1974): 57–87.

———. "Games, Prizes, Athletes and Ideology: Some Aspects of the History of Sport in the Greco-Roman World." *Stadion* 1 (1975): 49–89.

Poellner, Peter. *Nietzsche and Metaphysics*. Oxford: Clarendon, 1995.

Porter, James I. *The Invention of Dionysus: An Essay on The Birth of Tragedy*. Stanford, CA: Stanford University Press, 2000.

———. *Nietzsche and the Philology of the Future*. Stanford, CA: Stanford University Press, 2000.

———. "Untimely Meditations: *Zeitatomistik* in Context." *Journal of Nietzsche Studies* 20 (Spring 2000): 58–81.

Prinz, Jesse. "Where Do Morals Come From?" In *Philosophical Implications of Empirically Informed Ethics*, ed. M. Christen. New York: Springer, forthcoming.

Przybyslawski, Artur. "Nietzsche contra Heraclitus." *Journal of Nietzsche Studies* 23 (Fall 2002): 88–95.

Ranulf, Svend. *The Jealousy of the Gods and Criminal Law at Athens: A Contribution to the Sociology of Moral Indignation*. Vol. 1. London: Williams Norgate, 1932.

Raschke, Wendy, ed. *The Archeology of the Olympics: The Olympics and Other Festivals in Antiquity*. Madison: University of Wisconsin Press, 1988.

Raubitschek, Anthony. "The Agonistic Spirit in Greek Culture." *The Ancient World: Athletics in Antiquity* 7, nos. 1–2 (1983): 6–7.

Redfield, James. "Homo Domesticus." In *The Greeks*, ed. Jean-Pierre Vernant, trans. Charles Lambert and Teresa Lavender Fagan, 164–65. Chicago: University of Chicago Press, 1995.

Rée, Paul. "The Origin of Moral Sensations." In *Basic Writings*, trans. and ed. Robin Small, 85–164. Urbana: University of Illinois Press, 2003.

Reginster, Bernard. *The Affirmation of Life: Nietzsche on Overcoming Nihilism*. Cambridge, MA: Harvard University Press, 2006.

Renfrew, C. *Towards an Archaeology of Mind*. Cambridge: Cambridge University Press, 1982.

———. "The Minoan-Mycenaean Origins of the Panhellenic Games." In *The Archaeology of the Olympics: The Olympics and Other Festivals in Antiquity*, ed. Wendy Raschke, 13–25. Madison: University of Wisconsin Press, 1988.

Rethy, Robert. "Schein in Nietzsche's Philosophy." In *Nietzsche and Modern German Thought*, ed. Keith Ansell-Pearson, 59–87. London: Routledge, 1991.

Richardson, John. *Nietzsche's System*. New York: Oxford University Press, 1996.

———. *Nietzsche's New Darwinism*. New York: Oxford University Press, 2004.

———. "Nietzsche's Freedoms." In *Nietzsche on Freedom and Autonomy*, ed. Ken Gemes and Simon May, 127–49. Oxford: Oxford University Press, 2009.

Ricoeur, Paul. *The Rule of Metaphor: Multi-Disciplinary Studies of the Creation of Meaning in Language*. Translated by Robert Czerny. Toronto: University of Toronto Press, 1977.

Ridley, Aaron. "Nietzsche and the Re-Evaluation of Values." *Proceedings of the Aristotelian Society* 105 (2005): 171–91. Reprinted in *Critical Essays on Nietzsche's On the Genealogy of Morals*, ed. Christa Davis Acampora, 77–92 (Lanham, MD: Rowman & Littlefield, 2006).

Romano, David G. "The Ancient Stadium: Athletes and Arete." *The Ancient World: Athletics in Antiquity* 7, nos. 1–2 (1983): 9–16.

Rouse, Joseph. *How Scientific Practices Matter: Reclaiming Philosophical Naturalism*. Chicago: University of Chicago Press, 2002.

Salin, Edgar. *Nietzsche und Burckhardt*. 2nd ed. Heidelberg: Rowohlt, 1948.

Sallis, John. *Crossings: Nietzsche and the Space of Tragedy*. Chicago: University of Chicago Press, 1991.

Salomé, Lou Andreas. *Friedrich Nietzsche in seinen Werken*. Vienna: C. Konegen, 1894.

Schacht, Richard. *Nietzsche*. Boston: Routledge & Kegan Paul, 1982.

———. "Nietzsche's *Gay Science*: How to Naturalize Cheerfully." In *Reading Nietzsche*, ed. Robert C. Solomon and Kathleen Marie Higgins, 68–86. New York: Oxford University Press, 1989.

———, ed. *Nietzsche, Genealogy, Morality: Essays on Nietzsche's Genealogy of Morals*. Berkeley and Los Angeles: University of California Press, 1994.

———. *Making Sense of Nietzsche: Reflections Timely and Untimely*. Urbana: University of Illinois Press, 1995.

———. "Nietzsche's Naturalism." *Journal of Nietzsche Studies* (forthcoming).

Schank, Gerd. *Dionysos gegen den Gekreuzigten: Eine philologische und philosophische Studie zu Nietzsches Ecce homo*. New York: Peter Lang, 1993.

Schiller, Friedrich. *On the Aesthetic Education of Man in a Series of Letters*. Edited and translated by Elizabeth M. Wilkinson and L. A. Willoughby. Oxford: Clarendon, 1982. English and German facing. Also translated by Reginald Snell as *On the Aesthetic Education of Man: In a Series of Letters* (New Haven, CT: Yale University Press, 1954).

Schopenhauer, Arthur. *World as Will and Representation*. Translated by E. F. J. Payne. Mineola, NY: Dover, 1966.

———. *Essays and Aphorisms*. Translated by R. J. Hollingdale. New York: Penguin, 1970.

Schrift, Alan D. *Nietzsche and the Question of Interpretation: Between Hermeneutics and Deconstruction*. New York: Routledge, 1990.

———. *Nietzsche's French Legacy: A Genealogy of Poststructuralism*. London: Routledge, 1995.

———. "Rethinking Exchange: Logics of the Gift in Cixous and Nietzsche." *Philosophy Today* 40, no. 1 (Spring 1996): 197–205.

———. "Rethinking the Subject; or, How One Becomes-Other Than What One Is." In *Nietzsche's Postmoralism: Reassessments of Nietzsche's Philosophy*. Edited by Richard Schacht, 47–62. Cambridge: Cambridge University Press, 2001.

Sealey, Raphael. *A History of the Greek City States, ca. 700–338 BC*. Berkeley: University of California Press, 1976.

Shapiro, Gary. "Nietzsche on Envy." *International Studies in Philosophy* 15, no. 2 (1983): 3–12.

———. *Nietzschean Narratives*. Bloomington: Indiana University Press, 1989.

———. "Beyond Peoples and Fatherlands: Nietzsche's Geophilosophy and the Direction of the Earth." *Journal of Nietzsche Studies* 35/36 (2008): 9–27.

———. "Nietzsche's Unmodern Thinking: Globalization, the End of History, and 'Great Events.'" *American Catholic Philosophical Quarterly* 84, no. 2 (Spring 2010): 205–30.

Shapiro, H. A. "Herakles and Kyknos." *American Journal of Archaeology* 88, no. 4 (1984): 523–29.

Siemens, Herman. "Nietzsche's Hammer: Philosophy, Destruction, or the Art of Limited Warfare." *Tijdschrift voor Filosofie* 2 (June 1998): 321–47.

———. "Nietzsche's Political Philosophy: A Review of Recent Literature." *Nietzsche-Studien* 30 (2001): 509–26.

———. "Agonal Communities of Taste: Law and Community in Nietzsche's Philosophy of Transvaluation." *Journal of Nietzsche Studies* 24 (Fall 2002): 83–112.

———. "Nietzsche contra Liberalism on Freedom." In *A Companion to Nietzsche*, ed. K. Ansell-Pearson, 437–54. Oxford: Blackwell, 2006.

———. "Umwertung: Nietzsche's 'War-Praxis' and the Problem of Yes-Saying in *Ecce Homo*." *Nietzsche-Studien* 38 (2009): 182–206.

Siemens, Herman, and Vasti Roodt, eds. *Nietzsche, Power and Politics: Rethinking Nietzsche's Legacy for Political Thought*. Berlin: Walter de Gruyter, 2008.

Silk, M. S., and J. P. Stern. *Nietzsche on Tragedy*. New York: Cambridge University Press, 1981.

Small, Robin. "Boscovich contra Nietzsche." *Philosophy and Phenomenological Research* 46 (1984): 419–35.

———. *Nietzsche in Context*. Aldershot: Ashgate, 2001.

———. Introduction to *Basic Writings*, Paul Rée, trans. and ed. Robin Small, xi–liii. Urbana: University of Illinois Press, 2003.

———. *Nietzsche and Reé: A Star Friendship*. Oxford: Oxford University Press, 2005.

Smith, Angela M. "Control, Responsibility, and Moral Assessment." *Philosophical Studies* 138 (2008): 367–92.

Solomon, Robert C. *Living with Nietzsche: What the Great "Immoralist" Has to Teach Us*. Oxford: Oxford University Press, 2003.

Stack, George. *Lange and Nietzsche*. Berlin: Walter de Gruyter, 1983.

———. *Nietzsche: Man, Knowledge, and Will to Power*. Durango, CO: Hollowbrook, 1994.

Stegmaier, Werner. "Schicksal Nietzsche? Zu Nietzsches Selbsteinschätzung als Schicksal der Philosophie und der Menschheit (*Ecce Homo*, Warum Ich Ein Schicksal Bin 1)." *Nietzsche-Studien* 37 (2008): 62–114.

Stich, Stephen, John Doris, and Erica Roedder. "Altruism." In *The Moral Psychology Handbook*, ed. J. M. Doris and the Moral Psychology Research Group, 147–205. Oxford: Oxford University Press, 2010.

Strong, Tracy. "Genealogy, the Will to Power, and the Problem of a Past." In *Critical Essays on Nietzsche's On the Genealogy of Morals*, ed. Christa Davis Acampora, 93–106. Lanham, MD: Rowman & Littlefield, 2006.

Tauber, Alfred I. "A Typology of Nietzsche's Biology." *Biology and Philosophy* 9 (1994): 25–44.

Theognis. *Elegies*. Translated by Dorothea Wender. In *Hesiod and Theognis*. New York: Penguin, 1973.

Thiele, Leslie Paul. "The Agony of Politics: The Nietzschean Roots of Foucault's Thought." *American Political Science Review* 84, no. 3 (September 1990): 907–25.

———. *Friedrich Nietzsche and the Politics of the Soul: A Study of Heroic Individualism*. Princeton, NJ: Princeton University Press, 1990.

Thucydides. *The Peloponnesian War*. Translated by Rex Warner. New York: Penguin, 1954.

van Tongeren, Paul. *Die Moral von Nietzsche's Moralkritik*. Bonn: Bouvier, 1989.

———. "Nietzsche's Greek Measure." *Journal of Nietzsche Studies* 24 (Fall 2002): 5–24.

van Tongeren, Paul, Paul Sars, Chris Bremmers, and Koen Boey, eds. *Eros and Eris: Contributions to a Hermeneutical Phenomenology: Liber Amicorum for Adrian Peperzak*. Dordrecht: Kluwer Academic, 1992.

Van Wees, Hans. *Status Warriors: War, Violence and Society in Homer and History*. Amsterdam: J. C. Gieben, 1992.

Vernant, Jean-Pierre, ed. *Myth and Society in Ancient Greece*. Translated by Janet Lloyd. New York: Zone, 1988.

———. *The Greeks*. Translated by Charles Lambert and Teresa Lavender Fagan. Chicago: University of Chicago Press, 1995.

Villa, Dana R. "Democratizing the *Agon*: Nietzsche, Arendt, and the Agonistic Tendency in Recent Political Theory." In *Why Nietzsche Still? Reflections on Drama, Culture, and Politics*, ed. Alan D. Schrift, 224–46. Berkeley and Los Angeles: University of California Press, 2000.

Vlastos, Gregory. "The Paradox of Socrates." In *The Philosophy of Socrates: A Collection of Critical Essays*. Garden City, NY: Doubleday, 1971.

———. *Socrates: Ironist and Moral Philosopher*. New York: Cambridge University Press, 1991.

———. *Socratic Studies*. Edited by Myles Burnyeat. New York: Cambridge University Press, 1994.

Vogt, Ernst. "Nietzsche und der Wettkampf Homers." In *Antkie und Abendland*, ed. Bruno Snell and Ulrich Fleishcher, 103–13. Hamburg: Marion von Schröder, 1962.

Vondung, Klaus. "Unity through *Bildung*: A German Dream of Perfection." *Journal of Independent Philosophy* 5/6 (1988): 47–55.

Walcot, Peter. *Envy and the Greeks*. Warminster: Aris & Phillips, 1978.

Ward, Janet Lungstrum. "Nietzsche's Transvaluation of Jewish Parasitism." *Journal of Nietzsche Studies* 24 (Fall 2002): 54–82.

Ward, Joe. "Nietzsche's Value Conflict: Culture, Individual, Synthesis." *Journal of Nietzsche Studies* 41 (Spring 2011): 4–25.

Watson, Gary. "Two Faces of Responsibility." *Philosophical Topics* 24 (1996): 227–48.

Weiler, Ingomar. *Der Agon in Mythos: Zur Einstellung der Griechen zum Wettkampf*. Darmstadt: Wissenschaftliche Buchgesellschaft, 1974.

Whitlock, Greg. "Roger Boscovich, Benedict de Spinoza and Friedrich Nietzsche: The Untold Story." *Nietzsche-Studien* 25 (1996): 200–220.

———. "Roger J. Boscovich and Friedrich Nietzsche: A Re-Examination." In *Nietzsche, Epistemology, and Philosophy of Science*, ed. Babette E. Babich and Robert S. Cohen, 187–202. Boston: Kluwer, 1999.

———. "Investigations in Time Atomism and Eternal Recurrence." *Journal of Nietzsche Studies* 20 (2000): 34–57.

Whitman, James. "Nietzsche and the Magisterial Tradition of German Classical Philology." *Journal of the History of Ideas* 47, no. 3 (1986): 453–68.

Williams, Bernard. *Shame and Responsibility.* Berkeley and Los Angeles: University of California Press, 1993.

———. *Truth and Truthfulness: An Essay in Genealogy.* Princeton, NJ: Princeton University Press, 2002.

Wittgenstein, Ludwig. *Philosophical Investigations.* Oxford: Oxford University Press, 1958.

Wolf, Susan. *Freedom within Reason.* New York: Oxford University Press, 1993.

Woodruff, Martha K. "The Ethics of Generosity and Friendship: Aristotle's Gift to Nietzsche?" In *The Question of the Gift*, ed. Mark Osteen, 118–31. New York: Routledge, 2002.

———. "The Music-Making Socrates: Plato and Nietzsche Revisited, Philosophy and Tragedy Rejoined." *International Studies in Philosophy* 34, no. 3 (2002): 171–90.

Young, Julian. *Nietzsche's Philosophy of Art.* Cambridge: Cambridge University Press, 1992.

———. "Richard Wagner and the Birth of *The Birth of Tragedy*." *International Journal of Philosophical Studies* 16, no. 2 (2008): 217–45.

INDEX

12 - DIMINISHED Socratic AGŌN
17 - COMMUNITY → AGON
19 - 2 ways TO Defeat - superlative & diminish
20 - playing TO WIN v. playing well
22 - TYPES OF AGŌN
25 - AGON → INDIVIDUALITY VIA performances
27 - Alētheia - Defined
31 - ABUNDANCE vs. conservation in Pindar
32 - Excellence is dependent ON COMMUNITY
40 - BAD history / Accounting OF FACTS
44 - N.'s praise of Homer - what Homer Brought.
61 - TRAGEDY offers: NOT A MORAL judgment
62 - new symbolic forms & meaning making
65 - Euripedies case for Dionysus
72 - ECSTATIC Logic
75 - Socratic contest IS NOT AGORA
77 - "ARTFUL NATURALISM"
81 - great LIFE QUOTE
84 - MUSIC SOCRATES
87 - CRITERION OF INTELLIGIBILITY
89 - Semblance as morally BANKRUPT
90 - "mere / mere" Schein
92 - Science needs artfice TO ADVANCE
102 - ATOMISM
105 - WILL TO POWER AS CONTEST
113 - CRITIQUE OF Christian Agon
114 - Values FROM the Agon are TANGIBLE
117 - Paul in Luthean BIBLE - how N. SAW him
119 - ANTAGONISM
121 - Homer & invent agon BUT Refines it
125 - Luther
136 - promising not crucial
138 - ASZ project TO see IF values can be
        challenged thru agon
141 - Responsibility & DEEDS: 3 ways
149 - we are what we do